ZEW Economic Studies

Publication Series of the Centre for
European Economic Research (ZEW),
Mannheim, Germany

ZEW Economic Studies

Further volumes of this series can be found at our homepage:
springeronline.com/series/4041

Vol. 8: H. Legler et al.
Germany's Technological Performance
2000. X, 191 pp. ISBN 3-7908-1281-1

Vol. 9: O. Bürgel
**The Internationalization of British
Start-up Companies in High-Technology
Industries**
2000. XIV, 230 pp. ISBN 3-7908-1292-7

Vol. 10: J. Hemmelskamp et al. (Eds.)
**Innovation-Oriented Environmental
Regulation**
Theoretical Approaches and Empirical
Analysis
2000. VI, 348 pp. ISBN 3-7908-1313-3

Vol. 11: K. L. Brockmann, M. Stronzik (Eds.)
**Flexible Mechanisms
for an Efficient Climate Policy**
Cost Saving Policies and Business
Opportunities
2000. VIII, 130 pp. ISBN 3-7908-1314-1

Vol. 12: W. Smolny
**Endogenous Innovations
and Knowledge Spillovers**
A Theoretical and Empirical Analysis
2000. VIII, 277 pp. ISBN 3-7908-1320-6

Vol. 13: M. Lechner, F. Pfeiffer (Eds.)
**Econometric Evaluation
of Labour Market Policies**
2001. X, 242 pp. ISBN 3-7908-1372-9

Vol. 14: M. Beise
Lead Markets
Country-Specific Success Factors of the
Global Diffusion of Innovations
2001. XVI, 305 pp. ISBN 3-7908-1430-X

Vol. 15: O. H. Jacobs, C. Spengel
Effective Tax Burden in Europe
Current Situation, Past Developments and
Simulations of Reforms
2002. X, 131 pp. ISBN 3-7908-1470-9

Vol. 16: U. Kaiser
**Innovation, Employment, and Firm
Performance in the German Service Sector**
2002. X, 164 pp. ISBN 3-7908-1481-4

Vol. 17: J. Köke
Corporate Governance in Germany
An Empirical Investigation
2002. VIII, 184 pp. ISBN 3-7908-1511-X

Vol. 18: E. Wolf
What Hampers Part-Time Work?
An Empirical Analysis of Wages, Hours
Restrictions and Employment from a
Dutch-German Perspective
2003. X, 174 pp. ISBN 3-7908-0006-6

Vol. 19: P. Cecchini et al. (Eds.)
**The Incomplete European Market
for Financial Services**
2003. XII, 255 pp. ISBN 3-7908-0013-9

Vol. 20: C. Böhringer, A. Löschel (Eds.)
**Empirical Modeling of the Economy
and the Environment**
2003. VI, 326 pp. ISBN 3-7908-0078-3

Vol. 21: K. Rennings, T. Zwick (Eds.)
**Employment Impacts of Cleaner
Production**
2003. VIII, 322 pp. ISBN 3-7908-0093-7

Vol. 22: O. Bürgel, A. Fier, G. Licht,
G. Murray
**The Internationalisation of Young
High-Tech Firms**
An Empirical Analysis in Germany
and the United Kingdom
2003. XII, 291 pp. ISBN 3-7908-0120-8

Vol. 23: F. Hüfner
**Foreign Exchange Intervention
as a Monetary Policy Instrument**
Evidence for Inflation Targeting Countries
2004. X, 175 pp. ISBN 3-7908-0128-3

Vol. 24: E. Lüders
**Economic Foundation
of Asset Price Processes**
2004. XII, 121 pp. ISBN 3-7908-0149-6

Vol. 25: F. Reize
**Leaving Unemployment
for Self-Employment**
An Empirical Study
2004. XII, 241 pp. ISBN 3-7908-0168-2

Christoph Böhringer · Andreas Löschel

Climate Change Policy and Global Trade

With 43 Figures
and 109 Tables

Physica-Verlag

A Springer-Verlag Company

ZEW

Zentrum für Europäische
Wirtschaftsforschung GmbH

Centre for European
Economic Research

338.927
C639

Series Editor
Prof. Dr. Dr. h.c. mult. Wolfgang Franz

Editors

Prof. Dr. Christoph Böhringer
Dr. Andreas Löschel
Centre for European Economic Research (ZEW)
L 7,1
68161 Mannheim
Germany

ISBN 3-7908-0171-2 Physica-Verlag Heidelberg New York

Cataloging-in-Publication Data applied for
A catalog record for this book is available from the Library of Congress.
Bibliographic information published by Die Deutsche Bibliothek
Die Deutsche Bibliothek lists this publication in the Deutsche Nationalbibliografie; detailed bibliographic
data is available in the Internet at <http://dnb.ddb.de>.

Physica-Verlag is a part of Springer Science+Business Media

springeronline.com

© Physica-Verlag Heidelberg 2004
Printed in Germany

Cover design: Erich Dichiser, ZEW, Mannheim

SPIN 10981269   88/3130-5 4 3 2 1 0 – Printed on acid-free paper

Preface

This book contains a synthesis of the results of the project "Climate Change Policy and Global Trade" financed by the European Commission under the Energy, Environment and Sustainable Development programme within the Fifth Framework Programme (Contract N° EVK2-CT-2000-00093). The project aimed at providing quantitative insights into the impacts of two important international policy initiatives: (i) multilateral agreements on climate protection strategies, and (ii) trade agreements towards global trade liberalisation. Research in this project involved several institutions: Zentrum für Europäische Wirtschaftsforschung, Mannheim (ZEW – Centre for European Economic Research, coordinator), ICCS of National Technical University of Athens (ICCS/NTUA), Tinbergen Institute, Erasmus University Rotterdam (TI), Middlesex University Business School, London (MUBS), University of Rostock (UROS), and Metroeconomica Limited, Bath (MET).

Nikolaos Christoforides (European Commission, DG Research) supervised the project and provided valuable input. We would like to thank him as well as Pierre Valette (DG Research) and Katri Kosonen (DG Taxation) for their helpful comments. The views expressed in this volume are those of the authors and do neither reflect the opinion of the Commission nor of its officials.

We are obliged to Frauke Eckermann for diligent and dedicative management assistance throughout the project.

Furthermore, we would like to thank Andreas Pfeiff, Elisabeth Baier, Patrick Jochem, and Christoph Skupnik for assistance in putting together this book.

January 2004,   Christoph Böhringer and Andreas Löschel

Contents

Introduction
by Christoph Böhringer and Andreas Löschel.. 1

PART A: Policy Background

Climate Policy
by Christoph Böhringer and Andreas Löschel 3

Trade Policy
by Nikos Kouvaritakis, Nikos Stroblos, Leonidas Paroussos,
and Spyridon Tsallas 21

Multilateral Environmental Agreements and the Trade and
Environment Nexus
by Tim Taylor, Alistair Hunt, and Anil Markandya.. 85

PART B: Analytical Framework

A Computable General Equilibrium Model for Climate and
Trade Policy Analysis
by Christoph Böhringer, Andreas Löschel, and Joseph Francois 111

Imperfect Competition: Modelling Alternatives and Sensitivity
by Dirk Willenbockel 145

Risk and Transaction Costs
by Frauke Eckermann, Marcus Stronzik, Alistair Hunt,
and Tim Taylor 175

Leakage

by Michael Rauscher and Benjamin Lünenbürger 205

PART C: Policy Simulations

Climate Policies: Trade Spillovers, Joint Implementation and
Technological Spillovers, Market Power, Investment Risks

by Christoph Böhringer and Andreas Löschel 231

Trade Liberalisation and Climate Policies

*by Nikos Kouvaritakis, Nikos Stroblos, Leonidas Paroussos, and
Spyridon Tsallas* 297

Introduction

Christoph Böhringer and Andreas Löschel

Centre for European Economic Research, P.O. Box 103443, 68034 Mannheim, Germany
boehringer@zew.de, loeschel@zew.de

This book investigates the potential global impacts of two important international policy initiatives: (i) multilateral agreements on climate protection strategies and (ii) trade agreements towards global trade liberalisation. First, climate change has been framed by natural science as one of the most important problems facing the world community. Beyond fundamental incentive problems in the provision of climate protection as a global public good, policies to combat climate change are challenged with complex societal aspects such as the magnitude and distribution of abatement costs. Second, future trade-liberalisation agreements under the auspices of the World Trade Organisation (WTO) bear considerable promise of raising global welfare; however, such gains might be quite unevenly distributed across regions.

Although these initiatives are not directly linked, they interrelate in subtle, yet important ways. First, climate change policies in open economies not only cause adjustment of domestic production and consumption patterns but also influence international prices via changes in exports and imports. Changes in international prices, i.e. the terms of trade, imply a *secondary* benefit or burden which can significantly alter the economic implications of the *primary* domestic policy. Likewise, countries which do not undertake any abatement policies will nevertheless be affected through international spillovers. In the context of unilateral action, energy-intensive industries of abating developed countries might call for border adjustment measures, such as countervailing carbon tariffs on imports from non-abating countries, in order to protect international competitiveness. Such border interventions could be damaging to the trade interest of developing countries and might threaten to overturn global gains from trade liberalisation. On the other hand, border interventions may reduce negative international spillovers from leakage – a phenomenon referring to the increase in emissions in countries without emission control due to sub-global abatement policies. Thus, there is an important international trade dimension to climate protection strategies. Second, the ongoing liberalisation of world trade has implications on emission evolution and, in particular, on their regional allocation. Hence, there is an important climate change dimension to trade policies.

A large amount of economic research, meanwhile, provides "isolated" expertise on either climate change or trade liberalisation initiatives. However, there is hardly any literature that provides a comprehensive link between both issues. This book aims at filling this research gap by investigating the multiple cross-linkages between climate change mitigation and global trade agreements. Its primary objective is to develop and apply an appropriate analytical framework for the combined quantitative assessment of trade and climate policy initiatives.

The book is organised in three parts: PART A "Policy Background" provides an overview of recent developments and policy issues in climate policy and international trade. The qualitative analysis identifies key economic mechanisms on both fields that must be reflected within an appropriate quantitative framework. The theoretical foundations of mechanisms at work will be laid out based on trade theory and environmental economics to explain the effects of trade and environmental policy intervention.

PART B "Analytical Framework" deals with the development of an appropriate analytical framework and its parameterisation. State-of-the-art quantitative analyses of either trade or climate change policies build on multi-regional, multi-commodity computable general equilibrium (CGE) models. However, these models have generally not combined the key mechanisms from both perspectives, such as imperfect competition on commodity markets and the representation of (non-)tariff barriers (from the stance of trade policy analysis), or the deliberate representation of energy flows and emission substitution possibilities (from the stance of climate change policies). The book starts with the description of an established, well-documented global CGE model that has been previously used for the analysis of climate change policies and enforces the trade policy angle by incorporating market imperfections and existing trade agreements. Beyond the basic (generic) structure of the model, all extensions will be linked to the initial theoretical discussions and laid out in non-technical as well as algebraic form. Furthermore, the interested reader will be provided with details on data sources and model parameterisation.

PART C "Policy Simulations" resorts to the initial step by taking up selected policy scenarios. After the description of how the scenarios are implemented, detailed discussions about the simulation results based on sound economic theory will take place and policy conclusions will be drawn.

Climate Policy

Christoph Böhringer and Andreas Löschel

Centre for European Economic Research, P.O. Box 103443, 68034 Mannheim, Germany
boehringer@zew.de, loeschel@zew.de

1 Introduction

Despite the withdrawal of the USA under President Bush in March 2001, the Kyoto Protocol marks a milestone in climate policy history. For the first time, industrialised countries as listed in Annex B of the Protocol have agreed on quantified emissions limitations and reduction objectives. The negotiations around the Protocol have been dominated by two fundamental issues whose reconciliation is crucial for any substantial international agreement on climate protection: efficiency in terms of overall abatement costs, and equity in terms of a 'fair' distribution of these costs across countries. These issues are relevant in other fields of international environmental policy as well, but their importance in the greenhouse context is unique, given the potential magnitude of abatement costs at stake.

With regard to efficiency, the Kyoto Protocol allows for the use of emissions trading, joint implementation (JI) or the clean development mechanism (CDM) in order to reduce total costs of abatement. However, the permissible scope and institutional design of these flexible instruments are controversial among signatory parties. Several Annex B parties, such as the EU, are concerned that the extensive use of flexible instruments will negatively affect the environmental effectiveness of the Kyoto Protocol.

They stress the principle of supplementarity and call for ceilings on the amount by which national reduction targets can be achieved through the use of flexible instruments mentioned by the Kyoto Protocol (Baron et al., 1999). Other Annex B parties, such as the USA, have been strongly opposed to any ceiling plans throughout the negotiations.

With respect to equity, the Convention on Climate Change states that 'Parties should protect the climate system ... on the basis of equity and in accordance with their common but differentiated responsibilities and respective capabilities' (UNFCCC, 1997, Article 3.1). The Kyoto Protocol backs this proposition, though concepts of equity have remained rather vague during the negotiation process. Industrialised countries and economies in transition – both referred to as Annex B countries – have committed themselves to reducing greenhouse gas emissions to varying degrees, apparently meaning to reflect differences in the 'ability to pay'. Equity has also been invoked to justify the fact that developing countries have, as yet, not made any commitment to greenhouse gas abatement because they carry only minor historical responsibility for the increase of global greenhouse concentrations in the atmosphere.

A naïve assessment of the Kyoto Protocol may suggest that the adoption of concrete reduction commitments for Annex B countries reflects a careful balancing of efficiency and equity issues. However, the subsequent controversial Conferences of Parties, as well as the fact that no Annex B country has ratified the Protocol so far, indicate the opposite. Policy makers are obviously aware that the concrete – yet undefined – implementation of the Protocol will have important implications for the magnitude and regional distribution of compliance costs. Unresolved policy questions surrounding the implementation of the Kyoto Protocol deal with the implications of flexibility on the economic costs of abatement for Annex B countries, international spillovers to non-abating regions and global environmental effectiveness. Answers to these questions demand quantitative assessment, i.e. the use of analytical economic models. Obviously, models of complex socio-economic systems require simplifying assumptions on system boundaries and system relationships. These assumptions determine the model results and the derived policy conclusions. A major challenge of economic modeling is, therefore, to capture the key entities and relationships of the policy issue at hand. Given some inevitable ambiguity in this process, a careful check of the underlying assumptions is necessary: How do differences in perspectives affect the outcome and what are the implications for the choice of policy options? This chapter provides a short summary of relevant policy issues and presents the main results from applied modeling.

2   Policy Issues

An economic assessment of climate change has to make a trade-off between costs and benefits. More specifically, rational climate policy making should weigh the benefits from avoided undesirable consequences of global warming against the costs of greenhouse gas emission abatement. To this end, the established technique of cost-benefit analysis (see e.g. Mishan, 1975; Maddison, 1995; Pearce, 1998) provides the appropriate framework for measuring all negative and positive policy impacts and resource uses in the form of monetary costs and benefits. An economically efficient policy for emissions reduction maximises net benefits, i.e. the benefits of slowed climate change minus the associated costs of emissions reductions. Net benefit maximisation requires that emissions reduction efforts are taken up to the level where the marginal benefit of reduced warming equals the marginal cost of emissions reduction.

Given complete information, cost-benefit analysis could tell us how much greenhouse gas (GHG) emissions should be abated, when and by whom. However, neither costs nor benefits of GHG abatement are easy to quantify. In particular, there are large uncertainties in external cost estimates for climate change. The chain of causality – from GHG emissions to ambient concentrations of GHGs in the atmosphere to temperature increase to physical effects such as climatic and sea level changes – is highly complex. Little agreement exists, therefore, on the desirable level of greenhouse gas emission concentrations in the atmosphere and the scope and timing of emission mitigation measures.

The large uncertainties in external cost estimates are reflected in the current climate policy debate. Emissions reduction objectives are not the outcome of a rigorous cost-benefit analysis, but must rather be seen as a first response to recommendations from natural science on tolerable emission levels. In this vein, we restrict our subsequent analysis of emission abatement strategies to a cost-effectiveness approach. Cost-effectiveness analysis aims at identifying the least expensive way of achieving a given environmental quality target.[1] Only the costs are assessed in relation to an environmental goal; the policy target which represents the level of benefits is taken as given. In climate policy, targets may be formulated with respect to different bases, such as the stabilisation of GHG emissions in a certain year, a long-run stabilisation of atmospheric concentrations of particular greenhouse gases or the prevention of physical consequences (e.g. sea level rise). For the cost-effectiveness analysis, we simply adopt the short-term GHG emissions reduction targets as formulated in the Kyoto Protocol. That is, we measure the economic costs of alternative policy strategies to meet the emissions reduction objectives which Annex B countries have committed to.

In the remainder of this section, we address key issues in the climate policy debate and summarise evidence from quantitative studies without discussing the details of the underlying models. Our objective is twofold. First, we want to justify the choice of the analytical framework. Secondly, we want to motivate the choice of policy scenarios and the design of sensitivity analysis. For the reasons mentioned, we do not enter the scientific debate on the benefits associated with GHG emissions reduction. Starting from some exogenous global emissions reduction objective, the policy debate comes down to the magnitude and the distribution of abatement costs across regions for alternative policy strategies. The ongoing negotiations around the Kyoto Protocol provide a prime example of the issues at stake. Individual contributions of the Annex B Parties to the Protocol were determined by two basic considerations. On the one hand, the potential costs of the committed reduction had to be 'sufficiently low'. Even voters in wealthy industrialised countries reveal a rather modest willingness to pay for climate protection

---

[1]   The equivalent (dual) formulation is to achieve the greatest improvement in some environmental target for a given expenditure of resources.

whose benefits are unclear and of long-term nature (Böhringer and Vogt, 2001). On the other hand, the expected pattern of costs across Parties had to comply with basic fairness principles (see e.g. Lange and Vogt, 2001). The latter inevitably involves ethically-based equity criteria (see IPCC, 1996 and 2001).

The standard approach of positive economics is to separate efficiency and equity considerations. Economics cares for the minimisation of the total costs to reach some exogenous reduction target. It is then left to other disciplines as to how these costs should be allocated across agents through lump-sum transfers in order to meet some equity criteria. In the structure of this section, we will take up the traditional distinction between efficiency and equity issues. It should be noted, however, that both issues are closely linked when lump-sum instruments are not available, which is typically the case in political practice.

Our short summary is far from being comprehensive. The informed reader will notice that we have omitted several topics which are not necessarily less important than those explicitly addressed in this chapter. Among these topics are offsets from CO_2 sinks (see Stavins, 1999; Reilly et al., 1999), the incorporation of non-CO_2 GHG mitigation options (see MacCracken et al., 1999; Reilly et al., 1999; Burniaux and Martins, 2000) and implications from intertemporal flexibility (see Richels and Sturm, 1996; Richels et al., 1996; Tol, 1999).

2.1   The Magnitude of Abatement Costs

People who search for empirical evidence on the economic impacts of GHG abatement policies are often puzzled about the diverging results across quantitative studies. Not only are there differences in the order of magnitude for abatement costs, but also the sign in reported costs may be opposite. In other words, while one study suggests that an abatement policy results in economy-wide losses, another one indicates economic gains. This 'battle over numbers' explains reservations with respect to the usefulness of quantitative modeling. The constructive approach to this problem is not to renounce insights from applied modeling but to develop some understanding of differences in results. Most of these differences can be traced back to different assumption on the status quo, i.e. the baseline, of the economic system without exogenous policy interference (see Section 2.1.1). Another major source for deviations in cost estimates are differences in the scope of economic interactions that are captured by the studies (see Section 2.1.2). The awareness of these determinants for economic impacts of exogenous policy changes is a prerequisite to properly understanding model results and drawing appropriate conclusions (Böhringer, 1999). Hence, a major task for applied modeling is to reveal the importance of subjective judgements, which are implicit in the choice of the baseline, system boundaries and system relationships, for quantitative model results by means of sensitivity analysis.

2.1.1   Baseline Assumptions

Projections

The economic effects of future emission constraints depend crucially on the extent to which quantified emission limitation and reduction objectives will bind the respective economies. In other words, the magnitude of costs associated with the implementation of future emission constraints depends on the Business-as-Usual (BaU) projections for GDP, fuel prices, energy efficiency improvements etc. High economic growth alone, for example, leads to high energy demands and emissions. In the context of the Kyoto Protocol, this would increase the effective abatement requirement, as the Kyoto targets refer to 1990 emissions levels and higher economic growth will therefore imply higher total abatement costs. The importance of baseline projections generally receives little attention in the literature. Most modelers are typically careful in specifying their BaU assumptions but they rarely report results from sensitivity analyses. Böhringer, Jensen and Rutherford (2000) study the implications of alternative baseline projections on the magnitude and distribution of emission abatement costs under the Kyoto Protocol within the EU.

Market imperfections

The incorporation of existing market imperfections is a key factor in explaining why economic adjustments towards more stringent emission constraints might lead to economic gains even when we ignore the benefits of avoided GHG emissions. If policy measures induce reactions that weaken existing distortions, the net outcome might be beneficial even if the policy measure standing alone, i.e. without initial market imperfections, were to cause economic adjustment costs. In the climate change debate, this phenomenon is sometimes referred to as a no-regrets option for abatement policies.

No-regrets options are, by definition, actions to reduce GHG emissions that have negative net costs because they generate direct or indirect benefits large enough to offset their implementation costs. The existence of no-regrets potentials implies that market forces are not operating perfectly. Market imperfections may be due to imperfect information, lack of competition or distortionary fiscal systems and limited financial markets. It should be noted, however, that the removal of market failures and market barriers can cause significant transaction costs (Grubb et al., 1993). Taking transaction costs into account, no-regrets options may be significantly reduced or even non-existent (see Jaffe and Stavins, 1991). This explains why economists are rather sceptical about the magnitude of the no-regrets options reported in bottom-up technology-based studies (Krause et al., 1999). These studies assume large initial 'efficiency gaps' between the best available technologies and the equipment actually in use, but they do not incorporate the transaction costs of removing these inefficiencies.

The debate on a double dividend from environmental regulation also builds on the notion of no-regrets policies. Instruments such as carbon taxes or auctioned tradable permits generate revenues to the government. If these revenues are used to reduce existing tax distortions, emission abatement policies may yield a double dividend, i.e., simultaneously improve environmental quality (first dividend) and offset at least part of the welfare losses of climate policies by reducing the overall costs of raising public funds (second dividend). The literature distinguishes two forms of double dividend (Goulder, 1995b). In its weak form, a double dividend occurs as long as the gross costs of environmental policies are systematically lower when revenues are recycled via cuts in existing distortionary taxes, rather than being returned as a lump sum. In its strong form, the existence of a double dividend requires that the net cost of the environmental policy is negative (for theoretical analyses see Goulder, 1995b; Bovenberg, 1999). The weak double dividend is confirmed by many theoretical and numerical studies (e.g. EMF-16, 1999). Evidence on the strong double dividend is rather mixed. In public finance terms, a strong double dividend occurs when the marginal distortionary effect of a carbon tax is lower than the marginal distortionary effect of the substituted taxes, given some constant level of tax revenues (Hourcade and Robinson, 1996).

The existence of a strong double dividend thus depends on a number of factors, such as pre-existing inefficiencies of the tax system along non-environmental dimensions, the type of tax cuts (reductions in payroll taxes, value added taxes (VAT), capital taxes, or other indirect taxes), labour market conditions (level of unemployment and functioning of labour markets), the method of recycling and the level of environmental taxes (i.e. the environmental target). Environmental taxes may well exacerbate rather than alleviate pre-existing tax distortions. This is because environmental taxes induce not only market distortions similar to those of the replaced taxes but also new distortions in positive impacts of using intermediate and final consumption. The negative impacts from levying additional environmental taxes (tax interaction effect) can dominate the additional revenues for cuts in existing distortionary taxes (revenue recycling effect). This result is suggested by the stylised numerical and theoretical studies of Bovenberg and de Mooij (1994) and Parry et al. (1999). Applied studies of economies with few distortions such as the USA find no strong double dividend, but cost reductions as compared to lump-sum recycling up to 30-50% (Jorgenson and Wilcoxen, 1993; Goulder, 1995a). Complementary analysis for EU countries with more distortionary tax systems and substantial labour market imperfections are more optimistic on the prospects for a strong double dividend (Barker, 1998, 1999). In general, it can be argued that existing market imperfections provide an opportunity for beneficial policy reforms independent of environmental policies. In this vein, the second dividend may not be fully attributable to environmental regulation. On the other hand, the taxation of pollution can be seen as a second-best instrument, given growing political constraints on traditional non-environmental taxes (Hourcade, 1993).

2.1.2   System Boundaries

The choice of system boundaries determines the extent to which the cost-effectiveness analysis accounts for policy-induced adjustment costs. The main challenge of modeling is to select only those system elements and their relationships which really matter for the question at hand. To put it differently: The exclusion of cost components that are outside the chosen system boundaries should not significantly affect the order of magnitude of quantitative results nor the ranking of alternative policy options. In modeling practice, this rule of thumb can hardly be kept because one often does not know beforehand if simplifications that are, after all, a key element of modeling, may turn out to be too simple. Obviously, there is a trade-off between the scope of the system to be captured and the level of detail. In our discussion of system boundaries, we start with the widespread distinction between energy-system analysis (bottom-up) and macroeconomic impact analysis (top-down) of emission abatement strategies. Another important issue in the choice of system boundaries is the degree to which international spillovers from domestic policies are taken into account. The common distinction made here is between single-country models and multi-region models. Finally, we point out that system boundaries do not necessarily have a spatial or temporal dimension, but refer – more generally – to the degree of adopted endogeneity for system relationships. We illustrate the latter in the discussion of technological change.

Bottom-up versus top-down

There are two broad approaches for modeling the interaction between energy, the environment and the economy. They differ mainly with respect to the emphasis placed on (1) a detailed, technologically based treatment of the energy system, and (2) a theoretically consistent description of the general economy. The models placing emphasis on (1) are purely partial models of the energy sector, lacking interaction with the rest of the economy.[2] In general, they are bottom-up engineering-based linear activity models with a large number of energy technologies to capture substitution of energy carriers at the primary and final energy level, process substitution, process improvements (gross efficiency improvement, emission reduction) or energy savings. They are mostly used to compute the least-cost method of meeting a given demand for final energy or energy services subject to various system constraints such as exogenous emission reduction targets. The models emphasising (2) are general economic models with only rudimentary treatment of the energy system. Following the top-down approach, they describe the energy system (similar to the other sectors) in a highly aggregated way by means of neoclassical production functions, which capture substitution possibilities by means of substitution elasticities. These models may be classified as open

---

[2]   One exception is ETA-MACRO (Manne, 1981) and its derivatives. It combines a fairly detailed linear technology model of energy supply with a highly aggregated (one-sector) macroeconomic model.

(demand driven Keynesian) or closed (general equilibrium) models (for a model classification see for example Weyant, 1999) and capture feedback effects of energy policies on non-energy markets such as price changes for factors or intermediate goods. In the literature it is often overlooked that the differences between top-down models and bottom-up models are less of a theoretical nature; rather, simply relate to the level of aggregation and the scope of ceteris paribus assumptions.[3]

International spillovers

Since world economies are increasingly linked through international trade, capital flows and technology transfers, emission abatement by one country has spillovers on other countries. In the policy debate over climate change, spillovers from Annex B countries' abatement to non-abating developing countries play an important role. The Kyoto Protocol explicitly acknowledges the importance of international spillovers in stipulating that unilateral abatement policies should minimise adverse trade effects on developing countries (UNFCCC, 1997, Article 2.3). Even more, the UNFCCC guarantees compensation by Annex B to the developing world for induced economic costs under Articles 4.8 and 4.9. On the other hand, the developed Annex B countries fear adverse impacts from unilateral abatement, because their energy use will be taxed, while there will be no taxes in the developing world, hence they can expect to lose competitiveness in energy-intensive production. In a more dynamic perspective, important spillovers may also stem from technology transfers. In the presence of induced technological change, cleaner technologies developed as a response to abatement policies in industrialised countries may diffuse internationally, generating positive spillovers for non-abating countries. The diffusion of cleaner technologies may offset some or all of the negative leakage effects (Grubb, 2000). Environmental implications of international spillovers concern the phenomenon of carbon leakage due to sub-global action, which may have important consequences for the design of unilateral abatement strategies. The following paragraphs discuss the implications of spillovers on regional adjustment costs, industrial competitiveness and global environmental effectiveness in more detail.

Carbon abatement in large open economies not only causes adjustment of domestic production and consumption patterns, but it also influences international prices via changes in exports and imports. Changes in international prices, i.e. the terms of trade[4], imply a secondary benefit or burden that can significantly alter the economic implications of the primary domestic policy. Some countries may shift part

---

[3]   In fact, recent developments in the solution of nonlinear systems of inequalities (Dirkse and Ferris, 1995) have promoted the synthesis of bottom-up and top-down models within one consistent general equilibrium framework (see Böhringer, 1998b).

[4]   The terms of trade are generally measured as the ratio of a country's exports to its imports in value terms.

of their domestic abatement costs to trading partners, while other abating countries face welfare losses from a deterioration of their terms of trade.

With respect to the aggregate terms-of-trade effects, the most important are changes in international fuel markets. The cutback in global demand for fossil fuels due to carbon emission constraints implies a significant drop of their prices, providing economic gains to fossil fuel importers and losses to fossil fuel exporters (van der Mensbrugghe, 1998; Bernstein et al., 1999; McKibbin et al., 1999; Tulpulé et al., 1999; Montgomery and Bernstein, 2000).

The economic implications of international price changes on non-energy markets are more complex. Higher energy costs implied by carbon taxes raise the prices of non-energy goods (in particular energy-intensive goods) produced in abating countries. Countries that import these goods suffer from higher prices to the extent that they cannot substitute them with cheaper imports from non-abating countries. The ease of substitution – captured by the Armington elasticity – not only determines the implicit burden shifting of carbon taxes via non-energy exports from abating countries, but also the extent to which non-abating countries achieve a competitive advantage *vis-à-vis* abating exporters. The gain in market shares due to substitution effects may be partially offset by an opposite scale effect: Due to reduced economic activity and income effects, import demand by the industrialised world declines, and this exerts a downward pressure on the prices of developing country exports. On average, non-abating regions or countries with very low carbon taxes gain comparative advantage on non-energy markets that, however, may not be large enough to offset potentially negative spillovers from international fuel markets.

Terms-of-trade changes affect the pattern of comparative advantage. This refers to the relative cost of producing goods in a particular country compared to the cost of producing these goods elsewhere. Since, in the neoclassical view, the location of production is determined by these relative cost differences, competitiveness and comparative advantage can be used interchangeably. Carbon taxes increase production costs and change international competitiveness, depending on the size of the carbon tax and the carbon intensity of the product. Particularly, energy-intensive industries such as chemicals, steel or cement in mitigating countries are negatively affected. However, surveys on the impacts of carbon abatement policies on international competitiveness have found only minor effects so far, which might be due to rather modest emission taxes and wide-ranging exemption schemes for energy-intensive production (Barker and Johnstone, 1998; Ekins and Speck, 1998). The use of flexibility instruments reduces the competitive advantage of non-Annex B countries.

Sub-global abatement may lead to an increase in emissions in non-abating regions, reducing the global environmental effectiveness. This phenomenon is referred to as 'leakage'. Emission leakage is measured as the increase in non-Annex B emissions relative to the reduction in Annex B emissions. There are three basic channels through which carbon leakage can occur. First, leakage can arise when, in countries undertaking emission limitations, energy-intensive industries lose in competitiveness and the production of emission-intensive goods relocates, raising emission levels in the non-participating regions (trade channel). Secondly, cutbacks of energy demands in a large region due to emission constraints may depress the demand for fossil fuels and thus induce a significant drop in world energy prices. This, in turn, could lead to an increase in the level of demand (and its composition) in other regions (energy channel) (see Welsch, 1994 for a theoretical analysis). Thirdly, carbon leakage may be induced by changes in regional income (and thus energy demand) due to terms of trade changes (Rutherford, 1995a). Leakage rates reflect the impact of sub-global emission abatement strategies on comparative advantage. Model-based results on carbon leakage depend crucially on the assumed degree of substitutability between imports and domestic production in the formulation of international trade. Other major factors influencing the leakage rates are the assumed degree of competitiveness in the world oil market, the supply elasticities of fossil fuels, the substitution elasticity between energy and other inputs in the production of abating regions and the level of emissions trading (see Oliveira-Martins et al., 1992; Pezzey, 1992; Manne and Oliveira-Martins, 1994; Bernstein et al., 1999; Burniaux and Martins, 2000; Paltsev, 2000a).

2.1.3   Technological Change

Technological change is an important determinant of the economic costs induced by mid- and long-run GHG emission constraints, as it may significantly alter production possibilities over time. Löschel (2001) provides an overview of how technological change is represented in applied environment-economy models. These usually account for technical progress through an exogenous technical coefficient called the autonomous energy efficiency improvement (AEEI) (e.g. Capros et al., 1997).[5] The AEEI reflects the rate of change in energy intensity, i.e. the ratio of energy consumption to gross domestic product, holding energy prices constant (IPCC, 1996). It is a measure of all non-price induced changes in gross energy intensity, including technical developments that increase energy efficiency, as well as structural changes. The higher (lower) the AEEI, the lower (higher) the baseline emissions, and the lower (higher) the costs to reach a climate target relative to a given base year. Estimates for AEEI rates range from 0.4% to 1.5% (Dean and Hoeller, 1992; Kram, 1998, and Weyant, 1998). Sensitivity studies demonstrate the crucial importance of the AEEI parameter. Even small differences in the number chosen for the AEEI result in large differences in energy demand and emissions in the baseline and, hence, the total costs of emissions reductions (Manne and Richels, 1990 and 1992).

---

[5]   In bottom-up models, technological innovation can be captured through explicit technologies. However, the evolution of future technologies is typically taken as exogenous inputs from expert projections and not treated as an endogenous variable.

The implication of the treatment of technological change using AEEIs in prevalent models is that technological progress is assumed to be invariant with respect to climate policy interference. The modeling of the rate and direction of technical change in climate policy models as exogenous must be considered as a severe limitation (Anderson, 1999). If climate policies lead to improvements in technology, then the total costs of abatement may be substantially lower as compared to results from conventional models with exogenous technical change. However, at present, the theory of induced technological change (ITC) is still in development. The main elements in models of technological innovation are (1) corporate investment such as research and development (R&D) as well as learning by doing (LBD) in response to market conditions, and (2) spillovers from R&D. Innovation as a product of explicit private investment incentives in the knowledge sector has its origin in firm level innovation theory, which focuses on private profit incentives from (at least partly) appropriable innovations. With learning by doing in technologies, the technology costs are modeled explicitly as a function of cumulative investment or of installed capacity in that technology. Spillover effects stem from macro-level endogenous or 'new' growth theory. Investments in human capital and technology result in positive externalities (spillovers).

Investment in R&D is presented in models by Goulder and Schneider (1999), Buonanno et al. (2000) and Goulder and Mathai (2000). Quantitative results from these models indicate only weak impacts of induced technical change on the gross costs of abatement. Concerning LBD, it is found that marginal returns from LBD vary greatly between industries at different stages of development. For example, learning-by-doing effects in the mature conventional energy industries may be rather small compared to renewable energy industries (Anderson, 1999; Goulder and Mathai, 2000). Knowledge spillovers from R&D are analysed by Goulder and Schneider (1999), Weyant and Olavson (1999) and Goulder and Mathai (2000). They found that R&D market failures (knowledge spillovers) justify R&D subsidies as a second policy instrument in addition to a carbon tax. A counter-example is given by Kverndokk et al. (2000).

With endogenous technological change, the derivation of the shape of the least-cost mitigation pathway becomes more complex (Grubb, 1997).[6] ITC from investments in R&D makes it preferable to concentrate more abatement efforts in the future since it lowers the relative costs of future abatement. Early emissions-reduction measures are more preferable when LBD is considered, since current abatement contributes to a learning process that reduces the costs of future abatement (Goulder and Mathai, 2000).

---

[6] With exogenous technical change, it is generally cheaper to wait for better technologies to come along.

2.2   Equity: Burden Sharing

The establishment of international trade in emission rights requires a decision on the initial allocation of these emission rights among nations. From the Coase Theorem we know that the allocation of permits has only minor effects on the global costs of abatement when transactions costs of exchange are nil and there are no important income effects. A very similar efficient (cost-effective) outcome is reached for different initial permits allocations after all gains from trade are realised, i.e. marginal abatement costs across countries are equalised (Manne and Richels, 1995). However, the initial allocation of emission rights has major effects on the distribution of gains and losses and thus on the perceived equity of the agreement. Since there is no unique definition of equity or the objectives to which it should be applied, it is a political issue that requires the solution of serious political differences on burden sharing between industrialised countries on the one hand, and between developed and developing countries on the other hand.

Several alternative equity criteria can be found in the literature (see Kverndokk, 1995; Rose and Stevens, 1998; Rose et al., 1998; Ringius et al., 1999): Under the egalitarian criterion it is assumed that all nations have an equal right to pollute or be protected from pollution. Emission rights are allocated in proportion to population ('equal per capita emissions'). Under the sovereignty criterion current emissions constitute a status quo right now and emission rights are distributed accordingly ('grandfathered'). The no-harm criterion states that some (poor) nations should not incur costs. Emission rights are distributed to these countries according to their baseline emissions. The Kyoto Protocol may be seen as yet another *ad hoc* equity criterion. The differentiation in commitments follows some implicit equity considerations (UNFCC, 1997, Article 3.1).

There are several modeling studies that analyse the effects of different schemes for allocating emission rights (Edmonds et al., 1995; Manne and Richels, 1995; Rose and Stevens, 1998; Rose et al., 1998; Böhringer and Welsch, 1999). Most of these studies deal with global abatement strategies beyond Kyoto and impose emission constraints on developing countries to assure long-term reduction of global GHG emissions. A robust policy conclusion from these studies is that the problem of burden sharing implicit in alternative permit allocation schemes (i.e. equity rules) will be significantly relaxed through efficiency gains from world-wide emissions trading.

The separability of efficiency and equity under marketable permits allows us to concentrate on the former in our model simulations. Equilibrium abatement costs are only slightly affected by different permit distributions. However, as was previously pointed out, in international treaties such as the Kyoto Protocol, equity considerations may be crucial (Rose, 1990). The pursuit of equity consideration may even promote efficiency, since more parties with relatively lower abatement costs may be enticed into the agreement if it is perceived to be fair, which, in the case of many developing countries, may be an equal per capita allocation of permits (see for example Morrisette and Plantinga, 1991; Bohm and Larsen, 1994).

References

Anderson, D. (1999), *Technical Progress and Pollution Abatement: An Economic Review of Selected Technologies and Practices*, Working Paper, Imperial College, London.

Armington, P.A. (1969), *A Theory of Demand for Products Distinguished by Place of Production*, IMF Staff Papers 16 (1), 159-178.

Barker, T. (1998), The Effects on Competitiveness of Coordinated Versus Unilateral Fiscal Policies Reducing GHG Emissions in the EU: An Assessment of a 10% Reduction by 2010 Using the E3ME Model, *Energy Policy* 26 (14), 1083-1098.

Barker, T. (1999), Achieving a 10% Cut in Europe's CO_2 Emissions Using Additional Excise Duties: Coordinated, Uncoordinated and Unilateral Action Using the Econometric Model E3ME, *Economic Systems Research* 11 (4), 401-421.

Barker, T. and N. Johnstone (1998), International Competitiveness and Carbon Taxation, in: Barker, T. and J. Köhler (Eds.), *International Competitiveness and Environmental Policies*, Cheltenham, 71-127.

Baron, R., M. Bosi, A. Lanza, and J. Pershing (1999), *A Preliminary Analysis of the EU Proposals on the Kyoto Mechanisms*, Energy and Environment Division, International Energy Agency.

Bernstein, P., D. Montgomery, and T.F. Rutherford (1999), Global Impacts of the Kyoto Agreement: Results from the MS-MRT Model, *Resource and Energy Economics* 21 (3-4), 375-413.

Bohm, P. and B. Larsen (1994), Fairness in a Tradable Permit Treaty for Carbon Emissions Reductions in Europe and the Former Soviet Union, *Environmental and Resource Economics* 4, 219-239.

Böhringer, C. (1998a), Unilateral Taxation of International Environmental Externalities and Sectoral Exemptions, in: Fossati, A. and J. Hutton (Eds.), *Policy Simulations in the European Union*, London, 140-155.

Böhringer, C. (1998b), The Synthesis of Bottom-Up and Top-Down in Energy Policy Modeling, *Energy Economics* 20 (3), 233-248.

Böhringer, C. (1999), Die Kosten von Klimaschutz: Eine Interpretationshilfe für die mit quantitativen Wirtschaftsmodellen ermittelten Kostenschätzungen, *Journal of Environmental Law and Policy* 22 (3), 369-384.

Böhringer, C., M. Ferris, and T.F. Rutherford (1998), Alternative CO_2 Abatement Strategies for the European Union, in: Braden, J. and S. Proost (Eds.), *Climate Change, Transport and Environmental Policy*, Cheltenham, 16-47.

Böhringer, C., G.W. Harrison, and T.F. Rutherford (2003), Sharing the Burden of Carbon Abatement in the European Union, in: Böhringer, C. and A. Löschel (Eds.), *Empirical Modeling of the Economy and the Environment*, ZEW Economic Studies, Vol. 20, Heidelberg.

Böhringer, C. and C. Helm (2001), *Fair Division with General Equilibrium Effects and International Climate Politics*, ZEW Discussion Paper 01-67, Mannheim.

Böhringer, C., J. Jensen, and T.F. Rutherford (2000), Energy Market Projections and Differentiated Carbon Abatement in the European Union, in: Carraro, C. (Ed.), *Efficiency and Equity of Climate Change Policy*, Dordrecht, 199-220.

Böhringer, C., A. Ruocco, and W. Wiegard (2001a), Energiesteuern und Beschäftigung: Ein Simulationsmodell zum Selberrechnen, *WISU* 30 (1), 117-123.

Böhringer, C., A. Ruocco, and W. Wiegard (2001b), Energiesteuern und Beschäftigung: Einige Simulationsergebnisse, *WISU* 30 (4), 596-612.

Böhringer, C. and T.F. Rutherford (forthcoming), Carbon Abatement and International Spillovers, *Environmental and Resource Economics*.

Böhringer, C. and T.F. Rutherford (2001), World Economic Impacts of the Kyoto Protocol, in: Welfens, P.J.J. (Ed.), *Internalization of the Economy and Environmental Policy Options*, Berlin, 161-180.

Böhringer, C., T.F. Rutherford, and A. Voss (1998), Global CO_2 Emissions and Unilateral Action: Policy Implications of Induced Trade Effects, *International Journal of Global Energy Issues* 18-22.

Böhringer C. and C. Vogt (2001), Internationaler Klimaschutz: nicht mehr als symbolische Politik?, *Aussenwirtschaft* 56 (II), 139-155.

Böhringer, C. and H. Welsch (1999), *C&C-Contraction and Convergence of Carbon Emissions: The Economic Implications of Permit Trading*, ZEW Discussion Paper 99-13, Mannheim.

Bovenberg, A.L. (1999), Green Tax Reforms and the Double Dividend: An Updated Reader's Guide, *International Tax and Public Finance* 6, 421-443.

Bovenberg, A.L. and R.A. de Mooij (1994), Environmental Levies and Distortionary Taxation, *American Economic Review* 84 (4), 1085-1089.

Buonanno, P., C. Carraro, and M. Galeotti (2000), *Endogenous Induced Technical Change*, Working paper, Fondazione ENI Enrico Mattei.

Burniaux, J.-M. and J.O. Martins (2000), *Carbon Emission Leakages: A General Equilibrium View*, Working Paper 242, Organisation for Cooperation and Development (OECD), Economics Department.

Capros, P., T. Georgakopoulos, D. van Regemorter, S. Proost, T.F.N. Schmidt, and K. Conrad (1997), European Union: The GEM-E3 General Equilibrium Model, *Economic and Financial Modelling, Special Double Issue* 4 (2/3).

Dean, A. and P. Hoeller (1992), Costs of Reducing CO_2 Emissions: Evidence from Six Global Models, *OECD Economic Studies* 19 (Winter).

DOE (Department of Energy) (1998), *Annual Energy Outlook*, Energy Information Administration.

Edmonds, J., M. Wise, and D. Barns (1995), Carbon Coalitions: The Cost and Effectiveness of Energy Agreements to Alter Trajectories of Atmospheric Carbon Dioxide Emissions, *Energy Policy* 23, 309-335.

Ekins, P. and S. Speck (1998), The Impacts of Environmental Policy on Competitiveness: Theory and Evidence, in: Barker, T. and J. Köhler (Eds.), *International Competitiveness and Environmental Policies*, Cheltenham, 33-70.

EMF-16 Working Group (1999), *Economic and Energy System Impacts of the Kyoto Protocol: Results from the Energy Modeling Forum Study*, Stanford Energy Modeling Forum, Stanford University.

Goulder, L.H. (1995a), Effects of Carbon Taxes in an Economy with Prior Tax Distortions: An Intertemporal General Equilibrium Analysis, *Journal of Environmental Economics and Management* 29, 271-297.

Goulder, L.H. (1995b), Environmental Taxation and the Double Dividend: A Reader's Guide, *International Tax and Public Finance* 2, 157-183.

Goulder, L.H. and K. Mathai (2000), Optimal CO_2 Abatement in the Presence of Induced Technological Change, *Journal of Environmental Economics and Management* 39 (1), 1-38.

Goulder, L.H. and S. Schneider (1999), Induced Technological Change, Crowding out, and the Attractiveness of CO_2 Emissions Abatement, *Resource and Environmental Economics* 21 (3-4), 211-253.

Grubb, M. (1997), Technologies, Energy Systems, and the Timing of CO_2 Abatement: An Overview of Economic Issues, *Energy Policy* 25, 159-172.

Grubb, M. (2000), Economic Dimensions of Technological and Global Responses to the Kyoto Protocol, *Journal of Economic Studies* 27 (1/2), 111-125.

Grubb, M., J. Edmonds, P. ten Brink, and M. Morrison (1993), The Costs of Limiting Fossil-Fuel CO_2 Emissions: A Survey and Analysis, *Annual Review of Energy and Environment* 18, 397-478.

Hourcade, J.-C. (1993), Modelling Long-Run Scenarios: Methodology Lessons from a Prospective Study on a Low CO_2 Intensive Country, *Energy Policy* 21 (3), 309-311.

Hourcade, J.-C. and J. Robinson (1996), Mitigating Factors: Assessing the Cost of Reducing GHG Emissions, *Energy Policy* 24 (10/11), 863-873.

IPCC (International Panel on Climate Change) (1996), *Climate Change 1995: Economic and Social Dimensions of Climate Change*, Contribution of Working Group III to the Second Assessment Report of the Intergovernmental Panel on Climate Change, Cambridge.

IPCC (International Panel on Climate Change) (2001), *Climate Change 2001: Mitigation*, Contribution of Working Group III to the Third Assessment Report of the Intergovernmental Panel on Climate Change, Cambridge.

Jaffe, B. and R.N. Stavins (1991), The Energy-Efficiency Gap: What Does It Mean?, *Energy Policy* 22 (10), 804-810.

Jorgenson, D.W. and P.J. Wilcoxen (1993), Reducing U.S. Carbon Emissions: An Econometric General Equilibrium Assessment, *Resource and Energy Economics* 15, 7-25.

Kram, J. (1998), The Costs of Greenhouse Gas Abatement, in: Nordhaus, W. (Ed.), *Economics and Policy Issues in Climate Change*, Resources for the Future, Washington, D.C., 167-189.

Krause, F., J. Koomey, and D. Olivier (1999), Cutting Carbon Emissions While Saving Money: Low Risk Strategies for the European Union: Executive Summary, in: F. Krause et al. (Eds.), *Energy Policy in the Greenhouse*, Vol. II, Part 2, El Cerrito, USA.

Kverndokk, S. (1995), Tradable CO_2 Permits: Initial Distribution as a Justice Problem, *Environmental Values* 4 (2), 129-148.

Kverndokk, S., K.E. Rosendahl, and T.F. Rutherford (2000), *Climate Policies and Induced Technological Change, Which to Choose: The Carrot or the Stick?*, University of Colorado, Boulder.

Lange, A. and C. Vogt (2001), *Cooperation in International Environmental Negotiations Due to a Preference for Equity*, ZEW Discussion Paper 01-14, Mannheim.

Löschel, A. (2001), *Technological Change in Economic Models of Environmental Policy: A Survey*, ZEW Discussion Paper 01-62, Mannheim.

MacCracken, C.N., J.A. Edmonds, S.H. Kim, and R.D. Sands (1999), The Economics of the Kyoto Protocol, in: Weyant, J. (Ed.), *The Costs of the Kyoto Protocol: A Multi-Model Evaluation*, *The Energy Journal* Special Issue.

Maddison, D. (1995), A Cost-Benefit Analysis of Slowing Climate Change, *Energy Policy* 23 (4/5), 337-346.

Manne, A.S. and J.O. Martins (1994), Comparisons of Model Structure and Policy Scenarios: GREEN and 12RT, in: OECD (Ed.), *Policy Response to the Threat of Global Warming*, Paris.

Manne, A.S. and R.G. Richels (1990), The Costs of Reducing CO_2 Emission: A Further Sensitivity Analysis, *Energy Journal* 11 (4), 69-78.

Manne, A.S. and R.G. Richels (1992), *Buying Greenhouse Insurance: The Economic Costs of CO_2 Emission Limits*, Cambridge, MA.

Manne, A.S. and R.G. Richels (1995), The Greenhouse Debate: Economic Efficiency Burden Sharing and Hedging Strategies, *Energy Journal* 16 (4), 1-37.

McKibbin, W., M. Ross, R. Shackleton, and P. Wilcoxen (1999), Emissions Trading, Capital Flows and the Kyoto Protocol, *The Energy Journal* Special Issue, 287-333.

Mishan, E.J. (1975), *Cost-Benefit Analysis*, London.

Montgomery, D.W. and P. Bernstein (2000), *Insights on the Kyoto Protocol: Impact on Trade Patterns and Economic Growth in 25 Countries*, Charles River Associates.

Morrisette, P. and A. Plantinga (1991), The Global Warming Issue: Viewpoints of Different Countries, *Resources* 103, 2-6.

Oliveira-Martins, J., J.-M. Burniaux, and J.P. Martin (1992), Trade and the Effectiveness of Unilateral CO2 Abatement Policies: Evidence from GREEN, *OECD Economic Studies* 19, 123-140.

Paltsev, S.V. (2000a), *The Kyoto Agreement: Regional and Sectoral Contributions to the Carbon Leakage*, Working Paper 00-5, University of Colorado, Boulder.

Paltsev, S.V. (2000b), *The Kyoto Protocol: 'Hot air' for Russia?*, Working Paper 00-9, University of Colorado, Boulder.

Parry, I.W.H., R. Williams, and L.H. Goulder (1999), When Can Carbon Abatement Policies Increase Welfare? The Fundamental Role of Distorted Factor Markets, *Journal of Environmental Economics and Management* 37 (1), 52-84.

Pearce, D. (1998), Cost-Benefit Analysis and Environmental Policy, *Oxford Review of Economic Studies* 14 (4), 84-100.

Pezzey, J. (1992), Analysis of Unilateral CO2 Control in the European Community and OECD, *The Energy Journal* 13, 159-171.

Reilly, J., R. Prinn, J. Harnisch, J. Fitzmaurice, H. Jacoby, D. Kicklighter, J. Melillo, P. Stone, A. Sokolov, and C. Wang (1999), Multi-Gas Assessment of the Kyoto Protocol, *Nature* 401, 549-555.

Richels, R., J. Edmonds, H. Gruenspecht, and T. Wigley (1996), *The Berlin Mandate: The Design of Cost Effective Mitigation Strategies*, Energy Modeling Forum 14, Working Paper.

Richels, R. and P. Sturm (1996), The Cost of CO_2 Emissions Reductions: Some Insights from Global Analyses, *Energy Policy* 24 (10/11), 875-887.

Rose, A. (1990), Reducing Conflict in Global Warming Policy: The Potential of Equity as a Unifying Principle, *Energy Policy* 18, 927-935.

Rose, A. and B. Stevens (1998), A Dynamic Analysis of Fairness in Global Warming Policy: Kyoto, Buenos Aires, and Beyond, *Journal of Applied Economics* 1 (2), 329-362.

Rose, A., B. Stevens, J. Edmonds, and M. Wise (1998), International Equity and Differentiation in Global Warming Policy, *Environmental and Resource Economics* 12, 25-51.

Rutherford, T.F. (1995a), *Carbon Dioxide Emission Restrictions in the Global Economy: Leakage, Competitiveness and the Implications for Policy Design*, American Council for Capital Formation, Washington, D.C.

Rutherford, T.F. (1995b), Extensions of GAMS for Complementarity Problems Arising in Applied Economics, *Journal of Economic Dynamics and Control* 19, 1299-1324.

Shoven, J.B. and J. Whalley (1984), Applied General Equilibrium Models of Taxation and International Trade: An Introduction and Survey, *Journal of Economic Literature* 22, 1007-1051.

Shoven, J.B. and J. Whalley (1992), *Applying General Equilibrium*, Cambridge.

Stavins, R. (1999), The Costs of Carbon Sequestration: A Revealed-Preference Approach, *American Economic Review* 89 (4), 994-1009.

Tol, R.S.J. (1999), Spatial and Temporal Efficiency in Climate Policy: Applications of FUND, *Environmental and Resource Economics* 14 (1), 33-49.

Tulpulé, V., S. Brown, J. Lim, C. Polidano, H. Pant, and B. Fisher (1999), An Economic Assessment of the Kyoto Protocol Using the Global Trade and Environment Model, *The Energy Journal* Special Issue, 257-285.

UNFCCC (United Nations Framework Convention on Climate Change) (1997), *Kyoto Protocol to the United Nations Framework Convention on Climate Change*, FCCC/CP/L.7/Add.1, Kyoto.

van der Mensbrugghe, D. (1998), A (Preliminary) Analysis of the Kyoto Protocol, Using the OECD GREEN Model, in: OECD (Ed.), *Economic Modelling of Climate Change*, Paris, 173-204.

Weyant, J. (1998), The Costs of Carbon Emissions Reductions, in: W. Nordhaus (Ed.), *Economics and Policy Issues in Climate Change*, Resources for the Future, Washington, D.C., 191-214.

Weyant, J. (Ed.) (1999), The Costs of the Kyoto Protocol: A Multi-Model Evaluation, *The Energy Journal* Special Issue.

Weyant, J. and T. Olavson (1999), Issues in Modeling Induced Technological Change in Energy, Environment, and Climate Policy, *Journal of Environmental Management and Assessment* 1, 67-85.

Trade Policy

Nikos Kouvaritakis, Nikos Stroblos, Leonidas Paroussos, and Spyridon Tsallas

National Technical University of Athens, 9, Iroon Politechniou str., 15773
Zografou Campus, Athens, Greece
kapros@central.ntua.gr

1 Recent Developments in World Trade – Stylised Facts

1.1 Introduction

Between 1950 and 1999 total world trade has risen by a factor of 14 (Nordström and Vaughan, 1999). The major drivers of world trade expansion are:

- Population growth. World population has increased from 2.5 billion in 1950 to 6 billion in 2000.

- Real GDP growth. During the last 50 years real GDP has risen by a factor of six.

- Globalisation. World integration has proceeded considerably during this period, mainly due to the reduction in trade barriers, and transportation and communication costs.

According to WTO data (Table 7), the value of total world trade in 1999 was $6823 billion. The share of world merchandise trade to total trade was 80.2% ($5473 billions), while services with a trade value of $1350 billion contributed 19.8% to total trade. The merchandise trade content of total trade, depending on the level and the structure of each economy, ranges from 73.3% in the United States to 89% in China[1].

The vast majority of international transactions are concentrated within and among the borders of 25 countries located in three major geographical areas of the world (the so-called triad): East Asia, Europe and North America. These 25 countries

---

[1] This variation would have been greater if we had taken into account a more detailed list of countries.

(Table 8), with 37.3% of the world population, participate with a share of 78% in world merchandise trade.

These data, combined with the various political and economic changes, lead many analysts to the conclusion that the world tends to divide into three commercial blocs: One is the American continent, with the United States as the economic center; another is the European Union; and the third is Pacific Asia, having Japan as the center (Thurow and Lester, 1992).

The series of events that opened the way towards this direction are the following: Concerning the American continent, at the Miami summit of 1994 the 34 countries of the American continent (except Cuba) decided to initiate the foundation of the Free Trade Area of the Americas (FTAA). In this summit was also decided a gradual reduction of the barriers to trade and investments through a procedure of negotiations which will come to an end in 2005.

A similar development took place in Europe in the context of the European Economic Area (EEA), which consists of the European Union and three out of the four (except Switzerland) members of the European Free Trade Association. Under the EEA umbrella, both goods and services travel with no restrictions. Similar provisions have been made for the enlargement of the EEA with the inclusion of the countries of Central and Eastern Europe.

In the case of Asia, the existence of a powerful and continuously broadening ASEAN (Association of South East Nations, for an analysis see pp. 29), as well as the informal, up to now, topology of a yen block with Japan as the center, point towards the creation of a big Asian economic block.

At the level of economic theory, there has been considerable debate on the impact of such developments. The discussion usually centres around Krugman's paradigm of regional trading blocks (Krugman, 1991a). This model predicts the existence of many similar countries that produce a diversified product. Each country specialises in the production of one variety of the product but all consumers consume all the varieties. Under these assumptions, the results in global social welfare are examined in the case that the countries included in the model form trading blocks and impose tariffs on imports from the countries that are outside this block. According to the predictions of the model, global social welfare is maximised when the number of blocks is either one or very big: If there is only one block, then we have perfect globalisation; if we have many trading blocks, then the optimal tariff should be close to zero. Based on this model, Krugman concludes that the worst-case scenario for global social welfare is the one that leads to three blocks. Therefore, the predicted evolution of the world trade towards a division into three blocks should have negative effects on global social welfare.

As it was expected, Krugman faced a lot of criticism, mainly for the assumptions he made. The basic drawback of Krugman's model was that he ignored completely transportation costs. As Krugman himself acknowledges (Krugman, 1991b), if trade blocks were set on the basis of continents and intercontinental transportation costs were restrictively high, then the results in global social welfare would be identical with the ones resulting from the case of global free trade. This newest of his conclusions is much more encouraging for the intercontinental evolution. If the world is divided into three trading blocks, one for each continent, and the intercontinental transportation costs are prohibitively high, then global social welfare will reach the highest possible level.

Within this logic, Krugman calls blocks created at the continental level natural, and intercontinental blocks unnatural. Consequently, Krugman's new result is based on the assumption of prohibitively high intercontinental transportation costs. If this assumption is relaxed, then the results are vague. As Frankel, Stein, and Wei (1994) have shown, global social welfare will be reduced for certain levels of intercontinental costs.

The analysis so far has focused on developed countries. The 49 least developed countries (LDCs) together accounted for 0.5% of merchandise trade taking place in the context of the so-called triad (Table 9). In fact this share has decreased constantly over the last two decades (it was 0.9% in 1980, and 0.6% in 1990).

The above tendencies are partly due to the changes in the structure of world trade over the last decades. Agricultural products, which in 1950 accounted for the largest proportion of the value of trade (around 45%), accounted for the smallest proportion (9.94%) in 1999. Manufactures, on the other hand, have increased their relative importance from 36.6% of total mechandise trade in 1950 to 76.5% in 1999 (Fig. 1).

Least developed countries traditionally specialise in the production of agricultural products. The majority of them also face domestic factors that hamper the transition to production of manufactures. Both of these reasons have resulted in a decline of their relative share of world trade.

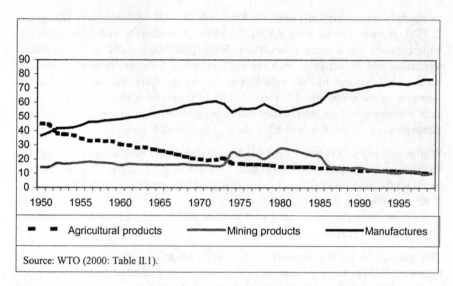

90
80
70
60
50
40
30
20
10
0

1950   1955   1960   1965   1970   1975   1980   1985   1990   1995

■ ■ Agricultural products   ▬▬Mining products   ▬▬▬Manufactures

Source: WTO (2000: Table II.1).

Figure 1:   Relative Share of Main Product Groups to Total Merchandise Trade.

A more detailed view on the product composition of regional trade is depicted in Table 10. The shares of manufactures in total trade in the regions where the most developing countries belong, like Latin America, Asia, Africa, and Middle East, are very high. Despite the low shares of LDCs in world trade, many developing countries become gradually producers and traders of manufactures.

World trade, except the aforementioned general features, is characterised by certain regularities that traditional and new theories attempt to explain. Four stylised facts of international trade are most cited in the bibliography:

- The rate of growth of trade of a country is higher than the growth rate of its GDP;

- products of the same industry (close substitutes) are both imported and exported by a given country – intra-industry trade (IIT);

- high IIT takes place between countries with similar development levels; and

- regional concentration of trade.

1.2   Increasing Openness

During the last 50 years the ratio of external trade (imports + exports) to GDP is increasing at the world level. The same tendency holds for most of the developed and developing countries.

From the data of Table 11 it can be inferred that, in comparison with their 1950 level, total merchandise exports have experienced an 88-fold increase while GDP, during the same period, has risen only by a factor of six. Regarding the increase experienced by the main components of total merchandise trade, exports of agricultural products have increased 19 times, mining products 63 times, and manufactures 184 times from their 1950 level.

The openness ratio is not uniform across the countries. From the data of the upper part of Table 12, there seems to be a positive correlation between the openness ratio and the level of income of a country. Most rich countries have the tendency to trade more intensively. But from the examination of the lower part of the table, referring to openness ratio of specific countries, it can be inferred that this is not the case. There are, for instance, countries like Singapore and Hong Kong with middle level of income and very high openness ratio. The high openness ratio of these countries is explained by the specific nature of their external trade. Both countries import large amounts of semi-finished goods for further processing and then re-export the processed product back to its primary producer or to third countries. Some other countries like Russia and China have low openness ratio due to political reasons.

In the literature there are numerous studies attempting to correlate the openness ratio with the rate of growth of GDP. The evidence, however, is far from being conclusive.

In a widely known article by Sachs and Warner (1995), the positive correlation between trade openness and economic growth was confirmed. A fundamental result of this study is that open developing countries grow with 3.5% more than similar closed ones.

However, openness is not the most important factor of growth. Ben-David and Papell (1998) studied a sample of 74 countries in relation to their economic evolution after World War II. One of the main conclusions of this research was that, in the cases of 46 out of the 74 countries, there was a negative correlation between the vector of growth rates and the corresponding openness vector.

The contradictory evidence in the econometric results is mainly due to the fact that the openness ratio, although it is an important factor in explaining economic growth, is not the most important one. In the literature of economic development there are many significant factors, such as human capital and public infrastructure, that affect GDP growth to a greater extent than the openness ratio.

Beyond econometric research, economic theory has attempted to explain the relationship between free trade and economic development. According to the traditional theory of Heckscher-Ohlin, which adopts the assumptions of constant returns to scale, fixed technologies, and perfect competition, free trade is correlated to income as follows: Every country specialises in the production of the goods where it has a comparative advantage and, therefore, distributes its resources more efficiently. This, consequently, increases productivity and, therefore, GDP. The logic, however, of the theory of Heckscher-Ohlin depends on the different ratios of endowments that every country has, so we should expect trade among countries to be more extensive when the difference in the endowments is bigger.

However a general empirical observation is that the greater volume of trade is conducted between countries with more-or-less the same structure of endowments. More on this issue can be found in the section below dealing with the analysis of IIT.

An additional disadvantage of traditional trade theory is also that the assumptions lead to static gains from free trade. Indeed, free trade increases the GDP level once and for all by introducing trade specialisation. It does not, however, provide a satisfactory explanation for the rate of growth of GDP, even less for the reasons that cause the more rapid increase of trade associated to increases of GDP.

The Heckscher-Ohlin theory represents a traditional static interpretation of trade. More recent research and notably the New Trade Theory has concentrated on dynamic aspects. The New Trade Theory is more realistic in its assumptions because it takes into account imperfect competition, increasing returns to scale, and evolving technologies. According to two of the most important representatives of the New Trade Theory, Helpman and Krugman (1985), a model of this category is more adequate in explaining the increase of trade associated with the increase of GDP in the industrial countries. The assumptions underlying their model are:

- The world consists of many countries.

- The producers produce varieties of a product.

- Production is characterised by increasing returns to scale.

- The market is characterised by a monopolistic competition framework.

- Consumers in all countries demand all varieties of this product because they are supposed to have a 'love of variety' demand structure.

- Trade among countries is balanced and free.

The intra-group trade volume E of a group of countries is:

$$E = s \cdot Y \cdot (1 - H) \tag{1}$$

where

Y is the sum of GDP of the countries that are included in the group,

s is the share of Y of the group in world GDP,

s_i is the share of GDP of the country i in Y

$$H = \sum_i s_i^2 \tag{2}$$

is the Herfindahl index of income inequality among the countries of the group. Differentiating the above relationship, and forming the rates of change, we get:

$$\frac{dE}{E} = \frac{dY}{Y} - \frac{sH}{(1-H)} \cdot \frac{dH}{H} \tag{3}$$

Therefore, it is safe to conclude that the increase in trade $\left(\frac{dE}{E}\right)$ exceeds the increase in GDP $\left(\frac{dY}{Y}\right)$ if $\left(\frac{dH}{H}\right)$ is negative. In other words, trade increases more rapidly than GDP if the income inequality among the countries decreases.

An empirical evidence of this conclusion could be found in a recent study of Ben-David and Kimhi (2001). One of the main conclusions is that when countries trade intensively with each other, there is a tendency to exhibit a relatively high incidence of income convergence.

1.3   Intra-Industry Trade (Takes Place Between Countries of Similar Development Levels)

Since the 1960s it has become obvious that countries simultaneously import and export products that are close substitutes and, therefore, belong to the same industry. Examples of this kind of trade can be taken from Table 13. For example, the European Union exports to the United States 'power generating machinery' worth $10.96 Billion and simultaneously imports $13.68 billion worth of the same commodities from the United States. Such an event of course could be attributed to an aggregation bias because under the heading 'power generating machinery' is not described a homogeneous good but a lot of similar individual products. Nevertheless this event is present also in studies using more detailed levels of disaggregation. (Sørensen et al., 1991).

This empirical evidence comes to an apparent contradiction with the traditional theories of international trade based on the concept of comparative advantage. According to the traditional theory, international trade can only take the form of inter-industry exchanges since each country specialises in the production of products most suited to its factor endowment. Hence the more different two countries are in their endowments the larger is the volume of bilateral trade that can be expected.

The persistence of IIT has led to new theories based on the concepts of horizontally and vertically differentiated products (Helpman and Krugman, 1985; Lancaster, 1980). According to these theories of international trade, products are not homogeneous but are differentiated horizontally in the sense that they are varieties of a product characterised by different attributes. The products can also be vertically differentiated in the sense that they are varieties of a product characterised by different qualities. On the demand side it is supposed that consumers will demand all the varieties of a product because 'they love variety'. Moreover, on the supply side, economies of scale induce the producers to produce differentiated products. It means that the higher the level of GDP of a country, the more the varieties of goods produced in that country and the volume of bilateral trade between two countries will be larger if the countries have similar levels of GDP. So the new theories of international trade sufficiently explain the stylised fact that 'intra-industry trade takes place between countries of similar development levels'.

According to aforementioned definitions, IIT is composed of horizontally and vertically differentiated products. For the new international trade theories it was necessary to have a measure, with the assistance of which total trade could be broken down to inter-industry trade and IIT.

The most widely used indicator measuring the scope of intra industry trade is the Grubel-Lloyd index (Grubel and Lloyd, 1975). The G-L index is given by

$$B_j = 1 - \frac{\left|X_j - M_j\right|}{X_j + M_j} \tag{4}$$

where

X_j: value of exports of commodity j by a country,

M_j: value of imports of commodity j by a country.

The G-L index calculates the overlap between imports and exports of similar traded commodities. The value of G-L index varies between 0 (all the trade is inter-industry) and 1 (all the trade is intra industry).

Table 14 includes calculated G-L indices for two sets of countries. The first set consists of countries with similar levels of GDP (EU, USA, Canada). The second set is composed of countries with different development levels.

Regarding the values for the set of 'rich' countries, two kinds of remarks can be made:

• IIT between the countries is substantial as the value of the G-L index indicates (with the exception of trade in mining products between USA and Canada).

• IIT trade is higher for total manufactures in comparison to the agricultural and mining products. This indicates that in the sector of manufactures there is more product differentiation and larger extent of economies of scale.

Both of the aforementioned remarks do not hold in the case of countries with different levels of GDP, with the exception of manufactures in the bilateral trade between Japan and Korea. This indicates that the trade between the countries of the second set is mainly inter-industry. Regarding the high G-L indices in the case of manufactures, it can be explained by the high level of trade in semi-finished goods, parts and components, which are dominant between the countries of East Asia. In East Asia the fragmentation and the sharing of manufacturing process between countries of the area has long been a major and evolving process (Ng and Yeats, 1999).

1.4   Regionalism

One of the characteristics of world trade is that intra-regional trade increases faster than world trade. The definition of the term 'region' is of vital importance, since it is related to opposing arguments in the modern theory of world trade. There are two definitions of this term: According to the first one, region is defined as a natural geographical area, such as Africa; according to the second one, region is an aggregation of countries, which are grouped under the framework of a specific regional trade agreement (for example NAFTA). The definitions in this case are significant because they are related to the conflicting arguments in the context of the theory of international trade.

The evolution of the intra-regional trade from 1960 to 1994 is depicted in Table 15. The term region in this table follows the second definition. The most common way, although not the ideal one, to estimate the evolution of the intra-regional trade is to calculate the share of the intra-regional trade of a specific region to the world trade, which is:

$$\frac{M_{IN} + X_{IN}}{M_{TOT} + X_{TOT}} \tag{5}$$

where

M_{IN} :   intra-regional imports,

X_{IN} :   intra-regional exports,

M_{TOT} :   total imports of the region,

X_{TOT} :   total exports of the region.

One of the main disadvantages of this index is that it does not take into account the relative importance of regional trade agreements within the total world trade. This may lead to inaccurate conclusions. For example, the most impressive increase of intra-regional trade in recent years was that of the ANDEAN PACT agreement, which increased the intra-regional trade by five times (1.8% in 1960 to 10% in 1994). However, the small share of the trade of this regional agreement within total world trade reduces considerably the significance of this increase. In addition, it should be noted that the share of exports of the ANDEAN PACT to world trade has decreased. Similar remarks can be made for the Economic Community of West Africa, the Latin American Free Trade Agreement, and the Central American Common Market.

The agreement with the highest increase of intra-regional trade and significant share in the world trade is ASEAN. For the period 1960-1994, its intra-regional trade increased more than two times (from 7,5% in 1960 to 19,1% in 1994). At the same time its share in the world trade was doubled.

Looking at Regional Trade Agreements that have a big share in the world trade, the conclusions are ambiguous. The intra-regional trade share of the European Union increased from 40% in 1960 to 55.4% in 1994. The actual increase was 60% in 1992, but it was influenced downwards by the 1993 recession. In 1999, this share stood at 63.5%. Moreover, it should be mentioned that the relative stagnation of the share of trade of the European Union in world trade reduces the significance of the increase of intra-EU trade (in 1960 it was 40.7% and in 1999 was 39%). Similar remarks can be drawn for the North American Free Trade Agreement.

Summing up the conclusions that can be drawn from the examination of Table 15, it can be pointed out that the only trade agreement that has increased significantly the intra-regional trade at the world level was ASEAN. The poor conclusions stemming from the previous analysis are due to the bias of the adopted index. Several authors Anderson and Norheim (1993), Drysdale and Garnaut (1982) and (1983) suggest that an important issue here is to examine whether a typical member of a Regional Trade Agreement trades more with the rest of its members than with countries that do not belong to the specific Regional Trade Agreement. The simplest way to verify this is to divide the intra-regional trade share, which was used above, by the share of the Regional Trade Agreement in world trade; this new index is called 'Simple Intra-Regional Trade Concentration Ratio' and is given by:

$$I = \frac{\dfrac{F_i}{E_i}}{\dfrac{M_i}{M}} \tag{6}$$

where

F_i :   intra-industry exports of regional trade agreement $_i$,

E_i :   total exports of regional trade agreement $_i$,

M_i :   total imports of regional trade agreement $_i$,

M :   world imports.

The rationale underlying this index is that, if the intra-regional trade as a share of the total exports of the Regional Trade Agreement is equal to the total imports of the Regional Trade Agreement as a share of the total imports of the world, i.e. the intra region trade has the same pattern with the world pattern, then the index equals 1. On the other hand, if there is a preference for intra-regional trade compared to the world trade, then the index should be greater than 1. The estimations of the simple concentration ratios for a number of Regional Trade Agreements are depicted in Table 16. The fact that all ratios in this table are greater than one shows that trade among members of the same Regional Trade Agreement is higher than the trade with the rest of the regions.

A number of studies (see, for instance, Frankel, 1997) reach the same conclusion by examining more Regional Trade Agreements and for more time periods. Furthermore based on the fact that the Simple Intra-Regional Trade Concentration Ratios are greater than one for almost all the Regional Trade Agreements, they concluded that world trade is regionally concentrated. Economists give different interpretations to the factors that lead to this stylised fact. The differences are based on whether the existing regional concentration can be justified by geographical proximity or by the trade facilitations that are provided in the context of Regional Trade Agreement (reduction of tariff and non tariff barriers etc).

According to Krugman (1991) and Summers (1991), the dominant explanation of high concentration is geographical proximity. Krugman specifically reports, as an example, the case of USA and Canada as well as the case of the four major traders of the European Union. The regression results indicated that the USA and Canada trade 13 times more than they would if they were not neighbour countries. Similarly, the four biggest economies of the European Union trade 7 times more than they would if they were not close enough. On the opposite side, there are Bhagwati (1992, 1993) and Panagariya (1995), who claim that the reason of the regional concentration of trade is the set of preferential relationships existing in the context of a Regional Trade Agreement.

Several subsequent studies have focused on establishing the relative importance of these two factors. The results are mixed, justifying either one side or the other (for a review see Frankel, 1997).

2 Global Trade Liberalisation: GATT/WTO

2.1 Introduction: The Challenge for a Rules-Based Trading System

One of the most important characteristics of the post Word War II period is the continuous increase in the globalisation of world economy. As the stylised facts of the previous chapter suggest, world trade during this period expanded steadily. One of the major drivers contributing to this evolution is the progressive reduction of barriers to trade and to foreign direct investments (FDI). The establishments of GATT (General Agreement on Tariffs and Trade) and WTO (World Trade Organisation) are considered cornerstones in the phasing out of trade and non-trade barriers, which characterises the post-1948 period.

In order for international agreements to be functional, the sovereign countries should, as far as trade policies are concerned, cede a part of their independence. The perception that trade policy is a national issue has many supporters both at government level and within groups of resistance to globalisation. Such views have been common mainly at the government level in the beginning of the 20th century. The way that national interests are served is through the distortion of world trade prices in order to achieve the desired distributional effects for the intervening country. This can be usually achieved by imposing a tariff or a non-tariff barrier in such a way that the terms of trade will be affected and the imposing country should be able to import more goods in exchange of a unit of its export good. It is obvious that the other countries will react in the same way to such a policy, resulting in 'beggar-thy-neighbour'-type phenomena. This phenomenon was prevalent during the Great Depression of the 1930s, when the US led the world in increasing trade barriers in order to assist the recovery of the US economy.

The negative results of this kind of policy for global social welfare have created the need of cooperation among countries in order to lessen protectionism. These types of cooperation should obey some criteria that will assure the interests of all participating countries. Two are the most important criteria on which international cooperations are based: the results-based criteria and the rules-based ones.

The results-based international agreements that came up during the 1960s and 1970s included mainly Communist countries or least developed countries. These agreements were at the level of products, and included barter trade, clearing trade, etc. After the fall of the Communist regimes, these agreements have lost most of their importance in international trade.

The rules-based agreements have been far more successful during the last century. The main idea of these agreements is that independent countries voluntarily undertake to respect certain world trade rules. Such a commitment from member states is definitely restricting their independence on trade policy.

In exchange though, the rules-based agreements provide new kinds of possibilities to participating countries. First of all, these rules are defined and discussed at group level and most of the times receive unanimous approval. Secondly, they improve the ability of the less powerful countries to negotiate, because it is easier for the stronger countries to use their market power at the bilateral than the multilateral level. Thirdly, the governments of such countries can utilise the existence of these agreements as a strong counterargument against any internal opposition to trade liberalisation.

2.2   A Brief History of GATT/WTO

The GATT was established as a provisional agreement for gradual tariff elimination after World War II. In order to correct the large overhang of protectionist measures that prevailed from the early 1930s, two parallel efforts were undertaken during the mid-40s, aiming to give a boost to trade liberalisation.

In the context of the first effort, 53 countries agreed on a draft Charter for International Trade Organisation (ITO), a new specialised agency of the United Nations. The ITO Charter was agreed at a UN Conference in Havana in 1948 and it was one piece of the so-called Bretton-Woods system, designed to promote and manage global economic development. (The International Monetary Fund and the World Bank were the other two main components).

Under the initiative of the US, as a parallel effort to the above, tariff negotiations opened among 23 countries in Geneva in April 1947. This first round of negotiations resulted in 45,000 tariff concessions affecting $10 billion (about 20%) of the world trade. At the end of negotiations in October 1947, it was also agreed that the importance of these concessions should be protected by the trade rules in the draft ITO Charter. The tariff concessions and rules together became known as the General Agreement on Tariffs and Trade and entered into force in January 1948. After the denial of the Senate of US government to agree with the ratification of Havana's Charter in 1950, ITO was effectively dead, so the GATT remained the only multilateral instrument governing international trade from 1948 until the establishment of WTO.

The main goals of GATT were to lower or to eliminate tariffs as well as other types of barriers to trade (non-tariff barriers). These goals have been achieved through multilateral trade negotiations, or 'Trade Rounds', under the auspices of GATT. From 1948 to 1994 eight negotiating 'Rounds' took place; the most important of them were:

- *Dillon Round (1961-1962)* – resulted in 20% reduction in custom duties of about 600 tariff lines (groups of products).

- *Kennedy Round (1964-1967)* – The main result was a new Anti-Dumping Agreement.

- *Tokyo Round (1973-1979)* – The results included a) an average of one third cut in customs duties in the world's nine major industrial markets, bringing the average tariff on manufactured products down to 4.7%, and b) a series of agreements, of which:

  ❖ 6 of them often referred to as 'codes'

    ▪ technical barriers to trade

    ▪ imports licensing procedures

    ▪ government procurement

    ▪ customs valuation

    ▪ subsidies and countervailing measures

    ▪ anti-dumping

  ❖ 3 sectoral agreements

    ▪ bovine meat arrangements

    ▪ international diary arrangement

    ▪ trade in civil aircraft.

- *Uruguay Round (1986-1993)* – The main result was the Marrakech Agreement Establishing the World Trade Organisation (WTO), with which the subsequent section deals.

The World Trade Organisation was established in 1995 in the context of the Uruguay Round, fully replacing the previous GATT Secretariat in the position of the organisation responsible for administering the international trade regime. Initially composed of 81 members, it became open later to all 125 members of GATT upon their ratification of the Uruguay Round Final Act. On 31 May 2001, WTO was composed of 141 members, while 31 countries were observers. Decisions are made by consensus of the entire membership; however, majority vote is also possible. The WTO's agreements have been ratified by all parliaments of the member countries.

The basic structure of WTO is depicted in Figure 2. The WTO's top-level decision-making body is the Ministerial Conference, which is composed of the ministers for international trade from all member countries and meets at least once every two years. The General Council, which is exactly below the Ministerial Conference, is composed of ambassadors who meet several times a year in the Geneva headquarters. The General Council also meets as the Trade Policy Review Body and the Dispute Settlement Body. At the next level, the Goods Council, Services Council, and Intellectual Property (TRIPS) Council report to the General

Council. Numerous specialised committees, working groups, and working parties deal with the individual agreements and other areas such as the environment, development, membership applications, and regional trade agreements (www.wto.org). The WTO is not a simple extension of GATT. The latter was not an international organisation with institutional foundation, but an intergovernmental treaty. The WTO is an international organisation administering multilateral agreements, pertaining to trade in goods as GATT did, and in addition to trade in services (GATS), and trade related aspects of intellectual property rights (TRIPs). The WTO dispute settlement system is also faster, more automated, and, in general, stronger than that of GATT.

Nevertheless, the GATT lives on as 'GATT 1994', the updated version of GATT 1947, which is an integral part of the WTO Agreement and which continues to provide the key rules affecting international trade in goods. The main functions of WTO are to:

- administer WTO trade agreements;

- provide a forum for trade negotiations;

- provide a dispute settlement system;

- review national trade policies;

- provide technical assistance and training programs to developing countries cooperating with other international organisations.

2.3   WTO Agreements – Overview

The table of contents of "The Results of the Uruguay Round of Multilateral Trade Negotiations: The Legal Texts" includes a catalogue of 60 agreements, supplements, decisions, and understandings. The plethora of these legal documents follows the simple structure of Figure 3.

The agreements regarding products and services can be divided into three parts:

- In the first part there are agreements that describe the general principles, as the 'General Agreement on Tariffs and Trade (GATT)', which refers to the trade of products, and the 'General Agreement on Tariffs in Services (GATS)', which refers to services.

- The second part also includes agreements and supplements, which deal with the more specialised sectors, and issues that concern trade of goods and services in general.

- In the third part there are also detailed catalogues with the commitments of the member states regarding the entrance of foreign products and related services in their markets. In the case of GATT, they refer to the upper bound on tariffs on imported goods decided for each member. Furthermore, it includes higher level of tariffs and quotas for agricultural products. In the case of GATS, these restrictions provide quantitative information regarding the number of foreign producers of services allowed access to approach the internal market. Finally, the catalogues of some special kinds of services for which the MFN (Most Favoured Nation) principle of non-discrimination (MFN exemptions) is not applicable are also included.

The agreement on Trade Related Aspects of Intellectual Property Rights (TRIPS), consisting of general principles that regard the specific form of trade, is not – up to now – accompanied by additional, more specialised agreements, as in the case of GATT and GATS.

The agreements mentioned above, having the form of large and complex legal documents that deal with many and conflicting issues, are characterised by two special principles, which are:

Non-discrimination principle: According to this principle member states have to treat all other members of WTO equally. This principle has two composites:

1.   the MFN Treatment,

2.   the National Treatment.

According to the MFN principle, if a member country provides a privilege to another member country, then it is obliged to provide the same privilege to all other member states of WTO. The MFN principle is very important in the WTO framework. However, some exclusions from the MFN principle are indeed possible in WTO. The most important exclusion is the creation of several Regional Trade Agreements in the framework of which privileges can be taken advantage of only by the members of these agreements and not all the members of WTO (article XXIV of GATT).

Following the National Treatment principle, imported goods, after satisfaction of imposed border rules, and goods produced in the home country should be treated equally. This means that imported goods existing in the home market should face the same taxation with the ones imposed on similar goods produced in the home market. The National Treatment principle is applied from the moment that imported goods have entered the home market. Therefore, imposing tariffs on imported goods does not violate the National Treatment principle, even if similar goods produced in the home market do not face an equal aggravation.

Transparency Principle: Member states of WTO are obligated, according to the Transparency Principle, to publish all trade-related measures taken, and create institutions that control governmental trade-related decisions. These are legal obligations included in the 10th article of GATT and the 3rd of GATS.

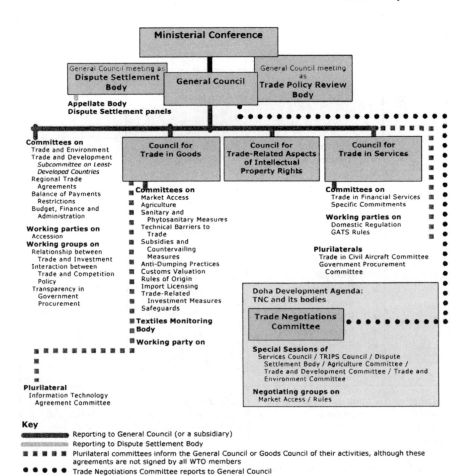

Source: www.wto.org/english/thewto_e/whatis_e/tif_e/org2_e.htm.

Figure 2:   WTO Organisational Chart.

	Goods	Services	Intellectual Property	Disputes
Basic Principles	GATT	GATS	TRIPS	Dispute Settlement
Additional Details	• Agriculture • Textiles and clothing • Health regulations for farm products • Products standards • Investment measures • Anti-dumping measures • Customs valuation methods • Pre-shipment inspection • Rules of origin • Import licensing • Subsidies and counter measures • Safeguards	• Movement of natural persons • Air transports • Financial services • Shipping • Telecommunications		
Market Access Commitments	Countries' schedules of commitments	Countries' schedules of commitments (and MFN exemptions)		

Figure 3:   The Basic Structure of the WTO Agreements (Source: WTO, 1999).

Internal acts and institutions that promote the transparency of trade are assisted by Trade Policy Reviews, which are country-level reports prepared from the WTO secretariat. Besides publication of measures, in the framework of agreements there are other transparency-of-trade promoting acts founded too. According to the 2nd article of GATT, member countries have to bound the tariff rates they impose on products of other WTO member countries, which means that they cannot exceed the agreed upper bound of the tariff for each product included in their tariff schedule. In this way, predictability of world trade is leveraged. Another way through which transparency and predictability of world trade is promoted is the discouragement of member states to impose quotas. On the contrary, tariffs imposed following the WTO framework are considered to be the best trade policy measures to serve this purpose. The arguments in favour of tariffs are the following (Hoekman and Kostecki, 2001):

- Tariffs assure direct linkage between the vectors of foreign and home prices, which is interrupted with the utilisation of quotas.

- By using tariffs, it is easier to assure nondiscrimination among imports from different countries. On the other hand, quotas are usually based on administrative decisions.

- Tariffs are more transparent because using tariffs makes it easier to calculate the customs' aggravation, whereas using quotas calculations are difficult.

- Tariffs contribute to the predictability because every seller knows the price of his product in the foreign market.

The analysis of quantitative results of the WTO agreements will follow the structure of Figure 3, separating the analysis into quantitative results regarding goods, and quantitative results regarding services.

2.4   Market Access for Goods

Because of the special way that agricultural products are treated, this section consists of two subsections: examining tariff and non-tariff barriers for industrial products in general, and on agricultural products respectively.

2.4.1   Market Access for Industrial Products

One of the most important contributions of the Uruguay Round was the radical improvement that has been achieved in market access for industrial products[2]. This improvement has two dimensions: One is related to the commitment of the member countries to bound their tariff rates, and the second to the commercial obstacles existing in the pre-Uruguay Round period.

Apart from a few cases, tariff cuts on industrial products took place in five equal time periods from 1995 to 1999. Therefore, we can hypothesise that, regarding industrial products, we are going through the post-Uruguay Round period. Thus, in this section, when we state 'post-Uruguay Round period' we mean the state under which there exists full implementation of the commitments that have been agreed at the Uruguay Round.

A synthetic picture of the pieces of information that come from the tariff schedules of member states is provided in Table 18 of the Annex. In the total of the member states of WTO, the share of industrial tariff lines subject to bound tariff has almost doubled in comparison to the pre-Uruguay Round period (increased from 43% to 83%).

---

[2]   For the definition of the term 'Industrial Products' see Table 17 of the Annex.

Developed economies as well as transition economies have bounded their tariff rates for all industrial products almost completely, with a coverage rate of 99% and 98% respectively; the percentages for the pre-Uruguay Round period were 78% and 73%. Developing countries have made the most impressive increase in the share of bounded tariff lines, more than tripling it from 21% to 73% for pre- and post-Uruguay Round periods respectively.

At the regional level, North American countries (Canada, US) have almost fully bounded all their industrial tariff lines. This percentage of bounded goods for these countries was very high (99%) even before the Uruguay Round. With the exception of tariff lines of Canada referring to transport equipment and mineral products (Table 19), all other tariff lines are 100% bounded.

Latin America has bounded 100% of its tariff lines. Latin American countries apply a uniform ceiling for all industrial products. The only exception is Brazil, which applies a uniform ceiling to only a small part of industrial products. Nevertheless, even this country has bounded tariffs in all industrial products (WTO, 2001). The smallest increase in bounded shares of tariff lines has occurred in Western Europe (from 78% to 82%). This small share is mainly due to Turkey that has left unbounded about 64% of its industrial products. In contrast, the European Union has bounded all its industrial products. The largest share of bounded goods (about 98%) after North and Latin America is observed in the countries of Central Europe.

The smallest shares of boundness can be found in Asian and African countries with 68% and 69% respectively. It must be noted though that the share for Africa in the post-Uruguay Round period has increased more than five times (from 13% to 69%) while for Asia it has increased more than four times (from 16% to 68%).

At the country level, there are great differences in the shares of bounded lines. In Asia, the largest shares are found in East Asian and Pacific countries – New Zealand (100%), Japan (99%), Australia (96%), Indonesia (93%), and Korea (90.4%). On the other hand, there are many developing countries with much lower rates; a characteristic case is Sri Lanka, which has bounded only 8% of its industrial tariff lines. This idiosyncratic situation also stands for Hong Kong and Macao. These countries have left unbounded a large share of their industrial products (76% and 90% respectively), while the tariffs imposed are zero.

In the case of Africa, apart from Cabon (100%) and South Africa (98%), all other countries have left unbounded more than half of their tariff lines. Cameroon, for instance, has bound only three out of its 4721 tariff lines.

According to the share of bounded tariff lines for every category of industrial products, important information can be extracted from Table 19. Based on the sample of countries included in the Table, we can make the following marks: Larger shares of bounded lines in relation to the average of every country can be observed in the non-electric machinery sector. In 32 out of the 41 countries included in the sample, the share of bounded tariff of non-electric machinery is larger than the share of bounded tariff lines of the country. It should be noted that this does not apply to 9 countries in Africa and Asia. The same stands for the sector of chemical and photographic supplies (31 out of 41 countries, where 9 of them are in Asia and Africa), as well as the sectors of wood pulp, paper and furniture, and textiles and clothing (11 out of 41).

In contrast, smaller shares from the average of the country can be observed in the sectors of transport equipments (17 out of 41 countries, where 13 of them are in Asia and Africa), fish and fish products, and mineral products and precious stones (14 out of 41 countries).

Apart from bounding their tariff lines, WTO member states agreed to reduce the level of tariff rate bounds existing before the Uruguay Round on a number of tariff lines. The part of the total tariff lines that the member countries agreed to reduce is provided in Table 20. According to the data of this Table, developed economies have accepted reductions of 67% of their tariff lines, developing countries 46%, and transition economies 83%.

At the regional level, North America and Western Europe accepted to reduce the total of bounded tariff lines (100% and 99% respectively). Latin American countries also agreed to reduce the bounded rates significantly; it is worth mentioning though that they are much higher than applied rates. The results of these reductions in bound rates can be seen in Table 21.

On average, on a trade-weighted basis, tariffs imposed by developed countries on their imports from all around the world have been reduced by 40%. These reductions proved to be useful to the developed countries themselves, since tariffs coming from the developed and developing countries (37% and 25%) were reduced less than the average. This is because the tariffs imposed by the developed countries on textiles and fish products were reduced less than the average. Regarding developing countries, the reduction of tariffs coming from developed countries was 25% when the corresponding percentage for imports from developing countries was 21%.

The biggest reductions (see Table 22) were on the sectors of wood, pulp, paper, and furniture (69%), metals (62%), and non-electric machinery (60%). In relation to imports from developing countries, there has been an important decrease in tariff rates for the mineral products and precious stones sector (69%).

The smallest reductions have occurred in the sectors textiles and clothing, and leather products, where the cuts of tariff rates were 22% and 18% respectively for imports from all countries, while for developing countries these cuts were 23% and 19% respectively. The same kind of small reduction in tariffs (23%) was observed in the sector of transport equipment.

There are important variations in average bound rates per category of industrial good. In most of the countries of the world, the highest average bound rates, compared to the average bound rates of the country, are in the sectors textiles and clothing, and leather, rubber footwear and travel goods; to a lesser extent, this also applies in transport equipment, and fish and fish products. The higher tariffs on textiles are in India (87.8%) and in Turkey (80%), and lower ones (except from Hong Kong and Macao, where tariffs are zero), are in Switzerland (4.6%) and EU (7.9%). Also noticeable are the relatively high and to a great extent uniform tariffs imposed by the Latin American countries. This is due to the fact that these countries have applied a flat ceiling bounding all products. In the analysis up to now we dealt with post-Uruguay Round tariff rates. In reality though, many countries have much lower tariff rates. Therefore, these countries can retain the option of increasing substantially actual tariff rates without violating their commitment to the WTO. A more detailed picture for the differences between average bound rates and average applied tariffs per country and kind of industrial product is in Table 24.

As it can be seen in this Table, the bigger differences between bound and applied tariff rates appear in the countries of Latin America, in Turkey, in Poland, in Romania, and in the Philippines. In some countries the differences are negligible, meaning that these countries have stated as bound tariff rates the tariff rate actually imposed. This is the case for Canada, Norway, Switzerland, Singapore, and the Republic of Korea.

For a series of other countries there exist negative signs, leading us to the conclusion that applied tariff rates are higher than bound rates. This happens because of the different dates to which the data of the Table refer to. In particular, the elements of bound tariff rates refer to the end of the implementation period of tariff reduction. For most of the countries, this period ended in 2000[3]. The data for applied tariff rates correspond to years before 1999, which means that these countries have been applying higher tariff rates from the bound tariff rates, since the implementation period of rate reduction had not finished. Examples of such countries are the European Union, the United States, Japan, Czech Republic, Hungary, etc.

2.4.2   Market Access for Agricultural Products

Agricultural products were subjected under the general regulations of GATT agreements, as the latter were modified in the different Rounds, even before the Uruguay Round. But the loopholes in these regulations rendered them technically less functional than the regulations on the industrial products. The main features of the agricultural products before the Uruguay Round were:

---

[3]   Many countries have asked and were granted an extension to 2005 for the end of the implementation period. Such countries are Argentina, Chile, Colombia, Cost Rica, Mexico, Peru, Hong Kong, Republic of Korea, Macau, Philippines, Singapore, Cameroon, Chad, and Cabon.

- variety of export subsidies,

- broadness of quantitative import restrictions (quotas and other non-tariff barriers).

In the opening of the Uruguay Round many agricultural products had tariff rates as the only protection measure. These rates, either bound or unbound, corresponded to 75% of the total tariff lines of the agricultural products. For the rest, the protection measure applied was non-tariff barriers in the form of quotas.

Given the opposition of WTO to quantitative restrictions, one of the primary measures that were taken during the Uruguay round was the tariffication of the non-tariff barriers. This tariffication procedure consisted of replacing the non-tariff measures with tariff measures that granted the same protection. Another crucial point during the round was the determination of the base rates of duties upon which the tariff reduction would take place later on. These base rates were included in the tariff schedules negotiations of the countries during the Uruguay Round.

The determination of the base rates was different for each country, depending on the pre-Uruguay Round state of the country. For the tariff lines that had a bound rate before the Uruguay Round, it became the base rate for the Uruguay Round. In the case where tariff lines are characterised by an unbound tariff rate, the base rate for the developed countries was considered the applied rate (September 1986). Developing countries were provided the possibility to have a ceiling bounding for all unbound goods in exchange of not reducing the tariffs on these products. Finally, for the products that went through the tariffication procedure, the base rate was considered to be equal to the tariff produced by this procedure.

A brief overview of this situation is given in Table 25. Comparing this table with the respective table for the industrial products it can be inferred that 100% of the agricultural products have bound tariff rates (thus there exists no column 'No offer'). This reflects the fact that all agricultural products have bound tariff rates. The second observation has to do with the 4th column of Table 25 with the title 'Binding without reductions'; as it was mentioned earlier, developed countries indicated the base rates subject to reduction in their tariff schedules. Therefore, where there is a zero, all agricultural products will go through a reduction. On the other hand, in the case of developing countries 15 indicates a ceiling binding for some products that will not go through any further reduction. Ceiling bindings were offered to the countries of Latin America, Africa, and Asia (see end of Table 25). Given the way that base rates or ceiling bindings were generated, the reduction of base rates was agreed in the following way: For the developed countries the anticipated unweighted average reduction is 36% under the restriction of more than 15% for every product. The implementation period for this reduction was five years (1995-2000). For developing countries an unweighted reduction of 24% was agreed, under the restriction of more than 10% for every product. The implementation period is 10 years (1995-2004).

The reductions of tariffs of developed countries at the end of the implementation period in comparison to the pre-Uruguay Round period situation is presented in Table 26. According to the data of this table, tariffs in agricultural products will be reduced by 37%. The smallest reduction will be in dairy products (26%) and the biggest in 'Cut flowers, plants and vegetable materials', and 'Other agricultural products' (48%). For the special category 'Tropical products' the reduction is 43%. The reductions in tariffs of the 2nd subcategory range from 37% (tropical nuts and fruits) to 52% (spices, flowers and plants). Information for the levels of bound tariff rates for selected economies can be found in Table 27. This table includes OECD and World Bank estimations for the average bound tariffs for both industrial and agricultural products (from "Market Access: Unfinished Business" of WTO). Although the two organisations have adopted different estimation techniques, the essence of their results is the same. According to the data presented in Table 27, the average bound tariff rates for the industrial and agricultural products are at similar low levels for North America and in similar high levels for Latin America. On the other hand, for the rest of the world, including the European Union, agricultural products have substantially higher average bound tariff rates compared to industrial products. The higher bound tariff rates are observed in Asia (e.g. India, Bangladesh and Korea are above 50%) and in Latin America (from 33% to 88%). The lowest bound tariff rates are observed in North America (5%), in Australia (3%), and in New Zealand (7%-8%).

Countries of Latin America and of Asia have applied ceiling bindings which are higher than the applied tariff rates. Bolivia for example applies an average tariff rate on agricultural products of 10% and its average bound tariff rate is 40%. On the other hand bound tariff rates in developed countries correspond to the applied tariff rates.

2.5   Market Access for Services

Trade in services accounts for over 20% of all trade. GATS was negotiated in the Uruguay Round and covers all different ways of providing services. These are:

• cross border supply (e.g. telecommunication services),

• consumption abroad (e.g. tourism),

• commercial presence (e.g. financial and insurance companies),

• presence of natural persons (e.g. consultants).

Moreover, GATS operates on four levels: i) the main part containing general principles and obligations, ii) annexes dealing with rules for specific sectors, iii) individual countries' commitments to provide access to their markets and iv) lists showing where countries are temporarily not applying the principle of non-discrimination.

The activities that are covered by the GATS are divided in 12 sectors:

1. business services (including professional and computer services),

2. communication services,

3. construction and engineering services,

4. distribution services,

5. educational services,

6. environmental services,

7. financial services,

8. health services,

9. tourism and travel services,

10. recreational, cultural and sporting services,

11. transport services,

12. other services.

According to GATS, the so-called MFN (Most Favoured Nation) treatment applies to all services. However, equal treatment of domestic and foreign service providers applies only in the context of specific commitments and exemptions are allowed[4]. Furthermore, in order to ensure transparency GATS dictates that governments should publish all relevant laws and regulations, they have also to notify WTO of any changes in regulations that apply to the services that come under specific commitments. For any regulatory change that a government makes in the service sector it should provide an impartial means of regulation. Another basic principle of GATS is the principle of "recognition" which states that all member countries should have equal opportunities in making agreements related to the recognition of professional qualifications.

Moreover, a certain goal of GATS is to take the liberalisation process further by encouraging more negotiations and increasing the level of commitments in schedules. Regarding the implication of GATS in developing countries it is expected that many new opportunities will rise for these countries and the areas in which they are expected to have comparative advantage or might develop one are:

• business services, including computer services,

• construction and engineering services,

• environmental services,

---

[4]   Under GATS a country does not have to apply national treatment in sectors where it has made no commitment.

- tourism and travel services,

- recreational, cultural, and sporting services,

- health services.

Additionally, once a government has made a commitment within GATS to open a service sector to foreign competition, it must not normally restrict money being transferred out of the country as payment for services supplied in that sector.

Regarding market access, commitments are negotiated as multilateral packages, although bilateral bargaining sessions are needed to develop the packages. A country is permitted to stipulate its commitments subject to specified conditions. These conditions can take the following forms (Article XVI):

1. limitations on the number of service suppliers allowed,

2. limitations on the value of transactions or assets (e.g. only 10% of the reinsurance value may be placed with foreign companies),

3. limitations on the total quantity of service output or total number of service operations,

4. limitations on the number of natural persons that may be employed,

5. limitations on the type of legal entity through which a service supplier is permitted to supply service,

6. limitations on participation of foreign capital.

A country is not permitted to impose any other conditions.

3   Regional Agreements

3.1   European Union

The European Union (EU) has a population of 375 million and a GDP of $7.8 trillion, and is the world's largest trading entity, accounting for around 20% of global merchandise exports, and importing about 18% of the world total. The corresponding figures for the United States and Japan, its main trading partners, are 16% and 9% for exports, and 21% and 6.5% for imports. Similarly, the EU accounts for 25% of world's commercial services exports, compared to 20% of US and 8.5% of Japan.

The European Union forms a Customs Union where circulation of goods is free, but the Common Customs Tariff, or CCT, although common to all members, is applied at different rates depending on the nature and origin of the product.

Having CCT as the cornerstone for world trade policy, the EU has participated in 8 tariff Rounds so far, having reduced tariffs considerably under GATT and WTO agreements.

The EU applies its trade measures through the Customs Tariff of the European Community and the tariff classification of goods, their origin (preferential or non-preferential), and their customs value.

Accounting for about 15% of world trade, even if we exclude intra-EU trade, the European Union is the largest trading bloc in the world. Apart from the WTO, which is the main multilateral framework for trade, the EU has signed special trade agreements with individual countries or groups of countries. As far as neighbouring countries are concerned, the EU participates in the European Economic Area (EEA) free trade agreement along with Iceland, Norway and Liechtenstein. The other member of older European Free Trade Area, Switzerland, has also signed a free trade agreement with EU, although it has not joined the EEA.

Bulgaria, Cyprus, the Czech Republic, Estonia, Hungary, Latvia, Lithuania, Malta, Poland, Romania, the Slovak Republic, and Slovenia, have also formed free trade area agreements with the EU. In all cases above, tariff reductions included in the agreements will promote trade benefiting all participants.

Finally, Customs Union agreements have been signed with Andorra, San Marino, and Turkey. Apart from its neighbours, the European Union has strengthened the links for cooperation and development with countries in Africa, the Caribbean, and the Pacific through the Arusha Convention and Yaoundé Convention, both in 1963, and the four Lomé Conventions. After decades of negotiations, the members of the last Lomé Convention have gained duty free access for all industrial products and for most agricultural products.

Algeria, Egypt, Israel, Lebanon, Morocco, the Palestine Liberation Organisation, Syria, and Tunisia enjoy special treatment in the context of the Mediterranean trade policy of the EU.

Asian and Latin American countries are allowed to export to the European Union at lower duty rates for manufactured goods and processed agricultural products. This is because these countries are under the General System of Preferences, an internationally accepted way of developing trade for the least developed countries based on previously existing trade agreements between LDCs and industrialised countries. However, these privileges are granted to the developing countries that adopt EU ideals on certain issues, for instance on environmental protection.

It is important to note that, given the structure of these preferential relationships, the external trade policy of EU is based on the sufficient defence of the rules of origin. In this direction, the EU has signed customs cooperation and mutual administrative assistance agreements with the United States, Canada and Korea against customs fraud.

Since the formation of free trade areas between the EU and other countries or groups of countries is considered useful for the former, multilateral trade and customs negotiations, in the WTO framework or outside it, are always on the agenda of EU trade officials.

3.2   Association of South East Asian Nations (ASEAN) Free Trade Area (AFTA)

The Association of South East Asian Nations (ASEAN) was formed by Indonesia, Malaysia, Philippines, Singapore, and Thailand, with Brunei Darussalam joining in 1984 and Vietnam in 1995. While its size is small, it has a significant average growth rate of 6.5% over the last 10 years before the financial crisis.

In 1991, ASEAN countries voted for the ASEAN Free Trade Area (AFTA) to be fully implemented by 2008. In 1994, a Common External Preferential Tariff, which is an effective tariff imposed on the goods originating from ASEAN Member States under AFTA, was agreed.

Under this scheme, tariffs were scheduled to be lowered to the level of 0% to 5%. Member States also rescheduled their tariff reductions from 15 years to 10 years, moving the year of full implementation back to 2003.

Table 1:   Main Indicators of ASEAN.

GDP	1995	1996	1997	1998	1999
Current US$ in Billions	642.2	713.3	676.6	463.7	536.1
% of World GDP	2.2	2.4	2.3	1.2	1.7
Population (in 1999)	446.0 million 7.46 % of world population				
Foreign Trade (in 1999)	7% of world trade				
Intra-Regional Trade (in 1999)	20.1% of foreign trade				

Source: WTO (2000) and World Bank.

3.3   Australia-New Zealand Closer Economic Relations Trade Agreement (ANZCERTA)

The Australia-New Zealand Closer Economic Relations Trade Agreement (ANZCERTA) was signed in 1993 between Australia and New Zealand, replacing an older limited free trade agreement between the two countries which covered only forest products in the beginning and some manufacturing ones by 1977. These two countries have been waiving gradually tariffs, non-tariff barriers, and subsidies; on the other hand, they have been practising antidumping policies and equal treatment in government procurement.

The earlier CER Agreement was built on a series of preferential trade agreements between Australia and New Zealand that had resulted in the removal of tariffs and quantitative restrictions on 80% of trans-Tasman trade.

The CER Agreement went under general review in 1988, having formed three protocols aiming at the acceleration of the process of tariff liberalisation in the trade of goods and the harmonisation of trade in services under the CER Agreement.

The ANZCERTA agreement went under several reviews focused on procedures to facilitate trade, including removing all remaining regulatory impediments to trade. The ANZCERTA agreement is widely acknowledged as one of the most comprehensive and WTO compatible bilateral regional trade agreements (RTAs) in existence today, and the first to include free trade in services.

Table 2:   Main Indicators of ANZCERTA.

GDP	1995	1996	1997	1998	1999
Current US$ in Billions	436.7	482.9	484.8	425.7	458.7
% of World GDP	1.5	1.6	1.6	1.4	1.5
Population (in 1999)	22.8 million 0.38% of world population				
Foreign Trade (in 1999)	3% of world trade				
Intra-Regional Trade (in 1999)	9% of foreign trade				

Source: WTO (2000) and World Bank.

3.4   Central American Common Market (CACM)

The Central American Common Market (CACM) was established in 1960 by a group of relatively small Central American countries: Costa Rica, Guatemala, Honduras, and Nicaragua.

Table 3:   Main Indicators of CACM.

GDP	1995	1996	1997	1998	1999
Current US$ in Billions	41.6	43.8	48.4	52.6	53.5
% of World GDP	0.14	0.15	0.16	0.18	0.17
Population (in 1999)	32.1 million 0.54% of world population				
Foreign Trade (in 1999)	0.6% of world trade				
Intra-Regional Trade (in 1999)	13% of foreign trade				

Source: WTO (2000) and World Bank.

In 1991 CACM members voted for partial inclusion of Panama in the new economic community. In 1992 a Transitional Multilateral Free Trade Agreement was signed.

The Central American countries found after the signing of the North American Free Trade Agreement (NAFTA) among Canada, Mexico, and the United States that the stabilisation of trade regimes in their main export markets assisted their own economic integration.

In 1992, the five Central American republics and Mexico signed a Framework Free Trade Agreement.

3.5   Caribbean Community and Common Market (CARICOM)

The Caribbean Community and Common Market (CARICOM) was created in 1973 by a group of formerly British colonies.

Altogether, the member countries (Antigua and Barbuda, the Bahamas, Barbados, Belize, Dominica, Grenada, Guyana, Haiti, Jamaica, Montserrat, St. Kitts and Nevis, Saint Lucia, St. Vincent and the Grenadines, Suriname, and Trinidad and Tobago) account for 0.1% of world output.

Table 4:   Main Indicators of CARICOM.

GDP	1995	1996	1997	1998	1999
Current US$ in Billions	18.6	19.9	19.2	20.1	20.2
% of World GDP	0.06	0.07	0.06	0.07	0.07
Population (in 1999)	6.5 million 0.11% of world population				
Foreign Trade (in 1999)	0.5% of world trade				
Intra-Regional Trade (in 1999)	6% of foreign trade				

Source: WTO (2000) and World Bank.

The integration of the group started in 1968, when the Caribbean Free Trade Association (CARIFTA) was created in order to lever the employment through the agricultural sector and implement a Free Trade Agreement.

CARICOM aimed at achieving economic integration through market forces, through trade liberalisation by removing duties, licensing arrangements, quotas, and other tariff and non-tariff barriers to trade. CARICOM members applied a Common External Tariff (CET), a Common Protective Policy (CPP), and trade arrangements such as the Agricultural Marketing Protocol and the Oils and Fats Agreement.

3.6   Common Market of the Southern Cone (MERCOSUR)

The Common Market of the Southern Cone (MERCOSUR) was established in 1991 by the nations of the eastern part of South America: Argentina, Brazil, Paraguay, and Uruguay. In 1986, Argentina and Brazil had already formed a coalition of economic cooperation, which was expanded in the form of MERCOSUR in order to create a union with common customs and a common market.

Table 5:   Main Indicators of MERCOSUR.

GDP	1995	1996	1997	1998	1999
Current US$ in Billions	989.8	1077.1	1127.8	1104.2	1063.2
% of World GDP	3.4	3.6	3.8	3.7	3.4
Population (in 1999)	213.2 million 3.57% of world population				
Foreign Trade (in 1999)	1.5% of world trade				
Intra-Regional Trade (in 1999)	20.1% of foreign trade				

Source: WTO (2000) and World Bank.

Since 1995, a Common External Tariff (CET) was established by the members of MERCOSUR, which is applied to partners under the MFN principle. During the transition period ending in 2001 for Argentina and Brazil and in 2006 for Paraguay and Uruguay, member countries have to converge in a linear manner to the tariff rate defined by CET. Free trade was established with Chile and Bolivia in 1996.

3.7   North American Free Trade Agreement (NAFTA)

NAFTA is an extension of CUFTA (Canada-United States Free Trade Agreement), which was signed in 1988 and came into force in 1999, but had its roots as early as 1937 in the form of limited tariff reduction measures. NAFTA came into force on January 1st, 1994.

NAFTA provided to the three member countries (USA, Canada, and Mexico) a 10-15 year horizon for tariffication of non-tariff barriers and reduction of the latter to a minimum level. Additional agreements were made for the labour market, agricultural products, and the environment.

Table 6:   Main Indicators of NAFTA.

GDP	1995	1996	1997	1998	1999
Current US$ in Billions	8203.8	8685.0	9264.2	9713.6	10270.7
% of World GDP	28.2	29.1	31.2	33.0	33.3
Population (in 1999)	405.3 million 6.8% of world population				
Foreign Trade (in 1999)	19.6% of world trade				
Intra-Regional Trade (in 1999)	54.1% of foreign trade				

Source: WTO (2000) and World Bank.

NAFTA improved market access conditions in a number of sectors, such as transportation, telecommunications, and financial services, as well as prepared the ground for freer movement of businessmen and professionals among the three countries. Furthermore, NAFTA includes agreements on trade in services; the right of establishment for investors and intellectual property rights; rules on government procurement and the operation of government enterprises; and a detailed system for dispute settlement.

Negotiations have begun aiming to add Chile to the bloc, which has already signed a bilateral FTA with Canada in 1996. Moreover, Caribbean Community (CARICOM) and Caribbean Common Market (CACM) nations have also expressed interest in joining NAFTA.

Appendix I

Table 7:   World Trade by Selected Region, 1999 (*Billion Dollars and Percentages*).

Region	Merchandise Trade		Commercial Services		Total Trade
	Value	Share in Total Trade	Value	Share in Total Trade	
World	5473	80.2	1350	19.8	6823
European Union (15)	2180	79.2	574	20.8	2754
United States	695	73.3	253	26.7	948
Japan	419	87.5	60	12.5	479
Canada	239	87.2	35	12.8	274
China	195	89.0	24	11.0	219

Source: WTO (2000: Tables III.01 and III.04).

Table 8:   Regional Structure of World Merchandise Trade, 1999 (*Billion Dollars and Percentages*).

	Exports			Imports			Population		
	Value	*Share in World Exports*	*Cumulative Share in World Exports*	*Value*	*Share in World Imports*	*Cumulative Share in World Imports*	*Number in Millions*	*Share in World Total*	*Cumulative Share in World Total*
European Union (15)	2180	39.8	39.8	2232	39.0	39.0	375.46	6.3	6.3
North America (USA-Canada)	934	17.1	56.9	1280	22.3	61.3	308.72	5.2	11.4
Six East Asian Traders	546	10.0	66.9	485	8.5	69.8	162.59	2.7	14.2
Japan	419	7.7	74.5	311	5.4	75.2	126.57	2.1	16.3
China	195	3.6	78.1	166	2.9	78.1	1253.60	21.0	37.3
Central and Eastern Europe	102	1.9	80.0	131	2.3	80.4			
Baltic States and the CIS	112	2.0	82.0	83	1.4	81.8			
Africa	112	2.0	84.1	133	2.3	84.2			
Middle East	170	3.1	87.2	150	2.6	86.8	3751.03	62.7	100
Latin America	297	5.4	92.6	335	5.8	92.6			
Rest Western Europe	172	3.1	95.8	186	3.2	95.9			
Rest of the World	232	4.25	100.0	237	4.1	100.0			
World	5473	100.0		5729			5977.97	100.0	

Source: WTO (2000: Tables I.3) and World Bank.

56   N. Kouvaritakis et al.

Table 9:   Merchandise Trade of Selected Regions with the Least Developed
Countries, 1980-99 (*Million Dollars and Percentages*).

	Exports			Share in Region's Total Exports			Imports			Share in Region's Total Imports		
	1980	*1990*	*1999*	*1980*	*1990*	*1999*	*1980*	*1990*	*1999*	*1980*	*1990*	*1999*
North America	2103	2079	2708	0.7	0.4	0.3	2625	4807	7208	0.8	0.7	0.6
Western Europe	10045	10232	9175	1.2	0.6	0.4	8510	10629	9884	0.9	0.6	0.4
Australia and New Zealand	285	403	421	1.0	0.8	0.6	92	86	173	0.3	0.2	0.2
China	446	707	2529	2.5	1.1	1.3	262	314	1396	1.3	0.6	0.8
Japan	1874	1707	1512	1.4	0.6	0.4	1356	1250	1015	1.0	0.5	0.3
Six East Asian Traders[5]	1390	2856	6811	1.5	1.1	1.2	556	1500	3871	0.5	0.5	0.8
Total of Above	16144	17983	23156	1.2	0.6	0.5	13400	18586	23547	0.9	0.6	0.5

Source: WTO (2000: Tables III.01 and III.04).

---

[5]   Six East Asian traders: Hong Kong, China, Malaysia, Republic of Korea, Singapore,
Taipei Chinese, and Thailand.

Table 10: Relative Shares of Main Product Groups to Total Merchandise Exports, by Region 1999 (*Percentages*).

	World	North America	Latin America	Western Europe	C./E. Europe/Baltic States/CIS	Africa	Middle East	Asia
Agricultural Products	9.94	10.60	20.24	10.03	10.11	19.77	3.68	7.07
Mining Products	10.16	5.67	18.86	5.49	28.02	47.23	69.34	6.25
Manu-factures	76.49	78.81	60.30	80.52	57.12	30.33	25.50	84.47
Total Merchandise Exports	100	100	100	100	100	100	100	100

Source: WTO (2000: Table A07).

Table 11:   World Merchandise Exports and Gross Domestic Product Changes, 1950-99 (*Percentage Changes at Nominal Prices Compared with the Amounts of 1950*).

Yr.	Exports				GDP	Yr.	Exports				GDP
	Total	Agric. Prod.	Mining Prod.	Manufac.			Total	Agric. Prod.	Mining Prod.	Manufac.	
51	31.15	28.57	33.33	39.13	7.9	76	1524.59	492.86	2577.78	2360.87	239.5
52	29.51	10.71	55.56	47.83	10.5	77	1744.26	571.43	2855.56	2717.39	255.3
53	32.79	10.71	55.56	52.17	18.4	78	2036.07	660.71	2966.67	3326.09	268.4
54	39.34	14.29	66.67	60.87	21.1	79	2580.33	835.71	4355.56	4008.70	281.6
55	52.46	17.86	88.89	82.61	28.9	80	3165.52	965.18	6219.27	4661.42	283.4
56	65.57	21.43	111.11	108.70	34.2	81	3118.08	945.27	6019.24	4628.67	291.7
57	78.69	32.14	122.22	126.09	39.5	82	2912.17	867.28	5371.07	4459.27	295.9
58	72.13	25.00	111.11	121.74	39.5	83	2854.30	853.42	4931.51	4483.92	308.0
59	86.89	35.71	122.22	143.48	47.4	84	3024.89	904.14	4885.98	4855.62	327.0
60	111.48	42.86	133.33	178.26	55.3	85	3018.02	847.06	4725.80	5045.66	342.0
61	119.67	46.43	155.56	195.65	63.2	86	3315.08	952.42	3574.91	6091.85	355.9
62	132.79	46.43	166.67	217.39	73.7	87	3906.00	1109.73	3977.80	7312.43	372.3
63	154.10	60.71	188.89	252.17	81.6	88	4444.31	1268.64	4013.09	8505.07	392.2
64	183.61	71.43	222.22	304.35	94.7	89	4795.67	1327.43	4648.78	9099.30	410.3
65	206.56	78.57	244.44	347.83	102.6	90	5430.25	1394.62	5373.57	10447.23	423.7
66	234.43	85.71	277.78	395.65	115.8	91	5515.03	1408.26	5048.79	10798.92	428.9
67	252.46	85.71	300.00	434.78	123.7	92	5874.39	1514.90	4980.50	11670.65	434.3
68	290.16	92.86	355.56	513.04	136.8	93	5824.56	1450.16	4716.69	11604.83	438.8
69	347.54	107.14	400.00	617.39	152.6	94	6607.82	1679.55	4896.81	13381.34	450.6
70	411.48	128.57	466.67	726.09	163.2	95	7932.92	1979.62	5794.85	15971.90	463.2
71	473.77	146.43	533.33	843.48	176.3	96	8294.40	2039.82	6826.07	16633.84	480.0
72	578.69	196.43	622.22	1026.09	192.1	97	8588.49	2026.86	6992.47	17512.81	498.9
73	840.98	332.14	966.67	1413.04	213.2	98	8453.34	1923.35	5530.94	17747.23	510.2
74	1270.49	428.57	2288.89	1895.65	218.4	99	8749.77	1853.77	6200.18	18391.06	526.7
75	1334.43	435.71	2200.00	2078.26	218.4						

Initial data: WTO (2000: Table II.01), World Bank.

Table 12:   Openness Ratio for Selected Ratios and Countries, 1995-99 Trade *(% of GDP, PPP).*

Region	1995	1996	1997	1998	1999
World	28.31	28.19	28.13	27.31	27.40
Low Income	8.81	9.19	9.18	8.14	7.80
Middle Income	17.92	18.26	18.63	17.26	16.90
High Income	37.83	37.55	37.38	36.97	37.36
European Monetary Union	51.51	51.36	49.54	51.54	52.66
Canada	52.31	53.20	56.38	55.92	57.30
Japan	26.18	24.06	23.75	21.75	23.18
United States	18.17	18.47	19.48	19.44	19.78
China	8.69	8.10	8.38	7.80	7.96
Russian Federation	13.31	15.06	15.30	13.14	10.56
Singapore	354.80	346.07	330.22	276.18	275.07
Hong Kong, China	271.11	259.58	262.04	255.90	239.20

Source: World Bank.

Table 13: Merchandise Trade by Product and Selected Trading Partner, 1999
(Billion Dollars).

	EU (15)-United States		United States-Canada		Japan Taipei		Korea, Rep		Hong Kong	
	exp	imp	exp	imp	exp	imp	exp	imp	exp	imp
Agricultural Products	9.45	11.31	10.52	20.94	0.59	1.23	0.42	2.15	0.49	0.07
Food	8.55	7.94	8.05	10.06	0.43	1.01	0.20	1.94	0.38	0.06
Raw Materials	0.87	3.40	2.48	10.88	0.17	0.22	0.22	0.21	0.10	0.00
Mining Products	7.97	5.07	6.11	25.16	1.05	0.23	1.01	2.15	0.45	0.04
Ores and Other Minerals	0.54	1.55	1.57	1.49	0.14	0.09	0.28	0.07	0.02	0.03
Fuels	5.43	1.69	2.24	17.64	0.12	0.01	0.19	1.96	0.09	0.00
Non-Ferrous Metals	2.05	1.79	2.31	6.03	0.79	0.12	0.53	0.12	0.34	0.01
Manufactures	168.54	154.29	143.05	140.43	26.16	10.93	20.84	11.55	20.17	1.44
Iron and Steel	3.54	0.66	2.77	2.68	1.35	0.37	1.92	1.08	0.91	0.00
Chemicals	28.60	23.68	14.82	10.34	3.98	0.63	3.50	0.87	2.08	0.02
Other Semimanufactures	14.66	8.46	13.87	21.26	1.35	0.54	0.93	0.78	1.26	0.13
Machinery and Transport Equipment	92.80	95.59	91.76	91.02	15.57	7.28	11.85	5.85	11.91	0.78
Power Generating Machinery	10.96	13.68	2.89	2.13	0.31	0.07	0.35	0.07	0.18	0.00
Other Non-Electrical Machinery	22.32	14.78	15.98	8.58	5.75	0.51	3.18	0.55	2.02	0.03
Office and Telecom. Equipment	13.85	35.79	18.98	10.46	5.34	5.66	4.65	4.52	6.05	0.56
Electrical Machinery and Apparatus	8.07	9.97	8.44	3.76	2.66	0.63	2.98	0.51	2.61	0.15
Automotive Products	26.21	6.12	38.60	59.37	1.09	0.18	0.49	0.09	0.72	0.00
Other Transport Equipment	11.00	15.34	6.87	6.71	0.42	0.23	0.20	0.09	0.32	0.03
Textiles	2.62	1.62	2.77	1.78	0.33	0.26	0.37	0.39	0.84	0.01
Clothing	2.48	0.59	0.75	1.76	0.10	0.14	0.02	1.03	0.05	0.10
Other Consumer Goods	23.50	23.77	16.31	11.59	3.48	1.72	2.24	1.55	3.13	0.40
Total Merchandise	188.89	173.16	163.90	201.43	28.74	12.79	22.86	16.03	22.00	1.79

Source: WTO (2000: Tables A9, A11, A15).

Table 14:   Grubel Lloyd (G-L) Index of IIT in Selected Products and Countries, 1999.

	EU (15)-United States	United States-Canada	Taipei	Korea, Rep	Hong Kong
Agricultural Products	**0.91**	**0.60**	**0.65**	**0.33**	**0.25**
Food	0.96	0.80	0.60	0.19	0.27
Raw Materials	0.41	0.34	0.87	0.98	0.00
Mining Products	**0.78**	**0.35**	**0.36**	**0.64**	**0.16**
Ores and Other Minerals	0.52	0.98	0.78	0.40	0.80
Fuels	0.48	0.17	0.15	0.18	0.00
Non-Ferrous Metals	0.93	0.52	0.26	0.37	0.06
Manufactures	**0.96**	**0.94**	**0.59**	**0.71**	**0.13**
Iron and Steel	0.31	0.95	0.43	0.72	0.00
Chemicals	0.91	0.85	0.27	0.40	0.02
Other Semimanufactures	0.73	0.75	0.57	0.91	0.19
Machinery and Transport Equipment	0.99	0.92	0.64	0.66	0.12
Power Generating Machinery	0.89	0.92	0.37	0.33	0.00
Other Non-Electrical Machinery	0.80	0.79	0.16	0.29	0.03
Office and Telecommunication Equipment	0.56	1.00	0.97	0.99	0.17
Electrical Machinery and Apparatus	0.89	0.72	0.38	0.29	0.11
Automotive Products	0.38	0.78	0.28	0.31	0.00
Other Transport Equipment	0.84	0.95	0.71	0.62	0.17
Textiles	0.77	0.83	0.88	0.97	0.02
Clothing	0.38	0.48	0.83	0.04	0.67
Other Consumer Goods	0.99	0.93	0.66	0.82	0.23
Total Merchandise	**0.96**	**0.83**	**0.62**	**0.82**	**0.15**

Source: WTO (2000: Tables A9, A11, A15 – Author Calculations).

Table 15:   Intra-Regional Shares of World Trade (1960-1994).

	1960	1970	1975	1980	1985	1990	1991	1992	1993	1994
1 European Community (EC, 1957)										
Trade Integration Ratio[a]	26.1	36.5	40.2	45.0	48.4	55.6	57.3	58.9	58.6	60.7
Share in Intra-Regional Trade[b]	40.0	51.7	51.2	52.4	53.5	59.2	59.6	60.2	55.5	55.4
Share in Total World Exports[c]	40.7	41.3	40.2	37.7	35.0	40.4	39.3	38.9	35.8	35.0
Share in Total World Imports[d]	40.7	41.8	39.7	40.4	34.1	40.4	40.5	39.4	34.3	33.7
2 European Free Trade Area (EFTA, 1960)										
Trade Integration Ratio[a]	35.8	44.9	47.8	53.8	57.9	63.9	64.0	66.3	66.9	69.5
Share in Intra-Regional Trade[b]	20.0	26.5	25.2	22.6	22.2	20.5	19.8	19.4	19.0	18.9
Share in Total World Exports[c]	18.5	15.3	13.7	13.3	12.6	13.6	13.0	12.7	11.8	12.0
Share in Total World Imports[d]	21.1	17.2	15.4	14.2	12.5	14.5	13.4	13.1	12.0	11.9
3 Central American Common Market (CACM, 1961)										
Trade Integration Ratio[a]	42.9	49.1	49.2	53.8	42.8	49.2	48.7	54.2	56.3	57.4
Share in Intra-Regional Trade[b]	6.7	25.1	20.2	21.7	12.5	11.9	13.8	15.5	13.5	12.7
Share in Total World Exports[c]	0.4	0.4	0.3	0.3	0.2	0.1	0.1	0.1	0.2	0.2
Share in Total World Imports[d]	0.5	0.4	0.4	0.3	0.3	0.2	0.2	0.2	0.3	0.3
4 Latin American Free Trade Area/Latin American Integration Association (LAFTA, 1960, 1980)										
Trade Integration Ratio[a]	27.6	25.7	23.9	26.6	24.0	30.1	32.2	35.5	36.7	38.4
Share in Intra-Regional Trade[b]	8.7	10.6	12.0	12.7	10.6	12.1	13.9	15.9	15.6	15.4
Share in Total World Exports[c]	6.9	4.5	3.9	4.4	4.6	3.4	3.3	3.2	3.8	4.0
Share in Total World Imports[d]	6.0	4.0	4.6	4.5	2.8	2.5	3.0	3.4	4.2	4.4
5 Australia-New Zealand Closer Economic Relations Trade Agreement (ANZCERTA, 1983)										
Trade Integration Ratio[a]	28.6	31.1	30.8	33.1	36.3	42.4	44.7	45.9	47.5	50.7
Share in Intra-Regional Trade[b]	5.1	5.9	6.2	6.4	6.7	7.4	7.4	7.5	8.1	8.7
Share in Total World Exports[c]	2.7	2.1	1.8	1.5	1.5	1.4	1.5	1.4	1.4	1.4
Share in Total World Imports[d]	2.9	2.1	1.7	1.5	1.6	1.5	1.4	1.4	1.5	1.6

Table 15 continued.

	1960	1970	1975	1980	1985	1990	1991	1992	1993	1994
6 Association of South East Asian Nations (ASEAN, 1967)										
Trade Integration Ratio[a]	48.9	58.3	67.4	83.9	78.9	106.9	112.6	112.6	119.7	131.0
Share in Intra-Regional Trade[b]	7.5	17.3	13.2	15.6	17.9	16.6	17.5	17.6	18.4	19.1
Share in Total World Exports[c]	1.6	2.2	2.8	3.9	3.9	4.2	4.7	4.9	5.6	6.0
Share in Total World Imports[d]	1.9	2.5	2.9	3.3	3.3	4.6	5.0	5.1	6.0	6.3
7 Andean Sub-Regional Integration Agreement (ANDEAN PACT, 1969)										
Trade Integration Ratio[a]	54.3	51.5	42.9	43.4	38.5	43.1	45.7	49.8	51.6	51.5
Share in Intra-Regional Trade[b]	1.8	2.9	6.0	6.0	5.7	6.0	7.3	8.1	9.2	10.0
Share in Total World Exports[c]	3.8	2.4	1.9	1.9	1.5	1.3	1.2	1.1	1.1	1.1
Share in Total World Imports[d]	2.4	1.6	1.6	1.5	1.0	0.7	0.8	1.0	1.1	1.0
8 Economic Community of West Africa (ECOWAS, 1975)										
Trade Integration Ratio[a]	51.4	61.9	71.2	91.7	69.3	54.9	54.9	55.4	54.8	50.7
Share in Intra-Regional Trade[b]	2.3	2.8	4.1	4.4	6.0	9.0	8.1	7.8	9.6	10.8
Share in Total World Exports[c]	1.1	1.1	1.5	1.4	1.1	0.6	0.4	0.6	0.5	0.5
Share in Total World Imports[d]	1.2	0.9	1.2	1.2	0.6	0.5	0.5	0.7	0.6	0.5
9 Preferential Trade Area for Eastern and Southern Africa										
Trade Integration Ratio[a]	N.A.	46.3	53.0	47.0	40.0	41.4	42.1	41.6	41.4	41.7
Share in Intra-Regional Trade[b]	N.A.	8.6	7.1	8.1	4.6	6.2	4.8	5.0	6.7	7.0
Share in Total World Exports[c]	N.A.	1.1	0.5	0.3	0.4	0.3	0.3	0.3	0.3	0.3
Share in Total World Imports[d]	N.A.	1.0	0.7	0.5	0.5	0.4	0.4	0.4	0.4	0.4
10 Canada-U.S. Free Trade Area/North American Free Trade Agreement										
Trade Integration Ratio[a]	10.7	14.2	16.1	18.5	20.0	25.0	25.8	27.2	28.5	30.4
Share in Intra-Regional Trade[b]	32.3	36.6	32.8	27.8	33.8	31.3	30.9	30.9	32.1	32.7
Share in Total World Exports[c]	26.0	22.2	19.5	16.8	17.8	16.3	16.6	16.6	17.4	17.1
Share in Total World Imports[d]	21.2	20.4	19.1	18.3	23.7	19.2	18.5	18.5	20.6	20.7

a. Export+import volumes of merchandise and services, ratio to GDP.
b. Intra-regional trade as percentage of the region's total trade (merchandise only).
c. Regional exports as percentage of total world exports (merchandise only).
d. Regional imports as percentage of total world imports (merchandise only).

Source: Shigeru OTSUBO (1998).

Table 16:   Simple Concentration Ratios of Selected Regional Integration
Arrangements, 1999 (*Billion Dollars and Percentage*).

Regional Trade Agreement	Imports/Exports		Value			Share in Total Exports/ Imports	Simple Concentration Ratios
		1999	1990	1998	1999	1999
EU (15)	Total exports	2180	100.0	100.0	100.0	
	Intra-exports	1385	64.9	63.1	63.5	1.56
	Extra-exports	796	35.1	36.9	36.5	
	Total imports	2232	100.0	100.0	100.0	
	Intra-imports	1389	63.0	62.8	62.2	
	Extra-imports	843	37.0	37.2	37.8	
NAFTA (3)	Total exports	1070	100.0	100.0	100.0	
	Intra-exports	579	42.6	51.2	54.1	2.08
	Extra-exports	491	57.4	48.8	45.9	
	Total imports a	1420	100.0	100.0	100.0	
	Intra-imports	575	34.4	40.3	40.5	
	Extra-imports	846	65.6	59.7	59.5	
ASEAN (10)	Total exports	359	100.0	100.0	100.0	
	Intra-exports	79	20.1	21.9	22.1	4.03
	Extra-exports	280	79.9	78.1	77.9	
	Total imports	299	100.0	100.0	100.0	
	Intra-imports	69	16.2	22.6	22.9	
	Extra-imports	231	83.8	77.4	77.1	
CEFTA (6)	Total exports	107	-	100.0	100.0	
	Intra-exports	13	-	13.0	12.0	4.87
	Extra-exports	94	-	87.0	88.0	
	Total imports	134	-	100.0	100.0	
	Intra-imports	13	-	9.7	9.5	
	Extra-imports	122	-	90.3	90.5	
MERCOSUR (4)	Total exports	74	100.0	100.0	100.0	
	Intra-exports	15	8.9	25.0	20.3	13.40
	Extra-exports	59	91.1	75.0	79.7	
	Total imports	83	100.0	100.0	100.0	
	Intra-imports	16	14.5	21.0	19.0	
	Extra-imports	67	85.5	79.0	81.0	
ANDEAN (5)	Total exports	43	100.0	100.0	100.0	
	Intra-exports	4	4.3	13.9	8.9	13.62
	Extra-exports	39	95.7	86.1	91.1	
	Total imports b	36	100.0	100.0	100.0	
	Intra-imports	4	7.7	11.7	11.7	
	Extra-imports	32	92.3	88.3	88.3	

Initial data: WTO (2000: Tables I9).

Appendix II

Table 17:   Definition of Industrial Product Categories.

Number	Category Description	Harmonised System Nomenclature HS 1996
01	Wood, pulp, paper and furniture	Ch.44, 45, 47, 4801-14, 4816-23, Ch.49, 9401-04.
02	Textiles and clothing	3005, 3306, 3921, 4202, Ch.50-63 (except 5001-03, 5101-03, 5201-02, 5301-02), 6405-06, 6501-05, 6601, 7019, 8708, 8804, 9113, 9502, 9612
03	Leather, rubber, footwear and travel goods	Ch.40, 41 (except 4101-03), 4201, 4203-05, Ch.43 (except 4301), Ch.64 , 9605
04	Metals	2601-17, 2620, Ch.72, 7301-20, 7323-26, Ch.74-76, 78-82, 8301-03, 8306-11
05	Chemicals and photographic supplies	2705, Ch.28-30 (except 3005), Ch.32-33 (except 3301and 3306), 3401-02, 3404-05, 3407, 3506-07, 3601-04, and Ch.37-39 (except 3823 and 3921).
06	Transport equipment	8601-07, 8609, 8701-07, 8711-14, 8716, 8801-03, 8901-08.
07	Non-electric machinery	7321-22, Ch.84, 8608, 8709.
08	Electric machinery	8501-18 and 8525-48.
09	Mineral products and precious stones and precious metals	Ch.25, 2618-19, 2621, 2701-04, 2706-08, 2711-15, Ch.31, 3403, 6801-06, 6808-15,

Table 17 continued.

	Category	Harmonised System Nomenclature HS 1996
Number	Description	
10	Manufactured articles not elsewhere specified	Ch.69-71 (except 7019). 2716, 3406, 3605-06, 4206, 4601-02, 4815, 6506-07, 6602-03, 6701-04, 6807, 8304-05, 8519-24, 8710, 8715, 8805, Ch.90, 9101-12, 9114, Ch.92-93, 9405-06 and Ch.95-97 (except 9502, 9605 and 9612).
11	Fish and fish products	Ch.03, 0509, 1504, 1603-05, 2301
97	Petroleum	2709-10.

Source: WTO (2001: Table 4).

Table 18:   Tariff Bindings on Industrial Products (*Percentages*).

Country Group	Percentage of Tariff Lines Bound	
	Pre-UR	Post-UR
Total	43	83
By Major Country Group		
Developed Countries	78	99
Developing Economies	21	73
Transition Economies	73	98
By Region		
North America	99	100
Latin America	38	100
Western Europe	79	82
Central Europe	63	98
Africa	13	69
Asia	16	68

Source: GATT (94: Table II.11).

Table 19: Bound Tariffs on Industrial Products. Scope of Bindings by Country and Product Category.

	Total Number of Tariff lines	Share of Bound Tariff Lines	1 Wood, Pulp, Paper and Furniture	2 Textiles, Clothing	3 Leather, Rubber Footwear and Travel Goods	4 Metals	5 Chemicals and Photog. Supplies	6 Transport Equipment	7 Non-Electric Machinery	8 Electric Machinery	9 Mineral Prod. & Precious Stones and Metals	10 Man. Articles Not Elsewhere Specified	11 Fish and Fish Products
North America													
Canada	6261	99.6	100	100	100	100	100	93.7	100	100	98.2	100	100
United States	7872	100	100	100	100	100	100	100	100	100	100	100	100
Latin America													
Argentina	10530	100	100	100	100	100	100	100	100	100	100	100	100
Brazil	10860	100	100	100	100	100	100	100	100	100	100	100	100
Chile	5055	100	100	100	100	100	100	100	100	100	100	100	100
Colombia	6145	100	100	100	100	100	100	100	100	100	100	100	100
Costa Rica	1546	100	100	100	100	100	100	100	100	100	100	100	100
El Salvador	4922	100	100	100	100	100	100	100	100	100	100	100	100
Jamaica	3097	100	100	100	100	100	100	100	100	100	100	100	100
Mexico	11255	100	100	100	100	100	100	100	100	100	100	100	100
Peru	4545	100	100	100	100	100	100	100	100	100	100	100	100
Venezuela	5974	100	100	100	100	100	100	100	100	100	100	100	100
Western Europe													
EU	7635	100	100	100	100	100	100	100	100	100	100	100	100
Iceland	5689	93.2	95	93.1	93.8	99.6	99	29.7	96.6	93.8	91.7	94.5	97.5
Norway	5326	100	100	100	100	100	100	100	100	100	100	100	100
Switzerland	6217	98.9	100	100	100	100	95.2	100	100	100	93	100	100
Turkey	15479	36.3	33.7	11.3	29.8	18.5	56.1	61.2	60.2	57.6	24.3	41.1	13.1

Table 19 continued.

Eastern Europe													
Czech Republic	4354	100	100	100	100	100	100	100	100	100	100	100	100
Hungary	5896	95.4	99.5	98.7	100	100	96.2	72.5	98.6	90.8	97.6	95.4	38.3
Poland	4354	95.8	100	99.4	100	100	99.6	57.4	99.4	100	99.4	95.7	4.7
Romania	4602	100	100	100	100	100	100	100	100	100	100	100	100
Slovak Republic	4354	100	100	100	100	100	100	100	100	100	100	100	100
Asia/Pacific													
Australia	5520	95.9											
Hong Kong, China	5110	23.5	93.2	2.4	24	54.2	5.8	5.1	16.8	4.2	39.7	20.9	100
India	4354	61.6	61.5	26	48.6	56.5	88.8	70.5	92.4	87.3	71.6	39.3	13.1
Indonesia	7735	93.2	98.8	99.6	99.3	93.7	96.7	32.8	92.5	91.6	97	81.9	100
Japan	7339	99.2	92.8	100	100	100	100	100	100	100	100	100	87
Korea, Rep. of	8882	90.4	92.2	99.7	82.3	99.3	95.5	62.7	94.6	64.4	92	95.3	35.8
Macau, China	5337	9.9	9.1	1.7	56	17.3	0	0	0	1.4	4.7	20.3	100
Malaysia	10832	61.8	20	94.8	87	49.8	72.9	39.5	89	77.5	65.1	84	43
New Zealand	5894	100	100	99.8	100	100	100	100	100	100	100	100	100
Philippines	5387	58.6	45.9	97.1	39.9	28.4	68.4	34.9	71.6	60.3	36.7	53.9	4.7
Singapore	4963	65.5	96	78	33.5	64.1	98.7	11.6	62	53.2	14.6	27.2	98.5
Sri Lanka	5933	8	9.1	0.4	6.1	4.6	4.5	4	13.1	11.6	7.7	17.9	95.7
Thailand	5244	67.9	85.9	94.4	45.6	54.3	54.6	24.3	88.2	57	43.8	68.7	92.3
Africa													
Cameroon	4721	0.1	0	0.4	0	0	0	0	0	0	0	0	0
Chad	4721	0.4	0	0	0	0	0	11.2	0	0	0	0	0
Senegal	4721	100	17	35.6	25.8	1	3	72.5	85.2	97.5	5.9	1.8	43.9
South Africa	2818	32.3	99.2	99.8	97.7	99.8	99.7	99.7	100	99.6	93.9	97.9	15.6
Tunisia	11677	98.1	35.2	93.3	40	25.4	37.7	48.8	52.2	45.2	10.7	43.9	4.2
Zimbabwe	5087	46.3	13.3	6.8	20	5.6	6.1	19.2	20.2	1	2.7	7	33.3
Average Share	1929	8.8	77.4	78.3	75.7	74.3	77	68.8	80.8	77.4	72.3	74.7	73

Source: WTO (2001: Tables II.1 and Appendix II.1).

Table 20:   Broad Pattern of Tariff Commitments on Industrial Products[1] (Percentages).

Country Group or Region	Already Bound Duty-Free[2]	Currently Dutiable and/or Unbound[3]		
	Share of Lines	Bindings with Reductions Share of Lines	Bindings Without Reductions Share of Lines	No Offer Share of Lines
By Major Country Group:				
Developed Economies	17	67	9	7
Developing Economies	0	46	24	29
Transition Economies	6	83	0	11
By Selected Region:				
North America	18	72	0	10
Latin America	0	72	26	2
Western Europe	16	58	1	25
Central/East Europe	6	67	17	10
Africa	4	24	38	35
Asia	2	43	21	33

[1]Excluding petroleum.
[2]Figures refer to tariff lines which were fully bound prior to the Uruguay Round.
[3]Figures include tariff lines with unbound zero duties and partially bound zero duties.

Source: GATT (1994: Table II.1).

Table 21:   Tariff Reductions on Industrial Products by Developed Countries from Selected Groups of Countries.

Imports from:	*Trade-Weighted Tariff Average*		
	Pre-UR	*Post-UR*	*Percentage Reduction*
All Industrial Products[1]			
All Sources	6.3	3.8	40
Developing Economies (Other Than Least Developed Economies)	6.8	4.3	37
Least Developed Economies	6.8	5.1	25
Excluding Textiles and Clothing, Fish and Fish Products			
All Sources	5.4	2.9	46
Developing Economies (Other Than Least Developed Economies)	4.8	2.4	50
Least Developed Economies	1.8	0.7	61

[1] Excluding petroleum.

Source: GATT (1994: Table II.4).

Table 22:   Developed Country Tariff Reductions by Major Industrial Product Group 1
(Percentages).

| Product Category | Tariff Averages Weighted by: | | | | | |
| | Imports from all Sources | | | Imports from Developing Economies | | |
	Pre-UR	Post-UR	% Red.	Pre-UR	Post-UR	% Red.
All Industrial Products	6.3	3.8	40	6.8	4.3	37
Fish & Fish Products	6.1	4.5	26	6.6	4.8	27
Wood, Pulp, Paper & Furniture	3.5	1.1	69	4.6	1.7	63
Textiles and Clothing	15.5	12.1	22	14.6	11.3	23
Leather, Rubber, Footwear	8.9	7.3	18	8.1	6.6	19
Metals	3.7	1.4	62	2.7	0.9	67
Chemicals & Photographic Supplies	6.7	3.7	45	7.2	3.8	47
Transport Equipment	7.5	5.8	23	3.8	3.1	18
Non-Electric Machinery	4.8	1.9	60	4.7	1.6	66
Electric Machinery	6.6	3.5	47	6.3	3.3	48
Mineral Products & Precious Stones	2.3	1.1	52	2.6	0.8	69
Manufactured Articles n.e.s.	5.5	2.4	56	6.5	3.1	52
Industrial Tropical Products	4.2	2	52	4.2	1.9	55
Natural Resource-Based Products	3.2	2.1	34	4	2.7	33

Source: GATT (1994: Table II.3).

Table 23: Bound Tariffs on Industrial Products. Simple Averages by Country and Product Category.

	1 Wood, Pulp, Paper and Furniture	2 Textiles and Clothing	3 Leather, Rubber Footwear and Travel Goods	4 Metals	5 Chemicals and Photographic Supplies	6 Transport Equipment	7 Non-Electric Machinery	8 Electric Machinery	9 Mineral Products & Precious Stones and Metals	10 Manufactured Articles Not Elsewhere Specified	11 Fish and Fish Products
North America											
Canada	1.3	12.4	7.6	2.8	4.5	6.8	3.6	5.2	3.1	4.2	1.8
United States	0.6	8.9	8.4	1.8	3.7	2.7	1.2	2.1	3.3	3.0	2.2
Latin America											
Argentina	29.4	35.0	35.0	34.4	23.5	34.6	34.9	34.7	32.8	33.7	34.5
Brazil	27.7	34.9	34.7	33.4	22.7	33.6	32.6	31.9	33.5	33.5	33.4
Chile	25.0	25.0	25.0	25.0	25.0	24.9	25.0	25.0	24.9	25.0	25.0
Colombia	35.0	36.8	35.2	35.0	35.0	35.8	35.0	35.0	35.1	35.0	47.7
Costa Rica	44.2	45.1	45.9	44.5	43.5	49.6	44.2	43.3	44.6	44.7	46.3
El Salvador	35.3	38.6	40.8	35.0	37.7	35.8	32.6	34.6	37.7	38.2	45.0
Jamaica	50.0	50.0	50.0	50.0	50.0	50.0	50.0	50.0	50.0	50.0	50.6
Mexico	34.0	35.0	34.8	34.7	35.2	35.8	35.0	34.1	34.4	34.6	35.0
Peru	30.0	30.0	30.0	30.0	30.0	30.0	30.0	30.0	30.0	30.0	30.0
Venezuela	33.7	34.9	34.5	33.6	34.1	33.6	33.2	33.9	34.1	33.4	33.8
Western Europe											
European Union	0.7	7.9	4.8	1.6	4.8	4.7	1.8	3.3	2.4	2.7	11.8
Iceland	11.9	9.7	13.8	6.8	2.8	17.1	7.0	19.4	11.5	21.9	3.6

Table 23 continued.

	Wood, Pulp, Paper and Furniture	Textiles and Clothing	Leather, Rubber Footwear and Travel Goods	Metals	Chemicals and Photographic Supplies	Transport Equipment	Non-Electric Machinery	Electric Machinery	Mineral Products & Precious Stones and Metals	Manufactured Articles Not Elsewhere Specified	Fish and Fish Products
Norway	0.4	8.5	2.2	1.1	3.0	3.3	2.7	2.7	0.7	2.2	7.3
Switzerland	2.1	4.6	2.0	1.1	1.5	2.2	0.6	0.7	1.5	1.3	0.5
Turkey	40.5	80.3	79.9	30.4	29.0	25.8	23.7	26.6	39.4	43.3	26.2
Eastern Europe											
Czech Republic	5.5	6.2	3.8	3.8	4.0	6.2	3.8	4.2	3.4	3.6	0.2
Hungary	5.4	8.1	6.7	4.9	5.5	15.9	8.4	9.5	5.0	7.8	17.1
Poland	8.0	13.1	11.9	9.9	8.7	16.1	8.9	9.7	6.9	11.6	16.3
Romania	31.4	32.9	30.7	31.7	30.6	32.1	29.5	27.3	32.2	29.3	28.1
Slovak Republic	5.5	6.2	3.8	3.8	4.0	6.2	3.8	4.2	3.4	3.6	0.2
Asia											
Australia	7	28.8	17.5	4.5	9.2	15.1	9.1	13.3	7	7	0.8
Hong Kong, China	0	0	0	0	0	0	0	0	0	0	0
India	56.4	87.8	67.8	58.3	44.1	53.9	36.2	44.8	47.2	72.4	68.6
Indonesia	39.6	39.9	39.6	36.4	37.4	58.5	36.6	38.7	39.2	36.9	40
Japan	1.2	6.8	15.7	0.9	2.4	0	0	0.2	1	1.1	6.2
Korea, Republic of	4.8	18.2	16.7	7.7	6.7	24.6	11.1	16.1	10.4	11.4	19.1
Macau, China	0	0	0	0	0	0	0	0	0	0	0
Malaysia	19.8	20.7	19.1	14.2	15.4	29.8	10.9	14.1	14.7	12.6	14.5
New Zealand	4.5	21.9	19.1	11.2	6.1	17	15.1	16.1	7.6	11.7	2.8
Philippines	31.8	27.7	32.7	22.9	22.6	26.1	22	26.2	28.5	29.5	29.4
Singapore	3.1	7.8	3.4	3.2	5	4.4	4.3	4.9	1.2	1.2	9.8

Table 23 continued.

	Wood, Pulp, Paper and Furniture	Textiles and Clothing	Leather, Rubber Footwear and Travel Goods	Metals	Chemicals and Photographic Supplies	Transport Equipment	Non-Electric Machinery	Electric Machinery	Mineral Products & Precious Stones and Metals	Manufactured Articles Not Elsewhere Specified	Fish and Fish Products
Africa											
Cameroon	21.8	22.8	21.2	15.9	11.6	14.9	12.2	16.8	18.5	22.9	23.8
Chad	21.8	22.7	21.2	15.9	11.6	20.2	12.2	16.8	18.5	22.9	23.8
Gabon	15.5	15.1	15	15.2	15.2	15	15.2	15	16.1	18.5	15
Senegal	17.6	16.1	16.3	15.1	15.2	14.1	6.7	7.2	15.1	15	12.9
South Africa	9.2	27.7	23.1	14.1	13.9	23.3	12	17.4	11.5	14.8	22.5
Tunisia	34.2	56.3	36.1	25.6	26.5	25.5	25.2	29.1	28.9	32.5	41.2
Zimbabwe	12.6	21.4	13.1	9.1	5.5	10.1	6.3	12.3	7.6	15.5	3.1
Sri Lanka	32.6	45	43	16.6	15.8	18.3	12.8	20.4	26.2	27.1	49.2
Thailand	21.3	29.2	34.1	25.6	29.3	38.5	23.4	30.5	25.9	29.5	12.5

Source: WTO (2001: Tables II.2).

Table 24: Difference Between Simple Average Bound Tariffs and Simple Average Applied Tariffs for Industrial Products.

	1	2	3	4	5	6	7	8	9	10	11
	Wood, Pulp, Paper and Furniture	Textiles and Clothing	Leather, Rubber Footwear and Travel Goods	Metals	Chemicals and Photographic Supplies	Transport Equipment	Non-Electric Machinery	Electric Machinery	Mineral Products & Precious Stones and Metals	Manufactured Articles Not Elsewhere Specified	Fish and Fish Products
North America											
Canada	-1.3	0.7	0.7	-0.2	0.8	1.4	1.8	2.5	1.0	1.2	0.2
United States	-0.6	-1.0	1.9	-0.9	-0.5	0.0	-0.2	-0.1	-0.2	0.7	0.0
Latin America											
Argentina	14.7	14.5	17.9	19.1	13.0	17.8	22.1	20.4	22.4	16.9	21.6
Chile	14.2	14.0	14.0	14.0	14.0	14.6	14.2	14.7	13.9	14.0	14.0
Colombia	22.2	18.6	22.5	25.0	27.7	22.5	25.8	24.9	25.0	24.3	29.4
Costa Rica	36.8	31.6	36.1	40.9	40.9	38.5	41.4	39.4	38.1	37.0	34.7
Mexico	22.2	13.3	16.7	22.2	26.2	22.0	24.9	21.2	22.6	21.3	16.2
Western Europe											
European Union	-2.2	-1.1	-0.1	-1.2	0.0	0.0	0.1	0.3	0.1	0.1	-0.3
Iceland	9.3	5.2	7.2	5.7	1.4	15.9	6.1	17.1	9.5	17.5	1.9
Norway	0.1	-2.5	-0.7	-0.2	-0.6	3.0	2.2	0.8	0.1	0.0	7.3
Switzerland	2.1	4.6	2.0	1.1	1.5	2.2	0.6	0.7	1.5	1.3	0.5
Turkey	36.2	70.3	69.8	25.1	23.6	18.5	20.9	22.0	36.1	39.4	-23.7
Eastern Europe											
Poland	8.0	13.1	11.9	9.9	8.7	16.1	8.9	9.7	6.9	11.6	16.3
Romania	31.4	32.9	30.7	31.7	30.6	32.1	29.5	27.3	32.2	29.3	28.1
Slovak Rep.	-0.4	-1.3	-1.2	-0.8	-0.3	-1.1	-0.5	-0.2	-1.3	-0.5	0.1

Table 24 continued.

	Wood, Pulp, Paper and Furniture	Textiles and Clothing	Leather, Rubber Footwear and Travel Goods	Metals	Chemicals and Photographic Supplies	Transport Equipment	Non-Electric Machinery	Electric Machinery	Mineral Products & Precious Stones and Metals	Manufactured Articles Not Elsewhere Specified	Fish and Fish Products
Asia/Pacif.											
Australia	3.3	13.4	9.6	0.8	6.9	9.7	5.3	8.5	4.7	4.4	0.8
Hong Kong, China	0.0	0.0	0.0	0.0	0.0	0.0	0.0	0.0	0.0	0.0	0.0
Japan	-1.1	-2.0	3.5	-1.1	-0.2	0.0	0.0	-0.1	-0.1	-0.2	-0.1
Korea, Rep. of	-1.3	8.4	7.9	1.0	-0.8	18.6	3.7	8.7	4.4	3.9	2.2
Macau, China	0.0	0.0	0.0	0.0	0.0	0.0	0.0	0.0	0.0	0.0	0.0
Philippines	19.9	10.3	20.9	14.2	17.5	13.8	17.3	18.9	20.5	20.5	17.4
Singapore	3.1	7.8	3.4	3.2	5.0	4.4	4.3	4.9	1.2	1.2	9.8
Africa											
Cameroon	0.0	0.1	0.0	0.0	0.0	0.0	0.0	0.0	0.0	0.0	0.0
Chad	0.0	0.0	0.0	0.0	0.0	0.0	0.0	0.0	0.0	0.0	0.0
Gabon	0.0	-7.6	0.0	0.0	0.0	0.0	0.0	0.0	0.0	0.0	0.0
Total average	6.9	8.4	9.6	6.8	7.0	8.4	7.9	8.5	7.9	8.2	5.4

Source: WTO (2001: Appendix II.6).

Table 25:   Broad Pattern of Tariff Commitments on Agricultural Products
(Percentages).

| Country Group or Region | Already Bound Duty-Free[1] | Currently Dutiable and/or Unbound[2] | |
		Bindings with Reductions	Bindings Without Reductions
	Share of Lines	Share of Lines	Share of Lines
By Major Country Group:			
Developed Economies	21	79	0
Developing Economies	9	76	15
Transition Economies	16	84	0
By Selected Region:			
North America	28	72	0
Latin America	2	72	26
Western Europe	13	87	0
Central/East Europe	13	87	0
Africa	13	55	31
Asia	20	76	4

[1]Figures refer to tariff lines which were fully bound prior to the Uruguay Round.
[2]Figures include tariff lines with unbound zero duties and partially bound zero duties.

Source: GATT (1994: Table II.7).

Table 26:   Developed Country Tariff Reductions on Agricultural Products.

Product Categories	Percentage Reduction in Tariffs
All agricultural products	**37**
Coffee, tea, cocoa, mate	35
Fruits and vegetables	36
Oilseeds, fats, and oils	40
Other agricultural products	48
Animals and products	32
Beverages and spirits	38
Flowers, plants, vegetable materials	48
Tobacco	36
Spices and cereal preparations	35
Sugar	30
Grains	39
Dairy products	26
Tropical products	**43**
Tropical beverages	46
Tropical nuts and fruits	37
Certain oilseeds, oils	40
Roots, rice, tobacco	40
Spices, flowers, and plants	52

Source: GATT (1994: Table II.8).

Table 27:   Bound Tariffs on Imports of Agricultural and Industrial Products.

	Agriculture		Industry	
	Simple Average Post-UR Bound Rate		Simple Average Post-UR Bound Rate	
	OECD Estimate	World Bank Estimate	OECD Estimate	World Bank Estimate
North America				
Canada	4.6	8.8	5.3	6.4
United States	5.5	9	3.8	4.6
Latin America				
Argentina	32.8	32.5	30.6	30.9
Brazil	35.3	35.2	29.7	29.5
Colombia	88.3	105.6	36.1	35.5
Mexico	42.9	25.1	34.8	34.7
Venezuela	55.4	67.7	33.8	33.3
Western Europe				
EU-15	19.5	20	4.1	4.1
Iceland	48.4	72.1	10	14.4
Norway	123.7	50.4	3.4	4.1
Switzerland	51.1	46.9	1.9	2.2
Turkey	63.9	74.3	40.7	16.6
Eastern Europe				
Czech Republic	13.3	18.9	4.5	4.8
Hungary	22.2	6.7	6.8	7.4
Poland	52.8	38.3	10.6	9.8
Romania	98.6	130.2	34.4	32.7
Asia/Pacific				
Australia	3.3	2.5	10.6	13
Bangladesh	83.8		83.5	
India	124.3	101	59	37.5
Indonesia	47.2	59.9	38.6	38.5
Japan	11.7	29.7	3.6	3
Korea	62.2	39.6	11.4	10.3
Malaysia	13.6	39	16.4	16.7
New Zealand	8.7	0.7	13.8	14.9
Philippines	35.3	46.9	25.1	23.2
Sri Lanka	50	50	50	26.8
Thailand	34.6	43.2	28.4	26.5
Africa				
Tunisia	116.7	15.1	41.2	36.8

Source: WTO (2001: Table III.3 p.49).

Table 28:   MERCOSUR Tariff Structure, 1995 and Final CET (2001/2006), % .

ISIC Code	Description	Argentina	Brazil	Paraguay	Uruguay	Average	Final
	Total	**10.5**	**11.9**	**9.4**	**10.8**	**10.7**	**11.2**
1	**Agriculture, hunting, forestry & fishing**	**7**	**7**	**6.9**	**6.9**	**7**	**7**
111	Agricultural and livestock production	7	6.9	6.8	6.8	6.9	7
12	Forestry and logging	4.6	4.7	4.4	4.6	4.6	4.6
121	Forestry	5.8	6	5.5	5.8	5.8	5.8
122	Logging	2	2	2	2	2	2
130	Fishing	8.7	8.7	8.7	8.7	8.7	8.7
2	**Mining & quarrying**	**3.4**	**3.6**	**3.4**	**3.4**	**3.5**	**3.4**
210	Coal mining	0	0	0	0	0	0
220	Crude petroleum and natural gas	0	6.8	0	0	1.7	0
230	Metal ore mining	2.2	2.2	2.2	2.2	2.2	2.2
290	Other mining	4.1	4.1	4.1	4.1	4.1	4.1
3	**Manufacturing**	**10.8**	**12.3**	**9.6**	**11.1**	**11**	**11.5**
31	Food, beverages and tobacco	11.6	11.7	11.5	11.7	11.6	11.6
311	Food products	11	11.2	10.9	11.2	11.1	11
312	Other food products and animal feeds	11.8	11.8	11.3	11.8	11.7	11.8
313	Beverages	18.1	17.3	18.6	17.6	17.9	18.6
314	Tobacco manufacturing	18.6	18.6	18.6	18.6	18.6	18.6
32	Textile, wearing apparel and leather	17.2	16.9	16.9	16.9	17	17.1
321	Textiles	16.8	16.7	16.6	16.7	16.7	16.9
322	Manufacture of wearing apparel	19.9	19.9	19.9	19.9	19.9	19.9
323	Leather products	13.2	12.4	13.2	12.8	12.9	13.2
324	Manufacture of footwear	24.6	19.4	18.8	19.4	20.6	19.4
33	Wood and wood products, inc. furniture	10.8	10.2	10.5	10.5	10.5	10.5
331	Wood and wood products, exc. furniture	8.1	7.7	8.1	8.1	8	8.1
332	Manuf. of furniture & fixtures exc. metal	18.9	18	18	18	18.2	18
34	Paper, paper prods, printing & publishing	11.7	10.7	10.7	10.4	10.9	10.9
341	Paper products	12.1	11	11.1	10.7	11.2	11.3
342	Printing, publishing & allied industries	10.1	9.4	9.4	9	9.5	9.4
35	Chemicals, petrol, coal, rubber, plastics	7.9	8.2	7.7	7.2	7.8	8.1
351	Industrial chemicals	7.2	7.5	7.1	6.4	7.1	7.5
352	Other chemicals, incl. pharm.	8.6	8.7	8.1	8.3	8.4	8.8
353	Petroleum refineries	0.9	12.7	0.9	0.9	3.9	0.9
354	Manuf. of misc. petrol. & coal prods.	2	3.2	2	2	2.3	2

Table 28 continued.

ISIC Code	Description	Argentina	Brazil	Paraguay	Uruguay	Average	Final
355	Rubber products	16.1	15.4	15.4	15.4	15.6	15.4
356	Manufacture of plastic products n.e.s.	17.4	17.4	17.4	16.8	17.3	17.4
36	Non-metal minrl prods exc. petrol & coal	10.9	10.5	10.6	10.9	10.7	10.9
361	Pottery and china	15.4	14.8	14.3	15.4	15	15.4
362	Manufacture of glass and glass products	12.6	12.6	12.4	12.6	12.6	12.6
369	Other non-metallic mineral products	9.2	8.6	9	9.2	9	9.2
37	Basic metal industries	10.9	9.9	9.6	9.3	9.9	9.9
371	Iron and steel basic industries	12.6	11.4	11	10.5	11.4	11.4
372	Non-ferrous metal basic industries	8.7	7.9	7.8	7.7	8	8
38	Fabricated metal prods, mach.& equip.	10.9	15.8	8	13.2	12	13.3
381	Fabricated metal products	16	16.4	14.7	16	15.8	16.1
382	Non-electrical machinery incl. computers	7.7	16.8	4.5	12.4	10.4	12.5
383	Electrical machinery	12.1	14.8	9.2	12.6	12.2	12.7
384	Transport equipment	13.5	15.2	11.5	14.6	13.7	14.6
385	Professional and scientific equipment	12.2	14.8	8.8	13.3	12.3	13.4
390	Other manufacturing industries	16.8	16.6	15.8	16.6	16.5	16.6

Note: CET to be completed by Argentina and Brazil by 2001 and by Paraguay and Uruguay by 2006.
Source: WTO Secretariat calculations, based on data supplied by MERCOSUR in Laird (1997).

References

Anderson, K. and H. Norheim (1993), Is World Trade Becoming More Regionalized?, *The Review of International Economics* 1 (2), 91-109.

Bhagwati, J. (1992), *Regionalism and Multilateralism: An Overview*, World Bank and CEPR Conference on New Dimensions in Regional Integration, April, Washington, D.C.

Bhagwati, J. (1993), Regionalism and Multilateralism: An Overview, in: de Melo, J. and A. Panagariya (Eds.), *New Dimensions in Regional Integration*, New York.

Ben-David and Papell (1998), Slowdowns and Meltdowns: Post-War Growth Evidence from 74 Countries, *Review of Economics and Statistics* 80, November, 561-71.

Ben-David and A. Kimhi (2001), *Trade and the Rate of Income Convergence*, NBER Working Paper No. W7642.

Drysdale, P. and R. Garnaut (1982), Trade Intensities and the Analysis of Bilateral Trade Flows in a Many-Country World, *Hitotsubashi Journal of Economics* 22, 62-84.

Drysdale, P.D. and R. Garnaut (1993), The Pacific: An Application of a General Theory of Economic Integration, in: Bergsten, C.F. and M. Noland (Eds.), *Pacific Dynamism and the International Economic System*, Washington, D.C.

Frankel, J.A., E. Stein, and S.-J. Wei (1994), *Trading Blocs: The Natural, the Unnatural and the Super-Natural*, Working Paper No. C94-034, Center for International and Development Economic Research, University of California at Berkeley.

Frankel J.A. (1997), *Regional Trading Blocs in the World Economic System*, Institute for International Economics.

GATT (1994), The Results of the Uruguay Round of Multilateral Trade Negotiations, *mimeo*, Geneva.

Grubel, H.G. and P.J Lloyd (1975), *Intra Industry Trade: The Theory and Measurement of International Trade in Differentiated Products*, New York.

Hackman B.M. and M. Kostecki (2000), *The Political Economy of the World Trading System: From GATT to WTO*, Oxford.

Nordström, H. and S. Vaughan (1999), Trade and Environment, *WTO Special Studies* 4.

Helpman, E. and P.R. Krugman (1985), *Market Structure and Foreign Trade, Increasing Returns Imperfect Competition and International Economy*, Cambridge, USA.

Lancaster K. (1980), Intra-Industry Trade Under Perfect Monopolistic Competition, *Journal of International Economics* 10, 151-175.

Ng and Yeats (1999), *Production Sharing in East Asia: Who Does What for Whom and Why*, Working Paper World Bank.

Krugman, P.R. (1991a), Is Bilateralism Bad?, in: Helpman, E. and A. Razin (Eds.), *International Trade and Trade Policy*, Cambridge, MA.

Krugman, P.R. (1991b), The Move to Free-Trade Zones, in: *Policy Implications of Trade and Currency Zones*, A Symposium sponsored by the Federal Reserve Bank of Kansas City, Jackson-Hole, Wyoming.

Laird, S. (1997), *MERCOSUR: Objectives and Achievements*, World Bank, Washington, D.C.

Otsubo, S. (1998), *New Regionalism and South-South Trade: Could it be an Entry Point for the South Toward Global Integration?*, APEC Discussion Paper No. 18.

Panagariya, A. (1995), Rethinking the New Regionalism, presented at the World Bank Conference on Trade Expansion Program, January 23-24, 1995. Forthcoming in Nash, J. and W. Takacs (Eds.), *Lessons in Trade Policy Reform*, Washington, D.C.

Sachs, J. and A. Warner (1995), Economic Reform and the Process of Global Integration, *Brookings Papers on Economic Activity* No. 1, 1-118.

Summers, L. (1991), Regionalism and the World Trading System, in: *Policy Implications of Trade and Currency Zones*, A Symposium Sponsored by the Federal Reserve Bank of Kansas City, Jackson Hole, Wyoming, 295-302.

Sorensen, N.K., B. Dalum, E.S. Madsen, and J.U.M Nielsen (1991), *Intra-Industry Trade in Denmark and Ireland*, A Comparison Memo 1991-19, Institute of Economics, Århus University.

Thurow, L. (1992), *Head to Head: The Coming Economic Battle Among Japan, Europe, and America*, New York.

World Bank Conference (1997), *Trade: Towards Open Regionalism*.

WTO (1996), *Trade Policy Review of Brazil*.

WTO (1999), *Trading into the Future*.

WTO (2000), *International Trade Statistics 2000*.

WTO (2001), *Market Access: Unfinished Business – Post Uruguay Round Inventory*, (Special study No. 6).

http://www.wto.org/english/thewto_e/whatis_e/tif_e/org2_e.htm

http://europa.eu.int/comm/trade/index_en.htm

Multilateral Environmental Agreements and the Trade and Environment Nexus

Tim Taylor, Alistair Hunt, and Anil Markandya

Department of Economics, University of Bath, Bath, BA2 7AY, United Kingdom
and Metroeconomica Limited, 108 Bloomfield Road, Bath BA2 2AR, United
Kingdom
ecstjt@bath.ac.uk, ecsasph@bath.ac.uk, hssam@bath.ac.uk

1 Introduction

The emergence of transboundary environmental problems, including climate
change and the depletion of the ozone layer, has led to the establishment of a
number of multilateral environmental agreements (MEAs). To date, over 200 such
agreements have been made. These MEAs may have important impacts on trade,
either directly through trade measures or indirectly through the changing of relative prices through mitigation measures. This chapter will investigate these impacts on trade of MEAs.

This chapter will review some of the main literature on the issue of trade impacts
of MEAs to date, including the Montreal Protocol, CITES and the Basel Convention, before examining the potential trade impacts of the Kyoto Protocol or its
successor. It then discusses issue linkage within a political economy framework
and investigates key determinants of implementation for future MEAs.

The trade and environment nexus within MEAs and likely implications for future
trade-environment issue-linkage within MEAs are then investigated.

2 Trade and Environment Nexus: Overview

The linkages between trade and environment are complex. Many studies have
attempted to identify and analyse these linkages, either through analysing the
impacts of trade liberalisation on the environment (e.g. CEC, 1999, Jha et al.,
1999) or through investigating the impacts of environmental agreements on trade
(e.g. Jha et al., 1999; Brack, 1996; Markandya and Milborrow, 1998). This section
will give a brief introduction to the key issues within the trade and environment

debate, before looking further at the latter case of the impact of multilateral environmental agreements on trade.

2.1   Trade Liberalisation and the Environment

The liberalisation of trade is a key part of the modern world. With the development of free trade areas such as the European Union, NAFTA and others, the impact that such liberalisation will have on the environment is of increasing concern. Trade liberalisation, thus, forms the backdrop to future multilateral environmental agreements and hence, we investigate briefly the impact that such liberalisation may have had on the environment to date.

The impact that the North American Free Trade Agreement (NAFTA) may have on the environment was investigated by CEC (1999), amongst others. They identified four key areas in which trade liberalisation was linked to environmental change, notably:

*   Changes in production, management and technology employed – which can affect the environment in that if cleaner production methods are used, as a result of increased access to the technology or environmental regulation contained within the trade agreement, then the level of environmental degradation could fall. There could also be negative impacts if trade liberalisation leads to increased output (the scale effect) and hence increased pollution.
*   Changes in physical infrastructure, including transportation networks – it is suggested that NAFTA could lead to changes in environmental quality depending on the capacity of existing traffic networks, and hence the need for possible expansion, and through shifts to more environmentally-friendly transportation methods.
*   Changes in social organisation – CEC suggested that "the NAFTA institutions may serve as the centre of a deepening North American community in which a sense of stewardship... grows."
*   Changes in government policy – government regulations may converge as a result of trade liberalisation. The implications of this on the environment are that the level of environmental quality in countries with lower environmental standards may be expected to rise as these standards converge with those of the other countries.

Studies on the effect that trade liberalisation may have on the environment have reached conflicting conclusions. Boyd et al. (1993) suggested that for the case of the Philippines tariff removal[1] would result in substantial increases in deforestation. Cruz and Repetto (1993) found similar results in another Philippine study. However, a study of 25 Latin American countries from 1960-88 found that open-

---

[1]   Boyd et al. (1993) considered removal of tariffs existing in 1988.

ness of the economy was significant in explaining pollution intensity, with increased openness implying reduced intensity (Birdsall and Wheeler, 1992).

Markandya (1999) reviewed the impacts of changes in trade regimes on developing countries and economies in transition by examining case studies commissioned by UNCTAD and UNDP. For Brazil the situation was found to be one where some small moves towards trade liberalisation have been accompanied by an upward trend in the level of environmentally harmful exports. In the case of China a more mixed picture was found. The use of new, cleaner technologies was accompanied by a dramatic expansion, particularly in small-scale industries. This expansion created significant ecological problems in some areas, including loss of biodiversity and natural resource depletion. For Poland, market reforms and trade liberalisation were not distinguished in the study. However, the economy was seen to be moving from energy-intensive, heavy engineering activities to a more Western mix of output. Markandya concludes that, for the eleven countries examined, the "studies do not provide emphatic evidence that trade liberalisation has systematically hurt the environment". In some cases the UNCTAD/UNDP studies identified cases in which environmental pressures had reduced and others where they had increased, though where the latter were the case policies were identified that would redress the situation with no negative impact on liberalisation.

To conclude, there is mixed evidence on the impact that trade liberalisation may have on the environment. With the potential enlargement of the European Union looming ever nearer, this forms the setting in which any potential future multilateral environmental agreement will have an impact on trade. Hence, studies of the trade impacts of future MEAs should consider the changing world environment. We now examine the impact that multilateral environmental agreements have on trade.

2.2   Multilateral Environmental Agreements and Trade

Trade and environment are not only linked in the case of trade liberalisation, but also when environmental protection measures may impact on trade. With growing awareness of transboundary environmental problems such as the depletion of the ozone layer and climate change the need for international agreement on ways in which to mitigate or adapt to environmental degradation has arisen. As a result, over 200 MEAs have been signed. These MEAs may have important implications for trade, either directly through trade restrictions[2] or indirectly through changing production costs and hence prices.

---

[2]   Brack et al. (2000) point out that of the 200 MEAs in existence, around 20 incorporate trade measures. These include the Basel Convention on Hazardous Waste, CITES and the Montreal Protocol.

Brack et al. (2000) identify four main objectives for which direct trade restrictions have been applied in the design of MEAs:

- to restrict markets for environmentally hazardous products or goods produced unsustainably,
- to increase the coverage of the agreement's provisions by encouraging governments to join and/or comply with the MEA,
- to prevent free-riding by encouraging governments to join and/or comply with the MEA,
- to ensure the MEA's effectiveness by preventing leakage[3.]

However, the trade restrictions introduced as part of an MEA may fall foul of WTO regulations established to promote free trade. A number of issues are of importance in this discussion, including:

- the hierarchical relationship between the WTO and MEAs: developing countries have resisted efforts to give MEAs superiority in dispute resolution (Shahin, 1999);
- the debate over Article XX: Article XX of GATT allows for measures "necessary to protect human, animal or plant life or health" or "relating to the conservation of exhaustible natural resources if such measures are made effective in conjunction with restrictions on domestic production or consumption". This Article is the subject of some debate as to whether it allows scope for trade restrictions under MEAs. Esty (1994) notes that the Article does not cover atmosphere, oceans, ozone layer and other elements of the global commons. The issue of the definition of "like products", which cannot be discriminated against under WTO rules, is also important. Article XX focuses on goods produced, not on the techniques used to produce them. Brack (1999) suggests that negotiations should be opened on a new WTO Agreement on MEAs with Trade Provisions.

Potential conflicts with the WTO must be taken into consideration in the design of trade measures in MEAs.

The implications of some of the major MEAs for trade are reviewed in the next section.

---

[3]   Brack et al. (2000) define leakage as "the situation where non-participants increase their emissions, or other unsustainable behaviour, as a result of the control measures taken by signatories".

3 Review of Past Experience with MEAs and Implications for Trade

This section presents a qualitative review of previous work on MEAs and the trade impacts associated with them. Three major MEAs have been the subject of much investigation, notably the Montreal Protocol on Substances that Deplete the Ozone Layer, CITES and the Basel Convention. These are reviewed below, along with some recent work on possible trade implications of the Kyoto Protocol.

3.1 Montreal Protocol

The Montreal Protocol on Substances that Deplete the Ozone Layer was established in 1987 as a result of growing international concern over the damage done to the ozone layer by ozone depleting substances, including chlorofluorocarbons (CFCs), halons and methyl bromide. The Montreal Protocol aimed to reduce consumption of Ozone Depleting Substances (ODS) and included a number of provisions which directly impacted on trade in ODS and products containing or made with ODS. The Protocol established a timetable for the phasing out of ODS, with industrialised countries aiming to phase out the main CFCs by the start of 1996 and industrialising countries by 2010 (Brack, 1996).

Trade provisions included restrictions on trade with non-signatories, which encouraged accession to the Protocol, and ensuring that no country gained a competitive advantage by not acceding to the Protocol. Brack (1996) concluded that the trade provisions contained in the Montreal Protocol were effective in reducing the extent of free riding and in preventing leakage, as there was no evidence of nations not signing in order to evade the controls. Markandya and Milborrow (1998) also concluded that trade restrictions, together with financial assistance to cover the costs of acceding to the Protocol, played a key role in the acceptance of the Protocol by all but 27 countries, a number of which are undergoing transition or have no stable government.

3.1.1 Trade Impacts of the Montreal Protocol

The trade impacts of the Montreal Protocol were examined in Markandya and Milborrow (1998). Markandya and Milborrow examined the impact of the Montreal Protocol through econometric analysis of the determinants of trade in ODSs for Belgium, the United Kingdom and the EU as a whole. The key results are presented in Table 1 below. As can be seen from the table, the Montreal Protocol had significant impacts on trade[4] between some of the areas considered in the study. In particular, ODS imports from developing countries rose by 25.6% in the UK, whilst European exports to the rest of the world fell dramatically.

Table 1:   Impact of Montreal Protocol on Trade in ODSs (in %).

		Rest of World	Other EU	Other Developed	Developing Countries
Belgium	Imports	ns	ns	-14	ns
	Exports	ns	13,4	ns	ns
	Years of Impact		1989-94	1985-94	
UK	Imports	19,6	-10,9	ns	25,6
	Exports	ns	-15,6	33,4	6,7
	Years of Impact	1987-94	1989-93	1987-94	1987-94
Europe	Imports	-11,5	na	-10,4	-10
	Exports	-139	na	ns	ns
	Years of Impact	1989-93		1989-93	1989-93

ns=not statistically significant, na=not applicable.
Source: Based on Markandya and Milborrow (1998).

The Montreal Protocol also contained trade measures for goods containing ozone depleting substances. The trade impacts for a number of regions and countries on trade in several goods containing ODSs were evaluated by Markandya and Milborrow (1998). The impacts of the Protocol identified using regression analysis are shown in Table 2. This regression analysis included GDP as a determinant variable and for individual countries exchange rate variables were tried but found to be insignificant. The impact of the Montreal Protocol varied from region to region, with negative impacts on imports of non-domestic and domestic refrigeration. The most notable change was that of EC imports of air-conditioning machinery, which rose by 77% over the period 1989 to 1993.

The trade impacts for some developing countries of the Montreal Protocol were presented in Jha et al. (1999). The main findings were:

• For Brazil, ODS-related exports declined by 45% between 1989 and 1992, compared with a decline in exports of manufactured goods to the OECD of 7%. Exports of products containing CFCs to developing countries rose quickly in the early 1990s, though this was side-by-side with growth in manufacturing exports.

---

[4]   The impact of the Montreal Protocol was estimated by regressing imports/exports on real GDP, exchange rate lagged one period and various 1-0 dummy variables to pick up trends after 1985 to proxy a protocol impact.

- For China, the volume of refrigerators exported fell 58% between 1988 to 1991, with similar declines in other ODS-related goods. This led to an expansion of the phase-out programme.

- For Malaysia, close cooperation between government and industry in the phase-out strategy meant that ODS phase-out had little or no impact on trade and competitiveness.

Table 2:   Impact of Montreal Protocol on Trade in Goods Containing ODSs (in %).

	Imports		Exports	
	Protocol Impact (%)	Years	Protocol Impact (%)	Years
Sector				
Non-Domestic Refrigeration				
EC	-30	1990-92	None	
OECD	-26	1990-92	None	
Asia	-24	1986-88	None	
Korea	None		None	
Air Conditioning Machinery				
EC	77	1989-93	-27	1986-88
OECD	37	1989-93	n.a.	
Asia	None		-28	1988-90
Singapore	-27	1989-91	n.a.	
Domestic Refrigeration				
EC	-28	1986-88	-35	1986-88
OECD	-28	1989-90	None	
Asia	None		-41	1988-90
Singapore	-28	1990-92	-37	1988-89
Malaysia	-54	1986-88	n.a.	
Turkey	n.a.	n.a.	None	
Korea	n.a.	n.a.	-53	1988-89

Source: Based on Markandya and Milborrow (1998).

3.1.2   Illegal Trade and the Montreal Protocol

Illegal trade is one potential problem for the credibility of the Montreal Protocol and other MEAs. Markandya and Milborrow recommended the following measures to counteract this:

- Demand-side measures to encourage industry to replace CFC-using equipment, for example fiscal exemptions or product endorsement for rapid conversions.
- Alternatively, controls could be established for CFC sales, holding stockpiles or imports of recycled materials.
- Closer monitoring of CFC production and trade.
- Greater cooperation between customs authorities and environmental agencies at national and international level, with a centralised intelligence unit being proposed.
- Credible penalties for breaking the Protocol are required.

3.1.3   'Pollution Havens' and the Montreal Protocol

The main findings in the literature on the Montreal Protocol and industrial location were:

- There was little evidence available to support the hypothesis that a shift in production location occurred as a result of the Montreal Protocol, in line with most other findings on industrial production.
- Cases of shifts of a number of CFC-using enterprises from Hong Kong (then a British protectorate) to China reported by Lu et al. (1993) may have been due to less stringent phase-out schedules in China. However, the shift may also have been caused by a desire to gain access to the Chinese market.
- In Thailand, one study found an increase in ODS consumption by subsidiaries of transnationals (UNCTAD, 1995).
- Evidence is not available of a shift in production by multinationals from established factories in developed to those in developing countries. Even if this were the case this should not be a matter of concern since ODSs will be needed in developing countries for some time. Targets established under the Montreal Protocol will still be met.
- Industrial migration is being restricted in some cases to prevent total consumption of ODSs rising above 0.3kg/head. Such is the case in Malaysia, where the government is reluctant to allow foreign companies that may raise the level of ODS to set up for fear of losing the benefits of being a non-Annex 5.1 member.
- Adaptation to the new market was shown to be advantageous in the Chinese case, where manufacturers of refrigerators had to adopt new non-ODS-using technologies in order to meet demands of international buyers.

Thus, it can be concluded that industrial migration or the creation of 'pollution havens' has not been a major issue as a result of the Montreal Protocol. This is possibly due to the fact that few countries have not become party to the Protocol, but also reflects wider evidence in the literature that other factors play a more important role in industrial location than environmental protection.

3.1.4   Conclusions

The Montreal Protocol has proven itself to be one of the most successful MEAs to date. A large part of this success can be attributed to the trade provisions laid down within the Protocol which encouraged accession and prevented free-riding. Statistical analysis shows that the Protocol was an important determinant in trade of ODS and ODS-containing goods. Important lessons can be drawn for other MEAs in terms of the time-lag between accession and impact and also in terms of measures that have been identified to prevent illegal trade in the substance under consideration. There is little or no evidence in the literature to date of a 'pollution haven' effect arising from the application of the Montreal Protocol, and where it does exist then there may be other factors, such as market access, which determine the enterprise decision to relocate.

3.2   Convention on International Trade in Endangered Species (CITES)

CITES came into force on July 1, 1975 and has a membership of 152 countries. (CITES, 2001). These countries have banned commercial international trade in an agreed list of endangered species and regulate and monitor trade in species that might become endangered.

CITES lists vulnerable species in one of three appendices:

- Appendix I – species "threatened with extinction and are or may be affected by trade", for which trade is banned for primarily commercial purposes.

- Appendix II – species not yet threatened with extinction, but which may become so if trade is not strictly regulated, for which trade is banned if the authorities in the exporting country deems export to be detrimental for species survival.

- Appendix III – species listed by governments as subject to exploitation and needing regulation to restrict exploitation. The presentation of appropriate export documents at the time of importation is required for such species.

3.2.1   Trade Impacts of CITES

Trade impacts under CITES are restricted to impacts on the trade in protected species or goods made with such species. Trade measures under this Convention have been suggested to cause unnecessary economic losses where the species under consideration are sustainably managed. Jha et al. (1999) give the example of Zimbabwe where there have been significant losses in trade of ivory and crocodiles, leading to stockpiling of ivory valued at US$12 million. Recent measures to alleviate this problem have included the downlisting of elephants to Appendix II, allowing limited trade. In April 1999, the first trade in ivory for 10 years took place between Zimbabwe and Japan (AFP, 1999).

Trade in products covered by CITES may represent only a small proportion of total exports. As such, only very small impacts on trade may be experienced. Such is the case in Costa Rica, though orchid dealers have complained of the impacts of a 5% tax on imports of wildlife species, claiming these have reduced competiveness (Markandya, 1999).

3.3   Basel Convention

The Basel Convention on the Control of Transboundary Movements of Hazardous Wastes and their Disposal entered into force on May 5, 1992, having received 20 ratifications. In December 1998 there were 122 Parties to the Convention, with the United States being the most important non-signatory (Krueger, 1999).

The trade provisions within the Basel Convention have been reviewed by Krueger (1999). They include the following:

- A ban on parties exporting wastes to countries that have prohibited their import;

- a ban on export of hazardous waste to "states that are neither parties to the Basel Convention nor to an agreement that is less environmentally sound than the Convention";

- a ban on hazardous waste export to Antartica.

- Prohibition of export if reason to believe environmentally sound management or disposal is not available at the destination.

Prohibition of trade with non-parties under Article 4.5 acts as a mechanism to encourage non-parties to join. The logic is similar to that of the trade provisions under the Montreal Protocol, in that non-parties must accede or lose trade with those that are party to the Convention. Krueger argues this measure has been undermined by Article 11, which allows for agreements with non-parties as long as they are not less environmentally sound. Moves to ensure conformity with the Convention were quashed by some industrialised countries due to fears over existing regional mechanisms not meeting the required standards.

3.3.1   Trade and Environment Impacts of the Basel Convention

The loopholes provided within the Basel Convention have been exploited to some extent, with such agreements being made between the US and Malaysia (1995), the US and Costa Rica (1997), Germany for exports to Kazakhstan and Namibia, amongst others. Krueger reports that by August 1997, 25 bilateral and nine regional or multilateral agreements were in existence. Hence, the trade impacts of the Basel Convention have not been as large as they may have been, due to this flexibility.

Impacts identified in the literature are diverse:

- That trade restrictions on recyclable hazardous waste may restrict access to secondary raw materials for non-OECD countries. Secondary raw materials are important in developing countries, for example imported battery scrap in India and the Philippines accounted for 60 to 70% of lead consumption in the early 1990s (UNCTAD, 1998).

- Definitions of the nature of "hazardous waste" are important in determining the trade impact (Johnstone, 1999).

- For LDCs the impact may be positive in terms of the environment, as they are protected against fake recycling schemes as a pretext for export.

- For Brazil, the impact of trade restrictions on the import of scrap metal could adversely impact on competitiveness, as scrap is imported to compensate for fluctuations in supply (Jha et al., 1999).

- For Poland, trade restrictions have resulted in a large decline in the import of wastes. Some of these wastes, in particular scrap paper, were useful inputs into production. Exports of scrap metal have also fallen which may have some benefits. The loss of revenue from transport of waste may be important, particularly for the corridor between Ukraine and Russia (Jha et al., 1999).

- In Thailand, imports of hazardous waste rose dramatically, but under new regulations these imports were expected to fall.

3.3.2   'Pollution Havens' and the Basel Convention

The Basel Convention has at its core the idea of preventing the dumping of hazardous waste in developing countries without the resources to manage such wastes. Insofar as this has resulted, such 'pollution havens' that existed due to differential regulations in these developing countries have been eradicated to a great extent. Illegal movements of waste are still of concern, however, and steps have been taken to prevent these.

In the intermediate years between accession to the Convention and the raising of environmental regulations, some impact on trade has been experienced. Jha et al. (1999) cite the case of Thailand, where the importation of toxic waste rose considerably, but were predicted to fall dramatically as regulations came into force. Such a pollution haven effect may be seen as a temporary phenomenon.

3.3.3 Conclusions

Trade restrictions form an important part of the Basel Convention. First, they encourage accession to the Convention, though the extent to which these measures are important has been blunted by the inclusion of Article 11 in the Convention. Second, they prevent the creation of pollution havens, though these have been seen in the short term in the immediate aftermath of the Convention.

Some significant trade impacts have been experienced as a result of the Convention, particularly in the trade of recyclable goods. These trade impacts may have important implications for competitiveness in developing countries which rely on these goods as inputs in the production process.

3.4 Kyoto Protocol

The potential for the application of trade measures within the framework of the Kyoto Protocol is discussed in Brack et al. (2000) in terms of feasibility, fairness and the interrelationship with the multilateral trading system. This section briefly reviews their main conclusions.

In terms of feasibility, four main criteria are identified for the successful application of trade restrictions. The products should be:

• limited in type and application;

• limited in origin;

• easily detectable; and

• easily substitutable.

Brack et al. conclude that for the Montreal Protocol these criteria were met by the main ozone depleting substance, CFCs. However, for the case of climate change trade restrictions would be more difficult to apply as green-house gases (GHGs) tend to be byproducts rather than traded products (though some GHGs, like Hydrofluorocarbonates (HFCs), are traded). For traded goods, Brack et al. suggest trade restrictions like those under the Montreal Protocol may be feasible. For byproducts the conclusions are that restrictions on GHG-related inputs or goods made with processes that produce GHGs would not meet any of the criteria for feasibility and if they were applied they would also result in a high welfare loss resulting from the severe restrictions on trade.

In terms of fairness, a climate change related treaty with trade provisions is argued to be relatively fair. This is due to the fact that the scientific evidence is becoming more credible and the FCCC contains scope for equity considerations, by differentiating between developed and developing nations.

The debate over the interaction between the WTO and multilateral environmental agreements continues, as mentioned earlier in the paper, and no firm conclusions are reached about the likely interactions between the Kyoto Protocol in particular and the WTO.

The current Climate Change and Global Trade project, of which this paper forms part, will examine the trade implications of the Kyoto Protocol, including focus on the flexibility mechanisms and impacts of EU enlargement. This will employ CGE modeling.

3.5   Effectiveness of Trade Measures Within MEAs

The assessment of the effectiveness of trade measures within MEAs is complex, as trade measures form only part of a wider set of measures to promote environmental improvement. The trade impacts identified above give some insight into the impacts of the MEAs on trade, but one question that remains is that of how influential are these trade measures on the successful implementation of the MEA under investigation. Clearly this will vary depending on the type of MEA. The issue of the impact of trade measures in defining accession to MEAs is discussed later in this chapter, but here we will discuss the broader issues of the impact on the success or failure of an MEA to meet its objectives.

OECD (1999) presents a review of the impacts that trade measures have had on the implementation of the Montreal Protocol, the Basel Convention and CITES. For the Montral Protocol the identification of the impact that trade based measures have had on the success of the Protocol is made complex by multilateral funding, however trade based measures were clearly important in encouraging accession.

CITES is a slightly different MEA from the Montreal Protocol, as it is made up of trade measures. However the success of CITES is not solely due to the banning or restriction of trade, CITES listing raises awareness of the risk of the extinction of species and can lead to actions by NGOs and others (OECD, 1999).

The Basel Convention is, like CITES, based on trade measures to promote environmental improvement. Inadequate data restricts the extent to which the effectiveness of the trade measures can be assessed – data on the physical quantities of transboundary waste transport is not precise and the valuation of total economic costs and benefits complex. The identification of the specific impact of the Basel Convention is also made more complex by the introduction of other control systems, including those enforced by the OECD and the European Union.

Hence, it is difficult to precisely assess the effectiveness of trade measures within MEAs. However, trade measures may lead to other positive impacts on environmental quality promoted by the MEA.

3.6 Conclusions

Trade measures have been used to some effect in multilateral environmental agreements. Such restrictions have been useful in encouraging countries to sign MEAs, particularly in the case of the Montreal Protocol and, to a lesser extent, the Basel Convention.

The impacts that some of the major MEAs have had on trade have been reviewed above. The main findings of this review are as follows:

Montreal Protocol

- Trade measures incorporated within the Montreal Protocol were important in encouraging countries to sign up to the Protocol.

- The trade impacts of the Montreal Protocol were significant, with large changes in the direction of trade of a number of goods, particularly refrigerators and air conditioning.

- The impact on developing countries varied from country to country, depending on the degree of government cooperation with industry, amongst other factors.

- Measures are needed to prevent against illegal traffic in prohibited substances.

- Industrial migration as a result of the Montreal Protocol has not been a major issue. This is possibly due to the number of parties, but also reflects wider evidence of the location of industry.

CITES

- Under CITES the trade impacts have not been large, in part due to the small proportion of total trade that trade in endangered species and related products represents.

- Some economic losses may have been experienced as a result of the listing of species as a whole rather than species in selected areas which are at risk of extinction. The Zimbabwean elephant case is one possible example, though steps have been taken to allow limited trade in ivory from Zimbabwe.

Basel Convention

- Trade provisions within the Basel Convention to encourage countries to become party to the convention have been weakened by allowances for waste to be traded with non-parties as long as agreements are not less environmentally sound (Article 11).

- For developing countries, impacts on the import of waste used as secondary sources of raw materials may be important for industrial competitiveness.

- There is some evidence of temporary increases in the import of toxic wastes to Thailand. However, as new legislation is passed this is predicted to fall dramatically.

It is difficult to assess the precise implications of trade measures for the implementation of MEAs. However, in the case of the Montreal Protocol it is clear that trade measures were instrumental in encouraging accession. In addition, under CITES, trade measures not only restricted trade in species and their byproducts but also raised awareness of the potential for species extinction.

4   Stakeholder Analysis

The preceding review of MEAs has shown that the adoption of trade sanctions within these Agreements has not noticeably reduced support for participation and seems likely to have acted as an incentive towards compliance with the Agreements. This is particularly the case for the Montreal Protocol, though there remains the possibility that the success to date for this policy is more dependent on the general recognition that ozone depletion is a real and serious threat to human health than of the threat of sanctions. The positive role of trade sanctions within future MEAs is, however, always likely to be contingent on the acceptability of the measure within society. Analysis of historical experience is therefore limited to the extent that interest groups are likely to have different influence in each new context. This section briefly indicates how stakeholder analysis can be used to add a layer of contextual realism to the overall analysis of whether trade sanctions are likely to be adopted within an MEA, using the climate change policy context as an example for illustrative purposes.

The aim of a stakeholder analysis is to identify those whose interests will be, or are being, affected by the suggested policy option, and to assess the potential influence they may have on the decision problem. The techniques used to identify the stakeholders can range from the formal (e.g. interviews) to the informal (e.g. press reviews). Option formulators and implementers should be expected to be aware of who the cast of stakeholders are likely to be, though this can be supplemented by the use of group consultations, etc.

Once a cast of stakeholders has been identified it is helpful to have systems of categorisation. One such system, shown in DFID (1995), categorises stakeholders as:

- Primary: those ultimately affected by the option, positively or negatively.

- Secondary: those involved in the delivering of the option, including those involved in the decision-making and those excluded.

- Key: those who may be indirectly affected by the option, but who may exercise a large degree of influence that can affect the intervention.

When considering whether to introduce trade sanctions to help enforce an MEA – such as those that may arise from the Kyoto Protocol or its successor – the primary stakeholder group may include households that have to pay higher prices for domestically produced goods and the industries in the signatory country that are affected by a shift in demand towards their products or by higher input costs. Within the non-signatory countries, energy intensive exporting industries and subsequently impacted households are also primary stakeholders. The secondary stakeholders might include the national governments of the signatory countries and perhaps the UNFCCC, as well as non-signatory country governments. The key stakeholders might include environmental NGOs and energy producers.

Having identified and categorised stakeholders the next step is to assess their interest in, and potential impact on, the option. Once again, a range of formal and informal research techniques may be used to gather information on the ways in which different stakeholders have an interest in the option and the ways in which they might influence an option. The importance of the different stakeholders in the policy objectives of the decision-maker, and the amount of influence that different stakeholders can bring to bear on an option, are therefore assessed. A matrix can then be constructed to locate stakeholders. The stakeholders identified in the climate change context are plotted in the matrix shown as Figure 1 below. Importance on the vertical axis means the extent to which the needs and interests of a particular group of stakeholders are regarded as a priority by the decision-maker. The horizontal axis ranks the amount of influence they may bring to bear. Clearly, the analytical framework is common to the consideration of decisions relating to accession to any MEA.

The matrix is used as an impressionistic tool to rank the importance and influence of stakeholders in relation to each other. An analysis of the relationships between the stakeholders views and the intervention objective – in this case, the imposition of trade sanctions – is the key output of a stakeholder analysis. In particular, it is necessary to assess the risks posed by the stakeholder views to the possibility of the option achieving its objective. Where stakeholders are identified as having considerable potential influence on the option, then they represent a considerable risk to its implementation. This then leads to consideration of how such risks should be managed.

	Low Influence	High Influence
High Importance	1, 2, 3, 4	5, 6, 10
Low Importance		7, 8, 9

Notes:

Primary stakeholders:

1 = households (signatory country)

2 = households (non-signatory country)

3 = import substitution industries (signatory country)

4 = energy intensive industries (non-signatory country)

Secondary stakeholders:

5 = signatory country governments

6 = non-signatory country governments

7 = UNFCCC

8 = WTO

Key stakeholders:

9 = environmental NGOs

10 = energy producers

Figure 1:   Climate Change MEA Stakeholder Matrix when Considering Imposition of Trade Sanctions.

In the climate change enforcement context, formal negotiation between UNFCCC participants has not begun on the possible use of trade sanctions as an enforcement tool. It is therefore not possible to ascertain all stakeholder views. Nevertheless, it is clear that the key relationship is likely to be between the signatory and non-signatory governments (both having high importance and high influence), now that the US is planning to reverse its signature. Specifically, since the US is a major export market for the EU it is foreseeable that the EU will not press for trade sanctions against non-signatory countries for fear of retaliatory action from the US. This is compounded by the uncertainty over the use of environmental trade barriers under the WTO rules, highlighted earlier.

The second dimension of the analysis is to identify what assumptions need to be made about how stakeholders should act for an option to achieve its objective. If the assumption is too ambitious, then it may be that it should be regarded as what is sometimes known as a 'killer-assumption' and the option specification should be revisited. In the climate change enforcement context, a principal assumption is that the trade sanction does not trigger a trade war, particularly between the EU and US. Whether this is the 'killer assumption' is not known since the EU has made no formal statement as to its intention regarding policy towards non-signatory countries.

To conclude, the views of different stakeholders are likely to have significant impacts on the implementation of any trade measures in climate-related MEAs. This section has identified some potential stakeholders that may be of importance and indicated some of the key issues that may dictate their actions in creating or responding to the threat of trade restrictions. A more rigorous analysis – soon to be conducted by the authors of this paper – will put more emphasis on the informal research approach by conducting in-depth interviews/surveys of stakeholder groups. This will hopefully allow a greater degree of understanding of the flexibility of the positions that the actors take and therefore allow a more realistic appraisal of the possibilities of the MEA-trade linkage to be made.

5   Political Economy of Accession to a Multilateral Environmental Agreement

Governments must weigh the cost of accession, including intertemporal considerations, with the benefits in terms of improved environment. The net benefits of accession to an environmental agreement may be expressed as:

$$NB = f(E_{(t\text{-}t+\infty)}, C, T, G, D, X) \tag{1}$$

Where E represents the (discounted) environmental benefit over period t to the infinite future, C the net direct costs of meeting the requirements of the treaty (including no-regrets options), T the trade impacts, G the level of environmental awareness and participation, D the distributional implications of the MEA and X all other factors.

The net environmental benefit will depend on a number of factors, including the natural of the environmental problem in question. The impact may vary according to location of the country, the level above sea-level, the population size and many other factors. In the case of a global pollutant, such as climate change, the impact may be felt globally though the distribution of the benefits of mitigation strategies and reduced damages may be felt differently from country to country. The benefits of reducing the level of local pollutants, such as hazardous waste covered under the Basel Convention, may only be felt in the country in question.

In weighing the decision of whether or not to accede to an MEA, it is obvious that the time horizon and discount rate applied may be crucial. Where the environmental benefit is felt a long time in the future, as is the case with climate change, then discounting the benefits has a large impact on the environment benefits derived from such a policy measure. For a discussion on intertemporal equity and climate change see Portney (2000). However, where the impact is felt in the nearer term, as is the case with a reduction in the depletion of the ozone layer, then this implies that the environmental benefit will be larger in the minds of decision-makers.

The net environmental benefit will depend not only on the timeframe of the environmental benefit but also on the environmental benefits that are taken into consideration by the government. This is particularly important in the climate change debate, with the contentious issue of ancillary benefits of climate change mitigation. Ancillary benefits[5] (or costs) are those benefits that arise as a consequence of a mitigation policy but are not the focus of the policy, for example health benefits. The inclusion or exclusion of such benefits (costs) may be of great importance in the decision of whether or not to accede to a climate change related MEA such as the Kyoto Protocol. Estimates of the ancillary benefits of GHG mitigation range from a small percentage of mitigation costs (defined as C above) to largely offsetting these costs (Krupnick et al., 2000). A framework for the estimation of these benefits (costs) is provided in Krupnick et al. (2000).

The costs of meeting environmental standards depend critically on the costs of installing new technologies and the efficiency with which these new technologies work. This component of the net benefit function should decline with time, thus delaying agreement may lower costs, although production may expand in the meantime, meaning that costs of adaptation would increase.

---

[5]   For a review of issues relating to ancillary benefits see IPCC (forthcoming) and OECD (2000).

The trade impacts would depend, as shown above in the review of trade and multilateral environmental agreements, on the nature of the commodity in question, the structure of the trade in that good and the extent to which trade sanctions may play a part in the MEA. This component may be crucial to signing a treaty, as was shown in the case of the Montreal Protocol. If the trade sanctions which may follow from non-signature of an MEA are large enough, these may affect the size and potentially the sign of the net benefits.

The level of environmental awareness and participation may affect the extent to which the environmental benefits of an agreement are valued. However, they also may cause changes in voting patterns towards more environmentally-friendly candidates. The extent to which this is important to accession may vary from country to country and across the electoral cycle.

The distribution of impacts resulting from the implementation of an MEA may have important implications in terms of political feasibility. Where the impact focuses on a politically active group, or an important interest group in society, then the implementation of such a policy may be stalled and render the policy infeasible. Thus, even if signing an MEA has a negative economic cost and has a low financial cost, if there are negative impacts on a key interest group this may affect the desirability of implementation in the eyes of the policy-maker. This problem was highlighted by Dixit (1996) who shows that, even in the case where compensation of the affected group is possible, credibility issues may render the policy impossible to implement. Thus, the distributional impacts on certain key interest groups in society may have important implications for the potential success of MEAs. As such stakeholder analysis, described above, will prove crucial to the design of the MEA to protect against barriers to implementation or accession.

The distribution of impacts may also be important in terms of political feasibility if poorer sectors of the community are impacted. The degree of inequality in a country has a number of potential impacts, including increased social unrest and slower economic growth. The impact on the environment may also be negative[6.]

The extent to which the different determinants are important in bringing about accession will vary across countries, governments and time. The nature of each variable will also vary according to the multilateral environmental agreement under consideration. First, we will examine the factors affecting the weights placed on each component of the payoff function. We will then examine the components within the frameworks of different MEAs.

The weights attributed to different components of the net benefit payoff function will vary for a number of reasons. As noted above, the electoral cycle may be of

---

[6]   For a recent review of the impact of increased poverty on the environment see Markandya (2001).

importance in determining these weights. The weight given to environmental participation in elections may increase as time to the next election falls if the 'green' vote is important. The discount rate applied to far-off benefits may also change. Likelihood of remaining in office may affect a government's willingness to commit to an environmental agreement. Where a government is unlikely to remain in office this may reduce the weight placed on the cost element, as it will fall on the incoming government.

Political ideology may be important in determining the weight placed on various components of the net benefit payoff function. First, 'green' parties may place a higher weight (or lower discount rate in the case of climate change) on the net environmental benefit from acceding to an MEA. Second, the weight placed on distribution may vary according to the political ideology of the government in terms of the impacts on the richer and poorer sections of society, as well as on different industries. Governments may be less concerned about negative impacts on groups that do not form a major part of their support base. Political funding may also play a role where impacts on major industries fund political activities. A government for which industrial funding forms a major part of party income may place a higher weight on impacts on the relevant industries.

The nature of government may also play a role in determining the weights. A democracy would probably be more likely to place weight on 'green' participation than a dictatorship.

The weight applied to trade impacts may vary according to the overall importance of trade in the economy. They may also be correlated with the distributional implications of trade impacts, following the industrial funding of political activities as described above. The expected likelihood of application of sanctions may also determine the value of the trade impacts, which may be defined in expected value terms.

The relationship between the components of the payoff function and the likelihood of accession (or put otherwise the net benefits) need not be linear. It may be the case that small losses are valued more highly than small gains by voters, for example.

5.1   Application of Framework to MEAs

The above framework can be applied to existing MEAs and the Kyoto Protocol. In Table 3 below, estimates of the size of the impact on different countries are given for the Montreal Protocol and the Kyoto Protocol, based on a review of the literature on these two MEAs. The size of impact and weights applied are open to some debate, though we believe the sizes given are defendable.

In the existing literature on the Montreal Protocol, the impacts of the trade regime have been identified as being particularly important in obtaining signatories to the

Protocol. However, as shown in the table below, other factors may also have been of importance, notably the level of 'green' participation. The costs of adaptation to non-ODS also fell, with the development of new technologies. Expectations of this may have played an important role in accession. The literature also suggests that a lengthier phase-out period and financial supports may have played an important role in reducing costs to developing countries.

For the case of the Kyoto Protocol, a major factor may be seen to be the expected environmental impact. Some scientific uncertainty as to the impacts has been identified, and some have argued that this uncertainty restricts the extent to which environmental benefits can be measured. Potential implications on industry also may be of importance to the Bush administration as a result of contributions by these stakeholders to campaign financing. These two factors may mean that the US government's payoff function is quite different from that of the EU. Hence, negotiations have been made to reduce the cost element (and likely negative impacts on industry) by expanding the scope of the Kyoto flexibility mechanisms. The EU, however, seems to be accepting the IPCC evidence that climate change is due in part to human-made pollutants, and thus values the net environmental benefits more highly than the US.

In different EU states the strength of industry and other stakeholders varies, as such the extent to which distributional concerns are important in the EU will vary from country to country.

The above is an illustrative view of the possible decision-making process undertaken by governments in the US, EU and developing countries. It represents a first step towards understanding the factors that may be of importance in determining accession to the Kyoto Protocol. Trade sanctions may play a role, however their scope may be limited by the extent to which they conflict with WTO rules. Also, the threat of retaliation may be significant enough to prevent parties from placing trade restrictions on countries which are non-parties.

6   Conclusions and Implications for Future Multilateral Environmental Agreements

This paper has examined the linkages between trade and environment in terms of multilateral environmental agreements. Firstly, we suggest that the trade impacts of MEAs must be considered in the context of increasing trade liberalisation, including the expansion of the European Union. Secondly, the impact of potential conflicts with the WTO and the MEA have to be considered.

Direct trade restrictions form part of a number of important multilateral environmental agreements, notably the Montreal Protocol, CITES and the Basel Convention. The trade impacts of these agreements vary, depending on the commodities concerned and the countries under consideration. Trade restrictions contained within MEAs have played an important part in expanding the coverage of the MEAs and thus should be considered important to the overall implementation of the agreement.

There is little evidence of pollution havens resulting from those multilateral environmental agreements reviewed. Some cases do exist, however, these can be explained through other factors such as attempts by industry to gain access to new markets through relocation. This is broadly in line with evidence in the literature on the location of industry.

The actions of stakeholders in response to a multilateral environmental agreement may be central to the success or failure of the MEA in question. The positive role of trade sanctions within future MEAs is always likely to be contingent on the acceptability of the measure within society. As such, a review of stakeholder opinions is important, as is the determination of the importance of the stakeholder to the decision maker and the amount of influence the stakeholder may bring to bear on the decision-making process. We present a framework for the evaluation of stakeholder opinions within the context of a climate change related MEA, which will be employed in a future study.

Factors other than trade may be important in determining a policy maker's attitude to accession to a multilateral environmental agreement. We develop a net benefit payoff function for governments deciding about whether or not to accede to an MEA, including discussion of the determinants of weights placed on the different factors by policy makers. This is then applied for the cases of the Montreal Protocol and the Kyoto Protocol.

Table 3:   Political Economy and MEAs[7].

MEA	Size of Impact (Weight)				
	E	C	G	T	D
Montreal Protocol					
OECD	Dependent on location (high)	Fairly low and reduced with R&D of ODS alternatives (fairly low)	High (variable)	High (high)	Low (variable)
Developing Country	Depends on location	Higher than OECD, but reduced with technology transfer, financial supports and lengthier phase-out period	Low (probably low)	Potentially High (variable)	Low (variable)
Kyoto Protocol					
US	Questionable - scientific uncertainty	Moderate (high) reducing with flexibility mechanisms and new technology	High (low)	Uncertain probably high (high)	High (high)
EU	High (high)	Moderate (high) reducing with flexibility mechanisms and new technology	High (high)	Uncertain probably high (high)	High (variable)
Developing Country	High (high)	Low - CDM and JI will reduce costs	Low (probably low)	Probably low but positive (low)	Low (low)

---

[7] The rankings in this table are based on what we believe may be the case, based on a review of the literature and of the media. For environmental impact, the Montreal Protocol is shown to be dependent on location, due to the nature of the problems presented by the hole in the ozone layer. For climate change, the same is true, however, overall the impact is expected to be quite large. The level of weight attributed to this in the EU and DCs reflects the high media interest and importance of the issue in these areas. The costs of mitigation in the US and EU are shown to be moderate. This is because they reflect only a relatively small percentage of GDP (see IPCC, 2001). Flexibility mechanisms provide potential opportunities for reducing these costs. Some also argue that there are 'no-regret' options available. The extent of the "green" vote varies by country, and the importance attributed may also do the same. In the case of the US, the weight attributed to this may be low as industrial perspectives may be given more weight due to political funding, employment and trade concerns. The trade impacts of the Kyoto Protocol are at present uncertain, though developed countries may be expected to bear the brunt of these impacts. The weight attributed in the US is high as the impact on competitiveness is a stated reason for non-ratification. The distributional implications may be seen to be high as the impacts on key stakeholders, particularly industry, may be high in developed countries. Impacts on the poorer groups in DCs may be considered under the environmental cost component.

References

AFP (1999), *Zimbabwe Resumes Ivory Trade After 10 Year International Ban*, International News, 13 April 1999. Available online at http://www.web.net/~nben/envnews/media/99/eleph.htm.

Birdsall, N. and D. Wheeler (1992), Trade Policy and Industrial Pollution in Latin America: Where Are the Pollution Havens?, in: Low, P. (Ed.), *International Trade and the Environment*, World Bank Discussion Papers No 159, Washington D.C.

Boyd, R., W. Hyde, and K. Krutilla (1993), *Trade Policy and Environmental Accounting: A Case Study of Structural Adjustment and Deforestation in the Philippines*, mimeo, Athens OH: Ohio University.

Brack, D. (1996), *International Trade and the Montreal Protocol*, RIIA, London.

Brack, D. (1999), Environmental Treaties and Trade, in: Sampson, G. and W.B. Chambers (Eds.), *Trade, Environment, and the Millenium*, New York.

Brack, D. with M. Grubb and C. Windram (2000), *International Trade and Climate Change Policies*, RIIA, London.

CEC (1999), *Assessing Environmental Effects of the North American Free Trade Association (NAFTA): An Analytical Framework (Phase II) and Issue Studies*, Commission for Environmental Cooperation, Montreal.

CITES (2001), CITES Website: www.cites.org.

Cruz, W. and R. Repetto (1993), *The Environmental Effects of Stabilization and Structural Adjustment Programs: The Philippines Case*, World Resources Institute, Washington DC.

Dixit, A. (1996), *The Making of Economic Policy: A Transaction-Cost Politics Perspective*. Cambridge, MA.

Esty, D. (1994), *Greening the GATT: Trade, Environment and the Future*, Institute for International Economics, Washington D.C.

IPCC(forthcoming), *Climate Change 2001: Mitigation*, Cambridge.

Jha, V., A. Markandya, and R. Vossenaar (1999), *Reconciling Trade and the Environment*, London.

Krueger, J. (1999), *International Trade and the Basel Convention*, RIIA, London.

Krupnick, A., D. Burtraw, and A. Markandya (2000), The Ancillary Benefits and Costs of Climate Change Mitigation: A Conceptual Framework, in: OECD (Ed.), *Ancillary Benefits and Costs of Greenhouse Gas Mitigation*, OECD, Paris.

Lu et al. (1993), cited in Markandya and Milborrow (1998).

Markandya, A. (1999), Overview and Lessons Learnt, Chapter 1 in: Jha et al. (1999).

Markandya, A. (2001), Poverty, Environment and Development, in: Folmer, H., H.L. Gabel, S. Gerking, and A. Rose (Eds.), *Frontiers of Environmental Economics*, Cheltenham.

Markandya, A. and I. Milborrow (1998), Trade and Industrial Impacts of a Multilateral Agreement to Phase out Ozone-Depleting Substances – A Case Study of the Montreal Protocol, *European Economy* (1), 39-90.

OECD (1999), *Trade Measures in Multilateral Environmental Agreements: Synthesis Report of Three Case Studies*, Joint Working Party on Trade and Environment, OECD, Paris.

OECD (2000), *Ancillary Benefits and Costs of Greenhouse Gas Mitigation*, OECD, Paris.

Shahin, M. (1999), Trade and Environment: How Real Is the Debate?, in: Sampson, G. and W.B. Chambers (Eds.), *Trade, Environment, and the Millennium*, New York.

UNCTAD (1995), Effects of Environmental Policies, Standards and Regulations on Market Access and Competitiveness, with Special Reference to Developing Countries, including the Least Developed Among Them, and in the Light of UNCTAD Empirical Studies: Environmental Policies, Trade and Competitiveness: Conceptual and Empirical Issues, 28 March 1995 (TD/B/WG.6/6), paras 103-5. Cited in Brack (1996).

A Computable General Equilibrium Model for Climate and Trade Policy Analysis[*]

Christoph Böhringer and Andreas Löschel

Centre for European Economic Research, P.O. Box 103443, 68034 Mannheim, Germany
boehringer@zew.de, loeschel@zew.de

Joseph Francois

Tinbergen Institute Rotterdam, Burg. Oudlaan 50, 3062 PA Rotterdam, Netherlands
francois@few.eur.nl

1 Overview

General equilibrium models provide a consistent framework for studying price-dependent interactions between all markets of the economy. The simultaneous explanation of the origin and spending of the economic agents' income allows addressing both economy-wide efficiency effects and distributional implications of policy interference. Therefore, computable general equilibrium (CGE) models have become the standard tool for the analysis of the economy-wide impacts of climate and trade policies on resource allocation and the associated implications for incomes of economic agents (see e.g. Weyant, 1999 for a recent survey on applications to climate policy; Shoven and Whalley, 1984 and 1992, provide an introduction to trade policy analysis).

Section 2 of this chapter contains the detailed algebraic description of a static multi-sector, multi-region general equilibrium model for integrated trade and climate policy analysis. Section 3 describes the model's parameterisation.

---

[*] Sections 2.1 to 2.5 are based on Böhringer, C. and A. Löschel (2002), Economic Impacts of Carbon Abatement Policies, in: Böhringer, C., M. Finus, and C. Vogt (Eds.), *Controlling Global Warming – Perspectives from Economics, Game Theory and Public Choice*, Cheltenham, 98-172.

2   Model Structure

This section outlines the main characteristics of a generic multi-sector multi-region general equilibrium model of global trade and energy use designed for the medium-run economic analysis of carbon abatement constraints and trade restrictions. It is a well-known Arrow-Debreu model of the interaction of consumers and producers in markets. Consumers in the model have a primary exogenous endowment of the factors of production and a set of preferences resulting in demand functions for each commodity. The demand function depend on all prices; they are continuous and non-negative, homogeneous of degree zero in factor prices and satisfy Walras' Law, i.e. the total value of consumer expenditure equals consumer income at any set of prices. Market demand is the sum of final and intermediate demand. Producers maximise profits given constant returns to scale production technology. Because of the homogeneity of degree zero of the demand functions and the linear homogeneity of the profit functions in prices, only relative prices matter in such a model. Three classes of conditions characterise the competitive equilibrium in the model: zero profit conditions for production activities, market clearance conditions for each primary factor and produced good and income definition equations with respect to the incomes of the economic agents. In equilibrium, (relative) prices are such that market demand equals market supply for each factor and commodity. Profit maximisation under constant returns to scale technology implies that no activity does any better than break even at equilibrium prices. It determines production levels in each industry in equilibrium. The model is a system of simultaneous, non-linear equations with – after the numeraire is fixed – the number of equations equal to the number of variables.

For an appropriate analysis of carbon abatement policies, the sectoral aggregation of energy markets should be rather detailed in order to reflect major differences in carbon intensities and the degree of substitutability across carbon-intensive goods. Our core model includes primary energy carriers – coal (COL), natural gas (GAS), crude oil (CRU) – as well as secondary energy carriers – refined oil products (OIL) and electricity (ELE). The disaggregating of non-energy markets typically includes important carbon-intensive and energy-intensive industries that are potentially most affected by carbon abatement policies. By default, endowments of primary factors in the model – labour (L), physical capital (K) and fossil fuel resources (R) – are exogenous, and factor markets are assumed to be perfectly competitive. Furthermore, labour and capital are treated as perfectly mobile across sectors whereas fossil-fuel resources are sector-specific. Factors are assumed to be immobile between regions, and agents behave according to the competitive paradigm. Sections 2.1 to 2.5 describe the algebraic setup of the generic CGE model. Section 2.6 describes the specification of market power on goods markets in order to represent important pro-competitive effects from trade liberalisation.

2.1   Production

Within each region (indexed by the subscript r), each producing sector (indexed interchangeably by i and j) is represented by a single-output producing firm which chooses input quantities of primary factors k (indexed by f), intermediate inputs x from other sectors, and production levels y in order to maximise profits, given input and output prices. The profit maximisation problem of a competitive firm i in region r is then:

$$\underset{y_{ir},x_{\cdot ir},k_{\cdot ir}}{Max} \quad p_{ir} \cdot y_{ir} - \sum_j p_{jr} \cdot x_{jir} - \sum_f w_{fr} \cdot k_{fir} \quad \text{s.t.} \quad y_{ir} \leq \varphi_{ir}\left(\vec{k}_{\cdot ir}, \vec{x}_{\cdot ir}\right), \tag{1}$$

where p_{ir} and w_{ir} are the prices for goods and factors, respectively, and $\varphi_{ir}\left(\vec{k}_{\cdot ir}, \vec{x}_{\cdot ir}\right)$ the production functions (assumed to be linear homogeneous in the model). When the profit maximisation problem has a solution for given prices, the profit function $\Pi_{ir}\left(\vec{p}_r, \vec{w}_r\right)$ gives the maximum profits of firm i in region r as a function of input and output prices. A necessary condition for profit maximisation is cost minimisation, i.e. there is no way to produce the same amount of output at a lower total input cost. The cost function $C_{ir}\left(\vec{p}_r, \vec{w}_r, y_{ir}\right)$ relates the minimum possible total costs of producing y_{ir} to the positive input prices, technology parameters, and the output quantity.

In the model, production of each good takes place according to constant elasticity of substitution (CES) production functions, which exhibit constant returns to scale. Therefore, the output price equals the per-unit cost in each sector, and firms make zero profits in equilibrium (Euler's Theorem). Firms are indifferent about the level of output at which they produce. Profit maximisation under constant returns to scale implies the equilibrium condition:

$$\pi_{ir}\left(\vec{p}_r, \vec{w}_r\right) = p_{ir} - c_{ir}\left(\vec{p}_r, \vec{w}_r\right) = 0 \qquad \text{(zero profit condition),} \tag{2}$$

where c_{ir} are the unit cost functions and π_{ir} the unit profit functions.

Demand functions for goods and factors can be derived by Shephard's Lemma. It states that the first-order differentiation of the cost function with respect to an input price yields the cost-minimising demand function for the corresponding input. Hence, the intermediate demand for good j in sector i is:

$$x_{jir} = \frac{\partial C_{ir}\left(\vec{p}_r, \vec{w}_r, y_{ir}\right)}{\partial p_{jr}} = Y_{ir} \cdot \frac{\partial c_{ir}\left(\vec{p}_r, \vec{w}_r\right)}{\partial p_{jr}}, \tag{3}$$

and the demand for factor f in sector i is:

$$k_{fir} = \frac{\partial C_{ir}\left(\vec{p}_r, \vec{w}_r, y_{ir}\right)}{\partial w_{fr}} = Y_{ir} \cdot \frac{\partial c_{ir}\left(\vec{p}_r, \vec{w}_r\right)}{\partial w_{fr}}. \tag{4}$$

The variable, price dependent input coefficients, which appear subsequently in the market clearance conditions, are thus:

$$a^x_{jir} = \frac{x_{jir}}{Y_{ir}} = \frac{\partial c_{ir}\left(\vec{p}_r, \vec{w}_r\right)}{\partial p_{jr}} = -\frac{\partial \pi_{ir}\left(\vec{p}_r, \vec{w}_r\right)}{\partial p_{jr}}, \qquad \text{and} \tag{5}$$

$$a^k_{fir} = \frac{k_{fir}}{Y_{ir}} = \frac{\partial c_{ir}\left(\vec{p}_r, \vec{w}_r\right)}{\partial w_{fr}} = -\frac{\partial \pi_{ir}\left(\vec{p}_r, \vec{w}_r\right)}{\partial w_{fr}}. \tag{6}$$

The model captures the production of commodities by aggregate, hierarchical (or nested) CES production functions that characterise the technology through substitution possibilities between capital, labour, energy and material (non-energy) intermediate inputs (KLEM). Each intermediate input represents a composite of domestic and imported varieties as described below (Armington assumption). Two types of production functions are employed: those for fossil fuels (v = COL, CRU, GAS) and those for non-fossil fuels (indexed by n).

Figure 1 illustrates the nesting structure in *non-fossil fuel production*. In the production of non-fossil fuels n, non-energy intermediate inputs M (used in fixed coefficients among themselves) are employed in (Leontief) fixed proportions with an aggregate of capital, labour, and energy at the top level. Material i for use in sector n in region r is thus a constant share of sector n output Y_{nr}. At the second level, a CES function describes the substitution possibilities between the aggregate energy input E and the value-added aggregate KL. For the sake of simplicity, the symbols α, β, ϕ and θ (and $\hat{\alpha}$, $\hat{\beta}$, $\hat{\phi}$ and $\hat{\theta}$) are used throughout the model description to denote the technology coefficients. We assume constant returns to scale, i.e. $\alpha + \beta = 1$. The production function then reads as:

$$Y_{nr} = \min\left\{(1-\theta_{nr})M_{nr}, \theta_{nr}\phi_{nr}\left[\alpha_{nr}E_{nr}^{\rho^{KLE}} + \beta_{nr}KL_{nr}^{\rho^{KLE}}\right]^{1/\rho^{KLE}}\right\}, \tag{7}$$

where $\sigma^{KLE} = 1/(1-\rho^{KLE})$ is the elasticity of substitution between energy and the primary factor aggregate and θ is the input (Leontief) coefficient. When the energy value share of an industry, α_{nr}, is small, the elasticity of substitution between the value added aggregate and the composite energy good, σ^{KLE}, is nearly equal to the own price elasticity of demand for energy. This elasticity determines how difficult it is for a region to adjust its production processes in response to changes in energy prices. Higher values imply that a region can more easily substitute value added for energy when the price of energy increases. Finally, at the third level, capital and labour factor inputs trade off with a constant elasticity of substitution $\sigma^{KL} = 1/(1-\rho^{KL})$:

$$KL_{nr} = \phi_{nr}\left[\alpha_{nr}K_{nr}^{\rho^{KL}} + \beta_{nr}L_{nr}^{\rho^{KL}}\right]^{1/\rho^{KL}}. \tag{8}$$

As to the formation of the energy aggregate E, we employ several levels of nesting to represent differences in substitution possibilities between primary fossil fuel types as well as substitution between the primary fossil fuel composite and secondary energy, i.e. electricity. The energy aggregate is a CES composite of electricity and primary energy inputs FF with elasticity $\sigma^E = 1/(1-\rho^E)$ at the top nest:

$$E_{nr} = \phi_{nr}\left[\alpha_{nr}A_{ELE,nr}^{\rho^E} + \beta_{nr}FF_{nr}^{\rho^E}\right]^{1/\rho^E}. \tag{9}$$

The primary energy composite FF is defined as a CES function of coal and the composite of refined oil and natural gas with elasticity $\sigma^{COA} = 1/(1-\rho^{COA})$. The oil-gas composite is assumed to have a simple Cobb-Douglas functional form with value shares of oil and gas given by θ and $1-\theta$, respectively:

$$FF_{nr} = \phi_{nr}\left[\alpha_{nr}A_{COA,nr}^{\rho^{COA}} + \beta_{nr}\left(A_{OIL,nr}^{\theta_{nr}} \cdot A_{GAS,nr}^{1-\theta_{nr}}\right)^{\rho^{COA}}\right]^{1/\rho^{COA}}. \tag{10}$$

The hierarchical structure of demand admits two elasticities which govern inter-fuel substitution: σ^{COA} determines the ease with which coal can substitute for liquid fuels, and σ^{LIQ} determines the potential for substitution between oil and gas.

Production of fossil fuels v, i.e. crude oil, gas, and coal, has the structure shown in Figure 2. It is characterised by the presence of a fuel-specific factor of production R_{vr} that represents the fuel resource in each region. The specific resource provides positive profits (rents) to the owners of the fixed resource, i.e. the representative agent in region r.

Mine managers minimise production costs subject to the technology constraint:

$$Y_{vr} = \phi_{vr}\left[\alpha_{vr}R_{vr}^{\rho_{vr}^f} + \beta_{vr}\left[\min\left(\theta_{vr}^K K_{vr}, \theta_{vr}^L L_{vr}, \theta_{vr}^E E_{vr}, \theta_{vr}^M M_{vr}\right)\right]^{\rho_{vr}^f}\right]^{1/\rho_{vr}^f}. \tag{11}$$

The substitution elasticity between the specific factor and the Leontief composite of capital-labour-energy-material at the top level is $\sigma_{vr}^f = 1/(1-\rho_{vr}^f)$. This substitution elasticity is calibrated consistently with an exogenously given supply elasticity for exhaustible energy ε_{vr} according to:

$$\varepsilon_{vr} = \frac{1-\gamma_{vr}}{\gamma_{vr}} \sigma_{vr}^{f},$$ (12)

where γ_{vr} is the resource value share (Rutherford, 1998). The resource value share represents major differences between fossil fuel sectors across regions. The resource cost share is rather high, e.g., in oil-exporting countries, while it is low in regions with less accessible resources (Babiker et al., 2001).

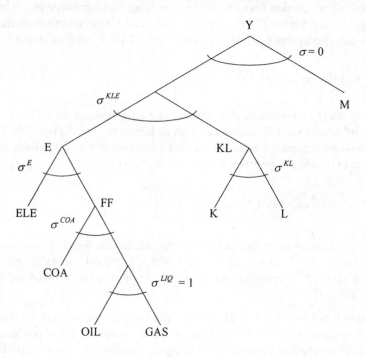

Figure 1:   Nesting Structure of Non-Fossil Fuel Production.

We now turn to the derivation of the factor demand functions for the nested CES production functions, taking into account the duality between the production function and the cost function. As an example, we derive the variable input coefficients for labour and capital in non-fossil fuel production, a_{nr}^{L} and a_{nr}^{K}. The input coefficients for labour and capital in fossil fuel production, a_{vr}^{L} and a_{vr}^{K}, and the input coefficients for intermediate demand, a_{jir}^{Y} $(= A_{jr}/Y_{ir})$, can be determined in an analogous manner.

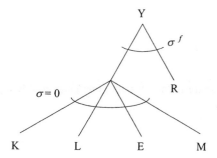

Figure 2:   Nesting Structure for Fossil Fuel Production.

The total cost function C^{KL} that reflects the same production technology as the CES production function for value added KL in non-fossil fuel production given by Equation (8), is:

$$C_{nr}^{KL}\left(PK_{nr},PL_{nr},KL_{nr}\right)=\frac{1}{\phi_{nr}}\left[\alpha_{nr}^{\sigma^{KL}}PK_{nr}^{1-\sigma^{KL}}+\beta_{nr}^{\sigma^{KL}}PL_{nr}^{1-\sigma^{KL}}\right]^{1/\left(1-\sigma^{KL}\right)}\cdot KL_{nr},\tag{13}$$

where PK and PL are the per-unit factor costs for the industry, including factor taxes if applicable. The price function for the value-added aggregate at the third level is:

$$PKL_{nr}=\frac{1}{\phi_{nr}}\left[\alpha_{nr}^{\sigma^{KL}}PK_{nr}^{1-\sigma^{KL}}+\beta_{nr}^{\sigma^{KL}}PL_{nr}^{1-\sigma^{KL}}\right]^{1/\left(1-\sigma^{KL}\right)}=c_{nr}^{KL}\left(PK_{nr},PL_{nr}\right).\tag{14}$$

Shephard's Lemma gives the price-dependent composition of the value-added aggregate as:

$$\frac{K_{nr}}{KL_{nr}}=\phi_{nr}^{\sigma^{KL}-1}\left(\alpha_{nr}\cdot\frac{PKL_{nr}}{PK_{nr}}\right)^{\sigma^{KL}},\quad\frac{L_{nr}}{KL_{nr}}=\phi_{nr}^{\sigma^{KL}-1}\left(\beta_{nr}\cdot\frac{PKL_{nr}}{PL_{nr}}\right)^{\sigma^{KL}}.\tag{15}$$

In order to determine the variable input coefficients for capital and labour, $a_{nr}^{K}=K_{nr}/Y_{nr}$ and $a_{nr}^{L}=L_{nr}/Y_{nr}$, one has to multiply Equation (15) with the per unit demand for the value-added aggregate KL_{nr}/Y_{nr}, which can be derived in an analogous manner. The unit cost function associated with the production function in Equation (7) is:

$$PY_{nr}=\left(1-\theta_{nr}\right)PM_{nr}+\frac{\theta_{nr}}{\hat{\phi}_{nr}}\left[\hat{\alpha}_{nr}^{\sigma^{KLE}}PE_{nr}^{1-\sigma^{KLE}}+\hat{\beta}_{nr}^{\sigma^{KLE}}PKL_{nr}^{1-\sigma^{KLE}}\right]^{\frac{1}{1-\sigma^{KLE}}}.\tag{16}$$

The demand for the value added per unit of production is:

$$\frac{KL_{nr}}{Y_{nr}} = \theta_{nr} \; \hat{\phi}_{nr}^{\sigma^{KLE}-1} \left(\hat{\beta}_{nr} \cdot \frac{PY_{nr}}{PKL_{nr}} \right)^{\sigma^{KLE}}, \tag{17}$$

where θ_{nr} is the KLE cost share in total production. The variable input coefficients for labour and capital are then:

$$a_{nr}^{L} = \theta_{nr} \; \phi_{nr}^{\sigma^{KL}-1} \; \hat{\phi}_{nr}^{\sigma^{KLE}-1} \left(\beta_{nr} \cdot \frac{PKL_{nr}}{PL_{nr}} \right)^{\sigma^{KL}} \left(\hat{\beta}_{nr} \cdot \frac{PY_{nr}}{PKL_{nr}} \right)^{\sigma^{KLE}} \quad \text{and}$$

$$a_{nr}^{K} = \theta_{nr} \; \phi_{nr}^{\sigma^{KL}-1} \; \hat{\phi}_{nr}^{\sigma^{KLE}-1} \left(\alpha_{nr} \cdot \frac{PKL_{nr}}{PK_{nr}} \right)^{\sigma^{KL}} \left(\hat{\beta}_{nr} \cdot \frac{PY_{nr}}{PKL_{nr}} \right)^{\sigma^{KLE}}. \tag{18}$$

2.2   Households

In each region, private demand for goods and services is derived from utility maximisation of a representative household subject to a budget constraint given by the income level m. The agent is endowed with the primary factors of production f (natural resources used for fossil fuel production, labour and capital). The budget constraint equates the value of energy and non-energy consumption to wage income, earnings on the capital stock, rents on fossil energy production, and tax revenues. The household's problem is then:

$$\underset{\overline{d}_r}{Max} \; U_r\!\left(\overline{d}_r\right) \quad \text{s.t.} \quad m_r = \sum_f w_{fr} \overline{k}_{fr} + TR_r \; \geq \sum_i p_{ir} d_{ir} \,, \tag{19}$$

where U_r is the utility of the representative household in region r, d_{ir} denotes the final demand for commodities, $\overline{k}_{fr}$ is the aggregate factor endowment of the representative agent and TR_r are total tax revenues. The utility function in the model is linearly homogeneous: $U_r\!\left(\lambda \overline{d}_r\right) = \lambda \cdot U_r\!\left(\overline{d}_r\right)$. This is a convenient cardinalisation of utility, because percentage changes in the utility level U are then equivalent to percentage Hicksian equivalent variations in income and U_r can be used directly as a welfare measure. The indirect utility function, $V_r\!\left(\overline{p}_r, m_r\right)$, says how much utility the consumer receives at his optimal choice at prices p and income m. The unit expenditure function $e_r\!\left(\overline{p}_r\right)$ (or utility price index PU) indicates the minimum level of expenditure required to reach unity utility. Market final demand functions are derived using Roy's Identity as:

$$d_{ir}\left(\vec{p}_r,m_r\right)=-\frac{\partial V_r\left(\vec{p}_r,m_r\right)}{\partial p_{ir}}\bigg/\frac{\partial V_r\left(\vec{p}_r,m_r\right)}{\partial m_r}. \tag{20}$$

In our model, total income of the representative agent consists of factor income, revenues from taxes levied on output, intermediate inputs, exports, imports, final demand, and CO_2 taxes (TR) and a baseline exogenous capital flow representing the balance of payment deficits B less expenses for exogenous total investment demand. In our comparative-static framework, regional investment demand I is fixed at the reference level. The composite price for investment is $PI_r = \Sigma_i a_{ir}^I \cdot PA_{ir}$, where PA_{ir} is the price of the different inputs. The budget constraint of the representative agent is then given by:

$$INC_r = PL_r \cdot \overline{L}_r + PK_r \cdot \overline{K}_r + \sum_v PR_{vr} \cdot \overline{R}_{vr} + TR_r + \overline{B}_r - PI_r \cdot I_r = PU_r \cdot U_r, \tag{21}$$

where INC_r is the income level of the representative agent and PR_{vr} is the price of the fuel-specific resources.

Household preferences are characterised by a CES utility function in our model. Utility of the representative agent is represented as a CES consumption composite of an aggregate of energy goods EC and non-energy goods NEC. The CES utility function is:

$$U_r=\left[\alpha_r EC_r^{\rho^c} + \beta_r NEC_r^{\rho^c}\right]^{1/\rho^c} \tag{22}$$

where the elasticity of substitution between the energy and the non-energy composites is given by $\sigma^C = 1/(1-\rho^C)$. End-use energy is composed of an (Armington) CES-aggregate of electricity and the various fossil fuels (ec = COL, GAS, ELE, OIL), while substitution patterns within the non-energy aggregate (nec = AGR, EIS, OTH) are reflected via a Cobb-Douglas function:

$$EC_r=\left(\sum_{ec}\phi_{ec,r}A_{ec,r}^{\rho^{EC}}\right)^{1/\rho^{EC}} \quad \text{and} \quad NEC_r=\prod_{nec}A_{nec,r}^{\theta_{jr}}, \tag{23}$$

where the elasticity of substitution within the energy aggregate is given by $\sigma^{EC} = 1/(1-\rho^{EC})$ and θ_j are the value shares in non-energy consumption. The structure of final demand is presented in Figure 3.

The indirect utility function that corresponds to Equation (22) is:

$$V_r\left(PEC_r,PNEC_r,INC_r\right)=INC_r\cdot\left[\alpha_r^{\sigma^c}PEC_r^{1-\sigma^c}+\beta_r^{\sigma^c}PNEC_r^{1-\sigma^c}\right]^{1/1-\sigma^c}. \tag{24}$$

The unit expenditure function e_r (utility price index, PU_r) is then given by $e_r = PU_r = \left[\alpha_r^{\sigma^c} PEC_r^{1-\sigma^c} + \beta_r^{\sigma^c} PNEC_r^{1-\sigma^c} \right]^{1/1-\sigma^c}$. The associated demand functions that have been derived by Roy's identity are:

$$EC_r = \left(\frac{\alpha_r PU_r}{PEC_r} \right)^{\sigma^c} \cdot U \text{ and } NEC_r = \left(\frac{\beta_r PU_r}{PNEC_r} \right)^{\sigma^c} \cdot U, \tag{25}$$

where the utility level is given by $U_r = INC_r / PU_r$.

Final demand coefficients $(a_{ir}^C = A_{ir} / U_r)$ are:

$$a_{ec,r}^C = \left(\frac{\phi_{ec,r} PEC_r}{PA_{ec,r}} \right)^{\sigma^{EC}} \cdot \left(\frac{\alpha_r PU_r}{PEC_r} \right)^{\sigma^c} \text{ and}$$

$$a_{nec,r}^C = \left(\frac{\beta_r PU_r}{PNEC_r} \right)^{\sigma^c} \cdot \theta_{nec,r} \cdot \frac{PNEC_r}{PA_{nec,r}}. \tag{26}$$

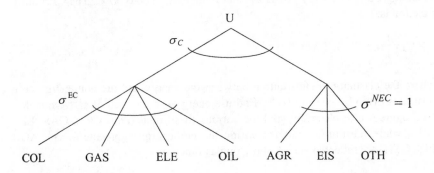

Figure 3:   Structure of Household Demand.

2.3   Foreign Trade

All commodities are traded in world markets. Crude oil and coal are imported and exported as homogeneous products with single world prices determined by global demand and supply, reflecting empirical evidence that these fossil fuel markets are fairly integrated due to cheap shipping possibilities. All other goods are characterised by product differentiation: There is imperfect substitutability between imports and domestically sold domestic output. Bilateral trade flows are subject to export taxes, tariffs and transportation costs.

On the output side, production of each good may be supplied either to domestic markets (D) or export markets (X):

$$Y_{ir} = D_{ir} + X_{ir} \,. \tag{27}$$

The exports of sector i in region r are equal to the imports of region s from region r, M_{irs}, over all trading partners:

$$X_{ir} = \sum_s M_{irs} \,. \tag{28}$$

Regarding imports, the standard Armington convention is adopted in the sense that imported and domestically produced goods of the same kind are treated as incomplete substitutes (i.e. wine from France is different from Italian wine). The aggregate amount of each (Armington) good A is divided among imports and domestic production:

$$A_{ir} = \phi_{ir} \left[\alpha_{ir} D_{ir}^{\rho^D} + \beta_{ir} M_{ir}^{\rho^D} \right]^{1/\rho^D} \,. \tag{29}$$

In this expression, $\sigma^D = 1/(1\text{-}\rho^D)$ is the Armington elasticity between domestic and imported varieties. Imports M_{ir} are allocated between different import regions s according to a CES function:

$$M_{ir} = \hat{\phi}_{ir} \left[\sum_s \hat{\alpha}_{isr} X_{isr}^{\rho^M} \right]^{1/\rho^M} \tag{30}$$

where X_{isr} is the amount of exports from region s to region r and $\sigma^M = 1/(1 - \rho^M)$ is the Armington elasticity among imported varieties. Typically, elasticities are chosen such that $\sigma^M > \sigma^D$, i.e. imported goods from two different sources are closer substitutes than are aggregate imports and domestic goods. Intermediate as well as final demands are, hence, (nested CES) Armington composites of domestic and imported varieties. Consumers and producers choose between domestically produced goods and imports in response to relative prices. The input coefficients for domestic and imported goods are:

$$a_{ir}^D = \frac{D_{ir}}{A_{ir}} = \phi_{ir}^{\sigma^D-1} \left[\alpha_{ir} \cdot \frac{PA_{ir}}{PY_{ir}} \right]^{\sigma^D} \quad \text{and} \tag{31}$$

$$a_{isr}^M = \frac{M_{isr}}{A_{ir}} = \phi_{ir}^{\sigma^D - 1} \hat{\phi}_{ir}^{\sigma^M - 1} \left[\beta_{ir} \cdot \frac{PA_{ir}}{PM_{ir}} \right]^{\sigma^D} \left[\hat{\beta}_{ir} \cdot \frac{PM_{ir}}{PY_{is}} \right]^{\sigma^M}, \tag{32}$$

where the aggregate import price of sector i in region r is given by:

$$PM_{ir} = \frac{1}{\hat{\phi}_{ir}} \left[\sum_s \hat{\alpha}_{isr}^{\sigma^M} PY_{is}^{1-\sigma^M} \right]^{1/(1-\sigma^M)}. \tag{33}$$

The assumption of product differentiation permits us to match the model with bilateral trade with cross-hauling of trade and avoids unrealistically strong specialisation effects in response to exogenous changes in tax policy. Small changes in costs across regions for a given good do not lead to large shifts away from existing trade patterns. On the other hand, the results may then be sensitive to the particular commodity and regional aggregation chosen in the model (Lloyd, 1994).

2.4   Carbon Emissions

Greenhouse gases and related gases have direct radiative forcing effects in the atmosphere. The various emissions of gases result from industrial production, fossil fuel consumption and household activities. The Kyoto Protocol includes carbon dioxide (CO_2), methane (CH_4), nitrous oxide (N_2O), hydrofluorocarbons (HFCs), perfluorocarbons (PFCs), and sulfur hexafluoride (SF_6) as gases subject to control.

We do not consider the abatement of a complete basket of GHG emissions from all energy-related sources as in the Kyoto Protocol, but instead focus on carbon dioxide abatement from fossil fuel consumption, since it constitutes the largest contribution to global warming. Carbon emissions are associated with fossil fuel consumption in production, investment, and final demand. Carbon is treated as a Leontief input into production and consumption. Each unit of a fuel emits a known amount of carbon, where different fuels have different carbon intensities. The carbon coefficients that we use are 25 MT carbon per EJ for coal, 14 MT carbon per EJ for gas and 20 MT carbon per EJ for refined oil.

Carbon policies are introduced via an additional constraint that holds carbon emissions to a specified limit. The solution of the model gives a shadow value of carbon associated with this carbon constraint. This dual variable or shadow price can be interpreted as the price of carbon permits in a carbon permit system or as the CO_2 tax that would implement the carbon constraint in the model. The shadow value of the carbon constraint equals the marginal cost of reduction; it indicates the incremental cost of reducing carbon at the carbon constraint.

The total economic costs induced by carbon abatement policies represent the resource cost or dead-weight loss to the economy of imposing carbon constraints. Carbon emission constraints induce substitution of fossil fuels with less expensive energy sources (fuel switching) or employment of less energy-intensive manufacturing and production techniques (energy savings). The only means of abatement are hence inter-fuel substitution, fuel-/non-fuel substitution, and the reduction of intermediate or final consumption. There are no economically feasible end-of-pipe technologies available for carbon abatement.

Given an emission constraint, producers as well as consumers must pay the price of the emissions resulting from the production and consumption processes. Revenues coming from imposing the carbon constraint are given to the representative agent. If we take CO_2 emission restrictions into account, the total cost function that corresponds to the Armington production function in Equation (29) is:

$$C_{ir}^A = \left[\frac{1}{\phi_{ir}} \left(\alpha_{ir}^{\sigma^D} PY_{ir}^{1-\sigma^D} + \beta_{ir}^{\sigma^D} PM_{ir}^{1-\sigma^D} \right)^{1/(1-\sigma^D)} + \tau_r \cdot a_i \right] \cdot A_{ir}, \qquad (34)$$

where a_i is the carbon emissions coefficient for fossil fuel i and τ is the shadow price of CO_2 in region r associated with the carbon emission restriction:

$$\overline{EMIT}_r = \sum_i a_i \cdot A_{ir}, \qquad (35)$$

where $\overline{EMIT}_r$ is the endowment of carbon emission rights in region r.

2.5   Zero Profit and Market Clearance Conditions

Mathiesen (1985) proposed a representation of an Arrow-Debreu model in which two types of equations define an equilibrium: zero profit conditions and market clearance conditions. The corresponding variables defining an equilibrium are activity levels and commodity prices. The zero profit conditions exhibit complementarity with respect to associated activity levels and the market clearance conditions with respect to market prices. The orthogonality symbol, $\perp$, shows the variable that is linked to a certain inequality condition in equilibrium.

Zero profit conditions as derived in Equation (2) require that no producer earns a positive profit in equilibrium. The total value of outputs must not exceed the total value of inputs per unit activity. The zero profit conditions for good Y_{ir}, using the variable input coefficient derived above, are:

$$a_{nr}^K \cdot PK_r + a_{nr}^L \cdot PL_r + \sum_j a_{jnr}^Y \cdot PA_{jr} \geq PY_{nr} \qquad \perp Y_{nr} \quad (36)$$

$$a_{vr}^K \cdot PK_r + a_{vr}^L \cdot PL_r + a_{vr}^R \cdot PR_{vr} + \sum_j a_{jvr}^Y \cdot PA_{jr} \geq PY_{vr} \qquad \perp Y_{vr}. \quad (37)$$

As an example, the complementarity condition for Equation (36) is:

$$\left(a_{nr}^K \cdot PK_r + a_{nr}^L \cdot PL_r + \sum_j a_{jnr}^Y \cdot PA_{jr} - PY_{nr} \right) \cdot Y_{nr} = 0. \qquad (38)$$

The zero profit conditions for Armington production are:

$$a_{ir}^D \cdot PY_{ir} + \sum_s a_{isr}^M \cdot PY_{is} + a_i \cdot \tau_r \geq PA_{ir} \qquad \perp A_{ir}. \quad (39)$$

The utility price index (unit expenditure) is:

$$\sum_i a_{ir}^C \cdot PA_{ir} \geq PU_r \qquad \perp U_r. \quad (40)$$

The market clearance conditions state that aggregate supply of each good and factor must be at least as great as total intermediate and final demand in equilibrium. The market clearance for good Y_{ir} states that total production is greater than or equal to total demand for domestic production at home and abroad:

$$Y_{ir} \geq a_{ir}^D \cdot A_{ir} + \sum_s a_{irs}^M \cdot A_{is} \qquad \perp PY_{ir}. \quad (41)$$

Markets clearance conditions for the Armington good require that total Armington good supply A_{ir} has to be at least as great as aggregate demand, which consists of intermediate demand, final demand, and investment demand:

$$A_{ir} \geq \sum_j a_{ijr}^Y \cdot Y_{jr} + a_{it}^C \cdot U_r + a_{ir}^I \cdot I_r \qquad \perp PA_{ir}. \quad (42)$$

Primary factor endowments are greater than or equal to primary factor demand:

$$\overline{L}_r \geq \sum_i a_{ir}^L \cdot Y_{ir} \qquad \perp PL_r, \quad (43)$$

$$\overline{K}_r \geq \sum_i a_{ir}^K \cdot Y_{ir} \qquad \perp PK_r, \quad (44)$$

$$\overline{R}_{vr} \geq a_{vr}^R Y_{vr} \qquad \perp PR_{vr}. \quad (45)$$

Total endowment with carbon emission rights is at least as great as total emission demand:

$$\overline{EMIT}_r \geq \sum_i a_i \cdot A_{ir} \qquad\qquad \perp \tau_r. \quad (46)$$

The inequality condition for utility is:

$$U_r \cdot PU_r \geq INC_r \qquad\qquad \perp PU_r, \quad (47)$$

where the income level INC_r is defined as

$$INC_r = PL_r \cdot \overline{L}_r + PK_r \cdot \overline{K}_r + \sum_v PR_{vr} \cdot \overline{R}_{vr} + TR_r + \overline{B}_r - PI_r \cdot I_r + \overline{EMIT}_r \cdot \tau_r. \quad (48)$$

An equilibrium is characterised by a set of prices and quantities for all goods and factors such that the zero profit conditions and market clearance conditions stated above hold.

2.6 Imperfect Competition

Quantitative evaluations of the static efficiency effects of trade policy reforms based on the analytical framework of traditional trade theory under perfect competition tend to end up with figures of small to negligible order. However, there is a widespread suspicion that these conventional studies miss the point by neglecting potential pro-competitive industrial organisation effects. These pro-competitive effects are trade effects emerging from the existence of scale economies and imperfect competition. They may relate to increased economies of scale, the falling of the production costs (lowering the markup) on the increase of product varieties (the expansion of output). Extending the standard perfect competition framework, we explicitly incorporate the former two effects. In addition, we account for demand side effects of economic integration, i.e. increased competition due to a greater substitutability of varieties, and the associated changes in markups.

To capture the pro-competitive effects we introduce increasing returns to scale (IRTS) on the plant or firm level. In sectors with imperfect competition we assume firm-level product differentiation, i.e. each firm produces its own variety of the good. In addition we choose a set-up in which domestic and foreign varieties are incomplete substitutes. This is in the spirit of Armington (1969), who introduced the theory of demand for goods distinguished by place of production. The setup follows Harrison, Rutherford and Tarr (1996 and 1997). It should be noted that firm-level competition among all firms independent of the country of origin is a special case of the model when the elasticity of substitution for varieties within a country equals the elasticity between domestic and imported goods and between foreign varieties. Firm-level product differentiation within an Armington structure is depicted in Figure 4. For concreteness, we illustrate the pro-competitive effects from the perspective of a new entrant to the EU (here: Poland) when Poland and the other Central and Eastern European Countries (CEEC) join the EU.

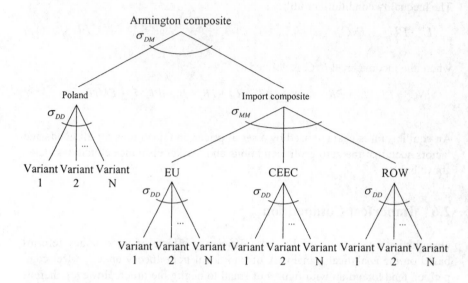

Figure 4:   Firm-Level Product Differentiation Within an Armington Structure.

Imperfect competition, if present, is due to fixed costs, not to regulation of entry. Fixed costs at the firm level are exogenous. As usual in oligopoly models, prices are a markup over marginal costs, where the markup rate reflects the number of firms and the elasticity of market demand. With free entry and exit combined with fixed costs, the number of firms is determined by the usual zero-profit condition, i.e. the number of firms changes in such a way that output price equals average cost. We assume a Cournot-type scenario, where the strategic variable is output. Producers compete based on a Cournot model with fixed conjectural variations. When markets are geographically segmented, the individual Cournot oligopolist located in one region (r) is able to choose the quantity supplied to each other region (s) separately. Correspondingly, there is a separate first-order condition for each market segment. Profit maximisation yields the equation for the markup on a variety of one commodity produced in country r and sold in country r ($m_{r,r}$) or country s ($m_{r,s}$):

$$m_{r,r} = \frac{1}{\sigma_{DD}} - \left(\frac{1}{\sigma_{DD}} - \frac{1}{\sigma_{DM}}\right)\frac{1}{n_r} - \left(\frac{1}{\sigma_{DM}} - \frac{1}{\Omega}\right)\frac{\theta_{r,r}}{n_r} \tag{49}$$

$$m_{r,s} = \frac{1}{\sigma_{DD}} - \left(\frac{1}{\sigma_{DD}} - \frac{1}{\sigma_{MM}}\right)\frac{1}{n_r} - \left(\frac{1}{\sigma_{MM}} - \frac{1}{\sigma_{DM}}\right)\frac{\theta_{r,s}^M}{n_r} - \left(\frac{1}{\sigma_{DM}} - \frac{1}{\Omega}\right)\frac{\theta_{r,s}}{n_r} \tag{50}$$

where σ_{DM} is the elasticity of substitution between domestic and imported goods, σ_{MM} denotes the elasticity of substitution between imports from alternative foreign countries, σ_{DD} is the substitution elasticities between different varieties, $\theta_{r,s}$ denotes the market share of firms from region r in region s's total commodity group expenditure, $\theta_{r,s}^M$ is the market share of region r in region s's total commodity group import expenditure, n_r is the number of firms in region r and Ω is the fixed conjectural variations parameter. Assuming firm-level competition among imports, i.e. elasticities of substitution between the domestic and the imported composite and between foreign firm varieties are the same, this formula is equivalent to Harrison, Rutherford and Tarr (1996, (1)) and in the case of a unit value for the conjectural variations parameter Ω, to Harrison, Rutherford and Tarr (1997, (2)).

As the abolition of tariffs leads to a shift in comparative advantage, the market shares will change. Domestic firms lose market share on the domestic market but gain share on the export markets. This affects the elasticity of market demand and the markup rates. If the elasticity of market demand rises, the markup drops and firms are driven out of the market. As a consequence, remaining firms increase their output and economies of scale become effective, and both unit costs and prices fall. This continues until rationalisation gains are sufficient to restore zero profit with the lowered markup. The reverse happens if the value shares change in such a way that the overall demand elasticity gets reduced. However, since changes in the market shares are typically not large, the rationalisation benefits and the associated welfare gains are expected to be small (Harrison, Rutherford and Tarr, 1997).

In addition, the integration of Poland and the CEECs into the EU will result in an increase in competition that can be attributed to the rise in trade from tariff reductions and border cost reductions from the European Single Market programme and the associated harmonisation of standards. These effects increase the willingness of EU, CEEC and Polish buyers to substitute among products from different regions of origin. Before integration, products from Poland, CEEC and the EU are perceived as differentiated due to the differences in regulations and technical standards. After integration, products from all regions of the Single Market programme are perceived as originating from the same region, i.e. the enlarged EU (Harrison, Rutherford and Tarr, 1997). The preference structure after integration is displayed in Figure 5.

After market integration, the markup is given by:

$$m_{r,s}^{\cdot} = \frac{1}{\sigma_{DD}} - \left(\frac{1}{\sigma_{DD}} - \frac{1}{\sigma_{DM}}\right)\frac{\theta_{r,s}^{REG}}{n_r} - \left(\frac{1}{\sigma_{DM}} - \frac{1}{\Omega}\right)\frac{\theta_{r,s}}{n_r} \tag{51}$$

where $\theta_{r,s}^{REG}$ is the market share of region r in region s's total commodity group expenditure from either the integrated EU region (for firm markups on trade between countries in the enlarged EU) or ROW (for firm markups selling to ROW).

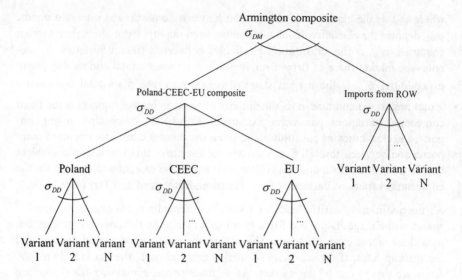

Figure 5:   Nesting Structure After Integration.

With a constant number of firms and market shares, the change in markup $(\Delta m = m' - m)$ induced by increased substitutability due to the integration of the Eastern European countries is given as:

$$\Delta m_{r,r} = \left(\frac{1}{\sigma_{DD}} - \frac{1}{\sigma_{DM}} \right) \frac{\left(1 - \theta_{r,r}^{REG} \right)}{n_r}. \tag{52}$$

$$\Delta m_{r,s} = \left(\frac{1}{\sigma_{DD}} - \frac{1}{\sigma_{MM}} \right) \frac{1}{n_r} + \left(\frac{1}{\sigma_{MM}} - \frac{1}{\sigma_{DM}} \right) \frac{\theta_{r,s}^{M}}{n_r} - \left(\frac{1}{\sigma_{DD}} - \frac{1}{\sigma_{DM}} \right) \frac{\theta_{r,s}^{REG}}{n_r}. \tag{53}$$

Since $\theta_{ROW,r}^{REG}$ equals one, the markup for ROW firms selling to the domestic market is unchanged while the markup on exports to the integrated EU regions increases given the ranking of elasticities $\sigma_{DD} > \sigma_{MM} > \sigma_{DM}$. The increased substitutability leads to a reduction of the markup on a variety produced and sold in any country of the enlarged EU. The effect on the markup on sales from one country of the enlarged EU to any other country is ambiguous.

3 Parameterisation

3.1 Core Data and Calibration

The model is based on a Social Accounting Matrix (SAM), i.e. a comprehensive, economy-wide data framework, representing the economy of a nation (see, e.g., Reinert and Roland-Holst, 1997). The main data source is the GTAP version 4 database that represents global production and trade data for 45 countries and regions, 50 commodities and five primary factors (McDougall et al., 1998). In addition, we use OECD/IEA energy statistics for 1995 (IEA, 1996). Reconciliation of these data sources (see Babiker and Rutherford, 1997) yields the benchmark data of our model.

In order to perform simulations with our model, we need values for the function parameters. Our large-scale model has many functional parameters that must be specified with relatively few observations. This renders an econometric estimation of the model parameters as a system of simultaneous equations impossible. The estimation of the parameters using single-equation methods, on the other hand, would not produce an equilibrium solution for the model that matches the benchmark data. The conventional approach is to determine parameters for the equations in the model using a non-stochastic calibration method (Mansur and Whalley, 1984). The model is calibrated to a single base-year equilibrium such that the base solution to the model exactly reproduces the values of the adjusted data. First order parameters for the CES production and utility functions are chosen in such a way that the general equilibrium model will have a benchmark equilibrium as its solution. Since we use CES production and utility functions, the assumptions of cost minimisation and utility maximisation leave us with one free parameter per function. Therefore, exogenously specified elasticity values from econometric literature estimates are also required. The other parameter values follow from the restrictions imposed by cost minimisation and utility maximisation. The substitution elasticities determine the curvature of isoquants and indifference surfaces, while their position is given by the benchmark equilibrium data. The given set of benchmark quantities and prices, together with the substitution elasticities given in Table 1, completely specify the benchmark equilibrium.

For example, consider again the value-added aggregate KL in non-fossil fuel production given by Equation (8). Deriving the first order conditions for cost minimisation and solving for α (where $\beta = 1 - \alpha$) gives:

$$\alpha_{nr} = \frac{PK_{nr} \cdot K_{nr}^{1/\sigma^{KL}}}{PL_{nr} \cdot L_{nr}^{1/\sigma^{KL}} + PK_{nr} \cdot K_{nr}^{1/\sigma^{KL}}} \tag{54}$$

where $PL = PL^*\cdot(1+tl)$ and $PK = PK^*\cdot(1+tk)$ are the cost of capital and labour including taxes tl and tk, respectively, and PL^* and PK^* are the benchmark net-of-tax factor prices.

Table 1:   Default Values of Key Substitution and Supply Elasticities.

Description	Value
Substitution Elasticities in Non-Fossil Fuel Production	
σ^{KLE} Energy vs. value added	0.8
σ^{KL} Capital vs. labour	1.0
σ^{E} Electricity vs. primary energy inputs	0.3
σ^{COA} Coal vs. gas-oil	0.5
Substitution Elasticities in Final Demand	
σ^{C} Fossil fuel composite vs. other final demand	0.8
σ^{FE} Coal vs. gas vs. oil	0.3
Elasticities in International Trade (Armington)	
σ^{D} Composite imports	4.0
σ^{M} Imports from different regions	8.0
Exogenous Supply Elasticities of Fossil-Fuels ε	
Crude oil	1.0
Coal	0.5
Natural gas	1.0

Since benchmark data are given in value terms (incomes, revenues and expenditures), we have to choose units for goods and factors to separate price and quantity observations. A commonly used units convention is to choose units for both goods and factors such that – where there are no distortions (such as taxes) that introduce a wedge between prices for the same good or factor – they have a price of unity in the benchmark ('Harberger Convention'). Quantities are then defined to be equal to the income, revenue or expenditure concerned. The benchmark net-of-tax factor prices PL^* and PK^* are thus set equal to one and Equation (54) can be written as:

$$\alpha_{nr} = \frac{\left(1+tl_{nr}\right)\cdot K_{nr}^{1/\sigma^{KL}}\Big/\left(1+tk_{nr}\right)\cdot L_{nr}^{1/\sigma^{KL}}}{1+\left(1+tl_{nr}\right)\cdot K_{nr}^{1/\sigma^{KL}}\Big/\left(1+tk_{nr}\right)\cdot L_{nr}^{1/\sigma^{KL}}} \qquad (55)$$

Since the unit conventions imply that the number of units of each factor equals the net of tax value of factor use, the values of L, tl, K and tk are available for each industry n from the underlying input-output tables and α can be calculated according to Equation (55) given an exogenous value for the substitution elasticity σ

^{KL}. β_{nr} is $(1 - \alpha_{nr})$. When we know α, β and $\rho = (\sigma - 1)/\sigma$, we can calculate ϕ using the zero-profit condition:

$$PK_{nr} \cdot K_{nr} + PL_{nr} \cdot L_{nr} = KL_{nr} \cdot PKL_{nr} \tag{56}$$

and

$$\phi_{nr} = \frac{\left(1 + tk_{nr}\right) \cdot K_{nr} + \left(1 + tl_{nr}\right) \cdot L_{nr}}{\left[\alpha_{nr} K_{nr}^{\rho^{KL}} + \beta_{nr} L_{nr}^{\rho^{KL}}\right]^{1/\rho^{KL}}}. \tag{57}$$

In a second step, we do a forward calibration of the benchmark economies to the target year under consideration (e.g. 2010 as the central year of the Kyoto commitment period), employing baseline estimates for GDP growth, energy demand and future energy prices as given in the International Energy Outlook (DOE/EIA 2001). The forward calibration entails three steps.

First, we fix the time profile of fossil fuel supplies from the model's regions to the exogenous baseline projections by making supplies inelastic and scaling sector-specific resources with the exogenous growth rates in fossil fuel production. This allows us to partially control the emission profile from the supply side. Within the BaU calculation, we endogenously adjust the resource endowments of fossil fuels to calibrate the model to given exogenous target prices. At the same time we incorporate exogenous, region-specific GDP growth rates to scale the labour and capital stock of our static model.

Second, we incorporate exogenous autonomous energy efficiency improvements (AEEI) to match the exogenous carbon emission profiles as provided by DOE/EIA. The AEEI reflects the rate of change in energy intensity, i.e. the ratio of energy consumption over gross domestic product, holding energy prices constant. It is a measure of all non-price induced changes in gross energy intensity including technical developments that increase energy efficiency as well as structural changes. The European Commission (EC 1996) mentions research or changes in public standards as sources of efficiency improvements. The higher (lower) the AEEI the lower (higher) the baseline emissions and the lower (higher) the costs to reach a climate target relative to a given base year. Estimates for AEEI rates range from 0.4% to 1.5%; sensitivity studies demonstrate the crucial importance of the AEEI parameter. Even small differences in the number chosen for the AEEI result in large differences for energy demand and emissions in the baseline and, hence, the total costs of emission reductions (Manne and Richels, 1994). The implication of the treatment of technological change using AEEIs in prevalent models is that technological progress is assumed to be invariant with respect to policy interference.

Third, we recalibrate fossil fuel supply functions locally to exogenous estimates of supply elasticities. The last step assures empirical reaction of fossil fuel production to policy induced changes in world energy prices of fuels.

To account for the importance of exogenous baseline projections (see Böhringer, Jensen and Rutherford, 2000), the model can be calibrated to alternative data sources in an automated way. In the current set-up, one can perform sensitivity analysis with respect to the three different core scenarios of DOE/EIA: low economic growth, reference case (middle), and high economic growth.

For concreteness, we consider output as a function of labour and some resource input. Consider the labour input to be variable and the resource input to be fixed. We then have a CES cost function, which in equilibrium defines the price of output:

$$p = c(r, w) \tag{58}$$

in which w is the exogenous wage rate and r is the residual return to the sector's fixed factor. Because this factor is fixed by Shepard's lemma we have the following relationship between output, the supply of the fixed factor and the return to the fixed factor:

$$y \frac{\partial c(r, w)}{\partial r} = \overline{R} \tag{59}$$

If we use the calibrated CES cost function (Rutherford 1995) of the form:

$$c(r, w) = (\theta r^{1-\sigma} + (1 - \theta) w^{1-\sigma})^{\frac{1}{1-\sigma}} \tag{60}$$

then the calibration problem consists of finding values for θ and σ for which:

$$\frac{\partial y}{\partial (p/w)} \frac{(p/w)}{y} = \eta \tag{61}$$

at the benchmark point.

To solve the calibration problem we proceed in two steps. First, we derive an analytical expression for the supply (production) function y. Second, we differentiate this function with respect to the relative price of output and substitute the resulting expression in (61) to obtain a relationship between the supply elasticity, benchmark values and the elasticity of substitution (see bottom). Note that we are free to choose units of the specific factor such that its benchmark price is unity. Hence, when we calibrate the share parameter, we are also determining the supply of the fixed factor:

$$\bar{R} = \theta\bar{y} \quad \text{(Scaling the benchmark price of output to unity.)} \tag{62}$$

If the relative price of output and the variable factor depart from their benchmark values, the supply constraint for the sector-specific resource can be inverted to obtain an explicit expression for the return:

$$r = p\left(\frac{\theta y}{\bar{R}}\right)^{1/\sigma} \tag{63}$$

where we have substituted the equilibrium price for the cost function.

Substituting back into the cost function, we have

$$p^{1-\sigma} = \theta p^{1-\sigma}\left(\frac{\theta y}{\bar{R}}\right)^{\frac{1-\sigma}{\sigma}} + (1-\theta)w^{1-\sigma} \tag{64}$$

$$y = \bar{R}\theta^{\frac{1}{\sigma-1}}\left[1 - (1-\theta)\left(\frac{w}{p}\right)^{1-\sigma}\right]^{\frac{\sigma}{1-\sigma}} \tag{65}$$

Differentiating this expression with respect to the relative price of output, and setting all prices equal to unit, we have:

$$\eta = \frac{\sigma(1-\theta)}{\theta} \tag{66}$$

This equation can be used in a variety of ways to calibrate the supply function. One approach would be to choose the value share of the fixed factor θ to match the base year profits, and then assign the elasticity according to:

$$\sigma = \frac{\theta\eta}{(1-\theta)} \tag{67}$$

Alternatively, one can choose to use a Cobb-Douglas function and set the specific factor value share accordingly:

$$\theta = \frac{1}{1+\eta} \tag{68}$$

Numerically, the model is formulated and solved as a mixed complementarity problem (MCP) using the Mathematical Programming Subsystem for General Equilibrium (MPSGE) described in Rutherford (1995b, 1999) within the General

Algebraic Modeling System (GAMS) mathematical modeling language (Brooke et al., 1996). The complementarity problem is solved in GAMS using the PATH solver (Ferris and Munson, 2000).

3.2   Markups, Post-Uruguay Round Tariffs, and Services Trade Barriers

3.2.1   Tariff Equivalents for Services Trade

This section describes the estimation of tariff equivalents for cross-border services trade. The basic methodology involves the estimation of sector-specific gravity equations vis-à-vis the United States, which reports detailed bilateral trading patterns in services. In this case, these equations have been estimated at the level of aggregation corresponding to the GTAP sectors "business services" and "construction services."

The gravity equations are estimated using ordinary least squares with the following variables:

$$X_i = a_1 \cdot \ln(PCY_i) + a_2 \cdot GDP_i + a_3 \cdot WHD_i + \varepsilon_i \tag{69}$$

where X_i represents U.S. exports, PCY_i represents per-capita income in the exporting country, WHD_i is a dummy for western hemisphere countries, and ε is an error term.

In the regressions, we break out the GTAP regions Hong Kong and Singapore as free trade 'benchmarks'. Deviations from predicted imports, relative to this free trade benchmark, are taken as an indication of barriers to trade. These tariff equivalent rates are then backed out from a constant elasticity import demand function as follows:

$$\frac{T_1}{T_0} = \left[\frac{M_1}{M_0} \right]^{\frac{1}{e}} \tag{70}$$

Here, T_1 is the power of the tariff equivalent $(1+t_1)$ such that in free trade $T_0 = 1$, and $[M_1/M_0]$ is the ratio of actual to predicted imports (normalised relative to the free trade benchmark ratio for Hong Kong and Singapore, as discussed above). This is a reduced form, where actual prices and constant terms drop out because we take ratios. The term e is the demand elasticity (taken to be -4).

Data stems from reports by the U.S. Bureau of Economic Analysis for 1997 (USITC, 1997). Adjustments have been made to construction services, on the observation that roughly 80% of exports with affiliates involves construction and related services. Regression results from this approach are reported in Table 2, while the relevant estimates of tariff equivalents for the model sectors and regions are reported in Table 3. Note that, for reasons of data availability and comparability, and because of the nature of trade in the sector, these estimates have not been extended to cover international transport and trade services.

Table 2:   Summary Output.

Construction Service Exports

Regression Statistics	
Multiple R	0.891091335
R Square	0.794043767
Adjusted R Square	0.69991627
Standard Error	1232.345397
Observations	18

ANOVA

	df	SS	MS	F
Regression	3	87826516.15	29275505.38	19.27700261
Residual	15	22780127.68	1518675.179	
Total	18	110606643.8		

	Coefficients	Standard Error	t Stat	P-value
Intercept	0	#N/A	#N/A	#N/A
log per capita Y	4.903911138	106.7484956	0.045938925	0.963964954
GDP	1.105489719	0.155176366	7.124085639	3.48293E-06
WH	1029.921296	784.7930289	1.312347662	0.209130473

Business Services

Regression Statistics	
Multiple R	0.890216861
R Square	0.79248606
Adjusted R Square	0.698150867
Standard Error	1993.514206
Observations	18

ANOVA

	df	SS	MS	F
Regression	3	227653474.5	75884491.5	19.09476678
Residual	15	59611483.37	3974098.891	
Total	18	287264957.9		

	Coefficients	Standard Error	t Stat	P-value
Intercept	0	#N/A	#N/A	#N/A
log per capita Y	55.85635939	172.6826286	0.323462527	0.750810694
GDP	1.677832014	0.251022392	6.683993409	7.30282E-06
WH	4063.153035	1269.527241	3.200524497	0.005957448

Table 3:   Estimated Tariff Equivalents.

	Finance and Business Services	Construction Services
European Union	0.085	0.183
Japan	0.197	0.297
ASEAN	0.021	0.103
India	0.131	0.616
United States	0.082	0.098
Brazil	0.357	0.572
Central and South America	0.047	0.260
Africa	0.040	0.095
Rest of World	0.204	0.463
Central and East European Associates	0.184	0.519
Former Soviet Union	0.184	0.519
Sub-Saharan Africa	0.157	0.421

+ U.S. estimates involve the assignment of North America (i.e. Canadian) values.

3.2.2   Markup Data

This section describes initial estimates of markups, to be used in the modelling of sectors under imperfect competition. The starting point is provided by recent estimated price-cost markups from the OECD (Martins, Scarpetta, and Pilat, 1996) based on methods pioneered by Hall (1988) and Roeger (1995). The Martins et al. (1996) paper provides an overview of the recent empirical literature on markups.

Both, Hall and Roeger, focus their work on the United States. In contrast, Martins et al. provide estimates for most OECD Members. However, because of data limitations, they were not able to estimate the full matrix of countries and sectors. To produce a complete matrix, we have run a cross-country regression, with dummy variables allowing for variations in markups by country (a general index of the degree of competition within a country) and by sector. The resulting coefficients were then used to fill in missing values. For developing countries, we have used industry and firm-level data from the World Bank.

Table 4 reports the estimate of markups for the OECD study. This includes our markup estimates for missing values. Table 5 reports regression estimates relating to missing values. Finally, Table 6 provides initial estimates of markups by model sector and region. Once refined and extended, they can be used either to calibrate the cost-disadvantage ratios and substitution elasticities (under monopolistic competition) or alternatively to calculate market power indexes under an oligopoly/cartel model.

Table 4:   Preliminary Estimated Markups from OECD Markup Data.

	United States	Japan	Germany	France	Italy	UK	Canada	Australia	Belgium	Denmark	Finland	Netherlands
Coal	1.11	1.10	1.09	***1.16***	***1.19***	1.06	1.31	1.33	***1.19***	1.39	1.16	***1.20***
Oil	1.11	1.10	1.09	***1.15***	***1.18***	1.06	***1.20***	1.33	***1.18***	1.39	1.16	***1.19***
Prfood	1.05	1.32	1.12	1.11	***1.14***	1.20	1.09	1.13	1.15	1.10	1.09	1.12
Textiles	1.08	1.19	1.15	1.10	1.16	1.03	1.20	1.14	1.12	1.11	1.22	***1.15***
Clothing	1.10	***1.13***	1.11	1.15	1.14	1.03	1.10	1.12	***1.12***	1.18	1.12	***1.13***
Leather Products	1.08	***1.17***	1.18	1.11	1.14	1.06	1.11	1.17	1.35	1.21	1.14	1.11
Paper Products	1.13	1.20	1.29	1.13	1.15	1.05	1.39	1.20	1.21	1.13	1.24	1.15
Publishing	1.19	1.10	1.09	1.24	1.18	1.09	1.21	1.21	1.16	1.10	1.20	1.22
Petroleum	1.03	1.04	***1.14***	1.19	***1.14***	1.07	***1.16***	1.21	***1.14***	***1.15***	1.22	***1.15***
Ind Chemicals	1.18	1.23	***1.23***	1.21	1.16	1.06	1.40	1.20	1.17	1.26	1.27	1.19
Drugs and Medicines	1.44	1.54	1.45	1.04	***1.38***	1.16	1.25	1.35	***1.37***	1.59	1.57	***1.38***
Chemicals Nec	1.26	1.26	1.24	1.19	***1.20***	1.08	1.20	1.25	1.13	1.12	1.26	***1.21***
Rubber	***1.10***	1.15	***1.16***	1.20	1.10	***1.05***	1.12	1.10	1.05	1.13	1.50	***1.16***
Plastics	1.07	1.15	***1.16***	***1.13***	1.08	***1.06***	1.17	1.21	***1.16***	1.16	1.34	1.14
Pottery, China, etc.	1.09	1.22	***1.31***	1.29	1.30	***1.21***	1.40	1.17	***1.31***	1.36	1.82	***1.32***
Glass Products	1.17	1.41	1.23	1.22	1.30	1.06	1.31	1.33	***1.26***	***1.27***	1.22	1.36
Non-Metallic Mineral Prods	1.18	1.26	1.26	1.24	1.30	1.15	1.32	1.21	1.09	1.25	1.39	***1.25***
Misc Manufactures	1.08	1.38	1.30	***1.15***	1.09	***1.08***	1.11	1.24	***1.18***	1.22	1.20	1.13
Wood Products	1.22	***1.21***	1.20	1.15	1.17	1.18	1.28	1.20	***1.20***	1.13	1.24	1.19
Furniture	1.06	1.25	1.15	1.21	1.21	1.19	1.16	1.13	1.29	1.15	1.31	***1.20***
Steel	1.10	1.19	1.14	1.16	1.17	***1.11***	1.25	1.31	1.30	1.09	1.30	1.39
Non-Ferrous	1.14	1.26	***1.20***	1.26	1.15	1.05	1.14	1.28	1.17	1.17	1.13	1.27
Other Metals	1.09	1.11	1.20	1.18	1.39	1.03	1.16	1.17	1.18	1.14	1.22	1.10
Motor	1.09	1.17	1.15	1.13	1.02	***1.03***	1.14	1.12	***1.13***	***1.14***	1.17	1.15
Office and Computer Machines	1.54	1.24	1.58	1.17	1.67	1.47	***1.50***	***1.50***	***1.48***	1.44	1.92	***1.49***
Other Machinery	1.06	1.09	1.06	1.12	1.19	***1.02***	1.15	1.15	***1.12***	1.12	1.22	***1.13***

Note that estimated values (i.e. those missing from the OECD reported estimates) are in bold-italics. Other values are from Martins et al. (1996).

Table 5:   Regression Results.

	Coefficient	Std. Error	t-Statistic	Prob.
Intercept (U.S. Glass Products)	1.200786	0.032978	36.41154	0
Australia	0.077526	0.026098	2.970581	0.0033
Belgium	0.056303	0.032057	1.756342	0.0802
Canada	0.080498	0.026743	3.010067	0.0029
Denmark	0.067479	0.026731	2.524345	0.0122
Finland	0.149373	0.025819	5.785429	0
France	0.024391	0.027071	0.900986	0.3685
Germany	0.058895	0.027784	2.119746	0.035
Italy	0.059665	0.027857	2.141843	0.0332
Japan	0.066326	0.026708	2.483407	0.0137
Netherlands	0.067091	0.031964	2.098943	0.0368
Norway	0.031608	0.027077	1.167333	0.2442
Sweden	-0.010474	0.028713	-0.364793	0.7156
UK	-0.041935	0.028213	-1.486393	0.1384
Chemicalsnec	-0.060785	0.038686	-1.571229	0.1174
Clothing	-0.133536	0.040487	-3.298261	0.0011
Coal	-0.066715	0.040484	-1.647943	0.1006
Drugs	0.115243	0.039459	2.92058	0.0038
Furniture	-0.071529	0.037918	-1.886406	0.0604
Leather	-0.100049	0.037885	-2.640836	0.0088
Mineralsnec	-0.016144	0.037918	-0.425759	0.6706
Miscmfgs	-0.079632	0.040467	-1.967845	0.0502
Motorvehicles	-0.123959	0.039349	-3.150215	0.0018
Indchemicals	-0.034467	0.037892	-0.909606	0.3639
Nonferrous Metals	-0.05648	0.038666	-1.460719	0.1453
Office Machines and Computers	0.223681	0.040472	5.526808	0
Oil	-0.078195	0.043185	-1.810682	0.0714
Other Machines	-0.136803	0.041617	-3.287162	0.0012
Other Metal Products	-0.089125	0.03722	-2.394511	0.0174
Paper and Publishing	-0.066268	0.03722	-1.78041	0.0762
Petroleum	-0.120066	0.047084	-2.550055	0.0114
Plastics	-0.095695	0.040461	-2.365111	0.0188
Pottery	0.050673	0.041718	1.214654	0.2256
Processed Foods	-0.124575	0.038578	-3.229213	0.0014
Publishing	-0.089125	0.03722	-2.394511	0.0174
Rubber	-0.104471	0.041852	-2.496225	0.0132
Steel	-0.046069	0.037894	-1.215732	0.2252
Textiles	-0.113067	0.037918	-2.981892	0.0031
Wood Products	-0.056962	0.038546	-1.477773	0.1407

R-squared	0.506646		
Adjusted R-squared	0.432545		
S.E. of regression	0.092072		
Sum squared resid	2.144757		
Log likelihood	303.0742		
F-statistic		6.837273	
Prob(F-statistic)		0	

Mean dependent var		1.195068
S.D. dependent var		0.122226
Akaike info criterion		-4.646604
Schwarz criterion		-4.155531
F-statistic		6.837273
Prob(F-statistic)		0
Sample(adjusted): 1 292		

Table 6:   Preliminary Markups by GTAP-4 Sectors.

Estimated Markups for Cournot Modeling

	European Union	Japan	ASEAN	India	United States	Brazil	Central and South America	Africa	Rest of World
Rice	1.00	1.00	1.00	1.00	1.00	1.00	1.00	1.00	1.00
Cereals	1.00	1.00	1.00	1.00	1.00	1.00	1.00	1.00	1.00
Vegetab	1.00	1.00	1.00	1.00	1.00	1.00	1.00	1.00	1.00
Oilseed	1.00	1.00	1.00	1.00	1.00	1.00	1.00	1.00	1.00
Canebeet	1.00	1.00	1.00	1.00	1.00	1.00	1.00	1.00	1.00
Fibers	1.00	1.00	1.00	1.00	1.00	1.00	1.00	1.00	1.00
Othagr	1.00	1.00	1.00	1.00	1.00	1.00	1.00	1.00	1.00
Fishing	1.00	1.00	1.00	1.00	1.00	1.00	1.00	1.00	1.11
Energyminer	1.16	1.08	1.09	1.11	1.08	1.17	1.17	1.11	1.07
Prfood	1.12	1.32	1.05	1.07	1.05	1.14	1.14	1.07	1.11
Texcloth	1.12	1.16	1.09	1.11	1.09	1.18	1.18	1.11	1.10
Othmanf	1.16	1.38	1.08	1.10	1.08	1.17	1.17	1.10	1.16
Wood	1.19	1.23	1.14	1.16	1.14	1.23	1.23	1.16	1.13
Metals	1.18	1.19	1.11	1.13	1.11	1.20	1.20	1.13	1.11
Motor	1.12	1.17	1.09	1.11	1.09	1.18	1.18	1.11	1.33
Machinery	1.30	1.17	1.30	1.33	1.30	1.41	1.41	1.33	1.17
Tradetrans	1.24	1.17	1.26	1.17	1.24	1.32	1.32	1.17	1.17
Finance	1.24	1.17	1.26	1.17	1.24	1.32	1.32	1.17	1.17
Othserv	1.24	1.17	1.26	1.17	1.24	1.32	1.32	1.17	1.17

3.2.3   Post-Uruguay Round Data

This section describes briefly the matrix of Post-Uruguay Round tariff rates for the GTAP-4E database, a condensed version of GTAP version 4 that incorporates IEA energy statistics (at the expense of a higher sectoral aggregation). In compiling this matrix, we have used two primary sources of Post-Round rate information: (1) version 3 of the GTAP database and (2) the GATT/WTO integrated database (IDB). Version 3 of the GTAP data is itself based, in large part, on the IDB. Throughout, we have assumed that the current applied tariff rates are correct as reported in GTAP-4E (i.e. the GTAP version 4 database).

Version 3 of the GTAP database provides carefully compiled Post-Uruguay Round protection vectors which draw heavily on the work by the World Bank. As a first step we have mapped the sectors and regions as of GTAP version 3 to the sectoral and regional disaggregation as of GTAP version 4. Whenever there is an exact match between bilateral sectors and regions, we use those post-Round rates. For Sweden and Finland, we use the average EU post Uruguay Round rates (rather than the EU3 rates from version 3), since they joined the EU in 1995 and subsequently harmonised their tariffs to EU levels as part of the accession process. Whenever there are no bilateral imports reported in the version 3 database, but imports appear in the benchmark version 4 database, we apply the average version 3 MFN (Most Favoured Nation) tariff to imports of that commodity.

For commodities without direct correspondence between version 3 and version 4, we employ the following technique. For those country-commodity combinations available directly from the IDB, we calculate the proportional cuts needed to move average version 4 tariffs to the average IDB post-Round bound rates. These percentage cuts are then applied to the bilateral tariffs, enabling us to exploit the IDB data while preserving the relative differences in tariff rates. Some countries are pulled out of regional groupings in the transition from version 3 to version 4. Rather than using aggregate version 3 regional tariff rates, for all commodities we have used the average individual IDB rates for individual commodities in these countries (i.e. Sri Lanka, Venezuela, Columbia, Uruguay, Turkey, South Africa).

Where regions and commodities have no direct GTAP version 3 match or no IDB post-Round rate is available, we map them as closely as possible to version 3. For version 4 regional groups, which are very similar to version 3, but differ slightly in composition, we map them to the version 3 region (i.e. the Rest of South Asia, Rest of South America, and Rest of World). There is also the problem of five new regional groupings introduced in version 4: Rest of the Andean Pact, Rest of Middle East, Rest of North Africa, Rest of Southern Africa, Rest of Sub-Saharan Africa. For these, we have simply mapped them to the closest version 3 region.

Once we assembled this matrix of post-Uruguay Round tariff rates, we simply multiplied it by the value of bilateral imports at world prices. Since tariff bindings only require that applied rates be no higher than the binding, we do not change the version 4 rates if the post-Uruguay Round bindings are higher than the initial tariff. As bindings are generally greater than or equal to zero, this also means that we do not apply post-Round bindings when the reported applied rate is negative (we use bindings from IDB and where this is not possible, we maintain the initial version 4 tariff rate.). Furthermore, for regions (Vietnam, China, Taiwan and the Former Soviet Union) that do not have any Uruguay Round obligations, we have left tariff rates as they are in the base data. For agricultural sectors, we assume that no cuts to the bilateral tariffs are needed to move from the 1995 benchmark version 4 database to Post-Round levels.

The final step involved aggregating the adjusted GTAP-4 data to the set of sectors and regions in GTAP-4E. Table 8 provides a comparison of the Pre- and Post-Uruguay tariff estimates we have arrived at as a result of this process.

Table 7:   GTAP Version 3 and GTAP-E (GTAP Version 4), Average Pre- and Post-Uruguay Round Tariff Rates (%).

	Advanced Economies	NIEs	Other East Asia	South Asia	Latin America	ME, N. Africa and CEEFSU	SSA	ROW	Developing Countries (Columns 3-7)	World Average
Pre-UR										
GTAP Version 3										
Agric. and processed food	47.80	57.69	47.70	16.69	10.86	16.34	16.57	65.02	20.48	40.14
Other primary products	0.97	3.19	10.45	8.88	6.33	8.47	9.46	22.89	8.54	2.61
Other manufactures	4.17	6.04	27.03	42.60	17.35	18.44	9.42	35.70	21.16	9.64
GTAP Version 4										
Agric. and processed food	15.95	28.29	23.67	39.85	5.02	14.76	12.51	70.61	16.14	17.39
Other primary products	0.32	2.54	2.86	10.19	10.09	5.92	2.12	22.41	6.28	1.67
Other manufactures	1.91	3.74	19.52	59.11	9.88	11.11	12.99	37.66	16.12	5.58
Post-UR										
GTAP Version 3										
Agric. and processed food	37.28	36.38	27.21	16.60	10.19	16.00	14.16	52.28	16.46	30.73
Other primary products	0.86	3.00	7.61	8.55	6.33	8.45	9.46	22.63	7.82	2.41
Other manufactures	2.85	4.29	24.79	31.64	15.89	18.08	9.34	31.41	19.50	8.12
GTAP Version 4										
Agric. and processed food	13.28	26.15	20.51	32.31	4.52	13.54	9.55	57.19	14.14	14.81
Other primary products	0.20	2.52	1.76	6.73	3.97	4.33	1.62	22.08	3.79	1.14
Other manufactures	1.59	3.58	18.56	30.51	9.56	10.67	8.42	33.36	13.98	4.84

References

Armington, P.A. (1969), A Theory of Demand for Products Distinguished by Place of Production, *IMF Staff Papers* 16 (1), 159-178.

Babiker, M.H., J.M. Reilly, M. Mayer, R.S. Eckaus, I.S. Wing, and R.C. Hyman (2001), *The MIT Emissions Prediction and Policy Analysis (EPPA) Model: Revisions, Sensitivities, and Comparisons of Results*, MIT Joint Program on the Science and Policy of Global Change Report.

Babiker, M.H. and T.F. Rutherford (1997), *Input-Output and General Equilibrium Estimates of Embodied Carbon: A Dataset and Static Framework for Assessment*, Working Paper 97-2, University of Colorado, Boulder.

Bergmann, L. (1990), The Development of Computable General Equilibrium Models, in: Bergman, L., D.W. Jorgenson, and E. Zalai (Eds.), *General Equilibrium Modeling and Economic Policy Analysis*, Oxford, 3-30.

Böhringer, C., J. Jensen, and T.F. Rutherford (2000), Energy Market Projections and Differentiated Carbon Abatement in the European Union, in: Carraro, C. (Ed.), *Efficiency and Equity of Climate Change Policy*, Dordrecht, 199-220.

Brooke, A., D. Kendrick, and A. Meeraus (1996), *GAMS: A User's Guide*, Washington, D.C.

DOE (2001), *International Energy Outlook 2001*, U.S. Department of Energy, Washington, D.C.

European Commission (1996), *Energy in Europe – European Energy to 2020 – a Scenario Approach*, European Commission, Brussels.

Fehr, F. and W. Wiegard (1996), *Numerische Gleichgewichtsmodelle: Grundstruktur, Anwendungen und Erkenntnisgehalt*, Ökonomie und Gesellschaft, Jahrbuch 13, Frankfurt, 297-339.

Ferris, M.C. and T.S. Munson (2000), Complementarity Problems in GAMS and the PATH Solver, *Journal of Economic Dynamics and Control* 24, 165-188.

Grubb, M., J. Edmonds, P. ten Brink, and M. Morrison (1993), The Costs of Limiting Fossil-Fuel CO_2 Emissions: A Survey and Analysis, *Annual Review of Energy and Environment* 18, 397-478.

Hall, R.E. (1986), Market Structure and Macroeconomic Fluctuations, *Brookings Papers on Economic Activity* No. 2, 285-338.

Harrison, G.W, T.F. Rutherford, and D.G. Tarr (1996), Increased Competition and Completion of the Market in the European Union: Static and Steady State Effects, *Journal of Economic Integration* 11 (3), 332-365.

Harrison, G.W, T. F. Rutherford, and D.G. Tarr (1997), Quantifying the Uruguay Round, *Economic Journal* 107, 1405-1430.

IEA (International Energy Agency) (1996), *Energy Prices and Taxes: Energy Balances of OECD and Non-OECD-Countries*, IEA publications, Paris.

Kehoe, P.J. and T.J. Kehoe (1994), A Primer on Static Applied General Equilibrium Models, *Federal Reserve Bank of Minneapolis Quarterly Review* (Spring).

Lloyd, P. (1994), Aggregation by Industry in High-Dimensional Models, *Review of International Economics* 2 (2), 97-111.

Mathiesen, L. (1985), Computation of Economic Equilibrium by a Sequence of Linear Complementarity Problems, in: Manne, A. (Ed.), *Economic Equilibrium – Model Formulation and Solution*, 144-162.

McDougall, R.A., A. Elbehri, and T.P. Truong (1998), *Global Trade, Assistance and Protection: The GTAP 4 Data Base*, Center for Global Trade Analysis, West Lafayette.

Martins, J.O., S. Scarpetta, and D. Pilat (1996), *Markup Ratios in Manufacturing Industries: Estimates for 14 OECD Countries*, OECD Working Papers 4 (24).

Peireira, A.M and J.B. Shoven (1992), Survey of Dynamic Computational General Equilibrium Models for Tax Policy Evaluation, *Journal of Policy Modeling* 10, 401-426.

Reinert, K.A., and D.W. Roland-Holst (1997), Social Accounting Matrices, in: Francois, J. F. and K.A. Reinert (Eds.), *Applied Methods for Trade Policy Analysis: A Handbook*, New York, 94-121.

Roeger, W. (1995), Can Imperfect Competition Explain the Difference Between Primal and Dual Productivity Measures? Estimates for US Manufacturing, *Journal of Political Economy* 103 (2), 316-330.

Rutherford, T.F. (1995), *Constant Elasticity of Substitution Functions: Some Hints and Useful Formulae*, Notes prepared for GAMS General Equilibrium Workshop in Boulder, Colorado.

Rutherford, T.F. (1998), *Economic Equilibrium Modelling with GAMS: An Introduction to GAMS/MCP and GAMS/MPSGE*, GAMS Development Corp., Washington, D.C.

Rutherford, T.F. (1999), Applied General Equilibrium Modelling with MPSGE as a GAMS Subsystem: An Overview of the Modelling Framework and Syntax, *Computational Economics* 14, 1-46.

Shoven, J.B. and J. Whalley (1984), Applied General Equilibrium Models of Taxation and International Trade: An Introduction and Survey, *Journal of Economic Literature* 22, 1007-1051.

Shoven, J.B. and J. Whalley (1992), *Applying General Equilibrium*, Cambridge.

USITC (United States International Trade Commission) (1998), *The Year in Trade: Operation of the Trade Agreements Program during 1997*, USITC Publication 3103, Washington, D.C.

Weyant, J. (Ed.) (1999), The Costs of the Kyoto Protocol: A Multi-Model Evaluation, *The Energy Journal* Special Issue.

Imperfect Competition: Modelling Alternatives and Sensitivity

Dirk Willenbockel

Middlesex University, Queensway, Enfield EN3 4SF, United Kingdom
d.willenbockel@mdx.ac.uk

1 Introduction

There is a widespread suspicion that traditional studies of trade policy reform under perfect competition miss a crucial part of the plot by neglecting potential pro-competitive industrial organisation effects such as scale economy gains and price mark-up reductions commonly emphasised by proponents of trade liberalisation and regional integration schemes. In order to account for industrial organisation effects, a model featuring imperfectly competitive supply behaviour and increasing returns to scale is required. Yet once the clear-cut world of perfect competition is left behind, a broad menu of a priori plausible alternative specifications of firm conduct opens up. As Helpman and Krugman (1989) put it, 'there is only one way to be perfect but many ways to be imperfect'. Since the empirical industrial organisation literature provides little guidance with respect to the appropriate model of firm conduct, an essentially subjective decision by the model-builder is required at this stage. The danger that the particular choice of specification may crucially predetermine the tenor of CGE simulation results calls for extensive sensitivity analyses across the spectrum of alternative oligopoly models in order to assess the robustness of results. However, practical feasibility constraints necessarily limit the scope for sensitivity analysis in large-scale multi-sector multi-region models like the GEM-E3 framework.

In order to clarify the rationale for the particular imperfect competition specification adopted in the large-scale model outlined in the previous chapter and to provide an indication of the robustness of the quantitative results presented in Part C to variations in the assumptions about firm conduct, the present chapter provides a systematic synopsis of alternative formulations of imperfectly competitive supply behaviour in applied general equilibrium trade models and examines the sensitivity of results to the specification choice within a stylised prototype world trade model.

The various formulations of supply behaviour in imperfectly competitive markets encountered in the existing CGE literature and included in the following synopsis differ along several dimensions: With respect to the type of strategic interaction among firms, the analysis distinguishes Bertrand-type competition, domestic and international Cournot competition, conjectural variations approaches, as well as large-group monopolistic competition. With respect to the type of international market regime, both market segmentation and market integration scenarios are considered. Here the world market for a commodity group is called *integrated*, if potential cross-border arbitrage ensures that firms are unable to engage in geographic price discrimination. Regional markets for a product group are labelled *segmented*, on the other hand, if firms have the power to set different price mark-ups for different geographic market segments. In other words, under market integration the law of one price reigns, while under market segmentation unexploited international commodity arbitrage opportunities are allowed to persist in equilibrium. Finally, with regard to the degree of product substitutability between the outputs of rival firms within an industry group, settings with product homogeneity across firms located in the same region and models with intra-industry product differentiation are considered under alternative assumptions about the degree of rivalry between domestic and imported goods in demand.

Since all models of firm conduct under consideration share the assumption of profit maximising behaviour, firms' pricing strategies are generically characterised by price mark-up functions, which relate equilibrium price-cost margins to firms' perceived price elasticities of demand. Section 2 provides a technical synopsis that describes the endogenous determination of these perceived elasticities for the various cases at hand. The algebraically explicit style of exposition intends to serve the needs of applied modellers, given that the derivation of the perceived elasticities for nested demand systems are tiresome and error-prone and the respective existing literature is notoriously opaque. Although the exposition follows the new trade theory literature by characterising the alternative models of oligopolistic interaction by resort to the language of classical oligopoly theory, it should be emphasised that all models except the conjectural variation models under consideration are compatible with a game-theoretic interpretation – i.e the equilibria under consideration are Nash equilibria of simultaneous-move one shot games in quantities or prices. Section 3 sets out the general equilibrium framework into which the various models of imperfectly competitive conduct are embedded. In order to assess the sensitivity of predictions to the choice of model, all specifications are calibrated to the same hypothetical benchmark data set as detailed in Section 4, and subjected to the same trade policy shock in Section 5. Section 6 draws conclusion.

2   Price-Cost Margins and Firm Conduct: A Synopsis

2.1   Models with Product Homogeneity Among Firms Located in the Same Region

Starting point for the endogenous determination of price-cost margins in imperfectly competitive industries is the nested Armington demand system specification underlying the large-scale model simulations in this volume. Since this demand system is commonly used in contemporary multi-country applied general equilibrium trade modeling[1], while the existing literature provides little reliable guidance with regard to the model-consistent determination of optimal mark-ups under imperfect competition, it appears worthwhile to provide a technically detailed exposition in this section.

The demand nesting hierarchy at the sectoral commodity group level (suppressing the commodity-group/sector subscript for notational convenience) is given by

$$A_r = \left[\delta_r D_r^{(\sigma_A - 1)/\sigma_A} + (1 - \delta_r) M_r^{(\sigma_A - 1)/\sigma_A} \right]^{\sigma_A/(\sigma_A - 1)}, \tag{1}$$

$$M_r = \left[\sum_{s \neq r} \gamma_{s,r} M_{s,r}^{(\sigma_M - 1)/\sigma_M} \right]^{\sigma_M/(\sigma_M - 1)}, \tag{2}$$

where A_r is an Armington composite good defined over all origin-specific varieties of a commodity group demanded by region r, D_r is the demand for domestically produced output by region r, M_r is the composite import demand by region r, $M_{s,r}$ represents imports of origin s demanded by region r, σ_A is the elasticity of substitution between domestic output and the import composite, and σ_M the elasticity of substitution between imports of different geographic origin.

The sectoral demand functions for output of origin r take the form

$$D_r(.) = \delta_r^{\sigma_A} \left(\frac{P_{r,r}}{PA_r} \right)^{-\sigma_A} A_r(.), \tag{3}$$

$$M_{r,s}(.) = \gamma_{r,s}^{\sigma_M} \left(\frac{P_{r,s}}{PM_s} \right)^{-\sigma_M} M_s(.) \ , \ M_s(.) = (1 - \delta_s)^{\sigma_A} \left(\frac{PM_s}{PA_s} \right)^{-\sigma_A} A_s(.), \tag{4}$$

---

[1]   Prominent examples are the GTAP model (Hertel and Tsigas, 1997) and the model of Harrison, Rutherford, and Tarr (1997).

where PA is the commodity group price index dual to A, PM the import price index dual to the aggregate import basket M, and $P_{r,s}$ the demand price for goods of origin r faced by region s.

Given that the actual relationship between A and PA in the model is quite complex, it is assumed that firms make simplifying assumptions about this relationship when estimating the price elasticity of demand for their output. In other words, in view of the information cost and computational complexity involved in finding their 'true' demand curve, firms are taken to be characterised by bounded rationality or limited cognition at this stage. Specifically, firms are taken to assume that top-level composite demands are governed by simple constant-elasticity functions

$$A_r(.) = bPA_r^{-\Omega}. \tag{5}$$

Note that (5) serves as a generic specification, which encompasses alternative particular formulations in existing models as special cases. Setting $\Omega=0$ corresponds to the assumption that firms perceive to have no influence on top-level composite demand *quantities*, as in Böhringer, Welsch and Löschel (2001), while the more common case $\Omega=1$ entails that firms perceive to have no influence on top-level commodity-group *expenditure* levels. The assumption of limited cognition of general equilibrium feedbacks also avoids the so-called price normalisation problem, which arises under imperfect competition when firms are furnished with the ability to assess the full general equilibrium consequences of their supply strategy.[2]

Let $X_r = n_r x_r$ denote the total output quantity of firms in an imperfectly competitive industry located in region r, where n_r is the number of symmetric firms and x_r is output per firm.

2.1.1   Domestic Cournot Oligopoly with Market Integration

Consider first the case of a Cournot-Nash game among domestic firms. With globally integrated markets, the individual Cournot oligopolist from region r chooses its profit-maximising supply quantity x_r to the world market under the assumption, that *domestic* rivals' supply quantities do not respond to changes in its own supply. The total demand function for output of origin r is

$$X_r(.) = D_r(.) + \sum_{s \neq r} M_{r,s}(.), \tag{6}$$

Profit-maximising behaviour entails the equalisation of marginal cost (mc) and perceived marginal revenue, i.e.

---

[2]   See Willenbockel (2003) for a detailed discussion of the price normalisation problem and references to the literature.

$$\frac{\partial(P_r x_r)}{\partial x_r} = P_r + \frac{\partial P_r}{\partial X_r}\frac{\partial X_r}{\partial x_r}x_r = P_r\left(1 + \frac{\partial P_r}{P_r}\frac{X_r}{\partial X_r}\frac{x_r}{X_r}\right) = P_r\left(1 - \frac{1}{\varepsilon_r n_r}\right) = mc, \tag{7}$$

where $\varepsilon_r = -\hat{X}_r / \hat{P}_r$ denotes the perceived elasticity of the total market demand function (6) and hat notation is used to indicate log derivatives. The perceived world market demand elasticity is found by log-differentiation of (6) with (3) to (5). Note that

$$\frac{P\hat{A}_s}{\hat{P}_r} = \frac{P\hat{A}_s}{P\hat{M}_s}\frac{P\hat{M}_s}{\hat{P}_r} = S_{r,s} \text{ and } \frac{P\hat{M}_s}{\hat{P}_r} = SM_{r,s},$$

where $S_{r,s}$ is the market share of region r in the total commodity group expenditure of region s and $SM_{r,s}=S_{r,s}/(1-S_{s,s})$ is the market share of region r in total commodity group *import* expenditure of region s. With these notational conventions for value shares, the perceived elasticity in (7) is determined by

$$\varepsilon_r = \frac{D_r}{X_r}(\sigma_A - (\sigma_A - \Omega)S_{r,r}) + \sum_{s \neq r}\frac{M_{r,s}}{X_r}(\sigma_M - (\sigma_M - \sigma_A)SM_{r,s} - (\sigma_A - \Omega)S_{r,s}). \tag{8}$$

In the special case $\sigma_A = \sigma_M$, the perceived elasticity formula simplifies to

$$\varepsilon_r = \sigma - (\sigma - \Omega)\sum_s w_{r,s}S_{r,s} \quad , \quad (w_{r,s} \equiv \frac{M_{r,s}}{Y_r}, \ M_{r,r} \equiv D_r). \tag{8'}$$

Note that (8') is in fact exactly equivalent (for $\Omega=1$) to (11.18)-(11.19) in Francois and Roland-Holst (1997).

2.1.2   International Cournot Oligopoly with Market Integration

A conceivable alternative to the domestic Cournot oligopoly specification arises when foreign rivals, which produce imperfect substitutes within the same commodity group, are recognised as players in the Cournot-Nash game. The determination of perceived elasticities for this case is a slightly more intricate affair, since the Cournot assumption that foreign rivals' quantities remain fixed implies that rivals' prices must respond to marginal variations in x_r, given that any variation in x_r entails a shift in foreign rivals' demand curves – and these Cournot-equivalent foreign rival price responses need to be determined simultaneously for all regions:

Let $VP_o^r = \hat{P}_o / \hat{P}_r$ denote the implicit Cournot-equivalent conjectural elasticity of rival price P_o with respect to P_r perceived by an individual firm located in r, which (for $o \neq r$) measures the change in P_o required to keep X_o constant when P_r changes. Due to product homogeneity across firms located in the same region,

$VP^r_r = 1$. The corresponding elasticities of aggregate industry price index PA_d and import price index PM_d in destination market d as perceived by a firm in r are then

$$VPA^r_d = \sum_o S_{o,d} VP^r_o \quad , \quad VPM^r_d = \sum_{o \neq d} SM_{o,d} VP^r_o \tag{9}$$

and the perceived global demand elasticity for output of origin r is expressed by

$$\varepsilon_r = -\frac{\hat{X}_r}{\hat{P}_r} = w_{r,r}[\sigma_A - (\sigma_A - \Omega)VPA^r_r]$$
$$+ \sum_{d \approx r} w_{r,d}[\sigma_M - (\sigma_M - \sigma_A)VPM^r_d - (\sigma_A - \Omega)VPA^r_d] \tag{10}$$

The Cournot assumption for foreign rivals of origin s $\neq$r is

$$0 = -\frac{\hat{X}_s}{\hat{P}_r} = w_{s,s}[\sigma_A VP^r_s - (\sigma_A - \Omega)VPA^r_s]$$
$$+ \sum_{d \approx s} w_{s,d}[\sigma_M VP^r_s - (\sigma_M - \sigma_A)VPM^r_d - (\sigma_A - \Omega)VPA^r_d] \tag{11}$$

For each region r, equations (9) to (11) constitute a separate linear m-equation system in the m unknowns ε_r and VP^r_s, s $\neq$r.

2.1.3   Cournot Oligopoly Under Regional Market Segmentation

When markets are geographically segmented, the individual Cournot oligopolist located in region r is able to choose the supply quantity to each regional market separately. Correspondingly, there is a separate first-order condition for each market segment:

$$P_{r,s}\left(1 - \frac{1}{\varepsilon_{r,s} n_r}\right) = mc, \tag{7'}$$

where

$$\varepsilon_{r,r} = -\frac{\hat{D}_r}{\hat{P}_{r,r}} = \sigma_A - (\sigma_A - \Omega)S_{r,r} \tag{12}$$

$$\varepsilon_{r,s} = -\frac{\hat{M}_{r,s}}{\hat{P}_{r,s}} = \sigma_M - (\sigma_M - \sigma_A)SM_{r,s} - (\sigma_A - \Omega)S_{r,s} \quad , \quad s \neq r. \tag{13}$$

2.1.4   Oligopoly with Conjectural Output Variations

The Cournot model presented above can be seen as special case of a general conjectural variations model in outputs, in which each oligopolist is assumed to conjecture that the relation between changes in domestic industry supply and changes in its own supply quantity is given by $dX = v\,dx$, where v is a constant parameter. In this case the mark-up formula under global market integration takes the form

$$\frac{\partial(P_r x_r)}{\partial x_r} = P_r\left(1 - \frac{v_r}{\varepsilon_r n_r}\right) = mc, \tag{7''}$$

whereby the perceived elasticity is still given by (8).

The conjectural variations approach has been used in a number of simulation studies, e.g. Dixit (1987; 1988), in order to break the link between observed price-cost margins in the benchmark data set and substitution elasticities: Given that benchmark firm numbers are set in accordance with extraneous industry concentration data, while the benchmark value shares in (8) as well as benchmark price-cost margins are predetermined by the benchmark data set, the substitution elasticities in (8) would have to be calibrated residually under specification (7) to ensure that the model replicates the price-cost margins of the benchmark data set. However, the resulting substitution elasticity values may imply implausible magnitudes for the price elasticities of model trade flows. By introducing an additional parameter, v, the conjectural variations approach allows to set substitution elasticity values extraneously, while v is calibrated residually.

2.2   Models with Intra-Industry Product Differentiation

We are now turning to models featuring horizontal product differentiation between firms within the same region and industry. It is straightforward to incorporate intra-regional product differentiation under the demand nesting structure (1)-(2) by redefining D_r and $M_{s,r}$ for imperfectly competitive sectors as Dixit-Stiglitz (1977)-type CES aggregators over firm-specific varieties produced in a region:

$$D_r = \left[\sum_{v=1}^{n_r} x_{r,r}^{(\sigma-1)/\sigma}\right]^{\sigma/(\sigma-1)}, \quad M_{r,s} = \left[\sum_{v=1}^{n_r} x_{r,s}^{(\sigma-1)/\sigma}\right]^{\sigma/(\sigma-1)}, \tag{14}$$

where σ (without subscript) denotes the elasticity of substitution between product varieties of different firms located in the same region.

Correspondingly, the $P_{r,s}$ must now be re-interpreted as price indices defined over firm-specific prices per variety $p_{r,s}$ dual to the quantity indices in (14). We will refer to the demand system (1,2,14) with $\sigma > \sigma_M \geq \sigma_A$ as *Armington-Dixit/Stiglitz*

(ADS) case.[3] In the special case $\sigma = \sigma_A = \sigma_M$ the demand side nesting hierarchy collapses to a pure 'love of variety' specification as used in theoretical intra-industry trade models in the tradition of Krugman (1979; 1980). We use the label *pure Dixit/Stiglitz (DS)* for this specification.

For clarity of exposition and to allow easier comparisons with the existing related theoretical and applied literature, it appears appropriate to treat the DS case first in Section 2.2.1, before dealing with the required modifications for the ADS case in Section 2.2.2.

2.2.1   Pure DS Demand System

The top-level commodity group composite demanded by region r takes the form

$$A_r = \left[\sum_{s=1}^{R} \delta_{s,r} n_r x_{s,r}^{(\sigma-1)/\sigma} \right]^{\sigma/(\sigma-1)}, \tag{1'}$$

i.e., the elasticities of substitution between firm-specific varieties are the same irrespective of origin, but preference intensity parameters are allowed to differ across regions to account for the home bias in observable trade patterns. Region r's demand for an individual firm's variety from origin s is

$$x_{s,r} = \delta_{s,r}^{\sigma} \left(\frac{PA_r}{p_{s,r}} \right)^{\sigma} A_r(.), \tag{15}$$

and as before firms assume that $A_r(.)$ is governed by (5).

2.2.1.1   *Market Segmentation*

Under market segmentation, a profit-maximising firm located in region r sets a separate price (quantity) for each market segment s according to the first-order conditions

$$p_{r,s} = mc_r \left[1 - 1/\varepsilon_{r,s} \right]^{-1}, \tag{16}$$

where $\varepsilon_{r,s}$ is the perceived price elasticity of demand for the firm's output in market segment s, which depends on the firm's perception of rivals' responses to changes in its own supply behaviour.

---

[3]   See Figure 4 in the foregoing chapter for a graphical representation.

2.2.1.1.1 Bertrand Oligopoly with Market Segmentation

Each firm conjectures that domestic and foreign rivals keep their supply prices in market s fixed when it varies its own price p* in market s. In this case

$$\varepsilon_{r,s} = -\frac{\hat{x}_{r,s}^{*}}{\hat{p}_{r,s}^{*}} = \sigma + (\Omega - \sigma)s_{r,s}, \quad s_{r,s} := \delta^{\sigma}(p_{r,s}/PA_s)^{1-\sigma} \tag{17}$$

where $s_{r,s} = p_{r,s}x_{r,s}/(PA_sA_s)$ is the market share of a *single firm* of origin r in market s.

2.2.1.1.2 Conjectural Price Variations with Market Segmentation

A generalisation of the Bertrand set-up can be developed by assuming that the firm under consideration conjectures that rivals respond to changes in its own price by a certain non-zero price reaction. Let v denote the constant conjectural elasticity of rivals' prices with respect to a change in p*, i.e.

$$\hat{p}_{j,s} = v\,\hat{p}_{r,s}*. \tag{18}$$

If the conjectural price response elasticity is the same for rivals from all regions competing in market s, the perceived elasticity becomes

$$\varepsilon_{r,s} = -\frac{\partial x_{r,s}^{*}}{\partial p_{r,s}^{*}} = \sigma + (\Omega - \sigma)(v + s_{r,s}(1-v)). \tag{19}$$

In the special case v=1, where any price change is fully matched by rivals, the perceived elasticity becomes Ω and unless $\Omega > 1$, a mark-up pricing equilibrium does not exist.

If the firm holds non-zero conjectural price variations only with regard to domestic rivals, we have

$$\varepsilon_{r,s} = \sigma + (\Omega - \sigma)(S_{r,s}v + s_{r,s}(1-v)). \tag{19'}$$

2.2.1.1.3 Cournot Oligopoly with Market Segmentation

Each firm conjectures that domestic and foreign rivals keep their supply quantities to market s fixed when it varies its own quantity x* in market s. To derive the perceived elasticity for this case, rewrite (15) with (5) in the inverse form

$$p_{r,s} = \delta\left[\frac{A_s}{x_{r,s}}\right]^{1/\sigma}\left[\frac{b}{A_s}\right]^{1/\Omega}.$$

Log-differentiation with respect to $x_{r,s}$* – taking into account that the Cournot conjecture entails the perception $\hat{A}_s / \hat{x}^*_{r,s} = s_{r,s}$ - yields

$$\varepsilon_{r,s} = \frac{\sigma\Omega}{(\sigma-\Omega)s_{r,s}+\Omega} \Leftrightarrow \frac{1}{\varepsilon_{r,s}} = \frac{1}{\sigma} - \left(\frac{1}{\sigma} - \frac{1}{\Omega}\right)s_{r,s} . \tag{20}$$

The same result can be obtained without prior inversion of the demand curves by taking consistent account of the conjectural rival price reactions implied by the Cournot assumption: For the firm under consideration, we have

$$\frac{\hat{x}^*_{r,s}}{\hat{p}^*_{r,s}} = -\sigma + (\sigma - \Omega)\frac{P\hat{A}_s}{\hat{p}^*_{r,s}} . \tag{21}$$

For rival firms from region j, the Cournot conjecture entails

$$\hat{x}_{j,s} = 0 = -\sigma\hat{p}_{j,s} + (\sigma - \Omega)P\hat{A}_s \Rightarrow \hat{p}_{j,s} = \frac{\sigma - \Omega}{\sigma} P\hat{A}_s . \tag{22}$$

Now

$$P\hat{A}_s = \sum_{j=1}^{R}\sum_{v=1}^{n_j} s_{j,s}\hat{p}_{v,j,s} = \sum_{j=1}^{R} n_j s_{j,s}\hat{p}_{j,s} + s_{r,s}(\hat{p}^*_{r,s} - \hat{p}_{r,s}) . \tag{23}$$

Using (22) in (23), we get

$$\frac{P\hat{A}_s}{\hat{p}^*_{r,s}} = \frac{\sigma s_{r,s}}{\Omega + s_{r,s}(\sigma - \Omega)} . \tag{24}$$

Using (24) in (21), we end up with (20), q.e.d.

For the case $\Omega=1$, the Cournot elasticity formula (20) has previously been derived in the existing literature by Norman (1990), Haaland and Wooton (1991), and Willenbockel (1994).

2.2.1.1.4 *Conjectural Output Variations with Market Segmentation*

A generalisation of the pure Cournot model can be obtained by assuming that the firm conjectures that domestic and foreign rivals' supply quantities to any market segment respond to changes in its own supply quantities according to

$$\hat{x}_{j,s} = v\hat{x}^*_{r,s} . \tag{25}$$

Given that the conjectural elasticity of rivals' quantities with respect to changes in own quantity, v, is assumed to be identical across rivals from all regions competing in destination s, we have $\hat{A}_s / \hat{x}^*_{r,s} = v + (1-v)s_{r,s}$. Using this result while proceeding analogous to the derivation of (20), one finds

$$\frac{1}{\varepsilon_{r,s}} = \frac{1}{\sigma} - \left(\frac{1}{\sigma} - \frac{1}{\Omega}\right)(v + (1-v)s_{r,s}), \tag{26}$$

which by construction encompasses (20) for $v=0$.

2.2.1.2   Market Integration

In the extreme case where all regions are integrated, regional price discrimination is ruled out since international arbitrage enforces the law of one price globally. Each firm resident in region r sets a single global supply price (or global supply quantity) according to the single first-order condition

$$p_r = mc_r\left[1 - 1/\varepsilon_r\right]^{-1}, \tag{27}$$

where ε_r is the perceived elasticity of the global firm-specific demand function

$$x_r = \sum_{s=1}^{R} x_{r,s}(.). \tag{28}$$

2.2.1.2.1   Bertrand Oligopoly with Market Integration

With Bertrand conjectures about rivals' responses, the perceived demand elasticity is simply the output-weighted average of the perceived Bertrand elasticities in the various destination markets as given by (17) above, i.e.

$$\varepsilon_r = -\frac{\hat{x}^*_r}{\hat{p}^*_r} = \sum_{s=1}^{R} w_{r,s}\varepsilon_{r,s} = \sigma + (\Omega - \sigma)\sum_{s=1}^{R} w_{r,s}s_{r,s} \quad, \quad w_{k,i} \equiv \frac{x_{k,i}}{x_k}, \tag{29}$$

provided that σ and Ω are identical across all destination regions.

2.2.1.2.2   Conjectural Price Variations with Market Integration

Similarly, with conjectural price variations as given by (18), the perceived demand elasticity is a weighted average of the destination-specific elasticities (19) or (19')

2.2.1.2.3   International Cournot Oligopoly with Market Integration

The model-consistent derivation of the perceived elasticity for this case is again a slightly more cumbersome task. The Cournot conjecture is now that domestic and foreign rivals keep their world-wide supply quantities fixed when the firm from region k under consideration varies its supply quantity. Since the rival price responses implied by the Cournot conjecture must now be determined simultaneously, some resort to matrix algebra is required in order to characterise the perceived elasticity in explicit form. In the following, bold-face symbols are used to indicate vectors or matrices of the corresponding scalar variables by region, and R is the number of regions.

For the firm in question we have

$$\hat{x}_r^* = -\sigma \hat{p}_r^* + (\sigma - \Omega)\mathbf{w_r}\mathbf{P\hat{A}}, \tag{30}$$

where $\mathbf{w_r} := [w_{r,1}, \ldots, w_{r,R}]$ is a $(1,R)$ row vector of quantity weights as defined above and $\mathbf{P\hat{A}}$ is the $(R,1)$ vector of top-level price index changes by region implied by the Cournot conjecture. For rivals the Cournot conjecture entails

$$\hat{x} = 0 = -\sigma \hat{\mathbf{p}} + (\sigma - \Omega)\mathbf{W}\,\mathbf{P\hat{A}} \;\Rightarrow\; \hat{\mathbf{p}} = \frac{\sigma - \Omega}{\sigma}\mathbf{W}\,\mathbf{P\hat{A}}, \tag{31}$$

where $\hat{\mathbf{p}}$ denotes the $(R,1)$ vector of rivals' price responses that would be required to keep their sales constant when the firm under consideration varies its output and price, and $\mathbf{W}=[\mathbf{w_1}', \ldots, \mathbf{w_R}']'$ is the (R,R) matrix of quantity weights for firms from all regions. Recalling that $s_{j,i}$ denotes the market share of a single firm/variety from region j in market i, the relation between conjectured Cournot-equivalent price and the top-level price index reactions as perceived by our representative firm in region r can be written as

$$P\hat{A}_i = \sum_{j=1}^{m} s_{j,i} n_j \hat{p}_j + s_{r,i}(\hat{p}_r^* - \hat{p}_r), \tag{32}$$

or in matrix notation, defining $\mathbf{S} = [S_{i,j}]= [s_{i,j}n_i]$ and $\mathbf{s_r} = [s_{r,1},\ldots, s_{r,m}]'$,

$$\mathbf{P\hat{A}} = \mathbf{S'\hat{p}} + \mathbf{s_r}(\hat{p}_r^* - \hat{p}_r). \tag{33}$$

From (31) we know that the Cournot-equivalent price reaction of *domestic* (i.e. region r) rivals is

$$\hat{p}_r = \frac{\sigma - \Omega}{\sigma}\mathbf{w_r}\,\mathbf{P\hat{A}}. \tag{34}$$

Using (31) and (34) in (33), we find

$$\mathbf{P\hat{A}} = \left[\mathbf{I} - \frac{\sigma - \Omega}{\sigma}(\mathbf{S'W} - \mathbf{s_r}\mathbf{w_r})\right]^{-1} \mathbf{s_r}\hat{p}_r^*. \tag{35}$$

Finally, inserting (35) in (30), we find that the perceived Cournot elasticity for our individual firm from region r takes the unappealing form

$$\varepsilon_r = \sigma - (\sigma - \Omega)\mathbf{w_r}\left[\mathbf{I} - \frac{\sigma - \Omega}{\sigma}(\mathbf{S'W} - \mathbf{s_r w_r})\right]^{-1}\mathbf{s_r}. \tag{36}$$

Existing studies simulating a Cournot scenario with market integration along these lines include Smith and Venables (1988), Haaland and Norman (1992) and Willenbockel (1994).

2.2.1.2.4 Domestic Cournot Oligopoly with Market Integration

Is the derivation of a Cournot elasticity less burdensome, if we assume in analogy to Section 2.1.1 above that the firm holds the Cournot conjecture only with respect to domestic rivals and neglects foreign rivals altogether? The answer is 'not really', since with product differentiation across domestic firms one still has to take account of the perceived domestic rivals' price reactions implied by the Cournot assumption:

In this case (31) is replaced by

$$\hat{x}_r = 0 = -\sigma\hat{p}_r + (\sigma - \Omega)\mathbf{w_r P\hat{A}} \Rightarrow \hat{p}_r = \frac{\sigma - \Omega}{\sigma}\mathbf{w_r P\hat{A}}, \tag{31'}$$

(32) simplifies to

$$P\hat{A}_i = S_{r,i}\hat{p}_r + s_{r,i}(\hat{p}_r{}^* - \hat{p}_r), \tag{32'}$$

and thus

$$\mathbf{P\hat{A}} = (\mathbf{S_r} - \mathbf{s_r})\hat{p}_r + \mathbf{s_r}\hat{p}_r{}^*. \tag{33'}$$

Using (31') with (33') in (30), we end up with

$$\varepsilon_r = \sigma - (\sigma - \Omega)\mathbf{w_r}\left[\mathbf{I} - \frac{\sigma - \Omega}{\sigma}(\mathbf{S_r} - \mathbf{s_r})\mathbf{w_r}\right]^{-1}\mathbf{s_r}. \tag{36'}$$

2.2.2   The ADS Case

This section shows how the perceived demand elasticities for the various oligopoly models considered in Section 2.2.1 have to be modified for the case $\sigma \neq \sigma_A \neq \sigma_M$ – i.e. we consider the deep demand nesting hierarchy given by (1) with (2) and

(14). In this case, the demand functions for an individual firm-specific variety produced in region r take the forms

$$x_{r,r} = \left(\frac{P_{r,r}}{p_{r,r}}\right)^{\sigma} D_r(.) \quad , \quad x_{r,s} = \left(\frac{P_{r,s}}{p_{r,s}}\right)^{\sigma} M_{r,s}(.) \, , \, s \neq r \, , \tag{37}$$

where $P_{r,r}$ and $P_{r,s}$ are the price indices over varieties of origin r dual to D_r and $M_{r,s}$ respectively and the functional forms for $D_r(.)$ and $M_{r,s}(.)$ are given by (3) and (4).

2.2.2.1   Market Segmentation

2.2.2.1.1   Bertrand Oligopoly with Market Segmentation

In this case, the perceived elasticities for an individual firm located in region r determining the price mark-ups via (16) take the form

$$\varepsilon_{r,r} = \sigma - (\sigma - \sigma_A)/n_r - (\sigma_A - \Omega)s_{r,r} \tag{38}$$

for its home market and

$$\varepsilon_{r,s} = \sigma - (\sigma - \sigma_M)/n_r - (\sigma_M - \sigma_A)SM_{r,s}/n_r - (\sigma_A - \Omega)s_{r,s} \tag{39}$$

for its export markets.

2.2.2.1.2   Conjectural Price Variations with Market Segmentation

With uniform conjectural price variations of the form (18) for both domestic and foreign rivals, it is straightforward to show that the perceived elasticities become

$$\varepsilon_{r,r} = \sigma - (\sigma - \sigma_A)(v + (1-v)/n_r) - (\sigma_A - \Omega)(v + (1-v)s_{r,r} \tag{40}$$

and

$$\begin{aligned}\varepsilon_{r,s} = \sigma - (\sigma - \sigma_M)(v + (1-v)/n_r) - (\sigma_M - \sigma_A)(v + (1-v)SM_{r,s}/n_r) \\ - (\sigma_A - \Omega)(v + (1-v)s_{r,s})\end{aligned} \tag{41}$$

If our firm holds non-zero conjectural price variations only with regard to domestic rivals as in Delorme and van der Mensbrugghe (1990), we have instead

$$\varepsilon_{r,r} = \sigma - (\sigma - \sigma_A)(v + (1-v)/n_r) - (\sigma_A - \Omega)(S_{r,r}v + (1-v)s_{r,r}) \tag{40'}$$

$$\begin{aligned}\varepsilon_{r,s} = \sigma - (\sigma - \sigma_M)(v + (1-v)/n_r) - (\sigma_M - \sigma_A)(SM_{r,s}v + (1-v)SM_{r,s}/n_r) \\ - (\sigma_A - \Omega)(S_{r,s}v + (1-v)s_{r,s})\end{aligned} \tag{41'}$$

2.2.2.1.3 Cournot Oligopoly with Market Segmentation

When the individual firm from region r conjectures that both domestic and foreign rivals' supply quantities to home market r and export markets s do not respond to changes in its own supply quantities, we have

$$\frac{1}{\varepsilon_{r,r}} = \frac{1}{\sigma} - \left(\frac{1}{\sigma} - \frac{1}{\sigma_A}\right)\frac{1}{n_r} - \left(\frac{1}{\sigma_A} - \frac{1}{\Omega}\right)s_{r,r} \tag{42}$$

and

$$\frac{1}{\varepsilon_{r,s}} = \frac{1}{\sigma} - \left(\frac{1}{\sigma} - \frac{1}{\sigma_M}\right)\frac{1}{n_r} - \left(\frac{1}{\sigma_M} - \frac{1}{\sigma_A}\right)\frac{SM_{r,s}}{n_r} - \left(\frac{1}{\sigma_A} - \frac{1}{\Omega}\right)s_{r,s}. \tag{43}$$

Since this is the specification alternative actually employed for the large-scale model simulations in this volume, we spell out the derivation of (42) in detail: Inverting the demand function (34) using (3) and (5) yields

$$p_{r,r} = \left[\frac{D_r}{x_{r,r}}\right]^{1/\sigma} P_{r,r} \quad \text{with} \quad P_{r,r} = \delta\left[\frac{A}{D_r}\right]^{1/\sigma_A} PA_r \quad \text{and} \quad PA_r = \left[\frac{a}{A_r}\right]^{1/\Omega}$$

Log-differentiation of these expressions with respect to $x_{r,r}^*$ – taking into account that the Cournot conjecture entails the perceptions $\hat{D}_r / \hat{x}_{r,r}^* = 1/n_r$ and $\hat{A}_r / \hat{x}_{r,r}^* = s_{r,r}$ - yields (42). (43) is derived in a similar manner.

(42) is equivalent to Harrison, Rutherford, and Tarr (1996: 346, equation 1) and in the case of a unit value for the conjectural variations parameter equivalent to Harrison, Rutherford, and Tarr (1997: 1420, equation 2). Compare also Willenbockel (1994), Capros et al. (1998), and Burniaux and Waelbroeck (1992) for similar efforts to derive Cournot-type perceived elasticity expressions for the ADS case.

2.2.2.1.4 Conjectural Output Variations with Market Segmentation

If one assumes, in analogy to case 2.2.1.1.4 above, that the firm holds conjectural output variations of the form (25), the mark-up rates are determined by

$$\frac{1}{\varepsilon_{r,r}} = \frac{1}{\sigma} - \left(\frac{1}{\sigma} - \frac{1}{\sigma_A}\right)\left(v + (1-v)/n_r\right) - \left(\frac{1}{\sigma_A} - \frac{1}{\Omega}\right)\left(v + (1-v)s_{r,r}\right) \tag{44}$$

and

$$\frac{1}{\varepsilon_{r,s}} = \frac{1}{\sigma} - \left(\frac{1}{\sigma} - \frac{1}{\sigma_M}\right)(v + (1-v)/n_r) - \left(\frac{1}{\sigma_M} - \frac{1}{\sigma_A}\right)(v + (1-v)\frac{SM_{r,s}}{n_r})$$
$$- \left(\frac{1}{\sigma_A} - \frac{1}{\Omega}\right)(v + (1-v)s_{r,s})$$

(45)

Harrison, Rutherford, and Tarr (1997:1492) incorporate conjectural output variations in a slightly more pragmatic manner, namely by simply multiplying the ordinary Cournot elasticities (42) and (43) with some fixed conjectural variations
parameter. If that parameter is literally meant to represent rivals' given uniform
conjectured output variation, this specification would be incorrect as elaborated by
de Santis (1999) at some length. Equations (44) and (45) show that when conjectural variations are entered via (25) – i.e. in a form which clearly spells out the
conjectural output response for each rival – the perceived elasticities are nontrivial
functions of the conjectural variation parameters v. However, the specification of
Harrison et al. may reasonably be seen as a pragmatic short cut to capture the
basic fact that if firms expect some sort of non-zero output reaction by rivals 'in
the aggregate', the perceived optimal mark-up differs from the pure Cournot
mark-up.

2.2.2.2   Market Integration

2.2.2.2.1   Bertrand Oligopoly with Market Integration

Analogous to case 2.2.1.2.1, the perceived Bertrand elasticity with integrated
markets is an output-weighted average of the corresponding Bertrand elasticities
(38) and (39) in the various market segments.

2.2.2.2.2   Conjectural Price Variations with Market Integration

The perceived elasticity is an output-weighted average of the elasticities (40),
(41).

2.2.2.2.3   International Cournot Oligopoly with Market Integration

The derivation of the perceived elasticity for this case is a particularly joyless task.
Proceeding along the lines of Section 2.2.1.2.3, it is possible if tedious to find a
closed-form matrix-algebraic expression for ϵ, yet the resulting formula is un-
wieldy and lacks intuitive appeal. Moreover, for programming purposes in
GAMS, it is more convenient to proceed in analogy to the product homogeneity
case in Section 2.1.2 above and determine the perceived demand elasticity for a
representative firm from region r as solution to the following linear R+1 equation
system in the unknowns ϵ_r and $vp_d = d\ln p_d/d\ln p_r{}^*$:

$$\varepsilon_r = \sigma - [\sigma - (\sigma_A - \sigma_M)w_{r,r} - \sigma_M]VP_r^r + (\sigma_A - \sigma_M)\sum_{d \neq r} w_{r,d}VPM_d^r$$

$$+ (\Omega - \sigma_A)\sum_d w_{r,d}VPA_d^r \qquad , \qquad (46)$$

$$0 = \sigma vp_s^r - [\sigma - (\sigma_A - \sigma_M)w_{s,s} - \sigma_M]VP_s^r + (\sigma_A - \sigma_M)\sum_{d \neq s} w_{s,d}VPM_d^r$$

$$+ (\Omega - \sigma_A)\sum_d w_{s,d}VPA_d^r \quad \forall s \in \{1,...,R\} , \qquad (47)$$

where

$$VP_d^r = \begin{cases} vp_d^r \text{ for } d \neq r \\ vp_r^r + (1 - vp_r^r)/n_r \text{ for } d = r \end{cases}$$

and the perceived Cournot-equivalent price index elasticities VPM and VPA are defined by (9) in Section 2.1.2. (47) represents the Cournot conjecture that domestic and foreign rivals keep their world-wide supply quantities fixed, when the firm from region r under consideration perturbs its supply quantity. The auxiliary variables v_d^r are the perceived Cournot-equivalent elasticities of rival prices with respect to p_r.

2.2.3   Large Group Monopolistic Competition

In all the cases considered in Section 2.2, the numerical value of the perceived elasticity converges towards $\epsilon = \sigma$ with a rising number of firms – i.e. in the limit all the cases considered in Section 2.2 converge to a Chamberlinian large-group monopolistic competition set-up with fixed mark-ups.

3   The Multi-Region General Equilibrium Framework

3.1   The Generic Prototype Model

In order to illustrate the comparative-static behaviour of the various specification alternatives and to assess the structural sensitivity of simulation results generated by the large-scale models in this volume to the specification of firm conduct, all models of imperfect competition considered in the previous section are embedded into a stylised low-dimensional general equilibrium world model, calibrated to the same hypothetical benchmark data set and subjected to the same trade policy shock.

The analytical framework distinguishes three regions (A, B, C), two sectors and commodity groups per region (PC, IC), and one primary production factor which is mobile across sectors but immobile across regions. The PC sector is perfectly competitive.

Demand for the top-level Armington commodity baskets (1) are governed by Cobb-Douglas preferences with expenditure shares α, i.e.

$$A_{i,r} = \alpha_{i,r} Y_r / PA_{i,r} \ , \ i \in I = \{PC, IC\} \ , \ r \in C = \{A, B, C\}. \tag{48}$$

Aggregate income is

$$Y_r = w_r L_r + \pi_r + T_r \tag{49}$$

where w is the factor price, L the inelastic factor endowment, π denotes pure profits, and $T_r = \Sigma_{o \neq r} \ p_{i,o,r} \ \tau_{i,o,r} M_{i,o,r}$ represents lump-sum distributions of tariff revenue.

Technologies in the PC sectors are characterised by constant returns to scale and are represented by linear production functions with factor productivity parameter $a_{PC,r}$. The imperfectly competitive sectors exhibit firm-internal globally increasing returns to scale, since a recurrent fixed factor requirement Lf_r is required in each firm before output can be produced according to a linear technology with factor productivity parameter $a_{IC,r}$. The factor market clearing conditions are thus

$$L_r = \frac{X_{PC,r}}{a_{PC,r}} + n_r \left(\frac{x_{IC,r}}{a_{IC,r}} + Lf_r \right) . \tag{50}$$

Profit maximising behaviour in the PC industries entails

$$p_{PC,r} = w_r / a_{PC,r} \tag{51}$$

Price-setting behaviour in IC industries is described by the generic first-order conditions

$$p_{IC,r} = \frac{w_r}{a_{IC,r}[1 - 1/\varepsilon_r(.)]} \tag{52}$$

if markets are internationally integrated, or

$$p_{IC,r,d} = \frac{w_r}{a_{IC,r}[1 - 1/\varepsilon_{r,d}(.)]} \tag{52'}$$

if markets are internationally segmented. The explicit functional forms for $\epsilon(.)$ are contingent on the assumed form of oligopolistic interaction as well as on the assumed demand nesting hierarchy as detailed ad nauseam in Section 2.

In all scenarios considered below we assume free entry or exit of firms in response to the occurrence of pure profits, so that equilibrium firm numbers are endogenously governed by the zero profit conditions

$$\pi_r = [(p_{IC,r} - w_r / a_{IC,r})x_{IC,r} - Lf_r]n_r = 0 \quad \text{or}$$

$$\pi_r = [\sum_d p_{IC,r,d} x_{IC,r,d} - w_r x_{IC,r} / a_{IC,r} - Lf_r]n_r = 0 \ , \ r \in C \qquad (53)$$

No integer constraint is imposed on n as this would in my view constitute a fallacy of misplaced concreteness at all practically feasible industry aggregation levels. Within the model n serves as a concentration index and is reasonably treated as a continuous variable.

3.2   Benchmark Data Set and Calibration

All model versions considered below are calibrated to the following benchmark data set: The matrix of aggregate commodity flows by origin and destination in value terms is given for both commodity groups by:

Origin/Destination	A	B	C
A	80	10	10
B	10	80	10
C	10	80	80

The matrix of sectoral factor allocations (value added) is given by :

Sector/Region	A	B	C
PC	100	100	100
IC	100	100	100

It is assumed that the benchmark equilibrium is a free trade equilibrium, i.e. consumer prices are equal to producer prices.

In all models of firm conduct under consideration, the perceived elasticity formula in conjunction with the given expenditure shares of the benchmark data set and the first-order conditions for a profit maximum establishes a relationship between benchmark equilibrium mark-ups m_0, the initial number of firms n_0, and the elasticities of substitution σ for each IC industry in each region. Unless the conjectural variations approach is adopted, two of these three parameters must be set extraneously while the remaining one has to be calibrated residually.

In principle, three alternative calibration strategies are conceivable, and as a matter of fact examples for each of these can be found in the literature: (i) determine n_0 and m_0 on the basis of extraneous information, e.g. on the basis of extraneous concentration statistics and scale elasticity estimates, and calibrate σ residually (e.g. Gasiorek, Smith and Venables, 1992; Haaland and Norman, 1992; Willenbockel, 1994); (ii) set n_0 and σ extraneously and calibrate m_0 residually (e.g. Brown and Stern, 1989); (iii) Set m_0 and σ and calibrate n_0 residually (e.g. Devarajan and Rodrik, 1991). [4]

We assume that data on the initial model-equivalent number of symmetric firms are available – e.g. computed on the basis of inverse Herfindahl concentration indices from production census data as exemplified in Capros et al. (1998) and Willenbockel (1994) – and given by $(n_a, n_b, n_c) = (10, 5, 20)$. For the models of Section 2.1 and Section 2.2.1, we adopt calibration strategy (ii) and assume that the choice of σ is based on an educated guess which takes into account the existing econometric evidence on trade flow elasticities. The factor productivity parameters a_{IC} and the fixed-cost parameters L_f must then be calibrated residually. This calibration strategy determines the initial potential for unexploited economies of scale as measured by the scale elasticity – that is the percentage increase in total cost associated with a one-percent increase in firm output – residually. The benchmark scale elasticities are here just equal to $1/a$, the benchmark marginal cost, and $a-1$ is the benchmark mark-up rate. For the ADS models of Section 2.2.2, calibration strategy (ii) is adopted for the following illustrative simulations.

4   Structural Sensitivity Analysis

In all simulations considered in this section, the counterfactual trade policy scenario is the introduction of a 20% ad valorem tariff unilaterally imposed by country A on imports of the imperfectly competitive good from all regions.

---

[4]   If the chosen model of firm conduct is the 'true' model and correct information on two of the three parameter sets would be available, the different calibration strategies would of course yield identical results. Willenbockel (2002) explores the potential sensitivity of simulation results to the choice of calibration strategy in the presence of incomplete information.

Starting with the product homogeneity case of Section 2.1, Table 1 reports the welfare effects for all regions measured by the Hicksian equivalent variation as a percentage of benchmark income as well as the effects on selected IC industry variables for the tariff-imposing country. As a yardstick for comparison, consider first the predictions of a corresponding model with price-taking behaviour and constant returns in both sectors.

The tariff raises the consumer price for imports of IC goods faced by residents of A relative to the domestic variety. The protected IC industry of country A expands in response to the increased demand by domestic residents while the PC sector contracts. The intersectoral factor reallocation effects in countries B and C are in the opposite direction. The drop in the demand by A for IC imports moves the terms of trade in favour of country A in order to restore external balance. As is typical for models with an Armington demand system, the terms of trade gain for the tariff-imposing country dominates the efficiency losses due to the domestic price distortion, so that A enjoys a welfare gain at the expense of the rest of the world under both elasticity configurations considered in Table 1.

The basic pattern of trade and intersectoral factor reallocation effects predicted by the perfect competition model carries over to the models with oligopolistic behaviour and increasing returns to scale. In the market integration scenarios, the tariff raises the mark-up for country A's oligopolists, since the perceived elasticity drops due to the rise in the home market share and the rise in the weight of home sales in overall sales according to (8). With barriers to entry, firms located in region A would enjoy pure profits. With free entry, new firms are attracted and equilibrium output per firm shrinks while unit costs rise, i.e. protection leads to inefficient entry a la Horstmann and Markusen (1986). Correspondingly, the predicted welfare gain for A is lower under imperfect competition compared to the perfect competition scenario. The difference in the simulated welfare effect is small for the low Armington elasticity scenario, but becomes more noticeable in the high-elasticity scenario. The calibrated initial mark-ups are lower and therefore the slopes of the average cost curves are less steep with higher σ_A. Thus more pronounced entry effects associated with stronger plant output reductions are required to drive profits back to zero in this case. It is noteworthy that IC industries in B and C experience mark-up increases and reductions in output size per firm with associated unit cost increases as well, as exemplified in Table 2.[5] For firms in B and C the loss of export sales to A is associated with an increase in their own home market share as well as with a higher weight of the low home market elasticity in (8), and thus with a drop in the perceived global elasticity.

In the market segmentation scenarios, the tariff-induced mark-up increase occurs only in the home market, while the export mark-ups drop slightly according to

---

[5]   The detailed effects on regions B and C for the other scenarios in Table 1 follow the same qualitative pattern as given in Table 2 and are therefore not separately reported.

(13). Nevertheless the signs and the orders of magnitude of the industrial organisation effects in A's IC industry are remarkably similar to the corresponding market integration case with the same Armington elasticity configuration.

In the conjectural variations simulations in Table 1, the parameter v in (7'') has been calibrated residually to support an *extraneous* benchmark price mark-up rate of m=25% and m=10%, i.e. to a higher mark-up rate than generated by the pure Cournot models for given σ and n. To support this given mark-up, oligopolistic interaction must be characterised by a certain degree of collusion as reflected in values for v above unity. Since the higher initial mark-ups are associated with considerably higher calibrated fixed costs per firm and a higher scale elasticity in relation to the other specifications, the tariff-induced inefficient entry process has now a far more significant negative effect on country A's welfare than in the pure Cournot scenarios. In the reported high-elasticity scenarios, this inefficient entry effect becomes in fact dominant. As a matter of course, the closer the assumed extraneous value for m in the conjectural variations scenario is set to the mark-up rate generated by the pure Cournot MI model, the smaller are the deviations of the simulated results between both models. The comparison of the conjectural variations scenario with the Cournot scenarios in Table 1 highlights the desirability of using extraneous information on benchmark price-cost margins or cost disadvantage ratios to inform the model specification choice and calibration process. It is thus worth reiterating at this point that the calibration of the large-scale simulation models used in this study draws upon disaggregated empirical estimates of sectoral price mark-up rates, as detailed in Section 2.2.2 of the preceding chapter.

A main general conclusion from Table 1 is that the simulation results are evidently far more sensitive to the choice of values for the elasticities of substitution in demand than to the choice of assumption about firm conduct – at least as long as this latter choice is restricted to Nash equilibrium specifications in which endogenous variations in mark-ups are explicitly based on optimising behaviour.

Tables 3 and 4 report results generated by the pure DS specifications with intra-industry product differentiation of Section 2.2.1. The results reinforce the main conclusions from Table 1. The global distribution of welfare effects and the signs of the industrial organization effects follow the same general pattern as in Table 1. Again all models predict positive entry effects with associated reductions in production run lengths in the tariff-imposing country, while the magnitude of these effects is far more sensitive to the direct or indirect choice of σ than to the choice of oligopoly model. In contrast to the models with intra-industry product homogeneity, the predicted entry effect is not necessarily inefficient, since the increase in product variety has per se a welfare-raising effect. A comparison across the low-elasticity high-markup and the high-elasticity low-mark-up scenarios in Table 3 again demonstrates the necessity to draw upon extraneous empirical information on sectoral price-cost margins, scale elasticities and/or cost disadvantage ratios in the calibration process.

Table 1:   Intra-Industry Product Homogeneity (Percentage Changes).

	EV_A	EV_B	EV_C	$X_{IC,A}$	x_A	n_A	ToT_A	$m_{A,0}$
$\sigma_A=2, \sigma_M=4$								
Perfect Competition	+0.49	-0.35	-0.35	+1.43	-	-	+3.72	-
Domestic Cournot – MI	+0.46	-0.49	-0.39	+1.40	-0.86	+2.28	+3.71	6.9
Domestic Cournot – MS	+0.52	-0.39	-0.36	+1.41	-0.85	+2.28	+3.72	7.9
International Cournot – MI	+0.47	-0.47	-0.38	+1.44	-0.39	+1.83	+3.65	7.1
Conjectural X Variations – MI	*+0.45*	*-0.45*	*-0.45*	*+1.38*	*-0.88*	*+2.28*	*+3.71*	*10.0*
Conjectural X Variations – MI	*+0.38*	*-0.59*	*-0.59*	*+1.30*	*-0.98*	*+2.31*	*+3.69*	*25.0*
$\sigma_A=5, \sigma_M=10$								
Perfect Competition	+0.11	-0.27	-0.27	+5.06	-	-	+3.00	-
Domestic Cournot – MI	-0.01	-0.50	-0.33	+4.86	-6.27	+11.2	+2.99	3.6
Domestic Cournot – MS	-0.01	-0.32	-0.28	+4.68	-8.56	+14.5	+2.96	5.9
International Cournot – MI	+0.06	-0.45	-0.31	+5.05	-1.85	+7.03	+2.99	5.4
Conjectural X Variations – MI	*-0.21*	*-0.58*	*-0.58*	*+4.36*	*-6.69*	*+11.8*	*+3.00*	*10.0*
Conjectural X Variations – MI	*-0.32*	*-0.89*	*-0.89*	*+2.95*	*-5.07*	*+8.45*	*+3.16*	*25.0*

Explanatory Notes: EV: Equivalent variation/Y_0; X: Industry output; x: Output per firm; n: Number of firms; ToT: Terms of trade; m_0: initial mark-up rate. MI: Market integration; MS: Market segmentation

Evidently, the simulated trade policy responses are far more sensitive to the respective parameter selections at the calibration stage than to the prior choice of oligopoly model type within the pure DS range.

In the illustrative conjectural variations simulations in Table 3, the conjectural elasticities v in (19) are calibrated residually to support prior information on *both* m_o and σ. Even if the assumed prior $m_o=0.25$ is significantly different from the initial mark-ups determined residually via calibration strategy (i) in the Nash equilibrium specifications, the conjectural variations models generate quite similar responses to the trade policy shock. Table 4 presents regionally disaggregated results for the Cournot specification with market integration. Again, the sign pattern of the effects on regions B and C is representative for the other specifications under consideration in Table 3.

Table 2:   Domestic Cournot Oligopoly Model with Market Integration; $\sigma_A = 2, \sigma_M = 4$
(Percentage Changes).

Change in	A	B	C
Welfare (EV/Y_0)	+0.46	-0.49	-0.39
Output PC	-1.46	+1.58	+1.49
IC	+1.40	-1.86	-1.56
Output per firm IC	-0.86	-2.15	-1.90
Terms of Trade	+3.71	-1.80	-1.85
Firm Number	+2.28	+0.30	+0.36
Mark-up	+0.86	+2.20	+1.94

Tables 5 and 6 report corresponding simulations for the ADS specification with calibration strategy (ii). Under this specification, the link between elasticities of substitution among firm-specific varieties σ and the price elasticities of trade flows, which are now governed by the Armington elasticities σ_A and σ_M, is broken.

As a consequence, the fact that different assumptions about firm conduct entail substantially different calibrated σ values when initial mark-ups are moderate matters far less for the aggregate welfare results than under a pure DS specification with residual calibration of σ. The high σ values resulting for the Cournot specifications in Table 5 imply that the varieties produced by different IC firms located in the same region are almost perfect substitutes. It is therefore not surprising that in these cases the simulation results are quite similar to the corresponding predictions of the models with intra-industry product homogeneity in Table 1.

Table 3:   Intra-Industry Product Differentiation – Pure DS Models; Calibration Strategy: Residual Calibration of Mark-Ups for Given σ and n (Percentage Changes).

	EV_A	EV_B	EV_C	$X_{IC,A}$	x_A	n_A	ToT_A	$m_{A,0}$
$\sigma=4$								
Bertrand – MS	+1.32	-0.89	-0.92	+2.49	-0.55	+3.05	+7.21	*36*
International Cournot – MS	+1.40	-0.86	-0.90	+2.15	-1.57	+3.79	+7.29	*45*
Bertrand – MI	+1.27	-0.95	-0.93	+2.49	-0.56	+3.07	+7.19	*36*
International Cournot – MI	+1.24	-1.01	-0.93	+2.23	-1.40	+3.69	+7.24	*40*
Domestic Cournot – MI	+1.23	-1.01	-0.93	+1.96	-2.38	+4.44	+7.31	*38*
Monopolistic Competition	+1.27	-0.93	-0.93	+2.64	0.00	+2.64	+7.19	*33*
Conjectural P Variations – MI	*+1.29*	*-0.91*	*-0.93*	*+2.53*	*-0.56*	*+3.10*	*+7.19*	*25*
Perfect Competition	*+0.44*	*-0.40*	*-0.40*	*+4.04*	-	-	*+4.28*	-
$\sigma=10$								
Bertrand – MS	+0.88	-0.69	-0.72	+3.08	-1.40	+4.54	+7.56	*12*
International Cournot – MS	+1.03	-0.68	-0.68	+2.23	-5.91	+8.64	+7.81	*21*
Bertrand – MI	+0.83	-0.74	-0.72	+3.07	-1.43	+4.56	+7.53	*12*
International Cournot – MI	+0.73	-0.87	-0.72	+2.52	-4.70	+7.57	+7.63	*16*
Domestic Cournot – MI	+0.70	-0.85	-0.71	+1.86	-10.2	+13.4	+7.82	*13*
Monopolistic Competition	+0.83	-0.72	-0.72	+3.22	0.00	+3.22	+7.51	*11*
Conjectural P Variations – MI	*+0.75*	*-0.84*	*-0.73*	*+2.91*	*-1.44*	*+4.42*	*+7.52*	*25*
Perfect Competition	*+0.63*	*-0.59*	*-0.59*	*+3.01*	-	-	*+7.06*	*0*

Table 4:   International Cournot DS Model with Market Integration – $\sigma=4$ (Percentage Changes).

Change in	A	B	C
Welfare (EV/Y_0)			
	+1.24	-1.01	-0.93
Output PC	-2.65	+2.11	+2.04
IC	+2.23	-2.60	-2.17
Output per Firm IC	-1.40	-1.55	-0.52
Terms of Trade	+7.24	-3.43	-3.56
Firm Number	+3.69	-1.07	-1.66
Mark-Up	+1.42	+1.57	+0.52

In line with the previous results, all models generate positive entry effects in the IC sector of the tariff-imposing country, yet in contrast to all other simulations, the Bertrand models predict in most cases moderate plant scale increases in the protected industry under the ADS demand system. The reason is that here the pro-competitive effect of new firm entry on home mark-ups dominates the contra-competitive effect of a higher total home market share $S_{A,A}$ in (38), so that the equilibrium mark-up drops and output per firm increases. Nevertheless, the aggregate welfare effects are again far more sensitive to variations in the Armington elasticity configuration and benchmark mark-ups than to the choice of oligopoly model.

Table 5:   Intra-Industry Product Differentiation: ADS Models (Percentage Changes).

	EV_A	EV_B	EV_C	$X_{IC,A}$	x_A	n_A	ToT_A	σ
σ_A=2, σ_M=4, m_A =8.1%								
Bertrand – MS	+0.54	-0.41	-0.41	+1.50	+0.11	+1.39	+3.80	14.76
International Cournot – MS*	+0.53	-0.39	-0.37	+1.45	-0.39	+1.58	+3.75	171.1
Bertrand – MI	+0.54	-0.41	-0.41	+1.50	+0.11	+1.38	+3.80	14.72
International Cournot – MI	+0.46	-0.48	-0.40	+1.31	-2.06	+3.44	+3.75	32.34
Domestic Cournot – MI	+0.47	-0.49	-0.39	+1.41	-0.82	+2.25	+3.72	92.86
Monopolistic Competition	+0.54	-0.41	-0.41	+1.50	0.00	+1.50	+3.82	13.4
Perfect Competition	+0.49	-0.35	-0.35	+1.43	-	-	+3.72	-
σ_A=5, σ_M=10, m_A =8.1%								
Bertrand – MS	+0.31	-0.38	-0.39	+5.59	+0.15	+5.44	+3.26	14.7
International Cournot – MS*	+0.21	-0.33	-0.30	+5.07	-2.51	+7.77	+3.17	92.2
Bertrand – MI	+0.31	-0.40	-0.39	+5.59	+0.14	+5.44	+3.25	14.6
International Cournot – MI	+0.15	-0.49	-0.35	+5.17	-2.41	+7.77	+3.11	28.6
Domestic Cournot – MI	+0.15	-0.53	-0.37	+5.05	-4.51	+10.0	+3.17	22.7
Monopolistic Competition	+0.33	-0.40	-0.40	+5.63	0.00	+5.63	+3.30	13.4
Perfect Competition	+0.11	-0.27	-0.27	+5.06	-	-	+3.00	-

Table 6:   International Cournot DS Model with Market Integration – $\sigma_A=2$, $\sigma_M=4$
(Percentage Changes).

Change in	A	B	C
Welfare (EV/Y_0)	+0.46	-0.48	-0.40
Output PC	-1.47	+1.58	+1.50
IC	+1.31	-1.88	-1.59
Output per Firm IC	-2.06	-2.95	-1.55
Terms of Trade	+3.75	-1.81	-1.88
Firm Number	+3.44	+1.10	-0.04
Mark-Up	+2.10	+3.04	+1.57

5   Concluding Remarks

This chapter has provided a technical synopsis of alternative optimisation-based specifications of non-collusive imperfectly competitive supply behaviour in multi-region applied general equilibrium models and has explored the robustness of trade policy simulation results to the choice of specification within a stylised miniature prototype model.

The main message from the illustrative structural sensitivity analysis in Section 4 may be summarised as follows: The simulated responses to a trade policy shock are far more sensitive to the direct or indirect choices of demand substitution elasticity figures at the calibration stage, than to the prior choice of firm conduct specification at the theoretical model design stage. When the different models of oligopolistic interaction are calibrated to the same substitution elasticity configuration, results remain generally remarkably robust to the choice of model. The practical implication for applied studies allowing for imperfect competition is, that it is more important to give careful consideration to the numerical specification choices at the calibration stage than to conduct structural sensitivity analyses across a wide spectrum of different models of imperfectly competitive conduct.

The analysis of this chapter suggests a reassuring inference with respect to the robustness of the large-scale model analyses of this study, which employ the ADS Cournot specification with market segmentation. The simulation results are neither critically dependent on the particular assumption of quantity rather than price competition among rival firms nor on the assumption of regional price discrimination in imperfectly competitive sectors.

References

Böhringer, C., H. Welsch and A. Löschel (2001), Environmental Taxation and Structural Change in an Open Economy: A CGE Analysis with Imperfect Competition and Free Entry, *ZEW Discussion Paper* No. 01-07, Mannheim.

Brown, D.K. and R.M. Stern (1989), U.S.-Canada Bilateral Tariff Elimination: The Role of Product Differentiation and Market Structure, in: Feenstra, R.C. (Ed.) *Trade Policies for International Competitiveness,* Chicago, 217-53.

Burniaux, J.M. and J. Waelbroeck (1992), Preliminary Results of Two Experimental Models of General Equilibrium with Imperfect Competition, *Journal of Policy Modeling* 14, 65-92.

Capros, P., T. Georgakopoulos, D. van Regemorter, and D. Willenbockel (1998), Aggregate Results of the Single Market Programme, in: European Commission (Ed.), *The Single Market Review* VI:5, Luxembourg/London.

Delorme, F. and D. van der Mensbrugghe (1990), *Assessing the Role of Scale Economies and Imperfect Competition in the Context of Agricultural Trade Liberalisation: A Canadian Case Study,* OECD Economic Studies, Vol. 13, 205-36.

Devarajan, S and D. Rodrik (1991), Pro-Competitive Effects of Trade Reform: Results from a CGE Model of Cameroon, *European Economic Review* 35, 1157-84.

Dixit, A.K. and J.E. Stiglitz (1977), Monopolistic Competition and Optimum Product Diversity, *American Economic Review* 67, 297-308.

Dixit, A. (1987), Tariffs and Subsidies Under Oligopoly: The Case of the US Automobile Industry, in: Kierzkowski, H. (Ed.), *Protection and Competition in International Trade: Essays in Honour of W.M. Corden,* Oxford, 112-27.

Dixit, A. (1987), Optimal Trade Policies for the US Automobile Industry, in: Feenstra, R.C. (Ed.), *Empirical Methods for International Trade,* Cambridge, MA, 141-65.

Francois, J.F. and D.W. Roland-Holst (1997), Scale Economies and Imperfect Competition, in: Francois, J.F. and K.A. Reinert (Eds.) *Applied Methods for Trade Policy Analysis: A Handbook,* New York, 331-63.

Gasiorek, M., A. Smith, A.J. Venables (1991), Completing the Internal Market in the EC: Factor Demand and Comparative Advantage, in: Winters, L.A. and A.J. Venables (Eds.), *European Integration: Trade and Industry,* Cambridge.

Gasiorek, M., A. Smith, A.J. Venables (1992), '1992': Trade and Welfare – A General Equilibrium Model, *CEPR Discussion Paper* No.672, London. Reprinted in: Winters, L.A. (Ed.), *Trade Flows and Trade Policy After '1992',* Cambridge, 35-66.

Haaland, J.I. and I. Wooton (1991), Market Integration, Competition and Welfare, *CEPR Discussion Paper* No.574, London. Reprinted in: Winters, L.A. (Ed.), *Trade Flows and Trade Policy After '1992',* Cambridge, 125-49.

Haaland, J.I. and V.D. Norman (1992), Global Production Effects of European Integration, *CEPR Discussion Paper* No.669, London. Reprinted in: Winters, L.A. (Ed.), *Trade Flows and Trade Policy After '1992',* Cambridge, 67-91.

Harrison, G.W., T.F. Rutherford, and D.G. Tarr (1996), Increased Competition and Completion of the Market in the European Union: Static and Steady-State Effects, *Journal of Economic Integration* 11, 332-65.

Harrison, G.W., T.F. Rutherford, and D.G. Tarr (1997), Quantifying the Uruguay Round, *Economic Journal* 107, 1405-30.

Helpman, E. and P.R. Krugman (1989), *Trade Policy and Market Structure*, Cambridge, MA.

Hertel, T.W. and M.E. Tsigas (1997), Structure of GTAP, in: Hertel, T.W. (Ed.), *Global Trade Analysis: Modeling and Applications*, Cambridge, 13-73.

Horstmann, I.J. and J.R. Markusen (1986), Up the Average Cost Curve: Inefficient Entry and the New Protectionism, *Journal of International Economics* 20, 225-47.

Krugman, P.R. (1979), Increasing Returns, Monopolistic Competition, and International Trade, *Journal of International Economics* 9, 469-79.

Krugman, P. (1980), Scale Economies, Product Differentiation, and the Pattern of Trade, *American Economic Review* 70, 950-9.

Marisliani, L., M. Rauscher and C. Withagen (Eds.) (2003), *Environmental Policy in an International Perspective*, Dordrecht, 219-245.

Norman, V.D. (1990), Assessing Trade and Welfare Effects of Trade Liberalization: A Comparison of Alternative Approaches to CGE Modelling with Imperfect Competition, *European Economic Review* 34, 725-51.

de Santis, R.A. (1999), Comments on the Harrison-Rutherford-Tarr CGE Model with Imperfect Competition and Increasing Returns to Scale, *Kiel Working Paper* No. 907, Kiel.

Smith, A. and A.J. Venables (1988), Completing the Internal Market in the European Community: Some Industry Simulations, *European Economic Review* 32, 1501-25.

Venables, A.J. and A. Smith (1986), Trade and Industrial Policy Under Imperfect Competition, *Economic Policy* 3, 621-72.

Willenbockel, D. (1994), *Applied General Equilibrium Modelling: Imperfect Competition and European Integration*, Chichester.

Willenbockel, D. (2002), *Specification Choice and Robustness in CGE Trade Policy Analysis with Imperfect Competition*, Middlesex University Business School Economics Discussion Paper No.105, London.

Willenbockel, D. (2003), The Numeraire Problem in General Equilibrium Models with Market Power: Much Ado About Nothing?, in: Bayar, A. and A. Dramais (Eds.) *Proceedings International Conference on Policy Modeling – ECOMOD 2003*, Brussels.

Risk and Transaction Costs

Frauke Eckermann and Marcus Stronzik

Centre for European Economic Research, P.O. Box 103443, 68034 Mannheim, Germany
frauke.eckermann@ruhr-uni-bochum.de, stronzik@zew.de

Alistair Hunt and Tim Taylor

Metroeconomica Limited, 108 Bloomfield Road, Bath BA2 2AR, United Kingdom
ecsasph@bath.ac.uk, ecstjt@bath.ac.uk

1 Introduction

Within the framework of the Kyoto Protocol the industrialised countries committed themselves to a reduction of their greenhouse gas emissions during the period from 2008 to 2012. The flexible mechanisms defined within the Kyoto Protocol are designed to achieve cost-effectiveness of emissions reduction by allowing countries to reduce emissions abroad, either in other Annex B countries, or in non Annex B countries. However, in determining the split of reduction measures between abroad and at home, transaction cost and risk elements that might be associated with the operation of these instruments are not usually taken into account. This paper evaluates the importance of transaction costs and risk premia with respect to the flexibility mechanisms of the Kyoto Protocol. It examines their effect on the up-take of these policy instruments and provides information on how to reduce these cost elements.

This paper is organised as follows: Section 2 provides a generic classification of various types of transaction costs. Section 3 presents estimates of transaction costs associated with the flexible mechanisms, and Section 4 those of project risk premia. Section 5 summarises and concludes.

2   The Nature of Transaction Costs

Transaction costs are those costs that arise from initiating and completing transactions, such as finding partners, holding negotiations, consulting with lawyers or other experts, monitoring agreements, etc. (Coase, 1937). Thus, simply being the costs that arise from the transfer of any property right, they occur to some degree in all market transactions. This feature of exchange therefore also applies to the so-called 'flexibility mechanisms' of the Kyoto Protocol (as they provide 'geographical flexibility' to Parties in fulfilling their commitments). These encompass Joint Implementation (JI) of projects among industrialised countries, Joint Implementation between industrialised and developing countries within the multilateral framework of the Clean Development Mechanism (CDM) and the establishment of a scheme for International Emissions Trading amongst industrialised countries (IET).

The most obvious impact of transaction costs is that they raise the costs for the participants of the transaction and therefore lower the trading volume or even discourage some transactions from occurring. The efficiency gains from the use of market based policy instruments are therefore constrained. Some empirical evidence is provided by Hahn and Hester (1989) for the emission trading programme of the 1977 Amendments of the U.S. Clean Air Act, where the trading scheme has failed to achieve its expected economic benefits due to high transaction costs. Coase (1960) argues that the transaction costs of implementation, enforcement, etc. should determine at the outset how pollution is controlled. In most policy simulations that provide magnitudes of efficiency gains from flexibility mechanisms, however, administrative or transaction costs are not taken into account (cf. for example Böhringer and Löschel, 2001 or Klepper and Peterson, 2002).

In this paper transaction costs refer to the costs associated with the process of obtaining JI or CDM recognition for a project and obtaining the resulting emission credits (OECD, 2001). Similarly for IET, transaction costs include the costs of obtaining emission credits. Table 1 below defines disaggregated cost components, which further sub-divide transaction costs into categories that parallel – in the case of JI and CDM projects – the project cycle. If a host country is out of compliance with certain eligibility requirements (Article 5 and 7 of the Kyoto Protocol), JI has to follow more or less the CDM project cycle, the so-called second track, which is considered in this paper. If a host country can demonstrate compliance with its inventory and reporting requirements and registries, the regulatory intensity is lowered.

Table 1:   Definition of Transaction Cost Components in the Kyoto Protocol Flexibility Mechanisms.

Transaction Cost Components	Description
Project Based (JI,CDM): Pre-Implementation	
Search Costs	Costs incurred by investors and hosts as they seek out partners for mutually advantageous projects
Negotiation Costs	Include those costs incurred in the preparation of the project design document (i.a. baseline determination and monitoring rules) that also documents assignment and scheduling of benefits over the project time period. It also includes public consultation with key stakeholders
Validation Costs	Review and revision of project design document by operational entity
Approval Costs	Registration and approval by UNFCCC Board and authorisation from host country
Project Based (JI,CDM): Implementation	
Monitoring Costs	Costs needed to ensure that participants are fulfilling their obligations
Verification Costs	Annual verification by the UNFCCC Executive Board/ Supervisory Committee
Certification Costs	Including issue of Certified Emission Reductions (CERs for CDM) and issue of Emission Reduction Units (ERUs for JI) by UNFCCC Executive Board
Enforcement Costs	Include costs of administrative and legal measures incurred in the event of departure from the agreed transaction
International Emissions Trading (IET)	
Search Costs	Same as project based; to include e.g. market brokerage fees
Negotiating Costs	To include legal and insurance fees associated with participation in the market
Monitoring Costs	Same as project based; to include annual verification
Certification Costs	Certification and issue of Assigned Amount Units (AAUs) by UNFCCC Executive Board
Enforcement Costs	Include costs of administrative and legal measures incurred in the event of departure from the agreed transaction

Based on: PriceWaterhouseCoopers (2000) and Dudek et al. (1996); concerning JI the Second Track has been considered.

The basic effects of transaction costs are illustrated in Figure 1 for the example of an emission trading scheme. Without transaction costs the trade of emission permits between companies will establish an international permit price that equals marginal abatement costs across companies. The inclusion of transaction costs leads to a left-shift (right-shift) of the supply curve (demand curve) if applied to sellers (buyers). As a consequence the volume of trade decreases and the price rises from P_0 to P_1, indicating that more abatement will be undertaken domestically compared to a situation with no transaction costs.

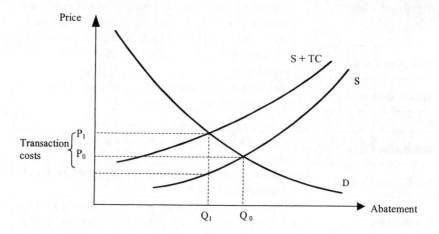

Figure 1:   Inclusion of Transaction Costs.

Particularly in the first stage of the use of the Kyoto Mechanisms, transaction costs are likely to be an essential element in determining the degree of use of the mechanisms and their shares. The level of these costs depends on the rules of the mechanism, the degree of utilisation of the respective mechanism and on the degree of standardisation of procedures. Presumably transaction costs will be higher in countries with an inefficient regulatory framework, leading to a competitive disadvantage vis-à-vis other countries. Whilst the paucity of country level data on transaction costs does not allow us to explore this issue in any depth in our analysis below, it is clearly a priority research area in the effective implementation of the flexibility mechanisms.

3   Estimation of the Transaction Costs Associated with the Flexibility Mechanisms Under the Kyoto Protocol

The great restriction under which this research has been undertaken is that since the Kyoto Protocol has not yet been implemented, the flexibility mechanisms are not formally in existence and so there is presently no real evidence of the magnitude of transaction costs. Evidence therefore has to be based upon:

- the pilot phase of the UNFCCC promoted Activities Implemented Jointly (AIJ) programme;

- the World Bank supported Prototype Carbon Fund;

- hypothetical estimates of cost components that have been constructed; or

- experience from the previous use of similar policy instruments – such as tradeable permit schemes – in other policy contexts.

3.1   World Bank Prototype Carbon Fund (PCF)

The PCF, operated by the World Bank, provides funding to host partners who wish to develop projects consistent with the JI/CDM mechanisms under the Kyoto Protocol. It presently has about 50 projects operating, or in development. One project has formally become a JI project, thereby accumulating emission reduction credits. As a result, it seems reasonable to assume that the transaction costs estimated for PCF projects approximate closely those that will exist under the implementation of JI in the Kyoto Protocol – at least in the first commitment period, 2008-2012.

Table 2:   PCF Range of Pre-Implementation Transaction Cost Components.

Pre-Implementation Phase	Typical Cost (€ 000s)	Low Cost (€ 000s)	High Cost (€ 000s)
Negotiation	290	160	573
Approval	NA	NA	NA
Validation	20	20	35
Sub-Total	310	180	608
10% Contingency	31	18	61
Total: Pre-Implementation	341	198	669

PCF transaction cost estimates are presented in Table 2 to Table 4. Data has been supplied by staff at the PCF, though is not yet published, or in public circulation. We have consequently been requested to make the country and project-specific data supplied more generic. Accordingly, we have not specified the project host country, but instead specified the world region in which the country is located. Table 2 presents the high and low ranges, together with 'typical' or average transaction costs associated with the pre-implementation phase of the project cycle for the PCF projects. The ranges reflect differences that exist in legal and institutional structures, data availability and consultant expenses in different countries.

Sufficient information exists on seven projects allowing us to derive transaction costs per tonne of carbon reduction; these estimates are presented in Table 3 and Table 4. Table 3 shows, for two individual projects hosted by Annex B countries (i.e. where JI projects would be located), the associated transaction costs. Table 4 gives the same information for non-Annex B countries where CDM projects would be located. We assume, therefore, that estimates of transaction costs presented in Table 3 apply to JI-type projects, while those in Table 4 apply to CDM-type projects.

To date, only one project has started and so there is little evidence on implementation costs (e.g. monitoring, verification, etc.). PCF estimates that these costs will total between € 100,000-200,000 (PCF, 2002). As a starting point, we have therefore assumed a mid-point of € 150,000 in our calculations.

The figures reveal a correlation between project size (in terms of carbon reductions) and transaction cost per ton of carbon reduced – as we would expect in the absence of any size-related streamlining. Table 4 allows further sectoral and geographical comparison, excepting the fact that the generic implementation cost is a constraint on drawing firm conclusions. There is no pattern of correlation between the agricultural sector and the electricity sector and their associated transaction costs per tonne of carbon. Indeed, the estimates for the agricultural sector provide the high and low range limits. It is notable that of the small number of projects for which we have data, the agricultural projects account for the largest and smallest total reductions in carbon – supporting the argument that project size dominates sectoral differences. One other pattern that is apparent is that those projects that are based in South America are lower than those in other CDM host regions, though the explanation is not clear from the data available.

Table 3:   JI Country Projects under PCF: Transaction Costs.

Country/ Region	Sector	Ton C Redn.	Proj- ect Life- Time	Ton C Redn. p.a.	Pre-Imple- mentation	Implemen- tation (Estimate)	Total Project TCs	TC/ Ton C
		000s	Yrs	000s	€ (000)	€ (000)	€ (000)	€
CEA	LUM	2880	15	192	220	150	370	0.13
CEA	SER	560	25	22.4	287	150	437	0.78

Table 4:   CDM Country Projects under PCF: Transaction Costs.

Country/ Region	Sector	Ton C Redn.	Proj- ect Life- Time	Ton C Redn. p.a.	Pre-Imple- mentation	Implemen- tation (Estimate)	Total Project TCs	TC/ Ton C
		000s	Yrs	000s	€ (000)	€ (000)	€ (000)	€
N. Afr	ELE	1590	20	80	397	150	547	0.34
CAM	AGR	684	8	86	482	150	632	0.92
S. Am 1	ELE	1081	50	22	150	150	300	0.27
S. Am 2	AGR	3070	21	146	220	150	370	0.12
S. Am 3	ELE	1600	20	80	176	150	326	0.20

Note: Where possible the GTAP nomenclature of countries/regions is used. For entries where country data is confidential, we classify the country according to world region. Thus, CEA = Central European Associates; S. Asia = South Asia; S. Am. = South America; CAM = Central America; N. Afr. = North Africa. There are three South American projects, and these are numbered to distinguish them; LUM = lumber and wood; SER = commercial and public Services; ELE = electricity and heat; AGR = agricultural products.

3.2   UNFCCC Activities Implemented Jointly (AIJ) Projects

The UNFCCC launched a pilot phase of Activities Implemented Jointly (AIJ) in 1995 – prior to the proposed implementation of the Kyoto Protocol – in order to learn more about the possible operation of JI and CDM projects under the Protocol's flexibility mechanisms and build confidence in this approach. The projects that have been implemented under this initiative are therefore thought likely to reflect current UNFCCC thinking on monitoring and other requirements for establishing JI and CDM projects, and the associated transaction costs.

Table 5 presents a selection of the project-based AIJ evidence on transaction costs available to date. Of the 157 AIJ projects proposed and/or initiated by March 2002, 70 have reported some of the above mentioned transaction cost elements whilst 25 projects have transaction costs identifiable for all categories in both the pre-implementation and implementation project phases. The cost categories reported in the Uniform Reporting Forms (URFs) on the UNFCCC website that can be attributed to transaction cost elements include:

- administration costs (for capacity building);

- technical assistance (of consultants until project commissioned);

- reporting (annual reporting to UNFCCC), and;

- follow-up (including monitoring and verification).

Table 5:   AIJ Project Cycle Transaction Costs (Totals and Per Ton Carbon Reduced).

Sector	Region	Lifetime	Ton C Redn. per annum	Total TC (Pre-Impl) '000 Euro	Pre-Impl Tran Cost/ Ton C	Total TC (Impl.) '000 Euro	Impl. Tran Cost/ Ton C	Total TC '000 Euro	Total TC/Ton C
Ele	CEA	10	39	160	410	53	136	213	547
Ser	CEA	10	39	126	322	32	83	158	405
Ele	CEA	10	46	165	356	43	93	208	449
Ele	CEA	6	80	76	158	10	22	87	180
Ele	CEA	10	71	164	232	33	46	197	279
Ele	CEA	10	82	26	31	30	36	55	67
Ele	CEA	10	90	77	85	32	35	109	120
Ele	CEA	10	92	108	118	32	35	140	153
Dwe	CEA	10	97	141	146	62	64	203	210
Dwe	CEA	10	104	129	124	27	26	156	150
Ele	CEA	10	115	155	135	78	67	232	202
Dwe	CEA	10	128	241	189	62	48	303	237
Ele	CEA	10	159	171	107	27	17	198	125
Ele	CEA	10	228	135	59	30	13	165	72
Ele	CEA	10	260	68	26	32	12	100	39
Ele	CEA	10	323	101	31	32	10	133	41
Ele	CEA	10	341	116	34	43	13	159	47
Ele	CEA	10	845	88	10	32	4	120	14
Ele	CEA	10	1119	154	14	30	3	184	16
Ele	CEA	10	1178	154	13	30	3	184	16
Ele	CEA	10	1510	114	8	32	2	147	10
Ele	CEA	10	1916	173	9	53	3	226	12
Ele	CEA	10	2082	35	2	30	1	65	3
Ele	CEA	10	30651	127	0.4	32	0.1	159	0.5
Agr	MEX	30	27994	153	0.2	43	0.1	196	0.2

Note: CEA = Central European Associates; MEX = Mexico; SER = commercial and public services; ELE = electricity and heat; AGR = agricultural products.
Source: UNFCCC (2002), own calculations.

We interpret the administration costs and technical assistance elements as pre-implementation costs, whilst the reporting and follow-up elements are taken to be implementation costs. However, the reporting categories are not transparent in relation to their interpretation as transaction costs. Therefore, in reality, there is likely to be some overlap of costs within these categories between the pre-implementation and implementation project phases. It should also be noted that the vast majority of the projects for which there is data have been undertaken by Sweden, whose implementing agency has presented average annual implementation costs across all projects in the individual project description.

Table 5 shows a wide variation in transaction costs per tonne of carbon reduced. The variation is explained not so much by the differing absolute project transaction costs as by the differing carbon emission reductions associated with each project, i.e. project size. The data has been sorted so that the lowest carbon reducing (smallest) projects are listed at the top, and the largest at the bottom of the table. A strong negative correlation between size of project and transaction cost per ton of carbon reduced is apparent. This reflects the fact that so far little flexibility – in relation to project size – has been granted to monitoring, verification etc., which determine transaction costs. In other words, no streamlining is evident.

3.3   PriceWaterhouseCoopers (PwC)

Estimates of PriceWaterhouseCoopers (2000) are constructed using different assumptions regarding the number of organisations, or 'operating entities' (OEs), that are involved in the activities that give rise to transaction costs over the project cycle. Three elements are identified, namely validation, verification, and certification, that require different OEs if possible conflicts of interests are to be avoided. Three 'levels' of transaction costs are therefore defined.

- Level 1 assumes a single OE (OE1) to undertake all elements of the project cycle.

- Level 2 assumes that OE1 undertakes the validation in the pre-implementation phase, whilst a second OE (OE2) undertakes the verification and certification in the implementation phase.

- Level 3 assumes the same as Level 2 except that the verification is undertaken by OE2 whilst a third OE (OE3) undertakes the certification.

Since the involvement of each additional OE requires that they have a detailed knowledge of the project in order to carry out the prescribed functions, there maybe a trade-off between the achievement of environmental goals of the project and the transaction cost. This is because the additional OE(s) spend time acquainting themselves with the project details, thereby adding to the transaction costs while ensuring (through the avoidance of conflicts of interest) the achievement of the carbon reductions being claimed. These assumptions, made in the year 2000, were primarily based on the Consolidated Text (FCCC/SB/2000/4), and before COP6. The Marrakesh Accords, agreed at COP7 in November 2001, explicitly rule out the possibility of Levels 2 and 3. Therefore, whilst the full range of transaction costs are presented below, we only include those from Level 1 estimates for further conclusions.

The transaction costs for five generic project types are presented in Table 7 to Table 11, based on the following assumptions on the daily rates of OE employees:

- Project developers: range Euro 750-1200; central value Euro 1000;

- Project consultants – local engineers/NGOs in host country: Euro 200;

- International management consultancy in host country: Euro 300;

- International management consultancy in OECD states: Euro 1500.

However, whilst the number of days are separately identified for the pre-implementation and implementation phases in the PwC report, the split between the different day rate categories is not made explicit. Nevertheless, as a first approximation, it is possible – using the split of total days – to apportion the percentage of total transaction costs to the two project phases.

The emissions reduction estimates are obtained by multiplication of energy (per lifetime, i.e. fifteen years for each of the projects) for the new plant (capacity x load factor x 131400 h) with the difference between old and new emissions. Table 6 provides the data for these calculations. Conversion from CO_2 to carbon is achieved through division by 3.65. As a baseline for emissions we chose 800g/kWh for a coal burning power station. PwC suggest a baseline of 944g/kWh for an Indian coal powered energy generator. However, with many power stations having emissions much below 944g/kWh, this baseline appeared to be too high. The figures for the load factor are rough estimates based on IKARUS (KFA, 1994), a comprehensive techno-economic database which has been developed for the German Federal Ministry of Education and Research.

Table 6:   Carbon Reduction for Technologies Considered in PwC (2000).

	G/kWh	Load Factor	Reduction (t/Lifetime)	Reduction (t/a)
Base (400 MW)	800	--	--	--
CCGT (400 MW)	365	0.79	4948560	329904
Retrofit CCGT (")	365	0.79	4948560	329904
Wind (50 MW)	0	0.30	432000	28800
PV (1 MW)	0	0.17	4896	326
PV (100 kW)	0	0.17	490	33

The resulting transaction costs (in Euro 2000 prices) are presented in Table 7 to Table 11 below in absolute terms, and as Euro/ton carbon reduced, for the range of five projects. PwC[1] points out that these results are to be taken as geographically generic in the sense that there is no distinction made between countries or regions where the CDM project would be located, since the data is averaged over a number of country experiences.

---

[1]   Ian Milborrow, PwC, personal communication, April 19, 2001.

Table 7:   Transaction Costs for New 400 MW Combined Cycle Gas Turbine (CCGT) Plant.

CDM Structure	Total TCs (€ 000s)	€/Ton C	Phase 1 TCs (€ 000s)	€/ Ton C	Phase 2 TCs (€ 000s)	€/ Ton C
Level 1	558	0.11	103	0.02	455	0.09
Level 2	675	0.14	103	0.02	582	0.12
Level 3	1057	0.21	103	0.02	986	0.20

Table 8:   Transaction Costs for 400 MW Retrofit Project.

CDM Structure	Total TCs (€ 000s)	€/Ton C	Phase 1 TCs (€ 000s)	€/ Ton C	Phase 2 TCs (€ 000s)	€/ Ton C
Level 1	489	0.10	73	0.02	416	0.08
Level 2	584	0.11	73	0.02	511	0.10
Level 3	897	0.18	73	0.02	824	0.17

Table 9:   Transaction Costs for 15 MW Wind Project.

CDM Structure	Total TCs (€ 000s)	€/Ton C	Phase 1 TCs (€ 000s)	€/ Ton C	Phase 2 TCs (€ 000s)	€/ Ton C
Level 1	392	0.91	61	0.14	331	0.77
Level 2	446	1.03	61	0.14	385	0.89
Level 3	610	1.41	61	0.14	549	1.27

Table 10:   Transaction Costs for 1 MW PV Project.

CDM Structure	Total TCs (€ 000s)	€/Ton C	Phase 1 TCs (€ 000s)	€/ Ton C	Phase 2 TCs (€ 000s)	€/ Ton C
Level 1	387	79.0	57	11.6	330	67.4
Level 2	441	90.1	57	11.6	386	78.8
Level 3	605	123.6	57	11.6	548	111.9

Table 11:   Transaction Costs for 100 kW PV Project.

CDM Structure	Total TCs (€ 000s)	€/Ton C	Phase 1 TCs (€ 000s)	€/ Ton C	Phase 2 TCs (€ 000s)	€/ Ton C
Level 1	387	790	57	116	330	674
Level 2	441	900	57	116	386	788
Level 3	605	1235	57	116	548	1119

The differing absolute transaction cost estimates reflect the fact that the renewable projects (shown in Table 9 to Table 11) with zero emissions require minimal verification effort in the implementation phase (phase 2). The results also confirm the fact, that total transaction costs increase when more OEs are involved in a project. More significant, however, is the fact, that the transaction costs expressed per ton of carbon reduced rise strongly as the size of the project becomes smaller.

Note that these results are for the first year of operation. PwC state that they would expect a learning curve effect in subsequent years such that the verification cost component of the project cycle would be 20% lower in these subsequent years.

Only recently, transaction costs became an issue in the discussion on the Kyoto mechanisms. Simplified modalities and procedures for small-scale CDM projects were adopted at the eighth Conference of the Parties in November 2002, in New Delhi. The elaboration of baselines and monitoring methodologies is currently being undertaken by the Methodologies Panel of the Executive Board.

3.4   EcoSecurities

EcoSecurities (2000) provides estimates of the transaction costs for JI electricity generation projects, assuming that JI requirements will be similar to the CDM project cycle. Transaction cost estimates are applied in net present value calculations for two project types:

- 150 MW gas plant, 20 years lifetime, resulting in reductions of 350000 t CO_2/year;

- 2 MW biomass plant, 20 years lifetime, resulting in reductions of 35000 t CO_2/year.

The data is presented in Table 12 and gives ranges of transaction costs on the basis of 50 similar energy sector projects. The ranges of transaction costs reflect the relative complexity – and therefore resource requirements – that these projects need. EcoSecurities suggest[2], for example, that a wind project is likely to be typical for the lower range of transaction costs whilst a bio-mass CHP or landfill project is more representative for the top end of the range.

The EcoSecurities estimates are country generic and do not differentiate according to size of project, since they argue that a similar amount of time/resources is required for the project cycle activities, regardless of project size. As a consequence, the transaction costs expressed as per ton of carbon reduced are lower, the larger the project (in terms of size of resulting emission reductions). The two above mentioned projects are both medium-sized or large projects with small costs per ton CO_2 reduced.

---

[2]   Paul Soffe, EcoSecurities, personal communication, May 15, 2001.

Jotzo and Michaelowa (2001) propose emission reduction unit (ERU) market price estimates of 1-5 € per t CO_2. This leads to the following transaction cost ranges for the above projects:

Table 12:   JI Transaction Cost Estimates for Gas Plant.

JI Project Cycle	Transaction Cost (€ 000s)		
Pre-Implementation Phase			
Search	12-20		
Negotiation	25-45		
Validation	10- 15		
Approval	10		
Total Pre-Impl. Phase	57-90		
Implementation Phase		*ERU value 1 €/t*	*ERU value 5 €/t*
Monitoring (annual)	3-15		
Certification	5-10% of ERU value		
Gas plant*		17.5-35	87.5-175
Biomass plant*		1.75-3.5	8.75-17.5
Enforcement (annual)	1-3% of ERU value		
Gas plant*		3.5-10.5	17.5-51.5
Biomass plant*		0.35-1.05	1.75 -5.15
Total Implementation Phase (20 years, undiscounted)			
Gas plant*		480-1210	2160-4830
Biomass plant*		102-391	270-753
Total Project Cycle			
Gas plant* (costs per t CO_2)		537-1300 (0.1-0.2€/t)	2217-4920 (0.3-0.7 €/t)
Biomass plant* (costs per t CO_2)		159-481 (0.2-0.7€/t)	327-843 (0.4-1.1 €/t)

* Reductions as quoted above.
Source: EcoSecurities (2000), own calculations.

The calculation shows that the bulk of costs are certification and enforcement costs. However, it is very unlikely that there will be no reduction of costs in later years of a project. In addition, certification costs are expected to decline with the amount of certificates and therefore to be not proportional to the amount of ERUs.

3.5   Comparison of JI/CDM Type Transaction Costs

The analysis above has identified estimates of transaction costs for the JI and CDM project types established under the Kyoto Protocol. The estimates are derived from different sources and reflect different institutional procedures. Consequently, the transaction costs may not be directly comparable. Nevertheless, due to the consistency in the range estimates of the values presented above, we are confident that these will approximate the transaction costs in the first commitment period. It is apparent, in any case, that a number of the current PCF and UNFCCC projects will convert to JI status – as one PCF project already has. The exception to this is the possibility for streamlining CDM – the details for which are still being worked out. This will be discussed separately.

The data is most usefully expressed in terms of transaction costs per ton of carbon reduced. Clearly, if the costs per ton of carbon are too high, this will prohibit an otherwise profitable carbon exchange. As can be seen from the data reported from the above mentioned individual sources, there is a strong correlation between the size of project in terms of carbon reductions, and costs per ton of carbon. This pattern is highlighted in Table 13 and Table 14, which present a categorisation that roughly fits the different data sources for JI and CDM projects respectively. Table 15 presents typical project types for the different project sizes.

Table 13:   Classification of Project Sizes for JI Projects.

Type	Reduction (t/a)	Low (€/ton C)	Central (€/ton C)	High (€/ton C)
Very large	> 50000	0.05	0.1	0.2
Large	5000-50000	0.5	1	2
Medium – upper	500-5000	3	10	15
Medium – lower	50-500	35	100	300
Small	< 50	400	500	600

Table 14:   Classification of Project Sizes for CDM Projects.

Type	Reduction (t/a)	Low (€/ton C)	Central (€/ton C)	High (€/ton C)
Very large	> 50000	0.08	0.2	1
Large	5000-50000	0.25	0.5	2
Medium – upper	500-5000	5	10	15
Medium – lower	50-500	67	100	300
Small	< 50	670	1,000	2000

Table 15:   Correlation of Projects and Project Size.

Type	Typical projects
Very large	Large hydro, gas power plants, large CHP, geothermal, landfill/pipeline methane capture, cement plant efficiency, large-scale afforestation
Large	Wind power, solar thermal, energy efficiency in large industry
Medium – upper	Boiler conversion, DSM, small hydro
Medium – lower	Energy efficiency in housing and SME, mini hydro
Small	PV

Whilst the data for JI and CDM projects are presented separately, the ranges that we have adopted to account for project specification, location, etc., do not allow us to identify significant cost differences between the two instruments. Indeed, communication with the PCF[3] suggests that estimates for both instruments will fall substantially over time as learning effects, combined with increased competition in these markets, bring cost reductions in both the pre-implementation and implementation project phases. The 20% cost reduction in the implementation phase assumed by PwC may therefore be seen as a minimum reduction.

As noted above, the provision of streamlined procedures for small scale CDM projects means that these projects will have significantly lower transaction costs than presented above. The Parties agreed that the following categories of small-scale project activities are eligible under simplified procedures:

- Renewable energy projects with a maximum output capacity of 15 megawatts;

- Energy efficiency improvement projects that reduce energy consumption by up to 15 gigawatt hours per year;

- other project activities that reduce anthropogenic emissions by source, which directly emit less than 15 kilotonnes of CO_2 equivalent annually.

Thus, the medium-low and small categories in Table 14 above can be adjusted to the levels presented in Table 16.

Table 16:   Transaction Costs for Streamlined Small-Scale CDM Projects (PwC).

Type	Reduction (t/a)	Low (€/ton C)	Central (€/ton C)	High (€/ton C)
Medium – lower	50-500	6	9	27
Small	< 50	60	90	180

The estimates presented in Table 16 may, however, differ from those generated when the CDM becomes operational. This is because two further streamlining rules – not anticipated in the PwC analysis – have been recommended. These are:

- the allowance for unilateral projects (where projects are developed, financed and implemented by the host country).

- The bundling of small-scale projects that are similar (so that the international CDM investor only has to deal with the organisation that bundles the projects).

The adoption of these two rules may mean that further reductions in transaction costs than identified in Table 16 may be possible. However, no quantitative estimates exist of such reductions at present.

---

3   Ken Newcombe, PCF, personal communication April 19, 2001.

3.6 International Emissions Trading (IET)

The estimation of transaction costs associated with IET is even more problematic than is the case for JI and CDM-type projects. This is because there has been little experience to date in the operation of internationally-based emission trading schemes. There is as yet no evidence on transaction costs that arise on domestic carbon trading e.g. in UK and Denmark. On the other hand, there is some evidence on transaction costs that have been incurred in domestic trading schemes for other pollutants than carbon, e.g. lead and SO_2 in the US. However, caution is urged in transferring transaction cost estimates from these schemes, since in international emissions trading search and negotiation costs are likely to be more significant, as the levels of technical competence will differ broadly among the firms in different countries, compared to domestic programs (Woerdman, 2001).

US SO_2 allowances trading

Tietenberg et al. (1999) emphasise that transaction costs play a key role in the success or failure of emission trading systems. Some national emissions trading schemes, like the U.S. SO_2 allowances trading programme introduced in the 1990 Amendment to the Clean Air Act, proved to be very successful. The evidence on transaction costs under this programme is not transparent. However, brokerage fees – which are likely to be the most significant component of transaction costs in trading schemes – are estimated to be in the range of 2% to 5% of the transaction value (Klaassen and Nentjes, 1997, and Joskow et al., 1998). This magnitude is supported by Solomon (1995) and Montero (1997), who estimate transaction costs to be 5% and 8% of the transaction value, respectively.

US lead trading

Kerr and Maré (1997) provide quantitative estimates for transaction costs in lead permit trading. They state that transaction costs in the market between 1982 and 1987 were equivalent to 10% of the total transaction value.

Transferring these estimates to the carbon IET context a key determining factor will be the number of participants in the market (Woerdman, 2001). Theory suggests that transaction costs will decline as the number of potential traders and the number of transactions per source increase (Stavins, 1995). The estimates from US experience presented above have been derived in national markets with a large number of participants. The number of participants in carbon IET context will depend on the detail of the market design that finally emerges from the Conference of Parties. The scheme for greenhouse gas emission allowance trading within the EU, which is envisaged for the period 2005 to 2008, covers large installations of energy-intensive industries. Therefore the number of participants will be large and we would expect to see transaction costs equal to 2-4% of total transaction value.

On the other hand, several problems will arise in the operation of trading schemes at an international level, that are not existent at a national level. These include the difficulty of installing appropriate monitoring and penalty systems and, for the national inventories, monitoring their overall emissions. An estimate of 10% (Barrett, 1995) has therefore been suggested. However, as for JI and CDM projects, a learning effect is expected in emissions trading so that transaction costs are likely to be higher in initial stages of a trading program. This is in line with the experience of the U.S. trading schemes (see studies by Gangadharan, 2000 and Aidt and Dutta, 2001) and suggests that over time 10% may be too high.

4   Estimates of Project Risk Premia

In addition to transaction costs, projects in different sovereign states may attract different risk premia owing to the perceived level of risk of default or project failure due to micro-level or macro-level factors. For instance, past actions such as default on loans may impact upon this perceived level of risk, as may macroeconomic variables such as inflation and the perceived level of economic development in the economy. This section focuses on the issue of the determination of the different types of risk faced by projects and identifies estimates for risk premia that can be used in the modelling applications.

4.1   Determining the Risk Premia

Dailami and Liepziger (1999) suggest that the required rate of return for a project in a given country is the sum of the risk-free interest rate and a risk premium that reflects the market's assessment of country and project risk.

Risk premia estimation can be based on a number of variables at both country and project level. These include: past projects, sovereign debt ratings, equity values, and risk. Econometric analysis tries to incorporate both country and project level risk, and separates these two levels of risk through the use of macroeconomic and project level indicators as explanatory variables in regression analysis. One study is Dailami and Liepziger (1999) which uses a sample of 26 greenfield infrastructure projects[4] to estimate the credit risk premium and relate these to macroeconomic and project-specific variables. The macroeconomic variables include the rate of inflation, GDP per capita, ratio of external debt to exports, ratio of short-term debt to foreign exchange reserves and the ratio of reserves to imports. Project size, leverage ratio (proportion of project loan to total project cost), and sector-

---

[4]   Note that this study was based on an initial sample of 78 projects. Of these projects, only 26 had sufficient data for the analysis of the risk premia.

specific dummy variables were used to estimate the impact of project-specific variables.

Given that CDM and JI projects are to be placed in developing countries and economies in transition, the above analysis suggests that differential risk premia may have to be used in project analysis. One technique is to calculate risk premia for different countries using equity returns and risk of default compared to a base country. Damadoran (undated) presents a methodological framework from which the risk premia for equities in different countries can be estimated. Damadoran (1999) calculates this for the USA relative to a number of other countries in the world, using average default spreads for different credit rankings. The results of this analysis are presented in Table 18. The estimates can be used as rough indicators of the country risk element to be applied to projects in the different countries since they relate the risk of failure to the countries own rating. The credit rating of an individual firm within a nation, and thus the cost of financing a project, is unlikely to be below that of the national government, given that financial resources are open to the government.

Table 17 reports the average risk premium attributed to countries of different credit ratings. Clearly, the level of risk rises as the credit rating falls.

Table 17:   Average Risk Premia by Credit Ranking.

Credit Ranking	Ave Risk premia
Aaa	0.00%
Aa1	0.60%
Aa2	0.65%
Aa3	0.70%
A2	0.90%
A3	0.95%
Baa1	1.20%
Baa2	1.30%
Baa3	1.45%
Ba1	2.50%
Ba2	3.00%
Ba3	4.00%
B1	4.50%
B2	5.50%
B3	6.50%
Caa	7.50%

Source: own estimates based on Damodaran (1999).

These average risk premia in different countries provide the basis for first estimations of the country risk premia to which projects under JI and CDM are exposed.

As noted above, one dynamic extension to the straight adoption of the values given in Table 18 is to relate forecast macro-economic indices for individual countries to the changes in credit rating (and therefore risk premia) that these indices would imply. This would be possible as long as the relationships between the indices and the credit rating are quantified. In a similar exercise, Cantor and Packer (1996) examined the extent to which sovereign credit ratings were determined by such variables, using econometric analysis of Standard and Poors' and Moodys' credit rating systems. Table 19 presents the main results of this analysis.

Table 19 shows that per capita income – an indicator of the level of political stability or the tax base from which a sovereign government can draw to repay debts – is statistically significant in all ratings. Similarly, inflation is significant in all equations, with a negative sign, indicating that a high level of inflation has a negative impact on the perception of risk of default. This one would expect as inflation is often associated with underlying structural problems in the economy. A negative relationship is shown between the ratings level and external debt, indicating that the higher the level of debt taken by a country the higher the level of risk involved with additional loans. Economic development, measured by a dummy variable showing whether a country is considered "industrialised" by the International Monetary Fund, has a positive effect on the ratings. Default history also has a significant impact, with the indicator showing whether a country has defaulted on a loan since 1970 having a negative influence on the ratings. GDP growth is significant at the 10% level in the equation with average ratings as the dependent variable. The adjusted R-squared values for all three equations based solely on ratings are high, suggesting a high level of accuracy, which is borne out by assessment of the strength of the equation system in predicting sovereign ratings, with no predictions for countries being very far from the actual rankings. This indicates that the parameters from this equation can be used to derive estimates of credit ratings for countries or regions that as yet do not have credit ratings.

Table 18:   Estimates of Country Risk Premia for Equities.

Country	Long-Term Rating	Adj. Default Spread	Total Risk Premium	Country Risk Premium
Alderney	Aaa	0	5.51%	0.00%
Andorra	Aa1	60	6.11%	0.60%
Argentina	B2	550	11.01%	5.50%
Australia	Aa2	65	6.16%	0.65%
Austria	Aaa	0	5.51%	0.00%
Bahamas	A3	95	6.46%	0.95%

Table 18 continued.

Country	Long-Term Rating	Adj. Default Spread	Total Risk Premium	Country Risk Premium
Bahamas – Off Shore Banking Center	Aaa	0	5.51%	0.00%
Bahrain	Ba1	250	8.01%	2.50%
Bahrain – Off Shore Banking Center	A3	95	6.46%	0.95%
Barbados	Baa2	130	6.81%	1.30%
Belgium	Aaa	0	5.51%	0.00%
Belize	Ba2	300	8.51%	3.00%
Bermuda	Aa1	60	6.11%	0.60%
Bolivia	B1	450	10.01%	4.50%
Botswana	A2	90	6.41%	0.90%
Brazil	B1	450	10.01%	4.50%
Bulgaria	B2	550	11.01%	5.50%
Canada	Aa1	60	6.11%	0.60%
Cayman Islands	Aa3	70	6.21%	0.70%
Cayman Isl. - Off Shore Banking Center	Aaa	0	5.51%	0.00%
Chile	Baa1	120	6.71%	1.20%
China	A3	95	6.46%	0.95%
Colombia	Ba2	300	8.51%	3.00%
Costa Rica	Ba1	250	8.01%	2.50%
Croatia	Baa3	145	6.96%	1.45%
Cuba	Caa1	750	13.01%	7.50%
Cyprus	A2	90	6.41%	0.90%
Czech Republic	Baa1	120	6.71%	1.20%
Denmark	Aaa	0	5.51%	0.00%

Table 18 continued.

Country	Long-Term Rating	Adj. Default Spread	Total Risk Premium	Country Risk Premium
Dominican Republic	B1	450	10.01%	4.50%
Ecuador	Caa2	750	13.01%	7.50%
Egypt	Ba1	250	8.01%	2.50%
El Salvador	Baa3	145	6.96%	1.45%
Estonia	Baa1	120	6.71%	1.20%
Eurozone	Aaa	0	5.51%	0.00%
Fiji Islands	Ba2	300	8.51%	3.00%
Finland	Aaa	0	5.51%	0.00%
France	Aaa	0	5.51%	0.00%
Germany	Aaa	0	5.51%	0.00%
Gibraltar	Aaa	0	5.51%	0.00%
Greece	WR	750	13.01%	7.50%
Guatemala	Ba2	300	8.51%	3.00%
Guernsey	Aaa	0	5.51%	0.00%
Honduras	B2	550	11.01%	5.50%
Hong Kong	A3	95	6.46%	0.95%
Hungary	A3	95	6.46%	0.95%
Iceland	Aa3	70	6.21%	0.70%
India	Ba2	300	8.51%	3.00%
Indonesia	B3	650	12.01%	6.50%
Iran	B2	550	11.01%	5.50%
Ireland	AA2	65	6.16%	0.65%
Isle of Man	Aaa	0	5.51%	0.00%
Israel	A2	90	6.41%	0.90%
Italy	WR	750	13.01%	7.50%
Jamaica	Ba3	400	9.51%	4.00%

Table 18 continued.

Country	Long-Term Rating	Adj. Default Spread	Total Risk Premium	Country Risk Premium
Japan	Aa1	60	6.11%	0.60%
Jersey	Aaa	0	5.51%	0.00%
Jordan	Ba3	400	9.51%	4.00%
Kazakhstan	B1	450	10.01%	4.50%
Korea	Baa2	130	6.81%	1.30%
Kuwait	Baa1	120	6.71%	1.20%
Latvia	Baa2	130	6.81%	1.30%
Lebanon	B1	450	10.01%	4.50%
Liechtenstein	Aaa	0	5.51%	0.00%
Lithuania	Ba1	250	8.01%	2.50%
Luxembourg	Aaa	0	5.51%	0.00%
Macau	Baa1	120	6.71%	1.20%
Malaysia	Baa2	130	6.81%	1.30%
Malta	A3	95	6.46%	0.95%
Mauritius	Baa2	130	6.81%	1.30%
Mexico	Baa3	145	6.96%	1.45%
Moldova	B3	650	12.01%	6.50%
Monaco	Aaa	0	5.51%	0.00%
Morocco	Ba1	250	8.01%	2.50%
Netherlands	Aaa	0	5.51%	0.00%
New Zealand	Aa2	65	6.16%	0.65%
Nicaragua	B2	550	11.01%	5.50%
Norway	Aaa	0	5.51%	0.00%
Oman	Baa2	130	6.81%	1.30%
Pakistan	Caa1	750	13.01%	7.50%
Panama	Baa1	120	6.71%	1.20%

Table 18 continued.

Country	Long-Term Rating	Adj. Default Spread	Total Risk Premium	Country Risk Premium
Panama – Off Shore Banking Center	Aa2	65	6.16%	0.65%
Papua New Guinea	B1	450	10.01%	4.50%
Paraguay	B2	550	11.01%	5.50%
Peru	Ba3	400	9.51%	4.00%
Philippines	Ba1	250	8.01%	2.50%
Poland	Baa1	120	6.71%	1.20%
Portugal	A3	95	6.46%	0.95%
Qatar	Baa2	130	6.81%	1.30%
Romania	B3	650	12.01%	6.50%
Russia	B2	550	11.01%	5.50%
San Marino	A2	90	6.41%	0.90%
Sark	Aaa	0	5.51%	0.00%
Saudi Arabia	Baa3	145	6,96%	1.45%
Singapore	Aa1	60	6.11%	0.60%
Slovakia	Ba1	250	8.01%	2.50%
Slovenia	A2	90	6.41%	0.90%
South Africa	Baa3	145	6.96%	1.45%
Spain	Aa1	60	6.11%	0.60%
Sweden	Aa1	60	6.11%	0.60%
Switzerland	Aaa	0	5.51%	0.00%
Taiwan	Aa3	70	6.21%	0.70%
Thailand	Baa3	145	6.96%	1.45%
Trinidad & Tobago	Baa3	145	6.96%	1.45%
Tunisia	Baa3	145	6.96%	1.45%
Turkey	B1	450	10.01%	4.50%

Table 18 continued.

Country	Long-Term Rating	Adj. Default Spread	Total Risk Premium	Country Risk Premium
Turkmenistan	B2	550	11.01%	5.50%
Ukraine	Caa1	750	13.01%	7.50%
United Arab Emirates	A2	90	6.41%	0.90%
United Kingdom	Aaa	0	5.51%	0.00%
United States of America	Aaa	0	5.51%	0.00%
Uruguay	Baa3	145	6.96%	1.45%
Venezuela	B2	550	11.01%	5.50%
Vietnam	B1	450	10.01%	4.50%

Source: Damodaran (1999).

4.2 Recommendations

The risk premia applied to projects in developing countries and economies in transition may be crucial in determining whether a project goes ahead or not. Hence the determination of the risk premia may play a central role in the development of CDM or JI projects in developing countries. Several studies have examined the determinants of such risk premia, and a number of investment organisations provide ratings for investment risk in developing countries. The work by Damodaran (1999, undated) is of particular use since it provides estimates of risk premia for different countries based on average levels of risk in equity markets. Combined with the estimation of the determinants of credit rankings by Cantor and Packer (1996) it may provide the basis for an iterative model of risk premia for countries as they develop through the timeframe of the simulation process. This would be valuable in future simulations since it may indicate the additional premia needed for CDM and JI projects to be accepted for financing by governments, international institutions and corporations seeking to gain carbon credits. These estimates, however, only give a lower bound of the *country risk* involved in project investment in any country. The same is true of estimates based on equity returns and risk of default. Analysis of project level data is required to examine the levels of project level risk and country level risk in developing countries. A study by Dailami et al. (2001) includes project-level variables but does not report complete econometric results and does not present the data set on which the econometric analysis is based.

Table 19:   Determinants of Sovereign Debt Ratings.

	Dependent Variable			
Explanatory Variable	**Average Ratings**	**Moody's Ratings**	**Standard and Poor's Ratings**	**Moody's/Standard and Poor's Rating Differences[a]**
Intercept	1.442	3.408	-0.524	3.932**
	(0.633)	(1.379)	(0.223)	(2.521)
Per Capita Income	1.242***	1.027***	1.458***	-0.431***
	(5.302)	(4.041)	(6.048)	(2.688)
GDP Growth	0.151*	0.130	0.171**	-0.040
	(1.935)	(1.545)	(2.132)	(0.756)
Inflation	-0.611***	-0.630***	-0.591***	-0.039
	(2.839)	(2.701)	(2.671)	(0.265)
External Balance	0.003	0.006	0.001	0.006
	(0.314)	(0.535)	(0.046)	(0.779)
External Debt	-0.013***	-0.015***	-0.011***	-0.004
	(5.088)	(5.365)	(4.236)	(2.133)
Indicator for Economic Development	2.776***	2.957***	2.595***	0.362
	(4.25)	(4.175)	(3.861)	(0.81)
Indicator for Default History	-2.042***	-1.463**	-2.622***	1.159***
	(3.175)	(2.097)	(3.962)	(2.632)
Adjusted R-Squared	0.924	0.905	0.926	0.251
Standard Error	1.222	1.325	1.257	0.836

Notes: The sample size is 49. Absolute t-statistics are in parentheses.
[a]The number of rating notches by which Moody's ratings exceed Standard and Poor's.
*Significant at the 10% level; ** Significant at the 5% level; ***Significant at the 1% level.
Source: Cantor, R. and F. Packer (1996).

5   Summary and Conclusion

It is evident that transaction costs are significant cost elements in the proposed implementation of the flexible mechanisms under the Kyoto Protocol. Moreover, it is likely that they will matter in the decision as to whether an individual JI or CDM project will be undertaken or not. The existing data illustrates that the absolute level of transaction costs is similar across all project types. Therefore the size of a project is significant for the costs per ton of carbon reduced. While the effect of transaction costs on large projects is negligible they will be prohibitive for small projects. This will therefore prevent the undertaking of projects that are otherwise cost effective and may even lead to the exclusion of some countries from participating in CDM-projects.

The strong impact of transaction costs on the uptake of small projects underlines the importance of simplified modalities for small-scale projects, which were decided in the Marrakech Accords. An elaborate project cycle may enhance up-front transaction costs but lower them ex post. Moreover, rules that enhance transparency will be critical to reduce search costs even if they entail ex-ante costs. Dudek and Wiener (1996) argue for a voluntary bulletin board; the UNFCCC CDM Executive Board will develop a website where project ideas can be posted. Funds like the Prototype Carbon Fund (PCF) can reduce transaction costs by developing generic procedures such as standardised contracts. They can also specialise in certain project types.

Further methods for reducing transaction costs include

- Bundling of projects to jointly undertake each step of the project cycle,

- verification and certification undertaken not annually but at long intervals,

- exemption of projects from one or more steps of the project cycle; this however endangers environmental credibility and could lead to moral hazard; and

- streamlining of information that is needed for each step of the project cycle.

It is worth noting at this point that the answer to the question of who bears the transaction costs may be important in determining their effect on the up-take of the flexible mechanisms. At this stage in the establishment of the mechanisms it is impossible to say whether public or private sector agents will be liable for the costs, and how this liability will affect the up-take. One can envisage, however, a future where the burden shifts from public to private sectors over time as learning effects reduce costs.

While the importance of project size is apparent, there is not enough data to draw detailed conclusions on which countries or sectors are likely to have lower or higher transaction costs. However, the renewable energy sector projects will have relatively low costs since monitoring in the implementation phase will have negligible costs.

The analysis on emissions trading showed that transaction costs are vital to the success or failure of an emissions trading scheme. Since there does not exist an international emissions trading scheme yet, transaction costs can only be quantified for national trading programmes. Data from such schemes, like the SO_2 or lead trading markets in the U.S., points out the importance of brokerage fees, which constitute the major part of transaction costs, and learning effects, which lead to an increase of trade and a decrease of transaction costs in later years of trading programmes.

In order to keep transaction costs low it will be desirable to build on the experience with past emissions trading schemes. Some problems do however occur in transferring the concept of national trading schemes to an international level. These include the difficulty to install appropriate monitoring and penalty systems and, for the national inventories, to precisely specify their overall emissions.

Experience with national emissions trading schemes provides transaction cost values given in percent of traded volume. We think that total average transaction costs at the beginning of a trading programme will constitute 10% of the traded volume and decrease gradually to approximately 2% of the traded volume, due to learning effects.

A key additional motivation for estimating the transaction costs associated with the different flexibility mechanisms is that the non-compliance penalty will be effective only if it is larger than the net costs of using the flexibility mechanisms. In a similar vein, if the net costs for JI and CDM, including transaction costs and risk premia, don't equal the net costs for IET, the up-take of individual flexible mechanisms will be affected. Continued monitoring of their current and proposed implementation will be necessary to determine which strategy should be taken in the next decade in promoting the different individual mechanisms. It is not yet clear, how much the transaction costs will be reduced through streamlining, learning effects, etc., however, it can be expected, that streamlining will lead to similar marginal costs for all three flexible mechanisms.

Risk premia constitute another important factor in the determination whether a project is undertaken or not. This holds in particular for projects in developing countries and economies in transition. We have determined country risk premia, based on Damodaran (1999), that can be used as rough estimates of the country risk element to be applied to projects in the different countries. Since project-specific risk premia were not yet available, further research in this area is recommended in order to better be able to analyse the take-up of the flexibility instruments.

References

Aidt, T.S. and J. Dutta (2001), *Transitional Politics: Emerging Incentive-Based Instruments in Environmental Regulation*, Nota di lavoro 78.2001, Fondazione Eni Enrico Mattei, Milan.

Barrett, S. (1995), *The Strategy of Joint Implementation in the Framework Convention on Climate Change*, United Nations, Geneva.

Böhringer, C. and A. Löschel (2001), *Market Power in International Emission Trading: The Impacts of U.S. Withdrawal from the Kyoto Protocol*, ZEW Discussion Paper No. 01-58, Mannheim.

Cantor, R. and F. Packer (1996), Determinants and Impact of Sovereign Credit Ratings, *FRBNY Economic Policy Review* (October), 37-53.

Coase, R.H. (1937), The Nature of the Firm, *Economica, New Series* 4, 386-405.

Coase, R.H. (1960), The Problem of Social Costs, *Journal of Law and Economics* 3, 1-44.

Dailami, M. and D. Leipziger (1999), *Infrastructure Project Finance and Capital Flows: A New Perspective*, Working Paper, Economic Development Institute, The World Bank, Washington D.C., available online at http://www.worldbank.org/html/dec/Publications/Workpapers/WPS1800series/wps1861/wps1861.pdf.

Dailami, M., I. Lipkovich, and J. Van Dyck (2001), *INFRISK: A Computer Simulation Approach to Risk Management in Infrastructure Project Finance Transactions*, Working Paper, World Bank Institute, available online at http://www.worldbank.org/wbi/infrafin/pubs/2083infrisk.htm.

Damodaran (1999), *Estimating Country Premiums*, Dataset, available online at http://www.stern.nyu.edu/~adamodar/.

Damodaran (undated), *Estimating Equity Risk Premiums*, Working Paper, New York University, available online at http://www.stern.nyu.edu/~adamodar/.

Dudek, D.J. and J.B. Wiener (1996), *Joint Implementation, Transaction Costs, and Climate Change*, OECD, Paris.

EcoSecurities (2000), *Financing and Financing Mechanisms for Joint Implementation (JI) Projects in the Electricity Sector*, Oxford.

Gangadharan, L. (2000), Transaction Costs in Pollution Markets: An Empirical Study, *Land Economics* 76 (4), 601-614.

Hahn, R.W. and G.L. Hester (1989), Marketable Permits: Lessons for Theory and Practice, *Ecology Law Quarterly* 16, 361-406.

Joskow, P.L., R. Schmalensee, and E.M. Bailey (1998), The Market for Sulfur Dioxide Emissions, *American Economic Review* 88 (4), 669-685.

Jotzo, F. and A. Michaelowa (2001), *Estimating the CDM Market Under the Bonn Agreement*, HWWA Discussion Paper No. 145, Hamburg.

Kerr, S. and D. Maré (1997), *Transaction Costs and Tradeable Permit Markets: The United States Lead Phasedown*, Paper EAERE Conference Tilburg, The Netherlands, June 26-28th.

KFA-Forschungszentrum Jülich (1994), *IKARUS-Instrumente für Klimagas Reduktionsstrategien*, Teilprojekt 4: Umwandlungssektor strom- und wärmeerzeugende Anlagen auf fossiler und nuklearer Grundlage, Teil 1 u. 2, Jülich.

Klaassen, G. and A. Nentjes, (1997), Sulfur Trading under the 1990 CAAA in the US: An Assessment of the First Experiences, *Journal of Institutional and Theoretical Economics* 153 (2), 384-410.

Klepper, G. and S. Peterson (2002), *Trading Hot Air: The Influence of Permit Allocation Rules, Market Power and the US Withdrawal from the Kyoto Protocol*, Working Paper, Kiel Institute of World Economics, available online at http://econpapers.hhs.se/paper/wopkieliw/1133.htm.

Montero, J.-P. (1997), Marketable Pollution Permits with Uncertainty and Transaction Costs, *Resource and Energy Economics* 20, 27-50.

OECD (2001), *Kyoto Mechanisms, Monitoring and Compliance from Kyoto to The Hague*, available online at http://www.oecd.org/env/cc/.

PCF (2002), *Learning from the Implementation of the PrototypeCarbonFund*. Presentation at a side event to the COP 6 Negotiations at The Hague, Netherlands, available online at http://www.prototypecarbonfund.org/router.cfm?show=DocLib.cfm&Item=5.

PriceWaterhouseCoopers (2000), *A Business View on Key Issues Relating to Kyoto Mechanisms*, London.

Solomon, B. (1995), Global CO Emissions Trading: Early Lessons from the US Acid Rain Program, *Climatic Change* 30, 75-76.

Stavins, R.N. (1995), Transaction Costs and Tradable Permit, *Journal of Environmental Economics and Management* 29, 133-148.

Tietenberg, T., M. Grubb, A. Michaelowa, B. Swift, and Z.X. Zhang (1999), *International Rules for Greenhouse Gas Emissions Trading*, UNCTAD, available online at http://www.unctad.org/ghg/Publications/intl_rules.pdf.

UNFCCC (2002), *Activities Implemented Jointly – List of Projects*, available online at http://unfccc.int/program/coop/aij/.

Woerdman, E. (2001) Emissions Trading and Transaction Costs: Analyzing the Flaws in the Discussion, *Ecological Economics* 38, 293-304.

Leakage[*]

Michael Rauscher and Benjamin Lünenbürger

University of Rostock, Ulmenstr. 69, 18057 Rostock, Germany
rauscher@wiwi.uni-rostock.de

1 Introduction

It is sometimes argued that globalisation undermines environmental policy because countries are tempted to use lax environmental standards to make domestic
industries more competitive on world markets. Since each country tries to be
competitive on world markets, environmental policy may suffer from a 'race towards the bottom'. To avoid such developments it is frequently suggested to har-
monise environmental standards or to introduce trade measures against 'dirty'
goods from abroad in order to level the playing-field. Such suggestions rather
contradict most trade and environmental economic theory. According to economic
theory, environmental policy – in a world of perfect competition – should be determined by the country-specific endowments with environmental resources and
not by internationally uniform standards. Factors influencing the endowments are
physical and geographical conditions but also the willingness of the people to pay
for environmental quality. Since these conditions can be different across countries,
uniform environmental standards and/or trade measures are likely to be inefficient
(see Bhagwati and Srinivasan, 1996, for instance). Consequently, trade policy
should be rather independent from environmental policy.

Even though this point of view holds true for many environmental problems, it
cannot be generalised. In the case of global environmental problems, the effectiveness of unilateral environmental policies is undermined. Besides free riding,
which leads to too lax unilateral environmental policies, another problem needs to
be considered: pollution leakage. Tighter environmental standards and domestic
emission reductions might lead to higher emissions abroad and this lowers the
incentives to introduce stricter standards. International cooperation would avoid
such incentives. However, in a second-best world without international cooperation, trade measures might be a supplement of environmental policy instruments in

---

[*] This paper was published in Marisliani, L., M. Rauscher, and C. Withagen (Eds.)
(2003), *Environmental Policy in an International Perspective*, Dordrecht, 219-245.
We gratefully acknowledge the permission by Kluwer Academic Publishers to reprint
this paper here.

order to achieve an optimal outcome. This paper will re-assess the leakage problem and will give some rough quantitative estimates of its magnitude. Trade interventions as a means against leakage effects will be discussed.

An example of a global environmental problem is climate change. Negotiations aiming to come to an agreement on emission reduction turned out to be difficult. Even though there was a broad consensus, that actions against climate change were needed, many countries resisted committing to substantial reductions of their emissions. Free riding proved to be a major problem. Since emissions contributing to climate change are quite unevenly distributed across the world, it seemed natural that countries contributing most to global warming should be the first ones to cut back their emissions. The Kyoto agreement, which constituted a major step in climate change policy, comprises the industrialised countries of the OECD (and a few others) leaving the rest of the world without any restrictions on their emissions. However, the withdrawal of the United States from the Kyoto protocol in 2001 demonstrated the relevance of the free riding problem once again, but also drew attention to another problem that hampers climate change policy: carbon leakage.

In a second-best world, where full cooperation is missing, pollution leakage can be the consequence of unilateral action. Emission reductions in one country or a group of countries (like the Annex 1 countries of the Kyoto protocol) might be accompanied by an increase of emissions in the rest of the world. Such an increase can partially or totally offset the initial reduction of emissions. Three main channels of leakage can be separated: leakage through final-goods markets, through factor markets and through energy markets.

On markets for commodities produced energy-intensively, tighter environmental policies lead to a reduction in domestic supply. These commodities become scarcer on international markets and their prices rise. This stimulates production, energy use and pollution abroad. On factor markets, tighter environmental policies tend to make factors of production less productive. If these are internationally mobile, they tend to relocate to less regulated countries, e.g. through international capital movements. Increased factor use abroad is likely to be accompanied by increases in energy demand and, thus, emissions tend to raise. On energy markets leakage can occur when environmental policy, aiming to reduce emissions, leads to higher domestic energy prices and less energy demand. This reduction in demand has a negative impact on world energy prices, thus stimulating energy demand and emissions abroad.

The question arises if an optimal environmental policy in a second best world should take leakage into account. The theoretical literature on global externalities and international trade investigated the optimal use of policy instruments. Besides environmental taxes, tariffs on trade as a means to achieve optimal policy outcomes were considered. In a two-country, two-goods model with a global externality Markusen (1975) shows the optimal tax on the consumption and the production of the environmental disruptive good and the optimal tariff on trade with the 'dirty' good. Rauscher (1997, Ch. 5) provides a generalisation of Markusen's model. However, leakage through trade with primary goods such as energy is not taken into account in those models. This is done by Hoel (1994). He shows that taxes on the domestic production of primary goods (e.g. energy) should be higher than taxes on their use. In a general equilibrium framework, Rauscher (2002) considers a stylised model with trade in a polluting intermediate input (energy) and with capital movements. He reproduces Hoel's result and shows that capital market interventions are part of a country's optimal policy.

In the following paper a simple partial-equilibrium model will be provided, which looks at leakage on final-goods markets and on energy markets. The third channel of leakage, through factor movements, is not taken into account. Three policy instruments will be considered: a production tax on the final good, a tariff on trade with final goods and a tariff on energy trade. Comparative-static effects and optimal policies will be determined. Policy responses of non-abating countries to changes in domestic environmental policies are not considered in this paper. This is done by Copeland and Taylor (2000). They argue that changes in domestic environmental policies have income effects in other countries via terms-of-trade changes. With changed incomes, these countries might wish to change their environmental polices since demand for environmental quality is income-dependent. In the case of increasing incomes, foreign environmental policies tend to be tightened. Copeland and Taylor (2000) call this the 'bootstrapping effect'. This effect, however, is not taken into account in this paper because it introduces an asymmetry between countries: The regulating country becomes the Stackelberg leader vis-a-vis the rest of the world. This may be realistic in the North-South context considered by Copeland and Taylor but not necessarily in the general case.

Besides optimal policies, the comparative statics are derived. Inserting plausible parameter values in the leakage expression gives a quantitative benchmark which may be used for comparing our simple analytical model with large scale computable general-equilibrium (CGE) simulation models. CGE models – which usually address positive rather than normative issues – have so far been the main source of quantitative assessments of leakage effects since empirical studies are not available. A summary on recent CGE models on leakage is given by Burniaux and Oliveira-Martins (2000). The estimates for the leakage rate of seven CGE models range between 21% on the higher bound and 2% on the lower bound. In these models the leakage rate is defined by the increase of foreign emissions (non-Annex 1 countries) in relation to domestic reduction (Annex 1 countries). Leakage rates are highly sensitive to the parameters used in the models. Particularly supply elasticities play a key role, e.g. the degree of the integration of China with its huge coal reserve into the world economy. Since leakage-rates estimates cover rather a wide range, CGE simulations give not yet a clear guideline of the practical relevance of the leakage problem.

This paper will re-assess the leakage problem from an analytical perspective. A simple model is used to calibrate it to plausible parameter values and to do some sensitivity analysis. The next section establishes the model, Section 3 looks at the comparative statics, and Section 4 presents some calibration results. Section 5 addresses optimal policy responses to leakage. This is first done using only one environmental policy instrument. In a next step optimal trade interventions are considered, too. Section 6 presents some considerations concerning non-competitive market structures. The last part summarises the results of this paper.

2 The Model

Consider a world consisting of two countries, home and foreign, producing an energy intensive tradable good. Denote the prices for final goods and energy by p and p^E, respectively. All variables of the home country are represented by lower-case letters, those of the foreign country by the corresponding upper-case letters. Initially, only the home country is considered, but all arguments carry over to the foreign country. Let there be a numéraire good, of which quantity x is consumed. The supply of x is exogenous; this is a partial-equilibrium approach. Consider a quasi-linear utility function of consumers

$$\omega(c,x) = u(c) + x - d(e + E),\qquad(0)$$

where c is consumption of the energy-intensive commodity, e and E are domestic and foreign energy use, u (.) is a utility function with $u' > 0$, $u'' < 0$, and d (.) is an environmental-damage function with $d' > 0$, $d'' \geq 0$. Environmental damage is an externality that the consumers cannot influence. Utility maximisation with respect to the budget constraint yields

$$u'(c) = p + \theta,\qquad(1)$$

p being the world market price and θ a tariff, both measured in units of the numéraire.

Producers of the final good use energy, e, as an input which is available to them at a price being the world-market price p^E plus the energy tariff θ^E plus and the energy tax t^E.[1] The first-order condition of profit maximisation requires that the marginal value product of energy equals the energy price, i.e.

$$(p + \theta)\ f'\ (e) = p^E + \theta^E + t^E\qquad(2)$$

---

[1]   Negative values of taxes denote subsidies. Positive values of θ in an exporting country stand for export subsidies, negative values of θ denote export tariffs. For importing countries, positive values of θ mean import tariffs, negative values mean import subsidies.

$f(e)$ is the production function with $f' > 0$ and $f'' < 0$.[2]

Energy supply, s, is generated at costs $g(s)$, $g' > 0$, $g'' > 0$. Again, due to the partial-equilibrium nature of this model, the factors and other resources which are represented by this cost function are not considered explicitly. Profit maximisation gives

$$g'(s) = p^E + \theta^E .$$ (3)

Similar first-order conditions hold for the foreign country:

$$U'(C) = p + \theta ,$$ (1')

$$(p + \Theta) F'(E) = p^E + \Theta^E + T^E ,$$ (2')

$$G'(S) = p^E + \Theta^E .$$ (3')

In equilibrium, demand equals supply in both the final-goods and the energy markets:

$$c + C = f(e) + F(E) ,$$ (4)

$$e + E = s + S .$$ (5)

These eight equations, (1) to (5) and (1') to (3'), completely characterise the interactions of the two markets in this two-country world. Note that in a partial-equilibrium model, a trade-balance equation is not required. The numéraire good, representing the rest of the economy balances international trade.

3   Leakage and Other Comparative Statics

Both countries are assumed to be large in the two markets considered here, i.e. prices p and p^E are endogenous. Thus, the equations contain eight endogenous variables (c, C, e, E, s, S, p, p^E) plus the taxes and tariffs as the exogenous policy variables. Domestic quantities c, e, and s depend on domestic policy instruments according to equations (1) to (3). Thus, taxes and tariffs determine quantities or

---

2   This production function can be thought of as a reduced form of a more general production function $\varphi(e, v)$ with v as a vector of other inputs. If these factors are fixed or if the factor prices are proportional to the producer price of the final good, $p + \theta$, then v can either be traded as fixed or it can be eliminated via the first-order conditions.

vice versa. In what follows, we will use quantities as the policy variables. The tariffs and taxes can then be interpreted either as shadow prices or as explicit prices of tradable import quotas and pollution permits, respectively.

The remaining five equations can be reduced to three by using (4) and (5) in (1') and (3'). This yields

$$U'\big(f(e)+F(E)-c\big)=p+\Theta\ , \tag{1''}$$

$$\big(p+\Theta\big)F'(E)=p^E+\Theta^E+T^E\ , \tag{2'}$$

$$G'\big(e+E-s\big)=p^E+\Theta^E\ . \tag{3''}$$

From the point of view of the home country, foreign policy instruments are given. Total differentiation gives

$$\begin{pmatrix} -1 & 0 & U''F' \\ F' & -1 & (p+\Theta)F'' \\ 0 & -1 & G'' \end{pmatrix} \begin{pmatrix} dp \\ dp^E \\ dE \end{pmatrix} = \begin{pmatrix} U'' & 0 & -U''f' \\ 0 & 0 & 0 \\ 0 & G'' & -G'' \end{pmatrix} \begin{pmatrix} dc \\ ds \\ de \end{pmatrix} . \tag{6}$$

Note that

$$\begin{pmatrix} \dfrac{dp}{de} & \dfrac{dp^E}{de} & \dfrac{dE}{de} \end{pmatrix} = \begin{pmatrix} -f' & -1 \end{pmatrix} \begin{pmatrix} \dfrac{dp}{dc} & \dfrac{dp^E}{dc} & \dfrac{dE}{dc} \\ \dfrac{dp}{ds} & \dfrac{dp^E}{ds} & \dfrac{dE}{ds} \end{pmatrix} . \tag{7}$$

This relation will be of some use when the optimal policies are determined.

Applying Cramer's rule to equation (6) yields the results that are summarised in Table 1. An increase in domestic demand for final goods tends to raise final-goods prices, energy prices, and foreign energy demand. And increase in domestic energy supply has the opposite effects on prices but also a positive impact on foreign energy demand. These results are intuitive. An increase in domestic energy demand has ambiguous impacts on the prices of energy and final goods, and a clearly negative impact on foreign energy use.

The ambiguity of the final-good price impact is somewhat surprising. One expects a negative relationship because increases in energy use increase the output of the final good thus generating excess supply and price reductions. However a negative price effect has to be taken into account, too: High energy demand tends to raise energy prices which might lead to a higher price of the final good. The other ambiguity of increased energy use is the energy-price effect. Again, one would expect a negative relationship. This may be turned around by an effect induced via the goods market. If the goods market price is reduced, the marginal value product of energy is reduced abroad. At a given energy price, foreigners reduce their energy demand. This creates an excess supply of energy with the consequence of energy-price erosion. If this effect dominates the other ones, the energy price may fall after an increase in domestic energy demand.

Table 1:   Comparative Statistics.

Dom. Policy Variables	Endogenous Variables		
	p	p^E	E
c	+	+	+
s	-	-	+
e	?	?	-

The leakage effect, finally, consists of two components:

- the energy-market effect. Higher energy demand at home raises the energy price and leads to a reduction in foreign energy demand.

- the goods-market effect. Higher energy demand at home increases domestic supply of final goods. This leads to a price reduction in the goods market and to a reduction of foreign production – and energy demand.

The magnitude of the leakage effect follows from equation (6):

$$\frac{dE}{de} = -\frac{G''-U''F'f'}{G''-U''F'^2-(p+\Theta)F''} < 0 \ . \tag{8}$$

Let us consider the case of symmetric countries, where symmetry here means equal productivities of energy, $f'=F'$. Then,

$$\left.\frac{dE}{de}\right|_{f'=F'} = -\frac{1}{1+\dfrac{(p+\Theta)F''}{U''F'^2-G''}} \ . \tag{9}$$

It is seen that the leakage effect is always less than 100% in this symmetric case. To interpret the term on the right-hand side, we re-state it in terms of elasticities. Let us use the following notation:

- $\eta \equiv \dfrac{U'}{U''C}$ is the price elasticity of demand for the final good.

- $\varepsilon \equiv -\dfrac{F'^2}{F''F}$ is the price elasticity of final-goods supply.

- $\eta^E \equiv \dfrac{F'}{F''E}$ is the price elasticity of energy demand.

- $\varepsilon^E \equiv \dfrac{G'}{G''S}$ is the price elasticity of energy supply.

Some basic but tedious transformations of equation (9) then yield

$$\left.\frac{dE}{de}\right|_{f'=F'} = -\frac{1}{1 - \dfrac{1}{\dfrac{\varepsilon}{\eta}\dfrac{F}{C} + \dfrac{\eta^E}{\varepsilon^E}\dfrac{E}{S}\dfrac{p^E + \Theta^E}{p^E + \Theta^E + T^E}}} \tag{10}$$

On the right-hand side of equation (10), the two effects responsible for leakage can be identified. They are related to the two terms in the lowest-level denominator. The first one is the goods-market effect: Tighter environmental policies at home tend to increase final-goods prices, which tends to increase foreign output and energy use. The second effect is the energy-market effect: tighter environmental policies at home lead to reductions in energy demand, to lower world energy prices and, thus, to an increase in foreign energy demand. The significance of the effect depends on elasticities, energy taxes, and supply-to-demand ratios. It is seen that leakage is substantial

- if the price elasticity of the foreign demand for final goods is low. Tighter environmental policy leads to higher goods prices. If this causes only minor reductions in foreign demand, a substantial leakage effect is likely.

- if the price elasticity of foreign supply of final goods is large. Then the increase in the goods price leads to a substantial increase in foreign supply – and energy use.

- if the supply-to-demand ratio is large. Then the supply impact of changing prices is large compared to the impact on demand.

- if foreign energy demand is price elastic. Then, small reductions in world energy prices lead to substantial increases in foreign energy demand.

- if foreign energy supply is price inelastic. Reduced energy prices lead only to minor reductions in foreign energy supply.

- if foreign energy taxes are low. If they are high, then the change of the price of energy in the foreign market is small compared to the change in the world market price.

- if the ratio of foreign energy demand to foreign energy supply is large.

4   A Calibration of the Model

In order to get an idea about the magnitude of leakage, specify $F(E)$ as a CES function such that

$$F\left(E\right)=\left(K+\alpha E^{\rho}\right)^{\frac{1}{\rho}}$$ (11)

with α and ρ as the parameters of the function and K as a constant factor of production. For such a function, we have

$$\frac{F'E}{F}=\frac{\alpha E^{\rho}}{K+\alpha E^{\rho}} \quad ,$$ (12a)

$$\frac{1}{\eta^{E}}=\frac{F''E}{F'}=\left(1-\rho\right)\left(\frac{\alpha E^{\rho}}{K+\alpha E^{\rho}}-1\right).$$ (12b)

Moreover, the price elasticity of final-goods supply can be determined by

$$\varepsilon=-\eta^{E}\frac{F'E}{F}.$$ (12c)

Let us assume the following parameter values for the elasticities:

$$\frac{F'E}{F}=0.1 \ ,$$ (13a)

$$\eta^{E}=-0.4 \ ,$$ (13b)

$$\varepsilon^{E}=0.8 \ ,$$ (13c)

$$\eta=-1 \ ,$$ (13d)

$$\varepsilon=-\eta^{E}\frac{F'E}{F}=0.04.$$ (13e)

The output elasticity of energy is rather small and the value chosen here probably overstates the true value. A price elasticity of energy demand of 40% is a realistic long-term value. In the short term, this value may be less than 20%. Supply elasticities vary quite a bit, ranging from approximately 40% for oil and gas to more than 100% in the case of coal. We chose a compromise with 80%. See Huntington (1992) for a survey of energy elasticities. The values chosen here are in accordance with the values Huntington reports. The price elasticity of final-goods supply is unity, which – admittedly – is chosen arbitrarily. Finally the price elasticity of supply is rather small given the direct link between energy demand and final-goods supply in this model. It will be argued below that this is an important feature of the model which drives some of its central results. Moreover, we assume symmetry of countries such that

$$E = S,$$
(13f)

$$F = C.$$
(13g)

With these parameters, we have for the leakage effect, $L=dE/de$,

$$L = -0.225.$$

In this model, the leakage effect is 22.5% or approximately one fourth. This is within the range of CGE results. Depending on the parameter values, leakage may be less or larger than 22.5%. The appendix presents sensitivity analyses with alternative parameter values.

Recall that we have from (10) that the leakage effect depends on the ratios of demand and supply elasticities for energy and final goods, η^E/ε^E and ε/η, which in our numerical example equal 0.5 and 0.04, respectively. It becomes clear that the goods market has only a small impact on leakage. The underlying reason is the loose link between energy inputs and final output as measured by the output elasticity of energy, EF_E/F. Compare equation (13e).

The energy-market effect and the final-goods market effect can be separated from each other if we assume that either final goods or energy are not traded. Alternatively, as a third case we look at a scenario where the country is small in the energy market but that it has a substantial impact in the final-goods market.

- If final goods are not traded, the comparative statics are determined by

$$U'\big(F\big(E\big)\big)F'\big(E\big) = p^E + \Theta^E + T^E \ ,$$

$$G'\big(e + E - s\big) = p^E + \Theta^E \ .$$

From total differentiation of these equations, we have

$$\frac{dE}{de}\bigg|_{F=C} = -\frac{G''}{G'' - U''F'^2 - U'F''} .$$ (14)

Rearranging terms, we obtain

$$\frac{dE}{de}\bigg|_{F=C} = -\frac{1}{1-\left(1-\dfrac{\varepsilon}{\eta}\right)\dfrac{p^E + \Theta^E + T^E}{p^E + \Theta^E}\dfrac{s}{E}\dfrac{\varepsilon^E}{\eta^E}} .$$ (14')

The qualitative impacts of the energy-market parameters (elasticities, prices, and supply-to-demand ratio) leakage effect are the same as before. Note that goods-markets elasticities still play a role since the demand for energy is a derived demand here. If final-goods demand is completely inelastic, the leakage effect is zero since a constant output requires a constant energy input.[3] Let us denote the leakage effect through energy markets only by L^E :

$$L^E = -0.194 .$$

Without commodity market interdependencies, the leakage effect is reduced to less than 20%. The appendix presents sensitivity analyses with alternative parameter values..

- If final goods are traded and energy is not, the foreign market equilibrium is determined by

$$U'\big(f(e) + F(E) - c\big) = p + \Theta ,$$

$$(p + \Theta)F'(E) = G'(E) + T^E .$$

The leakage effect is

$$\frac{dE}{de}\bigg|_{E=S} = \frac{U''F'f'}{G'' - U''F'^2 - U'F''} .$$ (15)

Rearranging the terms and assuming symmetry such that $f' = F'$, yields

$$\frac{dE}{de}\bigg|_{\substack{f'=F' \\ E=S}} = -\frac{1}{1 - \dfrac{\eta}{\varepsilon}\dfrac{C}{F}\left(1 - \dfrac{\eta^E}{\varepsilon^E}\dfrac{p^E}{p^E + T^E}\right)} .$$ (15')

---

[3]   Note that the possibility of substitution of energy by other factors of production is not taken into account here.

The qualitative impacts of the parameters are the same as in the general case. Leakage effects tend to be rather small since ε is small. Denoting by L^G the leakage effect in the absence of energy trade, we have for the calibrated model

$$L^G = -0.034$$

Leakage is now close to 3%. This confirms the conjecture that leakage through markets for final goods is not important.

- Let us finally consider the case of countries that are small in the energy market. The leakage effect is determined by

$$U'\big(f(e)+F(E)-c\big) = p + \Theta ,$$ (1")

$$(p+\Theta)F'(E) = p^E + \Theta^E + T^E ,$$ (2')

and turns out to be

$$\left.\frac{dE}{de}\right|_{p^E \text{ given}} = \frac{-U''F'f'}{U''F'^2 + U'F''} ,$$ (16)

or, with symmetry ($f'=F'$) and elasticities inserted

$$\left.\frac{dE}{de}\right|_{\substack{f'=F \\ p^E \text{ given}}} = -\frac{1}{1 - \dfrac{\eta}{\varepsilon}\dfrac{C}{F}} .$$ (16')

Denoting by L^{small} the leakage effect in the case of small open economies, we have numerically.

$$L^{small} = 0.038 .$$

Again the leakage effect is small, less than 4%.

Summarising, these simple calculations confirm the earlier result obtained by Rauscher (2002) that the largest part of the leakage effect is explained by energy-market interdependencies. See also Kuik and Verbruggen (2002). The simplicity of the present model allows the intuition behind this result to be derived. It seems to be that the price elasticity of supply of energy-intensive commodities is substantially lower than the price elasticity of demand. This implies that changes in world market prices for goods have only a small effect on foreign energy use.

5 Optimal Environmental Policies

An optimal environmental policy maximises domestic welfare subject to the behaviour of foreign firms and households as determined in equation (6) with respect to energy input, e. The domestic welfare function is

$$w = u(c) - p\big(c - f(e)\big) - p^E(e - s) - g(s) - d(e + E) , \tag{17}$$

i.e. utility from final consumption minus payments to foreigners for final-goods imports and energy imports minus the cost of domestic provision of energy minus environmental damage. For the time being, let us assume that there are no trade interventions, i.e. $\theta = \theta^E = 0$.

Note that environmental policy has an impact on domestic consumption, c and energy supply, s, as these variables depend on p and p^E, respectively, according to equations (1) and (3). The corresponding terms dc/de and ds/de, however, vanish due to the envelope theorem. The remainder implies

$$t^E = pf' - p_E = d'\left(1 + \frac{dE}{de}\right) + (c - f)\frac{dp}{de} + (e - s)\frac{dp^E}{de} . \tag{18}$$

The optimal environmental tax rate consists of four components:

- d' is the marginal environmental damage.

- $(dE/de)d'$ is the impact of leakage. Leakage reduces the environmental effects of strict environmental policy. Thus, with leakage, environmental policies should be less strict than without.

- $(dp/de)(c-f)$ is a terms-of-trade effect. If the country is an exporter of environmentally intensively produced commodities, it benefits from strict environmental standards since this raises the price of the exported good.

- $(dp^E/de)(e-s)$ is also a terms-of-trade effect, however, in the energy market. The sign of (dp^E/de) is ambiguous, but with indirect effects being not too strong it should be positive. This means that an energy-importing country should use stricter environmental policies than an energy-exporting country since strict policies reduce the demand for energy and, thus, the energy price.

If there were exogenous tariffs in the home country, two additional effects would show up. By changing its environmental policies, the country would be able to affect the tax bases of the tariffs. Taking this into account, a policy maker should modify its environmental policy.

The environmental policy considered here is not first best. There are multiple distortions and a single policy instrument cannot address them all appropriately. Let us now consider the possibility of trade interventions. The welfare function, (17), is now maximised with respect to c, s, and e. The first-order conditions are

$$\begin{pmatrix} \dfrac{dp}{dc} & \dfrac{dp^E}{dc} & \dfrac{dE}{dc} \\[2mm] \dfrac{dp}{ds} & \dfrac{dp^E}{ds} & \dfrac{dE}{ds} \\[2mm] \dfrac{dp}{de} & \dfrac{dp^E}{de} & \dfrac{dE}{de} \end{pmatrix} \begin{pmatrix} c - f(e) \\ e - s \\ d' \end{pmatrix} = \begin{pmatrix} u' - p \\ p^E - g' \\ pf' - p^E - d' \end{pmatrix}. \tag{19}$$

Noting that $u' - p = \theta$ and $p^E - g' = -\theta^E$, we can use equation (7) to obtain

$$\begin{pmatrix} \dfrac{dp}{de} & \dfrac{dp^E}{de} & \dfrac{dE}{de} \\[2mm] \\[2mm] \dfrac{dp}{de} & \dfrac{dp^E}{de} & \dfrac{dE}{de} \end{pmatrix} \begin{pmatrix} c - f(e) \\ e - s \\ d' \end{pmatrix} = \begin{pmatrix} -\theta f\ ' + \theta^E \\ pf\ ' - p^E - d' \end{pmatrix}.$$

It follows that

$$pf' - p^E - d' = -\theta f' + \theta^E$$

and, together with equation (2),

$$t^{*E} = d' . \tag{20}$$

The first-best optimal environmental tax is the Pigouvian tax, which equals the marginal environmental damage.

The optimal tariff rates then turn out to be

$$\theta^* = (c - f)\frac{dp}{dc} + (e - s)\frac{dp^E}{dc} + d'\frac{dE}{dc} , \tag{21a}$$

$$\theta^E * = -(c - f)\frac{dp}{ds} - (e - s)\frac{dp^E}{ds} - d'\frac{dE}{ds}. \tag{21b}$$

In each equation, there are two terms-of-trade components and a leakage component. The own-terms-of-trade components are straight forward: An importing country should tax its imports, an exporting country should tax its exports. Then there are cross-terms-of-trade effects. A tariff on final-goods imports or a subsidy on final-goods exports reduces the price of the final good. This in turn reduces foreign demand for energy and, therefore, the energy price. If the country is an energy importer, $e - s > 0$, this is a terms-of-trade improvement. Similar arguments apply to the opposite scenario. By tariffs on energy imports or subsidies on exports, the country reduces the world energy price. This leads to increased foreign supply of final goods. Since this reduces the world market price, an importer of final goods benefits from this whereas an exporter loses.

The leakage components will be subject to closer inspection. Omitting the terms-of-trade components, we obtain

$$\theta^* = \left(...\right) + d' \frac{-U''F'}{G'' - \left(p+\Theta\right)F'' - U''F'^2},$$

(22a)

$$\theta^E * = \left(...\right) - d' \frac{G''}{G'' - \left(p+\Theta\right)F'' - U''F'^2}.$$

(22b)

Inserting $t^E *$ for d' and using (14) in (22b) and (15) in (22a), we obtain

$$\theta^* = \left(...\right) - \frac{t^E *}{f'}\left[\frac{dE}{de}\Big|_{E=S}\right],$$

(23a)

$$\theta^E * = \left(...\right) + t^E *\left[\frac{dE}{de}\Big|_{C=F}\right].$$

(23b)

Finally rewrite (23a) such that

$$\frac{\theta^*}{p+\theta^*} = \left(...\right) - \frac{t^E *}{p^E + \theta^E * + t^E *}\left[\frac{dE}{de}\Big|_{E=S}\right].$$

(24)

Note that dE/de is always negative. This implies that $\theta^* > 0$ and $\theta^E * < 0$ if the terms-of-trade components are neglected. There should be an import tariff or an export subsidy for final goods. Both instruments lower the world market price and reduce foreign incentives to produce these energy intensive commodities. In the energy market, there should be an import subsidy or an export tax. Both instruments increase energy prices and, thus, have a negative impact on foreign energy demand. Import subsidies are difficult to be handled, however. If imports are subsidised, there is an incentive to re-import exported goods.[4] This can be avoided if a combination of tax instruments is used that mimics the effect of an import subsidy. Here one would combine a tax on energy use with a tax on energy production. See Hoel (1994) for the same result. Interestingly, in reality most countries subsidise rather than tax domestic energy production.

What are the magnitudes of optimal trade interventions that address the leakage problem?

---

[4]   Of course, a similar argument applies if exports of final goods are subsidised.

- The energy market. In the energy market, the tax or subsidy rate equals the leakage effect times the Pigouvian tax rate. See equation (23b). Thus, using the simple numerical example of the preceding section, $\theta^E *$ might be close to 20% of the emission tax rate.

- The final-goods market. It follows from equation (24) that the tariff rate as a percentage of the domestic commodity price equals the emission tax share of the domestic downstream price of energy times the leakage effect. Since the former is always less than one and the latter is rather small, possibly close to 3%, the leakage component in an optimal ad-valorem tariff is unlikely to be larger than 2%.

6   Non-Competitive Market Structures

The previous sections looked at trade in competitive markets. However, this is not always realistic. Large shares of international trade are intra-industry trade, which can hardly be the case in a perfect-competition world. Moreover, there are markets in which small numbers of suppliers are able to exert market power vis-a-vis the consumer and to extract oligopoly rents. What is the impact of leakage in these markets? In order to keep the algebra tractable, the following analysis will be restricted to a partial-equilibrium framework. In particular energy prices will be taken as given. The markets under consideration here have no significant effects on energy demand and supply.

Intra-industry trade and leakage have been considered by Gürtzgen and Rauscher (2000). They consider an intra-industry trade model á la Krugman (1979, 1980) with love-of-variety preferences and monopolistic competition. A feature of this model is that in its standard version with constant price elasticity of demand for differentiated goods, there is no leakage at all. Foreign emissions are determined by this price elasticity, by energy prices and emission taxes and by the parameters of technology. They are not affected by changes in domestic supply that are due to domestic changes in environmental policies. Matters change if the price elasticity is not constant but increases with the number of varieties available. However, what is the impact of environmental policy on product variety? One can show that it is ambiguous. Tighter environmental policies can increase or reduce product variety. As a consequence, the price elasticity of demand for differentiated goods may rise or be diminished. This is an effect spilling over to the foreign supply side and as one might expect, the result is ambiguous. Tighter environmental standards at home can have positive or negative effects on foreign emissions.

As the monopolistic competition framework is not too far from perfect competition (due to free entry, pure profits vanish), matters are different in an oligopolistic world. Usually, this is analysed within a Nash-equilibrium framework, where firms take as given the strategic variables of their competitors (prices or quantities). Tighter environmental policies change the production decisions of the regulated firms. The unregulated firms react according to their best-response functions and this generates leakage problems. Let us consider the simple case where there are two firms, a domestic and a foreign firm. The model set-up is basically that of Barrett (1994). The output is purchased by consumers in the rest of the world. Domestic consumption is not considered. Therefore, consumer surplus can be neglected. Firms exhibit Cournot behaviour: Quantities are the strategic variables. Using the notation of the previous sections, one can express domestic profits as

$$\pi = p\big(f(e)+F(E)\big)f(e)-\big(p^E+t^E\big)\;e\;. \tag{25}$$

$p(.)$ is the inverse-demand function and it can be derived from the consumers' utility function like in equation (1). Here it is sufficient to consider only one policy instrument. As will be seen below, the strategic objective of the home government in this game is to raise the output of the domestic firm. Output, however, is directly related to energy use. Thus, in this simple world, a tax on energy can be used as a multi-purpose instrument. The first-order condition of profit maximisation is

$$\big(p+p'f\big)f'=p^E+t^E\;,$$

which can be rewritten in terms of elasticities

$$\left(1+\frac{f}{f+F}\frac{1}{\eta}\right)pf'=p^E+t^E. \tag{26a}$$

By analogy,

$$\left(1+\frac{F}{f+F}\frac{1}{\eta}\right)pF'=p^E+T^E \tag{26b}$$

for the foreign firm. η is the price elasticity of demand in the rest of the world. For the sake of simplicity, assume that this elasticity is constant. Then total differentiation of (26b) with respect to e and E subject to given energy prices and foreign energy taxes yields

$$\frac{dE}{de}=-\frac{f'\left(1+\dfrac{F}{f+F}\left(\dfrac{1}{\eta}-1\right)\right)}{F'\left(1+\dfrac{f}{f+F}+\dfrac{1}{\eta}\dfrac{F}{f+F}-\dfrac{1}{\varepsilon}\left(1+\eta\dfrac{f+F}{F}\right)\right)}. \tag{27}$$

Under the assumption of symmetry (f'=F', f=F) and with the parameter values assumed in the previous sections, we arrive at a numerical value of the leakage effect, L^{oli}= -1/26.

$$L^{oli} = -0.038 .$$

That this is exactly the same as in the perfect-competition case, is an accident.[5] With other parameter values, in particular other values of the price elasticity of demand, the results may differ. What is decisive in this context, however, is the impact of the price elasticity of supply, which is rather low. This impact is omnipresent independent of which other parameter values have been chosen. The result is that leakage effects through commodity markets are rather insignificant even in the oligopoly case although the mechanism differs from the competitive one.

Finally, let us consider optimal environmental policies. Welfare is profits after taxes minus the cost of imported energy minus the environmental damage:

$$\omega = p\big(f(e)+F(E)\big)f(e)-p^E e-d(e+E) . \tag{28}$$

The first-order condition of welfare maximisation is

$$(p'f+p)f'-p^E -d'+p'fF'\frac{dE}{de}-d'\frac{dE}{de} = 0 .$$

The optimal emission tax rate is determined by

$$t^E = d'-p'fF'\frac{dE}{de}+d'\frac{dE}{de} . \tag{29}$$

The first term on the right-hand side is the marginal environmental damage. The second term is the rent-shifting effect of strategic trade policy. Laxer environmental standards induce the domestic firms to raise their output. This in turn results in a lower output abroad, implying a shift of oligopoly rents to the domestic firm as in Barrett.[6] Inserting for F' from (26b) yields

---

[5]   Note that under the symmetry conditions (27) is simplified such that

$$\frac{dE}{de} = -\frac{1+\frac{1}{2}\left(\frac{1}{\eta}-1\right)}{1-\frac{1}{\varepsilon}(1+2\eta)}$$ and compare this to (16').

[6]   In contrast to Barrett (1994), the domestic producer would be put into a Stackelberg position by the laxer environmental policy. The reason is that in this simple model there is an exact correspondence between inputs and outputs whereas Barrett uses more flexible functional forms.

$$t^E = d' - \frac{f}{F + \eta(f + F)} \frac{dE}{de}\left(p^E + T^E\right) + d' \frac{dE}{de} \tag{29'}$$

and the rent-shifting component of the domestic energy tax can be expressed as a share of the foreign energy price. The third component of the energy tax is the leakage component. Given the likely magnitude of the leakage effect, this effect turns out to be rather small.

7   Final Remarks

The paper has analysed the issue of leakage in a simple model where energy and final-goods markets interact. It was found

- that the major part of leakage is due to energy market interdependencies,

- that leakage through final-goods markets is of minor relevance,

- that non-competitive market structure does not make a big difference compared to the perfect-competition case,

- that domestic energy production should be taxed to avoid leakage or energy imports should be subsidised,

- and that imports of energy-intensive final goods should be subject to tariffs – albeit the tariff rates are very small.

These results have some policy implications for international environmental agreements. The Montreal protocol used trade restrictions both on primary and on final commodities. However, there were import bans rather than import subsidies on chlorofluorocarbons (CFCs). This may be explained by the fact that the Montreal protocol aimed at a complete phase-out of CFCs within a very short time interval. In the situation considered in this paper, the environmental-damage function is such that only a reduction in emissions is warranted. The protocol's provisions for trade with final commodities that have been produced with CFCs but do not contain CFCs is perfectly in line with the recommendations of our model. Such trade restrictions are in the self-interest of signatory parties of the agreement since they reduce leakage effects. Moreover, they serve as a disciplinary device by punishing non-signatories. The Kyoto protocol, in contrast, does not contain trade restrictions. The results of the preceding sections offer an explanation for why this may be the case. Import restrictions on energy-intensive commodities would be a real threat to non-compliants. However, the optimal tariff rates that are in the self-interest of signatory parties would be very low – almost zero. As regards import subsidies or export taxes, these instruments should be in the self-interest of countries implementing greenhouse-gas reducing policies. But would import subsidies or export taxes on energy be interpreted as sanctions by non-compliants? Probably not. Moreover, the anecdotal evidence rather shows that countries do the opposite of what they should be doing if they acted in their own self-interest. They should tax domestic energy production but instead they rather subsidise it. Of course, this is not irrational. But the underlying rationality has nothing to do with welfare objectives. The reasons must be sought in the political sphere, where powerful lobbies are able to capture domestic energy regulation. One major policy implication of this paper is that this is more harmful than usually thought. In a world with non-cooperative environmental policies and pollution leakage the first-best policy from a single country's point of view is to tax not only energy use but also energy production. In such a world, it is even more important to get rid of energy subsidies than in the traditional framework, where governments should not interfere in the supply of energy. Subsidies on energy supply should definitely be abandoned.

Appendix: Sensitivity Analysis

Leakage Through Energy and Final-Goods Markets

Partial variation of parameters of leakage total effect:

$$\frac{dE}{de}\bigg|_{f'=F'} = -\frac{1}{1 - \dfrac{1}{\dfrac{\varepsilon}{\eta}\dfrac{F}{c} + \dfrac{\eta^E}{\varepsilon^E}\dfrac{E}{S}\dfrac{p^E + \theta^E}{p^E + \theta^E + T^E}}}. \tag{10}$$

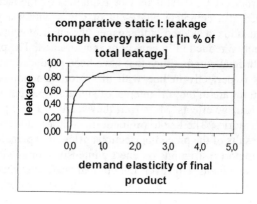

comparative static I: leakage through energy market [in % of total leakage]

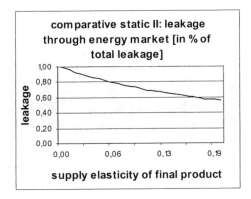

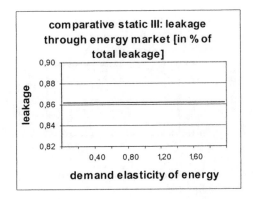

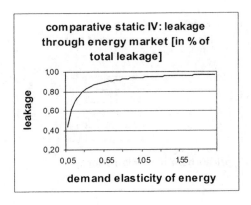

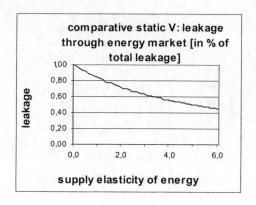

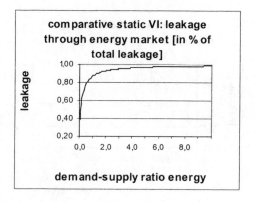

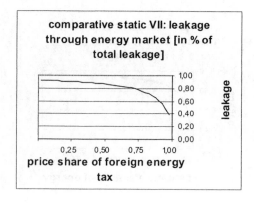

Leakage Through Energy Market Only

Partial variation of parameters of leakage effect through energy markets:

$$\frac{dE}{de}\bigg|_{F=C} = -\frac{G''}{G''-U''\,F'^{2}-U'\,F''} \,. \tag{13}$$

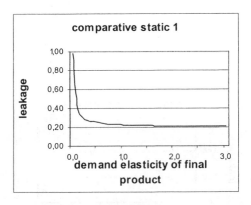

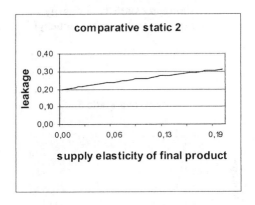

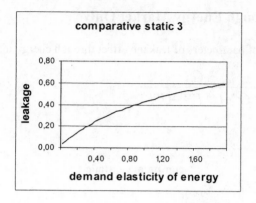

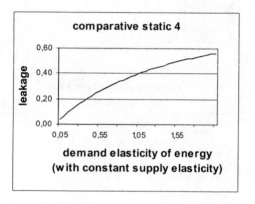

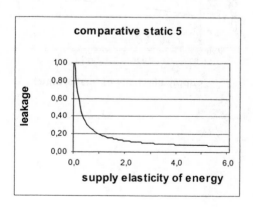

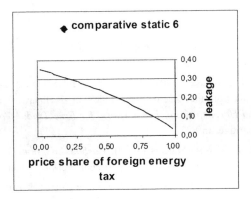

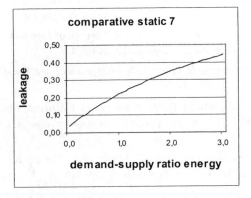

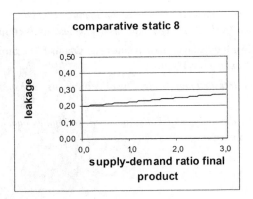

References

Barrett, S. (1994), Strategic Environmental Policy and International Trade, *Journal of Public Economics* 54, 325-338.

Bhagwati, J. and T.N. Srinivasan (1996), Trade and the Environment: Does Environmental Diversity Detract from the Case of Free Trade?, in: J. Bhagwati, R.E. Hudec (Eds.), *Fair Trade and Harmonization: Prerequisites for Free Trade? Volume 1: Economic Analysis,* Cambridge, 159-232.

Burniaux, J.M. and J. Oliveira-Martins (2000), *Carbon Emission Leakages: A General Equilibrium View,* OECD, Economics Department Working Paper 242, Paris.

Copeland, B.R. and M.S. Taylor (2000), *Free Trade and Global Warming: A Trade Theory View of the KyotoProtocol,* NBER Working Paper No. w7657, Cambridge, MA.

Gürtzgen, N. and M. Rauscher (2000), Environmental Policy, Intra-Industry Trade, and Transfrontier Pollution, *Environmental and Resource Economics* 17, 59-71.

Hoel, M. (1994), Efficient Climate Policy in the Presence of Free Riders, *Journal of Environmental Economics and Management* 27, 259-274.

Hoel, M. (1997), Environmental Policy with Endogenous Plant Locations, *Scandinavian Journal of Economics* 99, 241-259.

Huntington, H.G. (1992), Inferred Demand and Supply Elasticities from a Comparison of World Oil Models, in: Sterner, T. (Ed.), *International Energy Economics,* London, 239-261.

Krugman, P.R. (1979), Increasing Returns, Monopolistic Competition, and International Trade, *Journal of International Economics* 9, 469-479.

Krugman, P.R. (1980), Scale Economies, Product Differentiation and the Pattern of Trade, *American Economic Review* 67, 298-307.

Kuik, O.H. and H. Verbruggen (2001), *The Kyoto Regime, Changing Patterns of International Trade, and Carbon Leakage,* unpublished manuscript, Verbruggen.

Markusen, J.R. (1975), International Externalities and Optimal Tax Structures, *Journal of International Economics* 5, 15-29.

Rauscher, M. (1997), *International Trade, Factor Movements, and the Environment,* Oxford.

Rauscher, M. (2002), *Environmental Policy in Open Economies and Leakage Problems,* unpublished manuscript.

Climate Policies: Trade Spillovers, Joint Implementation and Technological Spillovers, Market Power, Investment Risks

Christoph Böhringer and Andreas Löschel

Centre for European Economic Research, P.O. Box 103443, 68034 Mannheim, Germany
boehringer@zew.de, loeschel@zew.de

1 Trade Spillovers

Policy interventions in large open economies not only affect the allocation of domestic resources but also change international market prices. The change in international prices implies an indirect (*secondary*) effect for *all* trading countries. This secondary terms-of-trade effect may have important policy implications. For example, international environmental agreements should account for induced changes in terms of trade when searching for 'equitable' burden sharing schemes. Section 1.1 presents a decomposition that splits the total effect of policy changes on individual countries into a *domestic market effect* holding international prices constant and an *international market effect* as a result of changes in international prices. Splitting the total effect into these components conveys important economic information as to why a country will benefit or lose from adjustments in domestic and international markets.

In applied policy analysis, it is often relevant to link changes in endogenous variables (e.g. regions' welfare or emissions of CO_2) to changes in the policy instruments (e.g. tariff rates). Such a decomposition of the total policy effect could, for example, be used to evaluate induced gains or losses from multilateral trade liberalisation at the bilateral level and set up transfer or compensation systems. Section 1.2 describes a decomposition technique (originated by Harrison et al., 2000) to measure bilateral spillovers from policy interference.

In order to highlight the relevance of the decomposition techniques for sustainable impact analysis, Sections 1.1 and 1.2 provide an application to climate change policy. The numerical simulations refer to a situation where industrialised countries apply domestic carbon taxes to meet their emission targets under the Kyoto Protocol (UN, 1997).

1.1   Decomposing International Spillovers[1]

The effects of policy intervention in large open economies can be broken down into a *domestic market effect*, assuming that international prices remain constant, and an *international market effect* as a result of changes in international prices. The key idea with respect to applied model analysis is that each region of a multi-region trade model (MRT) can be represented as a small open economy (SOE) in order to separate the domestic policy effect under fixed terms of trade. Policy induced changes in international prices from the multi-region model can then be imposed parametrically on the small open economy to measure the international market effect commodity by commodity (Böhringer and Rutherford, 2002a).

Figure 1 illustrates the steps involved in the decomposition procedure. Computation of the domestic market effect simply requires to keep international prices at the benchmark (reference) level and then impose the domestic policy change on the specific country. Hence, for the intermediate SOE equilibrium calculation (A→B), changes on the domestic market have no effect on international prices. The spillover effect for any economic or environmental activity of a specific country is then simply the residual between the SOE equilibrium solution at benchmark terms-of-trade and the full MRT solution for the specific country (C).[2]

Table 1 summarises results for the decomposition of economic effects induced by carbon abatement policies of industrialised countries under the Kyoto Protocol. The column *Total Policy Effect* reports aggregate consumption changes in % vis-à-vis the business-as-usual (BaU) that emerge from carbon taxes of industrialised countries introduced to comply with their Kyoto emission reduction targets in 2010.

Tax-induced reallocation of resources due to emission constraints (e.g. fuel shifting or energy savings) causes substantial adjustment costs for OECD countries. Furthermore, there are considerable international spillover effects from abating industrialised countries to non-abating countries: Adjustments on international markets induce welfare losses for FSU as well as MPC and, to a much smaller extent, for ROW. All other non-abating countries benefit to varying degrees from the changes in international prices associated with emission abatement in OECD countries.

---

[1]   This section is based on Böhringer, C. and T.F. Rutherford (2002), Carbon Abatement and International Spillovers, *Environmental and Resource Economics* 22 (3), 391-417.

[2]   A simple consistency check for the decomposition is as follows: Imposing the changes in international prices which are delivered by the MRT solution (A→C), one should be able to reproduce exactly the MRT solution from the SOE perspective (B→C).

Application of the decomposition method allows to gain insights into the different sources of welfare changes across regions. Table 2 lays out how the economic impact of carbon taxes turns from the domestic market effect into the total policy effect as changes in international prices are successively imposed upon the SOE sub-models. The column *International Spillovers* indicates the magnitude of international spillovers measured in percent of the total policy effect. Obviously, the international spillovers is identical to the total policy effect for those countries which do not undertake domestic abatement, i.e. countries whose domestic market effect is zero. As to abating countries, the decomposition provides information on the sign and relative magnitude of the primary domestic and the secondary international impacts. International spillovers are negative for USA, CAN and OOE, whereas CEA, EUR, and JPN benefit from the adjustments on international markets.

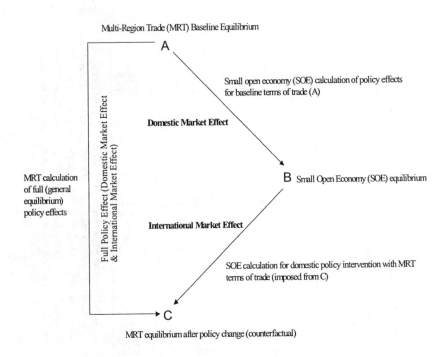

Figure 1:   The MRT-SOE Decomposition.

Table 1:   Decomposition of Total Consumption Changes for Carbon Tax Case NTR (No Trade).

	Domestic Market Effect** (in % of BaU Consumption)	Fossil Fuel Market Effect** (in % of BaU Consumption)	Total Policy Effect (in % of BaU Consumption)	International Spillovers* (in % of Total Policy Effect)	Carbon Tax (in USD$_{95}$ / Ton C)	Emission Reduction (in % vs. BaU)
CAN	-0.69	-0.86	-0.88	21	230	28
CEA	0.00	0.26	0.29	100	1	-6
EUR	-0.14	-0.06	-0.06	-116	107	14
FSU	0.00	-0.43	-1.03	100	-	-48
JPN	-0.44	-0.38	-0.30	-47	300	26
OOE	-0.13	-0.47	-0.65	81	76	16
USA	-0.36	-0.38	-0.40	9	160	27
ASI	0.00	0.26	0.14	100	-	-
BRA	0.00	0.08	0.09	100	-	-
CHN	0.00	0.26	0.20	100	-	-
IND	0.00	0.32	0.27	100	-	-
MPC	0.00	-0.77	-0.99	100	-	-
ROW	0.00	-0.05	-0.08	100	-	-

Key: CAN – Canada, CEA – Central European Associates, EUR – Europe (EU15 and EFTA), FSU – Former Soviet Union (Russian Federation and Ukraine), JPN – Japan, OOE – Other OECD (Australia and New Zealand), USA – United States, ASI – Other Asia (except for China and India), BRA – Brazil, CHN – China (incl. Hong Kong and Taiwan), IND – India, MPC – Mexico and OPEC, ROW – Rest of World

* Calculated as: 100* [(Total Policy Effect) – (Domestic Market Effect)] / (Total Policy Effect)

** Accounting for domestic market effect and international price changes for crude oil and coal

Regarding international spillovers, the adjustments on international coal and crude oil markets (see column *Fossil Fuel Market Effect*) are most important. The cutback in demand for fossil fuels from abating OECD countries depresses the international prices for oil and coal. As a consequence, countries which are net importers of coal and crude oil gain, whereas net exporting countries lose. For CAN, MPC, and ROW, which are net exporters of both coal and crude oil, the aggregate welfare effect is unambiguously negative. Likewise, net importers EUR, JPN, CHN, IND, BRA, and ASI experience welfare gains. For countries which are net importer of one fossil fuel *and* net exporter of the other, the aggregate effect depends on export and import quantities as well as the relative changes in international coal and crude oil prices.

The next step of decomposition accounts for international price changes in non-energy markets where traded goods are differentiated by region of origin. On these markets, developing countries typically face adverse spillover effects. Apart from higher export prices of developed countries, developing countries suffer from a scale effect as economic activity and hence import demand by developed countries decline. On the other hand, this effect can be (partially) offset by an opposite substitution effect. Developing countries gain market shares in Annex B countries because their exports become more competitive. The same mechanisms apply to trade between abating countries with large differences in imposed carbon taxes. As an example, OOE, which has low carbon taxes, suffers from increased export prices of trading partners with high carbon taxes, such as Japan.

To sum up: Application of the decomposition method to emission regulation under the Kyoto Protocol reveals that among signatory countries, Australia, Canada, New Zealand and USA bear a secondary burden through changes in international terms of trade, whereas Europe and Japan experience secondary benefits. Most developing countries gain a comparative advantage due to abatement in Annex B regions, but fossil fuel exporters such as Mexico and OPEC are seriously hurt. A major determinant for the differences in sign and magnitude of spillovers is the trade position of countries on international coal and crude oil markets: Depressed international prices for fossil fuels, that are due to the cutback in global fossil energy demand, provide gains for fossil fuel importers and losses for fossil fuel exporters.

1.2   Decomposing Bilateral Spillovers[3]

Harrison, Horridge, and Pearson (HHP) propose a generic linear decomposition methodology for calculating the contributions of multiple exogenous policy in-

---

[3]   This section is based on Böhringer, C. and T.F. Rutherford (2004), Who Should Pay How Much? Compensation for International Spillovers from Carbon Abatement Policies to Developing Countries – A Global CGE Assessment, *Computational Economics* 23 (2).

struments to the resulting changes in individual endogenous variables (Harrison et al., 2000). The HHP method can be explained along a simplified example in which an *endogenous* variable Z is expressed as an explicit function of a vector of *exogenous* variables $\vec{X}$ (the policy instruments):

$$Z = F(\vec{X}) = F(x_1, x_2, ..., x_n) \tag{1}$$

A change in the exogenous policy instruments $\vec{X}$ induces an endogenous change ΔZ in Z. For policy analysis, it is often useful to attribute changes in the endogenous variable to changes in the policy instruments. One way of decomposing the total change ΔZ in the endogenous variable with respect to the individual contributions from exogenous variables would be a sequential approximation of the impacts of *one* exogenous variable while keeping *all others* constant. Assuming that F is differentiable, the contribution of a change in the i-th exogenous variable to ΔZ (as x_i moves from the initial value x_i^0 to the new value x_i^1) can then be computed as the line integral:

$$\Delta Z\big|_{x_i} = \int_{x_i^0}^{x_i^1} \frac{\partial F}{\partial x_i} dx_i \tag{2}$$

For the numerical computation, the total change in the exogenous variable Δx_i is divided into sufficiently small steps to approximate the line integral through linearisation.

When F is nonlinear, the total change from shocks in exogenous variables cannot be decomposed in additive line-integrals for each exogenous variable starting from the initial value Z^0. The impact of a change in an exogenous variable must be calculated, taking into account the contributions of *previous* changes in other exogenous variables. This implies that the decomposition is potentially sensitive to the sequential ordering of changes in the exogenous policy variables. As there are $n!$ ways of sequential ordering of n exogenous variables, one quickly ends up with a large number of (possibly) different decompositions for relatively small-scale policy experiments. For many policy packages (including multilateral emission abatement contracts, such as the Kyoto Protocol) no sequential decomposition might be obviously more plausible than any other. HHP therefore suggest an order-independent 'natural' way of calculating contributions. On the 'natural' path, the exogenous variables move *together at the same rate* towards their final value along a straight line between their starting values $\vec{X}^0$ and the final values $\vec{X}^1$. The straight line between these points is obtained by changing the elements of $\vec{X}$ as a differentiable function H of some parameter t holding the rate of change in the exogenous variables constant along the path (where $\vec{X}^0 = H(t = t^0), \vec{X}^1 = H(t = t^1)$).

Figure 2 illustrates the difference between the sequential method of decomposition and the HHP approach. In contrast to moving along the *edges* of the policy cube, the HPP method follows a straight line between the pre- and post-simulation values.

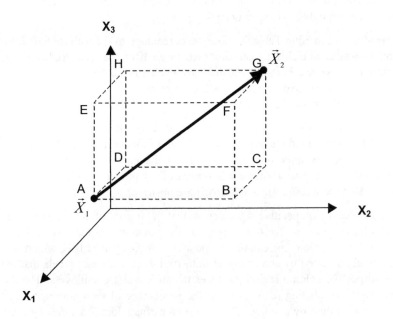

Figure 2:   Sequential Ordering Versus 'Natural'-Path.

For n exogenous variables, the total change in the endogenous variable is equal to:

$$\Delta Z = \sum_{i=1}^{n} \int_{t=t^0}^{t=t^1} \frac{\partial F}{\partial x_i} \frac{dx_i}{dt} dt \tag{3}$$

This concept is easily generalised to the case where the relationship between exogenous and endogenous variables is implicit, which is typically the case for computable general equilibrium models used for the economic analysis. As HHP point out, it is possible to calculate numerical values for the gradients $\frac{\partial F}{\partial x_i} \frac{dx_i}{dt}$ at all points of the 'natural' path by solving a system of linear equations. The individual contributions of changes in policy instruments x_i can then be approximated through linearisation of the respective line integral which involves solving a system of linear equations R times, where R renders a sufficiently small step-size $\Delta t / R$ (with $\Delta t = t^1 - t^0$).

Application of the HHP decomposition to climate change policies provides concrete estimates for bilateral spillovers that might be useful for the delicate policy issue of who should pay for adverse international spillovers to developing countries (Böhringer and Rutherford, 2004).[4] The HHP procedure avoids arbitrariness in the calculation of spillovers as compared to any sequential ordering of abatement policies in industrialised countries.

The results, presented in Table 2, show the percentage of the welfare cost for each region (rows) attributable to carbon taxes in each of the industrialised regions (columns). These numbers are obtained by evaluating a line integral where the carbon *taxes* across abating regions are change at equal rates starting from zero and ending with the final carbon taxes as reported in Table 1.

Matrix elements with negative signs indicate that the effect of the abatement policy by the column region is opposite to the sign of the total welfare change for the row region. For example, the value of -30 at the intersection of *row* ASI with *column* JPN means that abatement actions in JPN induce a welfare *loss* in ASI (since overall the welfare impacts for ASI are positive).

Matrix elements with positive signs denote that the impact of the abatement policy in the column region on the row region has the same sign as the total welfare impact of the row region. For example, a positive *row* entry for MPC, which in total is negatively affected by abatement in industrialised countries, reveals that action of the respective column region produces negative welfare spillovers. The diagonal elements for abating regions reveal the percentage of their aggregate welfare changes due to their own policy. The *own-policy* effect dominates the aggregate of the *foreign-policy* effects, except for OOE and, in particular, for CEA, which impose rather small domestic carbon taxes.

Reading down the *column* USA in Table 2, we find that abatement actions by the USA produce by far the largest spillovers to other countries. The main source for these spillovers are larger adjustments on the international fossil fuel markets due to the substantial cutbacks in US fossil energy demands. Emission constraints in the USA account for the bigger part of the decline in fossil fuel producer prices following multilateral abatement under the Kyoto Protocol. This produces positive bilateral spillovers to fuel importers, such as EUR, JPN and developing regions ASI, BRA, CHN, as well as IND. Fuel exporters, such as CAN, MPC or ROW, are negatively affected. At the other end of the impact spectrum, we find OOE and CEA, whose spillovers to other regions are rather negligible due to their moderate tax rates and small shares in overall trade volumes. Reading Table 2 by rows, we

---

[4]   The United Nations Framework Convention on Climate Change (UNFCC, 1992) guarantees compensation from industrialised countries to the developing world for adverse spillovers from emission abatement in the industrialised world (Articles 4.8 and 4.9).

obtain information on how a country is affected by the carbon taxes of abating industrialised countries.

Table 2:   Decomposition of Consumption Impacts from Carbon Taxes at the Bilateral Level.

	Consumption Change		Percentage of the Welfare Cost for Each Region (Rows) Attributable to Carbon Taxes in Each of the Annex B Regions (Columns)				
	in % vs. BaU	in bn USD$_{95}$	CAN	EUR	JPN	OOE	USA
CAN	-0.88	-0.62	87	6	4		2
CEA	0.29	0.10	11	24	18	1	47
EUR	-0.06	-0.69	-15	250	-25	-4	-105
FSU	-1.03	-0.51	3	40	4		52
JPN	-0.30	-1.65	-6	-12	148	-1	-29
OOE	-0.65	-0.33	3	13	12	33	39
USA	-0.40	-3.60	2	-4	-5	-1	107
ASI	0.14	0.24	12	19	-30	2	96
BRA	0.09	0.14	11	14	20	2	53
CHN	0.20	0.43	7	18	15	2	59
IND	0.27	0.16	7	17	15	2	59
MPC	-0.99	-1.71	9	19	20	1	51
ROW	-0.08	-0.19	15	31	51	6	-3
Total	-0.22	-8.23					

The percentage changes in welfare from individual policy action as reported in Table 3 can be translated into monetary units. Table 3 presents the matrix of compensating (net) transfer payments that must be assigned on a bilateral basis in order to provide compensation for spillovers from abatement policies in individual industrialised countries. A negative entry indicates compensation claims of the *row* region towards the *column* region.

Tables 2 and 3 reveal fundamental problems underlying the issue of compensation to developing countries for induced economic costs. A developing region may benefit from abatement in one industrialised country, but suffer from abatement in other industrialised regions. This raises the question of whether developing countries that are compensated for adverse spillovers on the one hand should pay for positive spillovers on the other hand. To put it differently, industrialised countries that compensate for adverse spillovers to some developing countries may well claim transfers from those developing countries which benefit from their abatement policy.

Table 3:   Compensating Transfers from Region (Rows) to Region (Column) in Billion Dollars Annually Between 2008 and 2012.

	CAN	CEA	EUR	FSU	JPN	OOE	USA
CEA	0.01						
EUR	0.14	-0.02					
FSU	-0.02		-0.2				
JPN	0.12	-0.02	0.03	0.02			
OOE	-0.01		-0.07		-0.06		
USA	-0.06	-0.05	-0.58	0.27	-0.3	0.17	
ASI	0.03		0.05		-0.07		0.23
BRA	0.02		0.02		0.03		0.07
CHN	0.03		0.08		0.06	0.01	0.25
IND	0.01		0.03		0.02		0.1
MPC	-0.15		-0.32		-0.34	-0.02	-0.87
ROW	-0.03		-0.06		-0.1	-0.01	0.01

2   JI and Technological Spillovers[5]

2.1   Introduction

In order to promote international climate policies, Germany has already committed itself to substantial unilateral emission reductions in the early 1990s: The German government set a carbon emission reduction target of 25% in 2005 as compared to 1990 emission levels which has been reconfirmed several times since then. Concerns regarding adverse employment effects of carbon emission con-

---

[5]   This section is based on Böhringer, C., K. Conrad, and A. Löschel (2003), Carbon Taxes and Joint Implementation: An Applied General Equilibrium Analysis for Germany and India, *Environmental and Resource Economics* 24 (1), 49-76.

straints for the national economy have induced policy makers to adopt an environmental tax reform as a key instrument for meeting the reduction target. Such a reform entails an increase in environmental taxes together with a revenue-neutral reduction in labour costs. This policy is supposed to yield a double dividend in the simultaneous reduction of harmful greenhouse gas emissions (first dividend) and alleviation of unemployment problems (second dividend). However, while the environmental dividend is generally beyond controversy, the employment dividend is not. Environmental taxes may well exacerbate rather than alleviate pre-existing tax distortions. This is because environmental taxes induce not only market distortions similar to those of the replaced taxes but in addition new distortions in intermediate and final consumption. The negative impacts on labour demand by levying additional environmental taxes (tax interaction effect) may dominate the positive impacts of using additional revenues for cuts in labour costs (revenue recycling effect). Theoretical and empirical results show that the prospect for the second dividend crucially depends on the existing inefficiencies of the tax system, labour market imperfections and the level of environmental taxes (i.e. the environmental target).[6]

The levying as well as the recycling of environmental taxes induce substitution and output effects. Under a higher emission or energy tax, employment benefits from a positive substitution effect of labour for energy. However, there is also a negative output effect due to increased prices and reduced domestic demand. The output effect could outweigh the substitution effect on labour demand. Given the latter, a policy which achieves an environmental goal with a weak negative output effect by reducing the level of environmental taxes and strengthening domestic demand is therefore of interest.

At the strictly domestic level, using lower environmental taxes to ameliorate negative effects on production activities and labour demand would directly trade off with higher emissions. Germany would then fall short of its stated reduction target. Yet, international treaties on climate protection allow for the supplementary use of flexible instruments to exploit cheaper emission reduction possibilities elsewhere. The concept of joint implementation has been incorporated into the Kyoto Protocol to the UN Framework Convention on Climate Change (UNFCCC, 1997).[7] Instead of meeting its reduction target solely by domestic action, Germany

---

[6]   For a survey on the double-dividend literature see Goulder (1995b) and Bovenberg (1997).

[7]   Under Article 6, countries with emission reduction targets (Annex I countries) may fund joint implementation projects in other Annex I countries in return for 'emission reduction units', which may be supplemental to domestic actions for the purpose of meeting the commitments. Article 12 defines the Clean Development Mechanism (CDM) as joint implementation between Annex I and non-Annex I countries. In the following, we only refer to joint implementation as the general concept.

could enter joint implementation with developing countries such as India, where Germany buys part of its emission reduction from abroad.[8]

In our analysis below, we investigate whether an environmental tax reform *cum* joint implementation (JI) provides employment and overall efficiency gains as compared to a *stand-alone* environmental tax reform (ETR). We address this question in the framework of a large-scale computable general equilibrium (CGE) model for Germany and India where Germany may undertake joint implementation with the Indian electricity sector. Our main finding is that joint implementation largely offsets the adverse effects of carbon emission constraints on the German economy. Whereas strictly domestic action by Germany (i.e. ETR) implies a loss in economic performance and employment, JI reduces substantially the welfare losses and provides employment gains. JI significantly lowers the level of carbon taxes in Germany and thus reduces the total costs of abatement as well as negative effects on labour demand. In addition, JI triggers direct investment demand for energy efficient power plants produced in Germany. This provides positive employment effects and additional income for Germany. For India, joint implementation equips its electricity industry with scarce capital goods leading to a more efficient power production with lower electricity prices for the economy and substantial welfare gains.

There have been several studies on the economic and environmental effects of green tax reforms for Germany based on numerical large-scale models and real data (e.g. Conrad and Wang, 1993; DIW, 1994; Buttermann and Hillebrand, 1996; Böhringer et al., 1997; Bach et al., 2001; Welfens et al., 2001). The evidence for employment and welfare effects is mixed, partly due to differences in the concrete tax reform scenarios considered but more so due to differences in modeling assumptions with respect to existing tax distortions, foreign closure and labour market imperfections. Our analysis complements the existing literature in several ways. From a policy point of view, it does not focus on a narrow discussion of the double-dividend hypothesis but investigates how flexibility through JI could improve the prospects for efficiency and employment gains from environmental tax reforms in Germany. From a methodological point of view, we provide an innovative application of the cost or productivity gap concept by Jorgenson and Nishimizu (1978): The effects of JI are evaluated taking into account efficiency improvements in developing countries through capital transfers.

The remainder of this chapter is organised as follows. First, the generic model structure complemented with extensions for representing joint implementation and measuring productivity changes is laid out. Then, the policy scenarios and our simulation results are described. Finally, conclusions and lines of future research are provided.

---

[8]   For detailed information on joint implementation see Kuik et al. (1994), Jackson (1995), and Jepma (1995).

2.2   Basic Model

The choice of production sectors and the nesting of functional forms capture key dimensions of the analysis of greenhouse gas abatement such as differences in carbon intensities and the scope for substitution across energy goods and carbon-intensive non-energy goods. The energy goods identified in the model are coal (COL), natural gas (GAS), crude oil (CRU), refined oil products (OIL) and electricity (ELE). The non-energy sectors include important carbon-intensive industries such as transportation services (TRN) and an aggregate energy-intensive sector (EIS). The rest of the production sector is divided into other machinery (OME), construction (CNS) and other manufactures and services (Y). Primary factors include labour, capital and fossil-fuel resources. Labour is treated as intersectorally mobile within each region, but not between regions. Capital is sector specific and internationally immobile. A sector-specific resource is used in the production of primary fossil fuels (crude oil, coal and gas), resulting in upward sloping supply schedules for those goods. Table 4 summarises the sectors, countries and primary factors incorporated in the model.

Table 4:   Overview of Sectors, Factors and Countries.

Sectors		Primary Factors		Countries
COL	Coal	CAP	Capital	GER Germany
CRU	Crude oil	LAB	Labour	IND India
GAS	Natural gas	RES	Sector-specific resource	
OIL	Refined oil products			
ELE	Electricity			
EIS	Energy-intensive sectors			
TRN	Transport equipment			
OME	Other machinery			
CNS	Construction			
Y	Manufactures and services			

2.2.1   Production

Nested constant elasticity of substitution (CES) cost functions are employed to specify the substitution possibilities in domestic production between capital (K), labour (L), energy (E) and material (M) intermediate inputs.

In the production of commodities other than primary fossil fuels and electricity, intermediate non-energy goods and crude oil (used as feedstock) are employed in fixed proportions with an aggregate of energy, capital and labour at the top level.

At the second level, a CES function describes the substitution possibilities between labour and the aggregate of capital and the energy composite. At the third level, capital and the energy composite trade off with a constant elasticity of substitution. The energy aggregate is, in turn, a nested CES composite of electricity and primary energy inputs. The primary energy composite is defined as a CES function of coal and a CES aggregate of refined oil and natural gas. In the production of electricity non-energy goods as well as crude oil and refined oil products, which do not constitute fossil fuel options in power generation, enter in fixed proportions with a composite of labour, energy, and capital. The latter is given as a CES function between labour inputs and a restricted CES sub-function of capital and energy. At the lower energy nest, gas and coal inputs trade off with a constant elasticity of substitution. The KLEM nesting structure for production in non-fossil fuel sectors reflects common perception of the substitution possibilities except for the trade-off between capital, labour and energy. Some models (see e.g. Manne and Richels, 1992) specify a trade-off between energy and the value-added aggregate, whereas other models (e.g. Welsch, 1996b) choose the trade-off between labour and an energy-capital composite. The latter disaggregation has been adopted for the current model since it reflects empirical evidence that labour is a substitute for both energy and capital (see Burniaux et al., 1992).

In the fossil fuel production activity (crude oil, natural gas and coal), labour, capital and energy inputs enter a CES composite at the lower nest. At the top level, this aggregate trades off with the sector-specific fossil-fuel resource at a constant elasticity of substitution. The latter is calibrated in consistency with empirical price elasticities of fossil fuel supplies.

2.2.2   Private Demand

Final private demand for goods and services in each region is derived from utility maximisation of a representative household subject to a budget constraint. In our comparative-static framework, overall investment demand is fixed at the reference level. Total income of the representative household consists of factor income and transfers. Final demand of the representative agent is given as a CES composite of an energy aggregate and a non-energy consumption composite. Substitution patterns within the energy aggregate and the non-energy consumption bundle are reflected via Cobb-Douglas functions.

2.2.3   Government Demand

The government distributes transfers and provides a public good (including public investment) which is produced with commodities purchased at market prices. In order to capture the implications of an environmental tax reform on the efficiency of public fund raising, the model incorporates the main features of the German tax system: (linear progressive) income taxes including social insurance contributions, capital taxes (corporate and trade taxes), value-added taxes and other indirect taxes (e.g. mineral oil tax). In all simulations, we impose revenue-neutrality in the sense that the level of public provision is fixed. Subject to this equal-yield constraint, additional revenues from environmental taxes get recycled through cuts in labour costs (social insurance payments). As to India, we do not incorporate details of taxation, but assume that constant public good provision is financed lump-sum by the representative consumer.

2.2.4   International Trade

All commodities are traded internationally. We adopt the Armington assumption that goods produced in different regions are qualitatively distinct for all commodities. Intermediate as well as final demands are (nested CES) Armington composites of domestic and imported varieties. Germany and India are assumed to be price-takers with respect to the rest of the world (ROW) which is not explicitly represented as a region in the model. Trade with ROW is incorporated via perfectly elastic ROW import-supply and export-demand functions. There is an imposed balance of payment constraint to ensure trade balance between Germany and India on the one hand, and ROW on the other hand. That is, the value of imports from ROW to Germany and India must equal the value of exports from these countries to ROW after including a constant benchmark trade surplus (deficit).[9]

2.2.5   Labour Market

The analysis of the employment effects associated with an environmental tax reform requires an appropriate specification of unemployment for the German economy. In our formulation, unemployment is generated by the existence of a 'wage curve', which postulates a negative relationship between the real wage rate and the rate of unemployment. The specific wage curve employed can be derived from trade union wage models as well as from efficiency wage models (Hutton and Ruocco, 1999). As to India, we assume that labour is in fixed supply and labour markets are perfectly competitive.

---

[9]   There are different types of macroeconomic closure rules (see, e.g., Dewatripont and Michel, 1987; Kehoe et al., 1995), but no clear-cut theoretical justification for the choice of a particular one. Our static model accommodates, e. g., different macroeconomic closure alternatives for the foreign sectors and the government. With respect to the foreign sector closure, we fix the trade deficit with ROW and determine exports and imports endogenously. For the government we assume an endogenous government deficit. The activity level of the government is then fixed. The sensitivity of simulation results to macroeconomic closure rules is analysed in Rattso (1982) and Kehoe et al. (1995).

2.3   Modelling Joint Implementation

The rationale behind joint implementation is the same as with emissions trading: Cost-effectiveness requires that measures to limit greenhouse gas emissions should be taken where they are cheapest, i.e. marginal abatement costs should be equalised across different sources. However, as compared to emissions trading, JI is based on concrete projects. The JI donor country receives emission credits that may count towards its own emission targets for carrying out climate protection projects in return for funds and technology given to the JI host. The implementation of project-based JI mechanisms in top-down models where sectoral production possibilities are given by aggregate functional forms raises some difficulties. Instead of using a discrete step-function for the abatement cost curve based on bottom-up estimates, emission abatement possibilities are implicit to the flexible functional form. The challenge is to specify and calibrate the functional form in such a way that it provides a reasonable approximation for the marginal abatement costs available from engineering data. For this purpose we employ flexible CES functions with a rather sophisticated nesting of energy inputs. Energy supply and demand calibration are based on physical energy flows and energy prices. In the model, JI is represented as a sectoral permit trade regime where sectors in non-abating countries qualifying for JI – in our case the Indian electricity sector – are endowed with sector-specific emission budgets. The amount of permit rights is set equal to the baseline carbon emissions of the Indian electricity sector. Under JI, the donor – here Germany – will demand emission rights (credits) from the JI host – here the Indian power industry – as long as the price of the emission credit is below its marginal abatement costs at home. On the other hand, the Indian power industry will deliver emission credits to Germany as long as the marginal costs of abating carbon in the power industry are lower than the price or revenue received for the emission credit. According to this arbitrage rule, the Indian electricity sector will allocate its baseline emission rights between credits for Germany and demand for its own domestic production. Without joint implementation, the quantity of available emission rights in Germany is fixed. Emission credits from joint implementation enlarge the total emission budget of Germany which allows for a reduction of the domestic carbon tax while complying with the overall carbon emission constraint.

The principal JI mechanism underlying our model simulations is illustrated in Figure 3. The flexibility mechanisms allow a redistribution of the emission reductions between the countries, although the overall target reduction is unchanged. Given the total emission reduction requirement $\bar{A}$ in Germany, only the volume A_G will be achieved by domestic action whereas the remainder A_I will be abated by the Indian power industry.[10] The carbon price under a strictly domestic environmental tax reform P_{ETR}^{CO2} is reduced to P_{JI}^{CO2} with JI. Total efficiency gains from JI are given by the shaded area KLM. Distribution of these gains are determined here via the market solution: The JI donor country receives a net gain NLM which is equal to its savings of abatement costs adjusted for the expenditure of purchasing emission credits. The electricity industry in India receives a net gain KLN which equals the difference between the revenues from the sale of emission credits and its undergone abatement costs.

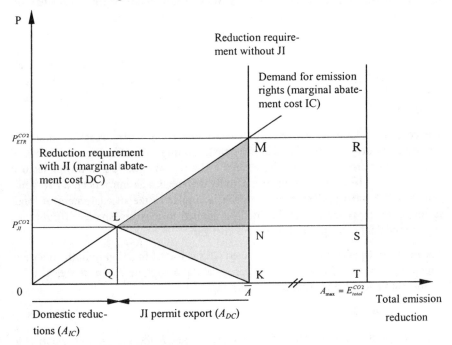

Figure 3:   Joint Implementation Mechanism.

Reflecting the project character of JI, the electricity industry in India uses the revenues from the sale of emission reductions to buy capital goods directly from Germany. The German capital goods (coal or gas power plants) increase the capital stock in the Indian electricity sector. This direct investment exerts a positive effect on employment in the German manufacturing industries. Additional revenues from permits reduce the electricity price in India. Tax revenue in Germany for reducing non-wage labour cost is the area MKTR before JI. After JI tax reve-

---

[10]   We assume that JI abatement is fully allowable against domestic abatement requirements and that there is no minimum share for domestic abatement. For other specifications see Cansier and Krumm (1996).

nue is only LQTS where LQKN is the amount of money paid by Germany for emission credits. The area NKTS is now left for reducing non-wage labour costs.

2.4   Joint Implementation Under Productivity Gaps in the Electricity Producing Industry

Reflecting empirical evidence we assume that there are productivity differences between Germany and India in the electricity sector. Since energy efficiency of fossil fuel fired power plants in Germany is significantly higher than in India, the German industry could invest in Indian power plants to reduce the productivity difference, hereby improving India's energy efficiency. In other words, India's energy producers use the JI revenues received from Germany for the replacement of older inefficient power plants by new highly efficient gas or coal power plants.[11] This results ceteris paribus in a decrease in variable costs or an increase in output.

The cost or productivity gap must be taken into account when assessing joint implementation projects based on capital transfer to improve efficiency. To measure such a cost or productivity gap between the German and the Indian power sector, we employ the measurement of productivity differences as introduced by Jorgenson and Nishimizu (1978). Our approach is similar to the measurement of total factor productivity over time, but will be applied to measure spatial differences. We use the dual concept of measuring a cost gap.

The point of departure is a joint restricted CES sub-cost function in both countries which describes production of the energy-capital aggregate EK in the electricity sector from a fossil fuel composite E and capital K:

$$C = C(PE, EK, K, D) \tag{1}$$

where PE is the price of fossil fuel, EK the output, K the capital stock, and D a dummy variable. The restricted cost function incorporates the short-run impact of quasi-fixed inputs' capacity restrictions on total factor productivity (TFP) growth, reflecting a temporary (short-run) equilibrium. Quasi-fixed inputs should then be evaluated at their shadow rather than their rental prices (i.e. the ex-post prices rather than the ex-ante prices) in order to derive accurate measures of TFP (Berndt and Fuss, 1986). We assume the cost function to be linear homogeneous in EK and K. Because output levels, capital stock and the factor price are expressed relative to India, the dummy variable takes on the value 0 for India (I) and 1 for Germany (G). The dummy variable catches country specific deviations from the joint

---

[11]   India's electricity sector is largely in the responsibility of State Electricity Boards (SEBs). Almost all SEBs are making losses and are nearly bankrupt. Therefore the electricity sector in India has been suffering a severe shortfall in investment resources. See Bose and Shukla (1999).

cost function. It shifts the cost function inwards or outwards. The difference in cost between India and Germany at a given point in time is calculated as the total differential of the cost function in Equation (1). In the form of logarithmic derivatives, we get:

$$\frac{d \ln C}{d D} = s_E \frac{d \ln PE}{d D} + \frac{\partial \ln C}{\partial \ln EK} \frac{d \ln EK}{d D} + \frac{\partial \ln C}{\partial \ln K} \frac{d \ln K}{d D} + \frac{\partial \ln C}{\partial D}$$

(2)

where $s_E = \frac{\partial \ln C}{\partial \ln PE} = \frac{PE \cdot E}{C}$ is the cost share of energy in this aggregate (Shephard's Lemma). In Equation (2) the partial derivatives of the variable cost function with respect to the capital stock K represent the savings in costs from a marginal increase in the stock. This savings in costs is the shadow price of the capital stock (PK_s). In logarithmic partial derivative with respect to K, it is the cost share (multiplied by -1), i.e.:

$$PK_s = -\frac{\partial C}{\partial K} \quad and \quad s_K = \frac{PK_s \cdot K}{C} = -\frac{\partial \ln C}{\partial \ln K}.$$

(3)

Under the additional assumption of profit maximising supply decisions, we have $PEK = \partial C / \partial EK$. The logarithmic partial derivative with respect to output then corresponds to the revenue cost-share. By rearranging Equation (2), we get:

$$\frac{\partial \ln C}{\partial D} = \frac{d \ln C}{d D} - s_E \frac{d \ln PE}{d D} - \frac{PEK \cdot EK}{C} \frac{d \ln EK}{d D} + s_K \frac{d \ln K}{d D}.$$

(4)

Equation (4) shows the sectoral difference in costs between India and Germany if the costs were adjusted for the differences in the levels of production, capital stock, and factor prices at a given point in time. If there is a disadvantage in costs of an Indian sector, then $\partial \ln C / \partial D$ is negative. The left-hand side means that with given Indian energy prices, output EK and capital stock K in the German industrial environment, cost would be lower. In the production function approach $EK = F(E, K, D)$, the equivalent interpretation is that output would be higher by that percentage if Indian EK was produced in Germany. Therefore, in Germany the resources are used more efficiently. The cost gap is calculated by adjusting the difference in costs by the weighted differences in PE, EK and K. Since under CRTS of $C(\cdot)$ in EK and K and under marginal cost pricing $PEK \cdot EK = C + PK_s \cdot K$, or

$$\frac{PEK \cdot EK}{C} - \frac{PK_s \cdot K}{C} = 1$$

(5)

we can cast Equation (4) into the expression

$$\frac{\partial \ln C}{\partial D} = \frac{d \ln C}{d D} - s_E \frac{d \ln PE}{d D} - \frac{d \ln EK}{d D} - \frac{PK_s \cdot K}{C} \frac{d \ln (EK/K)}{d D}.$$ (4')

An increase in capital productivity EK/K in India would lower the positive term $\frac{d \ln (EK/K)}{d D}$ and would therefore reduce the Indian productivity gap.

As a discrete approximation of the Divisia Index in Equation (4), we use the Törnquist index. Then the cost gap s_D can be calculated as:

$$s_D = \ln C(G) - \ln C(I) - \bar{s}_E \left(\ln PE(G) - \ln PE(I) \right)$$
$$- \bar{s}_{EK} \left(\ln EK(G) - \ln EK(I) \right) + \bar{s}_K \left(\ln K(G) - \ln K(I) \right)$$ (6)

with $\bar{s}_j = \frac{1}{2} \left(s_j(G) + s_j(I) \right)$ for $j = E, EK, K$.

Regional differences in the cost structure of two industries result from differences in the quantities of inputs which, in turn, are determined by the level of production, by factor prices, and by the capital stock. A descriptive analysis indicates which components are accountable for the differences in costs but does not determine their contribution in explaining the differences in factor demand. Therefore, the causes for the changes in the cost gaps have to be determined by employing an econometric model.

For our CGE analysis, we use a CES specification of the restricted cost function:

$$C = PE \cdot \left[\left(EK \cdot \exp(-a_0 - a_D \cdot D) \right)^{-\rho} - (d_K + d_{K,D} \cdot D) \cdot K^{-\rho} \right]^{-\frac{1}{\rho}} \cdot (d_E + d_{E,D} \cdot D)^{\frac{1}{\rho}}$$ (7)

where $\sigma = \frac{1}{1+\rho}$ is the elasticity of substitution. The cost shares s_E, s_{EK}, s_K and the gap $s_D = \frac{\partial \ln C}{\partial D}$ can be derived by differentiating the cost function with respect to PE, EK, K and D.[12] It is

$$s_D = \frac{\partial \ln C}{\partial D} = \frac{-a_D + \dfrac{d_{K,D}}{\rho} \left(\dfrac{EK}{K} \right)^{\rho} \exp(-a_0 \cdot \rho)}{1 - \left(\dfrac{EK}{K} \right)^{\rho} \exp(-a_0 \cdot \rho) \cdot d_K} + \frac{d_{E,D}}{\rho \cdot d_E}$$ (8)

---

[12]   See Appendix for the calibration of the parameters under a temporary equilibrium and a cost gap.

and $\dfrac{\partial s_D}{\partial \left(\dfrac{EK}{K}\right)} > 0$ gives the impact of $\dfrac{EK}{K}$ on the difference in costs. The positive

sign means that the difference in costs ($s_D < 0$) will be reduced if capital productivity can be raised in India.

The following Figure presents the situation. We assume that output is the same in both countries and that the relative price of energy with respect to capital is normalised to be one in both countries in a long-run equilibrium situation. Given capital shortage in India, the shadow price of capital, PK_s, in India is higher than in Germany, implying the less steep slope of the iso-cost line for India in its temporary equilibrium.

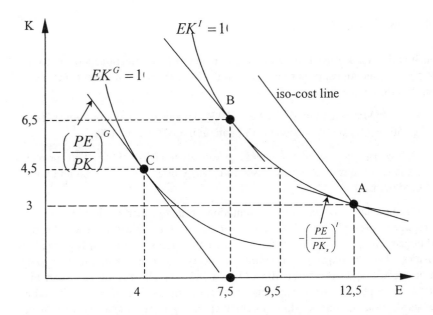

Figure 4:   Productivity Gaps in the Electricity Sector.

Since capital is quasi-fixed, India does not produce at its minimal cost combination B. It has to produce at A with $\bar{K} = 3$, $E = 12.5$. If India produced $EK = 10$ with 4.5 units of capital instead of its 3 units, it would save 3 units of energy (9.5 instead of 12.5). If it used only 4 units of energy, it would require about 3 times as much capital as Germany. Since the Indian electricity industry is in a short-run equilibrium (A), investment in capital through joint implementation would help to reach the long-run equilibrium in B. Since energy and capital are internationally traded goods, we assume that the slope of the iso-cost line in B and C is the same for India's and Germany's electricity sector. Since costs are lower in B compared to A, the cost gap will be reduced by becoming less negative. From the production side, the saving in costs can be used to buy more inputs and the increase in the resulting output will reduce the productivity gap. In the cost gap calculation in Equation (4) $\ln C(I)$ declines, the new s_D^{JI} will be less negative. Therefore the parameter a_0 in Equation (6) for s_D has to be revised.[13] Its new value enters into the variable cost function and thereby into the price determination of PEK. Since for electricity the demand side determines the size of the aggregate EK (electricity cannot be stored), only a CGE calculation can say whether capital productivity EK/K has changed. In a partial equilibrium framework, EK/K will not change if K changes because EK then changes by the same magnitude, due to constant returns to scale.

2.5   Parameterisation

Benchmark data are used to calibrate parameters of the functional forms from a given set of quantities, prices and elasticities. Data from two different sources are combined to yield a consistent benchmark data set for 1995:

- *GTAP4* (McDougall et al., 1998). GTAP includes detailed input-output tables for 50 sectors and 45 regions with bilateral trade flows for 1995.

- *IEA energy balances and energy prices/taxes* (IEA, 1996). IEA provides statistics on physical energy flows and energy prices for industrial and household demand.

We accommodate a consistent representation of energy markets in physical units by replacing GTAP's aggregate input-output monetary values for energy supply and demand by physical energy flows and energy prices as given in IEA's energy statistics. This 'bottom-up' calibration of energy demands and supplies yields sector-specific and energy-specific CO_2 coefficients. The advantage is that marginal abatement cost curves, and hence the cost evaluation of emission constraints, are based on actual energy flows rather than on aggregate monetary data, which strengthens the credibility of the quantitative results. The magnitude of efficiency gains from JI depend crucially on the emission structure in the Indian and German economy.

---

[13]   If policy instruments are to be considered to close the gap, then instruments like research and development or infrastructure have to be introduced as arguments into the cost function.

2.6   Scenarios and Results

Within the EU burden sharing agreement under the Kyoto Protocol, Germany is obligated to reduce its greenhouse gas emissions by 21% during the period 2008-2012 as compared to its 1990 emission level (EC, 1999b). Independent of this international commitment, the German government adopted a much more ambitious national climate policy plan which foresees a reduction of domestic carbon emissions by 25% in 2005 vis-à-vis the emission level in 1990. In our simulations, we refer to the 25% reduction target and apply it to our benchmark situation for 1995.[14]

We distinguish two alternative policy scenarios as to how Germany can meet its reduction target. The first scenario ETR refers to an environmental tax reform in Germany where carbon taxes are levied in order to meet the domestic emission constraint. Carbon taxes are recycled in a revenue-neutral way to lower labour costs. The second scenario JI allows for joint implementation with the Indian electricity sector. Germany's reduction target can be met by domestic abatement as well as emission reduction undertaken in the Indian power sector. Table 5 summarises the implications of the two different abatement scenarios for inframarginal welfare (measured in terms of Hicksian-equivalent variation), unemployment and marginal abatement costs.

Table 5:   Welfare, Unemployment, Marginal Abatement Cost, Emission Reductions.

	ETR	JI
Welfare in Germany [a]	-0.47	-0.26
Welfare in India [a]	-	2.49
Unemployment in Germany [a]	0.22	-0.49
Marginal Abatement Cost [b]	61	33
Emission Reduction in Germany [c]	242	154
Emission Reduction in Indian Electricity Sector [c]	-	88

[a] Percentage change.
[b] In USD_{95} per ton of CO_2.
[c] In million tons of CO_2.

---

[14]   To avoid speculation on the future economic development and baseline emissions for Germany (see e.g. Böhringer et al., 2000a), we abstain from the forward-calibration of the 1995 economy to 2005.

2.6.1   Welfare

A *stand-alone* environmental tax reform is far more costly for Germany than carbon taxes supplemented with joint implementation. Under ETR a carbon tax of roughly 60 USD per ton of CO_2 is required to cut down Germany's carbon emissions by 25%. With JI the carbon tax can be reduced to about 30 USD while ensuring the same overall environmental effectiveness. Lower domestic abatement efforts reduce costly reallocation of resources towards less carbon-intensive production (see Table 6 for the sectoral effects on production).[15] Except for direct efficiency gains from joint abatement under JI, Germany benefits from demand for energy-efficient power plants which triggers additional income. Whereas ETR induces welfare costs of roughly 0.5%, JI largely offsets these adverse effects of carbon emission constraints. As expected, India is not affected by ETR undertaken in Germany. With JI, however, India experiences a large increase in welfare (almost 2.5%). The latter stems from the substantial productivity increase in electricity production due to the capital stock augmentation through JI.

2.6.2   Unemployment

Our simulations indicate that higher carbon taxes as necessary under ETR are not likely to yield an employment double dividend given the initial tax distortions and labour market imperfections in Germany. Carbon tax revenues under ETR amount to nearly 45 bn USD which accommodates a reduction in labour costs of about 5%. The implied positive substitution effects are, however, more than offset by negative output effects due to higher energy prices. JI reduces the negative impact of carbon abatement on employment in Germany. With JI, carbon taxes are reduced and carbon tax revenues fall to 27 bn USD. As a consequence, labour costs can be lowered by only 3% which weakens the substitution effect in favour of labour. On the other hand, the negative output effect is reduced as well – with positive implications for labour demand. In addition, there are direct positive effects on output demand and employment associated with investment under JI.

2.6.3   Emissions

Under ETR Germany must cut down emissions from 972 m tons CO_2 to 730 m tons CO_2. Entering JI with India, Germany's emissions rise to 818 m tons CO_2. In

---

[15]   Coal production in India only decreases by 2.3% even though coal inputs into power generation under JI decline by 28% to accommodate the substantial cutback in carbon emissions in this sector. The reason is that the reduced coal demand in the electricity sector leads to a substantial fall in the output price of coal which, in turn, increases coal demand in other sectors. This also explains the 'sectoral leakage' effect described below. In addition, the large decrease in the market price of coal by about 40% exerts a strong cost pressure which results in the dismissal of 26% of the labour force in coal production.

other words, India takes over carbon abatement of 88 m tons CO_2 as emissions in the Indian electricity sector decline from 353 m tons to 265 m tons CO_2. Germany then only fulfils 64% of its national reduction target domestically – the remaining 36% is delivered by abatement measures in the Indian power sector. It should be noted, that JI only considers emission abatement in the Indian power sector, i.e. indirect (general equilibrium) effects on emissions by other sectors of the Indian economy are not taken into account. In fact, there is intersectoral carbon leakage for India since increased overall economic activity triggered by JI leads to a rise in carbon emissions of the non-electric production sectors.

Table 6:   Sectoral Effects on Production and Employment (% Change).

	GER		IND
	ETR	JI	JI
Production			
COL	-32.31	-20.96	-2.32
GAS	-4.22	-3.21	1.83
OIL	-4.76	-2.58	0.33
ELE	-4.95	-2.76	18.24
EIS	-3.11	-1.69	6.38
TRN	-0.06	-0.03	3.03
OME	0.69	0.50	2.65
CNS	-0.11	0.07	0.52
Y	-0.44	-0.18	1.22
Employment			
COL	-52.90	-38.67	-26.02
GAS	-6.98	-5.33	13.62
OIL	-6.66	-3.67	3.16
ELE	-0.43	-0.19	9.63
EIS	-1.86	-0.99	1.61
TRN	0.20	0.11	-0.87
OME	0.87	0.62	0.21
CNS	-0.03	0.12	-2.20
Y	-0.05	0.05	0.13

The 'intersectoral' leakage rate, which can be measured as the ratio of the emission increase in the non-electric sectors to the emission reduction in power generation, amounts to 56%. From the point of view of global environmental effectiveness, these non-negligible leakage effects of JI should be taken into account although – in political practice – severe problems with respect to the proper determination of the macro-baseline might occur.

2.6.4   Cost Gap Reduction

Through joint implementation the capital stock in the Indian electricity sector increases by about 14%. The reduction in costs due to the movement of the temporary equilibrium towards the long-run equilibrium (which is characterised by less energy and more capital input) results in a significant decline of the electricity price in India. The zero profit condition for the Indian electricity sector states:

$$PELE \cdot ELE = C(ELE; PE, PK, PL) + AC\left(A^I\right) - A^I \cdot P^{CO2}. \qquad (9)$$

The costs of abating CO_2 $\left(AC\left(A^I\right)\right)$ are added to the cost of production and the revenues from selling permits at the permit price P^{CO2} are subtracted. Since the revenue is higher than the cost of abatement, the resulting profit can be used to lower the price $PELE$ of electricity. Although the price PE of fossil fuel increases by the price of a permit (see Table 7), the price index of electricity in India declines significantly from 1 to 0.72. As the fossil fuel mix of India has higher CO_2 emission coefficients, the price PE in India is higher than this price in Germany. Energy intensity E/K drops from 0.40 to 0.27 for India and from 0.33 to 0.26 for Germany. Capital productivity EK/K increases from 1.19 to 1.22 for India and decreases from 1.33 to 1.25 for Germany. Overall, JI improves the performance of the Indian economy and narrows the productivity gap in the Indian electricity sector with respect to the German sector. The initial gap s_D = -0.67 is reduced to s_D^{JI} = -0.11 with JI.

Table 7:   Effects of JI on the Electricity Sector.

	Benchmark		JI	
	IND	GER	IND	GER
K (in bn USD)	1.46	2.39	1.68	2.39
PK	1.44	1	1.15	0.99
E (in bn USD)	0.58	0.79	0.45	0.63
PE	1	1	2.15	1.58
EK (in bn USD)	1.73	3.18	2.05	2.99
PEK	1.55	1	1.41	1.12
PELE	1	1	0.72	1.05

2.7   Conclusions

Carbon taxes which are sufficiently high to achieve substantial domestic emission reductions would have non-negligible adverse impacts on welfare and employment in Germany. JI can help to reduce these negative effects through the associated cost savings and additional investment demand from JI host countries. There are, however, some important remarks on the representation of JI in our analytical framework: Planning and implementation of JI projects in a developing country like India typically involve considerable control and transaction costs. These costs may reduce the attractiveness of JI. In our analysis we neglect this aspect, mainly because of a lack in accurate data. In addition, investments in emission reduction projects in developing countries are risky. We also do not consider the problem that JI between Annex I and non-Annex I countries provides an incentive for the parties to overstate baseline emission levels in order to generate additional emission rights. Furthermore, our analysis is restricted to carbon emission constraints for *one* industrialised country, Germany, that can be met through purely domestic action or via joint implementation with *one* developing country, India. A broader setting, which allows for the incorporation of emission constraints on several industrialised countries as well as joint implementation with all developing countries (as foreseen under the Kyoto Protocol) may affect our quantitative results: For example, a larger reduction of global fossil fuel demand by the industrialised world will depress international fossil fuel prices which provides substantial terms-of-trade gains for fuel importers and terms-of-trade losses for fuel exporters. Likewise, the demand and supply schedule for joint implementation projects will be affected by the increased number of participating countries. However, the key mechanisms of JI elaborated in our paper apply independently of such a more general setting.

The implications of our results for ongoing negotiations may be important. Many developing countries have reservations about joint implementation which might be considered as a pre-stage of binding international emission reduction objectives for the developing world. Moreover, some developing countries regard compensation projects as a cheap buy-out option for the industrialised world from their historic obligation to reduce greenhouse gas emissions. However, JI may be the only possibility for developing countries like India to equip its electricity industry with scarce capital goods yielding large welfare gains through more efficient power production and lower electricity prices. As to future research, an intertemporal analysis of the process of capital accumulation in developing countries towards the long-run equilibrium would be desirable in order to shed more light on the dynamic aspects of joint implementation.

2.8   Appendix: Calibration of Parameters Under a Temporary Equilibrium and a Cost Gap

In this Section the calibration of a joint production function for the electricity producing industry is described, where the Indian sector is in a temporary equilibrium including a productivity gap.

The joint CES production function is:

$$EK = \exp(a_0 + a_D \cdot D) \cdot \left[\left(d_E + d_{E,D} \cdot D \right) \cdot E^{-\rho} + \left(d_K + d_{K,D} \cdot D \right) \cdot K^{-\rho} \right]^{-1/\rho} \tag{10}$$

where $\sigma = \dfrac{1}{1+\rho}$ is the elasticity of substitution. The cost-minimising input coefficients are

$$\frac{E}{EK} = \left(d_E + d_{E,D} \cdot D \right)^{\sigma} \left(\frac{PEK}{PE} \right)^{\sigma} \cdot \exp\left[\left(a_0 + a_D \cdot D \right) \cdot \left(-\rho \cdot \sigma \right) \right] \tag{11}$$

$$\frac{K}{EK} = \left(d_K + d_{K,D} \cdot D \right)^{\sigma} \left(\frac{PEK}{PE} \right)^{\sigma} \cdot \exp\left[\left(a_0 + a_D \cdot D \right) \cdot \left(-\rho \cdot \sigma \right) \right] \tag{12}$$

where $(a_0 + a_D) = 0$.

Table 8:   Benchmark Data for the German Electricity Sector.

K^G (in bn USD)	2.386
PK^G	1
E^G (in bn USD)	0.794
PE^G	1
EK^G (in bn USD)	3.180
PEK^G	1

We start from benchmark data for Germany *(D=1)* (Table 8) and assume $\sigma = 0.5$, i.e. $\rho = 1$. We obtain from Equation (11) and Equation (12):

$$d_E + d_{E,D} = 0.062, \quad d_K + d_{K,D} = 0.563. \tag{13}$$

Energy input for India is $E^I = 0.582$. In order to construct a figure for the capital stock, we assume that energy efficiency is lower by 20% in India. Since $\left(E/K \right)^{\sigma}$ is 0.333 in Germany, we assume that $\left(E/K \right)^I = 0.333 * 1.20 = 0.399$.

We assume $PE^I = 1$ which implies a shadow price of capital for India larger than one. For calculating this shadow price PK for India we assume that India is in I on the isoquant in a temporary equilibrium. From $MRS = \left(PE/PK\right)^I$ we determine PK^I:

$$MRS = \frac{d_E + d_{E,D}}{d_K + d_{K,D}} \left(\frac{K}{E}\right)^{I\,\rho+1} = \left(\frac{PE}{PK}\right)^I \tag{14}$$

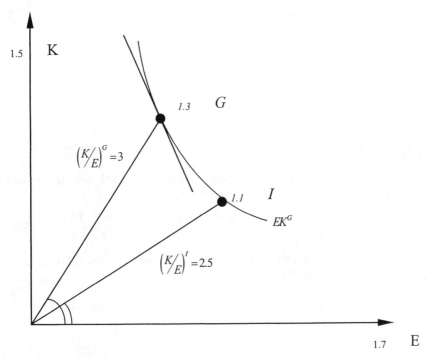

Figure 5: Energy Efficiency in Germany and India.

Since $\left(E/K\right)^I = 0.399$ and $E^I = 0.582$ we obtain $K^I = 1,457$ and from Equation (5) $PK^I = 1.44$. We finally assume an efficiency gap of 15%, i.e. $EK^I = 0.85\left(K^I + E^I\right) = 1,733$. The efficiency term in Equation (10) becomes therefore $\exp(-0.163 + 0.163 \cdot D)$, i.e. $a_0 = -0.163$, $a_D = 0.163$. The productivity gap will be higher than 15% because of the temporary equilibrium situation. The price PEK comes from the zero profit condition

$$PEK^I \cdot EK^I = PK^I \cdot K^I + PE^I \cdot E^I = 2.681 \tag{15}$$

that is, $PEK^I = 1.547$. The data for India are summarised in Table 9.

Table 9:   Calibrated Benchmark Data for the Indian Electricity Sector.

K^I (in bn USD)	1.457
PK^I	1.440
E^I (in bn USD)	0.582
PE^I	1
EK^I (in bn USD)	1.733
PEK^I	1.547

Using these data we can determine d_E and d_K from Equation (11) and Equation (A3):

$$d_E = 0.062, \ d_K = 0.560 \tag{16}$$

and from Equation (A4):

$$d_{E,D} = 0.0004, \ d_{K,D} = 0.003. \tag{17}$$

We can then calculate the productivity gap in terms of the dual cost gaps according to Equation (4):

$$s_D = \ln\frac{0.794}{0.582} - \frac{1}{2}\cdot\left(\frac{2.681}{0.582} + \frac{3.180}{0.794}\right)\cdot\ln\frac{3.180}{1.733} + \frac{1}{2}\cdot\left(\frac{2.098}{0.582} + \frac{2.386}{0.794}\right)\cdot\ln\frac{2.386}{1.457} = -0.672$$

In order to derive the variable or restricted cost function C(PE,EK,K,D) we insert E, derived from Equation (10), into $C = PE \cdot E$ and obtain:

$$C = PE\cdot\left[\left(EK\cdot\exp(-a_0 - a_D\cdot D)\right)^{-\rho} - \left(d_K + d_{K,D}\cdot D\right)\cdot K^{-\rho}\right]^{-1/\rho}\cdot\left(d_E + d_{E,D}\cdot D\right)^{1/\rho}$$

It is

$$PK^I = -\frac{\partial C}{\partial K} = 1.44 \tag{18}$$

and

$$s_D = \frac{\partial \ln C}{\partial D} = -\frac{EK^{-\rho}\cdot a_D\exp(a_0\cdot\rho) - \dfrac{K^{-\rho}\cdot d_{K,D}}{\rho}}{EK^{-\rho}\cdot\exp(a_0\cdot\rho) - K^{-\rho}\cdot d_K} + \frac{d_{E,D}}{\rho\cdot d_E}. \tag{19}$$

If $|s_D|$ gets smaller, a_0 in Equation (19) captures this effect and *PEK* from

$$PEK = \frac{C(\cdot)}{EK} + \frac{PK\cdot K}{EK} \tag{20}$$

will decline. If a new gap s_D has been calculated according to the residual method (4), then a_0 follows from Equation (19) by solving it for a_0, with $a_D = -a_0$, since Germany's efficiency is not affected by joint implementation ($a_0 + a_D \cdot D = 0$ for $D = 1$). With joint implementation the gap decreases to $s_D^{JI} = -0.109$ and a_0 becomes $a_0 = -0.038$.

Finally, from profit maximisation it is $PEK = \dfrac{\partial C}{\partial EK}$, or, in a revenue share:

$$\frac{PEK \cdot EK}{C} = \frac{EK^{-\rho} \cdot \exp((a_0 + a_D \cdot D) \cdot \rho)}{EK^{-\rho} \cdot \exp((a_0 + a_D \cdot D) \cdot \rho) - (d_K + d_{K,D} \cdot D) \cdot K^{-\rho}}. \tag{21}$$

With German or Indian data, given the calibration, this condition is satisfied. Solved for EK it is the supply function which we do not need because demand in the CGE framework will in any case be supplied.

3   Market Power[16]

3.1   Introduction

The Kyoto Protocol, adopted in December 1997, specifies quantified reduction targets for a basket of six major greenhouse gases (GHG) across industrialised countries as listed in its Annex B. One very contentious policy issue regarding the implementation of the Kyoto Protocol has been the degree to which emission reduction commitments by individual Annex B countries can be met through the use of tradable emission permits. On the one hand, emissions trading is straight-forward under basic cost-efficiency considerations: Total costs of achieving the overall Annex B abatement target will be lowest when marginal abatement costs across different emission sources are equalised under free competitive trade. On the other hand, unrestricted Annex B emissions trading will allow transitional economies of Eastern Europe (EIT) and the former Soviet Union (FSU) to sell 'excess' emission rights, i.e. rights that they would not use in the case of strictly domestic abatement. These excess emissions are referred to as *hot air* and stem from the fact that EIT and particularly FSU have been conceded emission entitle-ments under the Kyoto Protocol that are well in excess of their anticipated emis-

---

[16]   This section is based on Böhringer, C. and A. Löschel (2003), Carbon Taxes and Market Power and Hot Air in International Emissions Trading: The Impacts of U.S. Withdrawal from Kyoto-Protocol, *Applied Economics* 35 (6), 651-664.

sions (as a result of the economic turndown during the transition to market economies). Obviously, larger amounts of hot air can significantly decrease the environmental effectiveness of the Kyoto Protocol vis-à-vis strictly domestic action. Hot air has important implications not only for environmental effectiveness but also for the market structure under which intergovernmental emission trading will take place. In fact, a larger share of the effective emission reduction requirements across Annex B countries can be covered by hot air from FSU (Paltsev, 2000; Victor et al., 2001). The resulting dominant supply position enables FSU to exert monopoly power.

The issue of hot air was not 'resolved' prior to the withdrawal of the U.S. in March 2001, when President Bush declared the non-compliance of the U.S., reasoning that the costs of Kyoto to the U.S. economy would be too high. After the withdrawal of the U.S. – the biggest greenhouse gas emitter among Annex B parties – entry into force of the Kyoto Protocol would have been no longer possible without the participation of FSU that made unrestricted emission trading a condition sine qua non.[17] In this context, the concretions to the Kyoto Protocol at the climate conferences in Bonn (March 2001) and Marrakech (November 2001) did not include any restrictions to Annex B emissions trading in order to rescue the treaty.

The objective of this paper is to provide quantitative evidence on the consequences of U.S. withdrawal for environmental effectiveness, compliance costs, and excess costs of market power under the Kyoto Protocol. Based on a multiregion partial equilibrium framework of marginal carbon abatement cost curves generated by the POLES world energy model (Criqui et al., 1996), our key findings can be summarised as follows:

- *Environmental effectiveness:* Under U.S. compliance, monopolistic permit supply by FSU has no impact on environmental effectiveness as compared to a competitive trading system. The reason for this is that in both cases the total amount of hot air is traded. Aggregate emissions of Annex B regions fall by 10% compared to business-as-usual emission levels. Under U.S. withdrawal, monopolistic permit supply by FSU will assure some environmental effects of the Kyoto Protocol with aggregate Annex B emissions falling by 3% vis-à-vis the business-as-usual emission level. For competitive permit trade, environmental effectiveness would be reduced to zero, since the U.S. withdrawal implies an excess supply of permits, driving permit prices down to zero.

- *Compliance costs:* U.S. withdrawal provides substantial cost reduction to complying non-U.S. OECD countries since the reduced overall permit de-

---

[17]   The coming into force of the Protocol requires that countries which ratify the treaty must account in total for at least 55% of the industrialised world's CO_2 emissions in 1990, i.e. the Protocol's base year. Without U.S. *and* FSU, this requirement would not be fulfilled.

mand drives down the permit price. On the other hand, FSU and its competitive fringe EIT must bear a larger decline in revenues from permit sales.

- *Excess costs of market power:* Under U.S. compliance, relative excess costs of market power amount to 40% of total compliance costs under competitive permit trading, which achieves the same environmental target. Under U.S. withdrawal, these efficiency losses increase to 100%. However, in absolute terms the excess costs decline from 2.6 bn USD to 0.9 bn USD.

- Non-U.S. OECD countries could substantially increase the environmental effectiveness of Kyoto (without the U.S.) at moderate additional costs. If FSU and EIT were not allowed to trade hot air, total Annex B emission reduction would more than double from 3% to 6.6%. Competitive permit trading that minimises total compliance costs could be sustained by relatively small side-payments to EIT vis-à-vis the case with hot air and market power. In fact, no side-payments would be required for FSU to renounce hot air and market power. The reason for this is that the suppression of hot air greatly increases the permit price.

The economic and environmental impacts of U.S. withdrawal have been subject to several studies (see Buchner et al., 2001 for a synopsis). However, most of the analyses are based on the assumption of competitive permit trading and do not incorporate the most recent changes in emission reduction requirements of Annex B countries due to sink credits (i.e. forests and agricultural soils that can store CO_2) that have been finalised during the Marrakech meeting. Previous studies neither investigate the implications of U.S. withdrawal for the excess costs of market power, nor do they quantify policy options to bypass the problems of hot air and market power.

The remainder of the paper is organised as follows. Section 3.2 describes the effective emission constraints for Annex B regions (including sink credits) and lays out our basic reasoning on the potential for supply-side market power. Section 3.3 explains the analytical framework to study the effects of non-competitive permit supply behaviour under the new provisions of the Kyoto Protocol. Section 3.4 contains our policy simulations. Section 3.5 concludes.

3.2   Kyoto Emission Constraints

In its original version, the Protocol entails a reduction of GHG emissions for Annex B countries by 5.2% on average below their aggregate 1990 emission level during the commitment period 2008-2012. Table 10 lists historical GHG emissions for 1990 and projected emissions for 2010 across Annex B regions.[18] Fur-

---

[18]   Due to lack of appropriate data for non-CO_2 gases, most studies focus on the analysis of CO_2, which is by far the most important greenhouse gas for industrialised coun-

thermore, it contains the *nominal* percentage reduction commitment with respect to 1990 as well as the *effective* percentage reduction commitment with respect to 2010 for both the initial amendments of Kyoto (columns *Old*) and the Bonn updates (columns *New*). The latter are based on recent estimates for sink credits by the European Commission as listed in Appendix B. The last column of Table 10 reports the cutback requirements of the *New* regime in absolute terms.[19]

We see that all OECD countries are expected to have substantially higher emissions in 2010[20] since their economic growth is linked to higher fossil fuel consumption. On the other hand, EIT and, in particular, FSU, have emissions well below their 1990 levels as a result of a sharp decline in economic activity during the 90ies that will not be offset by the projected economic recovery of these regions between 2000-2010. In short, compliance to the Kyoto Protocol implies a drastic reduction in business-as-usual emissions for OECD countries even under sink credits, whereas the scope of hot air for FSU and EIT increases further.

The official DOE projections for 2010 (DOE, 2001), combined with the revised Kyoto targets (*New*), suggest a hot air volume of 302 MtC for FSU and 59 MtC for EIT, respectively. Accounting for the U.S. withdrawal from the Protocol, the figures on absolute cutback requirements in Table 10 indicate an excess supply of hot air of 78 MtC. If emission rights were fully tradable across Annex B regions, competitive permit markets would drive down the international permit price to zero such that no emission reduction at all would occur with respect to business-as-usual.[21]

---

tries. The usual approach is to apply reduction targets referring to the basket of six GHG to CO_2 only. We proceed in a like manner within the current paper.

[19] The aggregation of individual Annex B countries is based on the data available from the POLES model.

[20] In our comparative-static analysis, we refer to the commitment period in terms of a representative target year 2010.

[21] It has been agreed that the use of emissions trading "shall be supplemental to domestic action and domestic action shall thus constitute a *significant* element of the effort made by each Party ... to meet its quantified emission limitation and reduction commitments ..." (UNFCCC, 2001). The undefined term 'significant' gives sufficient leeway for comprehensive trading. The restrictive position of the EU with respect to the permissible scope of emissions trading between industrialised countries has not been held up since the Bonn conference. There are no concrete caps on the share of emissions reductions a country can meet through the purchase of permits from other industrialised countries, nor are there caps on the amount of permits it can sell.

Table 10:   Baseline Emissions, Percentage Reduction, Absolute Cutbacks.

Region	Baseline Emissions (MtC)[a]		Nominal Reduction (% wrt 1990)[b]		Effective Reduction (% wrt 2010)		Absolute Cutback (MtC wrt 2010)	
	1990	2010	Old	New	Old	New	Old	New
AUN	88	130	-6.8	-10.2	27.7	25.4	36	33
CAN	126	165	6.0	-7.9	28.2	17.6	47	29
EUR	930	1040	7.8	5.2	17.5	15.2	182	158
JPN	269	330	6.0	0.8	23.4	19.1	77	63
EIT	279	209	7.1	3.9	-24.0	-28.3	-50	-59
FSU	853	593	0	-4.9	-43.8	-50.9	-260	-302
Total US out[c]	2545	2467	4.3	0	1.3	-3.2	32	-78
USA	1345	1809	7.0	3.2	30.9	28.0	558	507
Total US in[d]	3890	4276	5.2	1.1	13.8	10.0	590	429

Key: AUN – Australia and New Zealand,
CAN – Canada, EUR – OECD Europe (incl. EFTA),
JPN – Japan, EIT – Central and Eastern Europe,
FSU – Former Soviet Union (incl. Ukraine).
[a] Based on DOE reference case (DOE, 2001)
[b] Estimates by the EU Commission based on UNFCC (http://www.unfccc.int)
[c] Annex B without U.S. compliance
[d] Annex B with U.S. compliance.

Paltsev (2000) has noted that, due to the variability of growth numbers in the gross domestic product for FSU, the projected amount of hot air may vary to some extent across different data sources. Lower estimates for hot air may prevent an excess supply of permits and thus competitive permit prices from falling to zero in the case of U.S. withdrawal. However, our simulations on supply-side restrictions in Section 4 confirm robustness of quantitative results with respect to larger deductions in hot air. The reason is that monopolistic permit supply will be smaller than the lower bound estimates for hot air in any case.

3.3   Determinants of Market Power

The issue of market power in tradable quota markets has been subject to extensive theoretical and empirical research that includes Hahn (1984), Sartzetakis (1997), Ellerman and Decaux (1998), Ellerman et al. (1998), Misiolek and Elder (1989), Malueg (1990), Westkog (1996 and 2001), Burniaux (1998), Ellerman and Wing

(2000), Godby (2000), and Löschel and Zhang (2003). Either dominant buyers (monopsony or oligopsony) or sellers (monopoly or oligopoly) may be able to exert market power in the permit market or use their market power in the permit market to gain power in the product market. In the following, market power refers only to the capacity to influence the market price of traded permits (so-called 'cost minimising manipulation').

Market power in emissions trading results in reduced demand in the case of a monopsony or reduced supply in the case of a monopoly. A monopsonist may thereby force the permit price below a monopolist above the competitive level. Thus, the extent of competition in a tradable permit market affects the efficiency of international permit trade and the degree to which potential cost savings are realised. Permit price manipulations result in additional overall economic costs to achieve the same level of abatement as under perfect competition.

There has been some discussion whether market power on international permit markets will be an issue under the Kyoto Protocol. In general, the likelihood of market power increases if the number of participants is smaller or if the size of some participants is larger than neo-classical firm-to-firm trading with many participants (Woerdman, 2000). Article 17 of the Kyoto Protocol creates an intergovernmental emissions trading market next to or instead of firm trading, so it is uncertain whether firms or governments will participate in international emissions trading. In the case of firm-to-firm trading, the scope for market power seems rather limited. However, it seem very unlikely that the FSU, as the dominant supplier of emission rights[22], will give up on market power by leaving permit trade to its domestic firms (whose entitlements with carbon rights are unclear anyway). On the demand side, competitive behaviour seems to be the appropriate assumption. The reason is that either firms of OECD countries may be allowed to engage in emissions trading directly[23], or – under the assumption of Party-to-Party trading – coordination of several individual OECD countries within a demand cartel seems rather difficult.

Figure 6 illustrates the effects of supply-side restrictions accounting for the excess supply of hot air. Under perfect competition, unrestricted (see index "u" in Figure 6) hot air supply of EIT and FSU exceed aggregate permit demand by non-U.S. OECD countries; the permit market price will drop to zero (P_u) and the quantity of hot air permits traded equals the total abatement requirement of non-U.S. regions (Q_u). Consequently, there will be no domestic emissions abatement of permit importers (here: non-U.S. OECD countries) with respect to business-as-usual

---

[22]   FSU holds 84% of total hot air, which exceeds market demand for any given price level (see Table 1 and Figure 2).

[23]   See e.g. the plans of the EU commission to implement an EU internal trading system starting in 2005 with firm-to-firm trading across energy-intensive industries (see Böhringer, 2001).

emission levels $\left(\bar{e}\right)$, and total revenues for permit exporting countries (here: EIT and FSU) equal zero. Quantity restrictions S_r (see index 'r' in Figure 6), which reduce the supply of hot air below the total abatement requirement Q_u, drive up the market price of permits by ΔP from P_u to P_r. Total permit trade is, then, reduced from Q_u to Q_r and effective total emission abatement amounts to ΔQ. Apart from increased environmental effectiveness, the exercise of monopoly power entails a redistribution of the gains from permit trade from buyers to sellers and a loss of economic efficiency, because marginal abatement costs (C') are no longer equalised across regions. In comparison to the competitive outcome, permit exporters receive the rectangle *HIK0* as income from permit sales. Hot air exporters benefit from further supply restrictions as long as the gains from higher prices are greater than the loss of revenues from a lower level of permits sold. Due to the higher price of permits, an importing country increases domestic abatement (a) and covers its remaining abatement requirements to its Kyoto emission target (k) through permit imports (q). Its costs of compliance increase to the area *LMNT*.

The existence of hot air complicates the usual textbook illustration of efficiency losses emerging from market power in tradable quota markets. In fact, the possibility of selling hot air changes the environmental effectiveness between the competitive solution vis-à-vis the non-competitive solution. While – in our case – hot air in competitive markets reduces environmental effectiveness to zero, supply-side restrictions below Q_u imply a real reduction in emissions. The concise measurement of efficiency loss from market power must then refer to the same emission abatement. In Figure 6, the triangle *IJK* visualises the induced efficiency loss: The same effective abatement ΔQ emerging from monopolistic supply could have been achieved at lower overall costs in a competitive setting (see index 'c' in Figure 6) if the hot air supplier had also undertaken some real abatement (Q_c-Q_r). The market price of permits would then fall to P_c.

Reference to the same target allows us to abstract from the benefit-side of emission abatement, which would otherwise require the use of rather uncertain and broad-ranged estimates for the external cost of GHG emissions. One should be aware that market power in the presence of negative environmental externalities may increase total welfare (economic efficiency) in contrast to the competitive solution as long as the loss from non-equalisation of marginal abatement costs is more than offset by the benefits from reduced environmental damages at the margin.

3.4   Analytical Framework

The analysis of non-competitive supply behaviour in Section 4 below is based on marginal abatement cost curves for different Annex B regions (see Appendix A for the algebraic exposition of the model). These curves represent the marginal cost of reducing carbon emissions by different amounts within an economy. Marginal costs of abatement may vary considerably across countries due to differences in carbon intensity, initial energy price levels, and the ease of carbon substitution possibilities. For the empirical specification of regional marginal abatement costs curves across regions i, we adopt a constant elasticity function of the form:

$$C_i'\left(\overline{e_i} - e_i\right) = \alpha_i \cdot \left(\overline{e_i} - e_i\right)^{\beta_i} \tag{1}$$

where C' is the marginal cost of reducing carbon emissions in country i, $\overline{e_i}$ are the business-as-usual emissions, e_i are the actual emissions, i.e. $a_i = \overline{e_i} - e_i$ denotes the level of abatement.

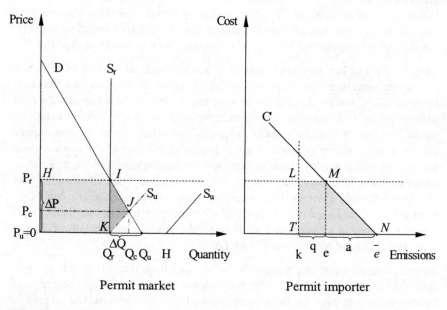

Figure 6:   Effects of Supply Side Restrictions Accounting for Hot Air.

In order to determine the coefficients α and β, we employ a least-square procedure based on a sufficiently large number of discrete observations for marginal abatement costs (or carbon taxes) and the induced emission reduction in each region. These values are generated by the world energy system model POLES (Criqui et al., 1996), which embodies a detailed bottom-up description of regional energy markets and world-energy trade. Table 11 lists the least-square estimates for the coefficients of marginal abatement cost curves across regions.

Table 11:   Coefficients of Marginal Abatement Cost Curve Approximations.

Coefficients	AUN	CAN	EIT	EUR	FSU	JPN	USA
α	0.675	1.567	0.316	0.114	0.046	0.718	0.020
β	1.442	1.379	1.388	1.369	1.482	1.338	1.427

Figure 7 illustrates the implied marginal abatement cost curves for those Annex B regions that face binding carbon constraints and are willing to comply with the Kyoto Protocol. As noted above, this set of region compromises all OECD countries except for the U.S.

The carbon taxes that the different regions would have to impose in order to reach their Kyoto commitment through strictly domestic action are indicated on the cost curves. We use the marginal abatement costs curves for the derivation of the aggregate permit demand curve under the *New* targets of the Kyoto Protocol. A region will demand permits as long as the market price of permits is lower than its marginal abatement costs. Conversely, it supplies permits as long as the market price is above its marginal costs of abatement. The aggregate demand curve, as depicted by Figure 7, is then obtained by simply adding up the demanded and supplied quantities of all regions at each market price. If the market price is equal to zero (as in the case of competitive permit markets), the aggregate demand amounts to 284 MtC, which is the sum of emission abatement requirements across all non-U.S. OECD regions. As the price increases, aggregate demand diminishes. When the market price reaches 105 USD/tC, AUN switches from being a permit supplier to being a permit demander, since the international permit price exceeds its marginal abatement costs associated with purely domestic compliance to the Kyoto Protocol. The same happens at a price of 117 USD/tC for EUR. At a price of 131 USD/tC, the amount of permits supplied by AUN (5 MtC) and EUR (13 MtC) just equals the demand by CAN (4 MtC) and JPN (14 MtC), resulting in an aggregate demand of zero.

3.5   Policy Simulations

Throughout the exposition in this Section, we refer to Annex B regions as those countries of the Annex B in the Kyoto Protocol that are willing to ratify. This means that the U.S. is not included unless explicitly specified otherwise. Furthermore, it should be noted that all our results refer to one target year, namely 2010.

3.5.1   Scenarios

In our simulations, we first consider the case in which Annex B countries meet their Kyoto reduction commitment by purely domestic action. Although this scenario is unlikely, it provides a useful reference point for the potential environmental effectiveness of the Kyoto Protocol if hot air is suppressed (see scenario *COMP-2*):

NTR   Annex B countries can trade emission rights as allocated under the Kyoto Protocol only within domestic borders. This is equivalent to a situation in which Annex B countries apply domestic carbon taxes that are high enough to meet their individual Kyoto commitments. Regions EIT and FSU do not face direct compliance costs, as their emission targets do not become binding but won't be able to sell hot air in this case either.

Considering international emissions trading, we start with the assumption of perfect competitive supply and demand behaviour:

TRD   All Annex B countries, including FSU and EIT, are allowed to trade emissions among each other. All regions behave as price takers. There is no market power exercised in the international permit market.

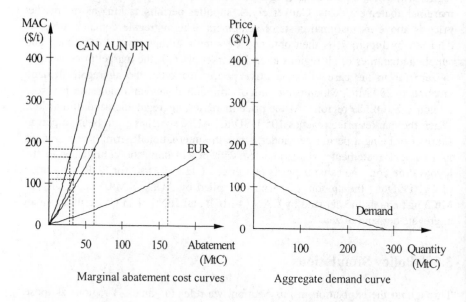

Marginal abatement cost curves   Aggregate demand curve

Figure 7:   Marginal Abatement Cost Curves and Aggregate Demand.

As has been elaborated in Section 3, competitive supply behaviour of FSU is neither realistic for the case of U.S. compliance nor for the case of U.S. withdrawal: FSU takes a dominant permit supply position due to its large entitlements with hot air. In the scenario *MONOP*, therefore, we assume monopoly power of the FSU:

MONOP FSU acts as a monopoly whereas all other regions are price takers, i.e. they minimise their permit trading or abatement costs given the permit price set by the FSU. EIT is treated as a competitive fringe (price taker) following the price leadership of the dominant region FSU.[24]

The scenario *COMP-1* is designed to provide information on the efficiency gains from competitive markets as compared to the monopolistic solution warranting the same environmental effectiveness:

COMP-1 Marginal abatement costs across all Annex B regions are equalised given the overall Annex B reduction target from scenario *MONOP*. In this case, the individual abatements by the various regions are cost-efficient from an overall point of view.

The final scenario, *COMP-2*, is the complement to the initial *NTR* scenario in the sense that it achieves the same environmental effectiveness under competitive permit trading:

COMP-2 FSU and EIT are only entitled with business-as-usual emissions and no longer dispose of hot air. The aggregate reduction level for Annex B regions amounts to the emission cutback achieved under *NTR*. Emissions can be fully traded across regions to assure a cost-efficient outcome.

The label *COMP* for the last two scenarios indicates that they incorporate monetary compensation to FSU and EIT up to the revenues from permit sales that occur in the case of monopolistic FSU supply behaviour (scenario *MONOP*). After compensation of FSU and EIT, *COMP-1* still provides some efficiency gains from competitive markets to allow for a Pareto-superior solution as compared to the *MONOP* outcome. *COMP-2* delivers information on the magnitude and distribution of compliance costs across Annex B regions if FSU and EIT are only entitled with their business-as-usual emissions in 2010. Once again, compensation to FSU and EIT for the *MONOP* revenues would be required. In a nutshell: The scenario *COMP-2* provides the lowest aggregate costs for non-U.S. OECD countries to achieve the *NTR* environmental effectiveness (including monetary compensations to FSU and EIT).

The three final scenarios *US-NTR*, *US-TRD*, and *US-MONOP* consider U.S. compliance for alternative assumptions on the scope of emissions trading and the underlying market structure. U.S. compliance is obviously not a realistic policy option given the current status of climate policy. Yet, these scenarios provide the necessary information on how U.S. withdrawal (as captured by the preceding scenarios) changes economic costs and environmental effectiveness vis-à-vis U.S. compliance:

---

[24] FSU knows how much EIT supplies at any given price and adjusts the residual demand curve accordingly.

US-NTR   All Annex B regions – including the U.S. – meet their reduction target by domestic action only.

US-TRD   Emission entitlements can be traded on perfectly competitive markets across all Annex B regions.

US-MONOP   Emission are freely tradable across all Annex B regions. FSU exerts monopoly power on international permit markets.

3.5.2 Results

Table 12 summarises the economic and environmental effects across all scenarios that assume non-compliance of the U.S. We begin with the interpretation of results for the *NTR* case. Without permit trading, each Annex B country has to meet its reduction target exclusively by domestic action. The associated marginal abatement costs are listed in Note 'c' of Table 12. Notice that the order in marginal abatement costs across OECD countries does not necessarily reflect the order of magnitude of percentage reduction requirements. The relative cutback requirement is only one determinant of marginal and inframarginal[25] abatement costs. Other major factors affecting marginal abatement costs include the energy/carbon intensity of the respective economies, initial energy prices[26], and the ease of carbon substitution in production and consumption. EIT and FSU do not face any binding abatement requirements. Therefore, their marginal costs of abatement are zero. In absolute terms, compliance costs for OECD countries sum up to 16.2 bn USD with EUR facing the highest compliance costs. However, if we adopt a meaningful relative cost measure (here: costs as percentage of projected GDP in 2010), EUR bears by far the smallest abatement burden. Compliance costs are rather small across OECD countries, ranging from 0.07% GDP loss for EUR up to 0.2% for AUN and CAN. Obviously, the real emission reduction under *NTR* for Annex B countries must be equal to the *New* effective reduction commitments under the Kyoto Protocol as listed in Table 12. Total emission reduction with respect to *BaU* amounts to 284 MtC or 6.6% of aggregate *BaU* emissions across all Annex B countries, including the U.S.

Under competitive Annex B emissions trading (scenario *TRD*), the permit price equals zero, since the amount of hot air exceeds the total amount of the emission reduction requirements. Consequently, the total costs as well as country-specific costs for meeting the *New* Kyoto targets without participation of the U.S. are zero. Total gains from trade as compared to the NTR scenario, hence, amount to 16.2 bn USD, i.e. the total of *NTR* compliance costs. However, there is no emission reduc-

---

[25]   The areas under the marginal abatement cost curves in Figure 2 reflect the total costs of compliance for the *NTR* case as listed in Table 3.

[26]   For example, higher initial energy prices due to prevailing taxes require – ceteris paribus – higher carbon taxes in order to reach the same relative cutback in energy demand.

tion at all with respect to *BaU*. In short, Kyoto boils down to business-as-usual; Annex B emissions in 2010 remain unchanged.

Under monopoly power, FSU reduces the hot air supply to maximise its profits given the reaction of EIT as a competitive fringe. The monopolistic profit of FSU amounts to 3 bn USD with a hot air supply of 94 MtC at a market price of 32 USD. The fringe supplier EIT delivers emission permits of 87 MtC to the market composed of 59 MtC hot air and 35 MtC from domestic abatement. EIT benefits from implementation of the Kyoto Protocol with a net revenue of 2.4 bn USD under *MONOP*. All OECD regions face substantially lower compliance costs under *MONOP* as compared to the *NTR* case, since their *NTR* marginal abatement costs are much higher than the monopolistic permit price. As a consequence, it is much cheaper for OECD countries to reduce their domestic abatement efforts (see rows *Real emission reduction* in Table 12) and pay for fictive (in the case of hot air) or effective emission abatement in FSU and EIT. However, the huge cost reduction under *MONOP* vis-à-vis *NTR* is not only due to cost savings from permit trading but also due to a substantial relaxation of the overall emission constraint. Environmental effectiveness drops by more than half from 6.6% to 3%. The monopoly case entails efficiency losses because marginal abatement costs across all Annex B regions are not equalised. In fact, FSU has marginal abatement costs of zero and does not abate any real emissions.

Scenario *COMP-1* reveals the excess costs of market power for the *MONOP* case. In absolute terms, these costs equal 0.9 bn USD. In relative terms, the costs of MONOP amount to 100% of total compliance costs for *COMP-1* that achieves the same environmental target. Marginal abatement costs under *COMP-1* drop by half and are now equalised across all trading partners. The row "Real emission reduction" in Table 12 indicates the efficient abatement share for each region under overall cost-effectiveness considerations. With regard to permit trade, emission exports reported for FSU and EIT now reflect real abatement; the additional row in Table 12, "Hot air", denotes the total feasible amount of hot air that can be sold by FSU and EIT in the competitive setting. Note, that this amount is the same as under *MONOP*, but an overall cost-efficient abatement now requires a (substantial) cutback of real emissions in FSU. Of course, FSU will only accept the *COMP-1* abatement policy when it is at least fully compensated up to its *MONOP* profits. Likewise, approval by OECD countries and EIT implies that no country is worse off as compared to the *MONOP* case. Given the gains in overall compliance costs, these requirements can be met, while nearly 1 bn USD can additionally be distributed across all trading partners. It is not appropriate to speculate at this point on a specific distribution mechanism.

The results for the final scenario *COMP-2* in Table 12 summarise the implications that would surface if Annex B countries were to achieve the same total emission reduction as for the *NTR* case. Total compliance cost for OECD countries decreases from 16.2 bn USD to 9.8 bn USD. As expected, all OECD countries would be better off than under *NTR* but undergo higher costs than in the *MONOP* case. Interestingly, *COMP-2* would not require additional compensation of the FSU; FSU profits slightly more from competitive permit trading under *COMP-2* (i.e. without hot air and *NTR* environmental effectiveness) than from monopolistic pricing under *MONOP*. The reason for this is that the increase in the permit price under *COMP-2* not only compensates FSU for the undertaken domestic abatement, but remaining profits are even higher than the profits from hot air sales under *MONOP*. EIT, however, is worse off, since its revenues from permit trade are not high enough to cover both domestic abatement costs and the profits occurring in the *MONOP* case. Hence, EIT must be considered a candidate for compensation up to its *MONOP* profits. The question remains whether OECD countries would accept the overall increase in total costs from 7.2 bn USD to 11.2 bn USD (including compensating transfers to EIT) and how these costs should be distributed.

Table 13 completes our analysis of alternative abatement policy scenarios. It provides a perspective on how U.S. compliance (or, in turn, U.S. withdrawal, if we make the reference to Table 13) affects environmental effectiveness and the magnitude as well as the distribution of compliance costs. For the scenario *US-NTR*, compliance costs of non-U.S. Annex B countries must be the same as under the *NTR* scenario in our partial analytical framework. In absolute as well as in relative terms, the U.S. bear the highest compliance costs. The importance of U.S. compliance for international climate policy becomes evident from the implied change in environmental effectiveness: Real emission reduction of Annex B countries triples compared to the *NTR* case under U.S. withdrawal. Competitive international permit trade under *US-TRD* accommodates a major cutback in total compliance costs while the real emission reduction vis-à-vis business-as-usual amounts still to 10% (compared to 18.5% for *US-NTR* and only 6.6% for *NTR*). In contrast to our results for the case of U.S. withdrawal, we see that monopoly power by FSU has no impact on environmental effectiveness; the aggregate emission cutback under *US-TRD* and *US-MONOP* are the same.

Table 12:   Summary of Results Without Participation of USA.

	NTR	TRD	MONOP	COMP-1	COMP-2
Absolute Cost of Compliance (bn USD)					
AUN	1.4	0	0.8	0.4	1.0
CAN	2.0	0	0.8	0.4	1.1
EIT	0	0	-2.4	-1.1	-1.0
EUR	7.8	0	3.9	2.2	5.3
FSU	0	0	-3.0	-2.0	-3.1
JPN	5.0	0	1.7	0.9	2.4
Total	16.2	0	1.8	0.9	5.6
Relative Cost of Compliance (% of Business-As-Usual GDP in 2010)					
AUN	0.209	0	0.116	0.065	0.154
CAN	0.208	0	0.080	0.043	0.111
EIT	0	0	-0.403	-0.184	-0.174
EUR	0.067	0	0.034	0.019	0.046
FSU	0	0	-0.351	-0.231	-0.363
JPN	0.104	0	0.036	0.019	0.050
Total [a]	0.083	0	0.009	0.004	0.029
Real Emission Reduction (% from Business-As-Usual in 2010)					
AUN	25.4	0	11.2	6.9	14.8
CAN	17.6	0	5.4	3.3	7.3
EIT	0	0	13.4	8.1	17.9
EUR	15.2	0	5.9	3.6	8.0
FSU	0	0	0	8.7	18.4
JPN	19.1	0	5.2	3.1	7.0
Total [b]	6.6	0	3.0	3.0	6.6
Total Real Emission Reduction (MtC)					
	284	0	130	130	284
Market Price (USD/tC)					
	- [c]	0	32	16	48
Permit Trade (MtC) [d]					
AUN	-	33	18	24	14
CAN	-	29	20	24	17
EIT	-	. [e]	-87 (-59) [f]	-17	-37
EUR	-	158	97	121	77
FSU	-	. [e]	-94 (-94) [f]	-52	-109
JPN	-	63	46	53	40
Hot air	-	-284	-153	-153	

[a] Percentage change with respect to business-as-usual GDP of Annex B in 2010 except for the U.S.

[b] Percentage change with respect to total Annex B emissions in 2010 under *BaU* including U.S. emissions.

[c] MAC without trade: 105 USD/tC for AUN, 163 USD/tC for CAN, 117 USD/tC for EUR, 184 USD/tC for JPN.

[d] Positive values indicate permit imports, negative values indicate permit exports.

[e] Exports of permits by EIT and FSU are undetermined.

[f] Numbers in parenthesis show export of hot air.

The reason is that in both cases the total amount of permits supplied by FSU (and EIT) exceeds the total stock in hot air. Given the same environmental impact, we can directly read off the efficiency losses induced by *US-MONOP* vis-à-vis *US-TRD*: Monopolistic supply by FSU drives up the permit price to 51 USD, which increases compliance costs by 40% as compared to competitive permit trading (in which the permit price is only 37 USD).[27]

Cross-comparison between scenarios *MONOP* and *US-MONOP* indicates that non-U.S. OECD countries face smaller compliance costs after U.S. withdrawal considering FSU market power. The reason for this is the fall in the emission permit price implied by a reduced permit demand after U.S. withdrawal. However, the reduction in compliance costs must be weighted against a substantial loss in environmental effectiveness (from 10% to 3% emission reduction). FSU and its competitive fringe EIT face a drastic decline in revenues from permit sales, since the permit price declines from 51 USD under *US-MONOP* to 32 USD under *MONOP*.

Figure 8 summarises the results of our policy simulations. Without U.S. compliance, the residual demand of competitive OECD countries (all of them facing binding emission constraints) is given by the curve D. Under competitive permit trading *TRD*, FSU supplies hot air in excess of market demand, which results in a market equilibrium at point *H*. If the FSU exercises monopoly power (*MONOP*), it sells hot air permits until the marginal revenues of permit sales (MR) are equal to the marginal costs of abatement, which are zero in our case (point *I*). Monopoly power by the FSU, thus, increases the international permit price, and initiates real emission reduction. Point *J* reflects the scenario *COMP-1*, which achieves the *same* emission reduction as under *MONOP* in a cost efficient way, since cheap reduction possibilities in FSU are exploited (to a level where marginal abatement costs are equalised across all regions). With U.S. participation, the residual demand faced by FSU is depicted by the curve D_{US}. In this case, the competitive permit market equilibrium (*US-TRD*) is given by point *K* whereas point *L* captures the situation of FSU monopoly power (*US-MONOP*). Note that monopolistic behaviour under U.S. participation does not affect environmental effectiveness, since the optimal monopolistic permit supply by FSU is larger than its amount of hot air.

---

[27]   We omit an additional scenario *US-COMP* (like *COMP-1*) to identify the efficiency losses from market power, since the latter would be (almost) identical to the scenario *US-TRD*.

Table 13:   Summary of Results with Participation of USA.

	US-NTR	US-TRD	US-MONOP
Absolute Cost of Compliance (bn USD)			
AUN	1.4	0.9	1.1
CAN	2.0	0.9	1.1
EIT	0	-2.8	-4.2
EUR	7.8	4.4	5.6
FSU	0	-13.2	-15.6
JPN	5.0	1.9	2.5
USA	30.3	14.5	18.6
Total	46.5	6.5	9.1
Relative Cost of Compliance (% of Business-As-Usual GDP in 2010)			
AUN	0.209	0.128	0.160
CAN	0.208	0.090	0.117
EIT	0	-0.474	-0.699
EUR	0.067	0.037	0.048
FSU	0	-1.522	-1.803
JPN	0.104	0.040	0.053
USA	0.230	0.110	0.142
Total [a]	0.142	0.020	0.028
Real Emission Reduction (% from Business-As-Usual in 2010)			
AUN	25.4	12.3	15.5
CAN	17.6	6.0	7.6
EIT	0	14.8	18.7
EUR	15.2	6.6	8.3
FSU	0	15.4	0.3
JPN	19.1	5.8	7.4
USA	28.0	10.7	13.5
Total [b]	18.5	10.0	10.0
Total Real Emission Reduction (MtC)			
	790	429	429
Market Price (USD/tC)			
	- [c]	37	51
Permit Trade (MtC) [d]			
AUN	-	17	13
CAN	-	19	16
EIT	-	-90	-98
EUR	-	90	72
FSU	-	-393	-304
JPN	-	44	39
USA	-	313	262

[a] Percentage change with respect to business-as-usual GDP of Annex B in 2010 including the U.S.

[b] Percentage change with respect to total Annex B emissions in 2010 under *BaU* including U.S. emissions.

[c] Marginal abatement cost in region without trade are 105 USD/tC for AUN, 163 USD/tC for CAN, 117 USD/tC for EUR, 184 USD/tC for JPN and 145 USD/tC for USA.

[d] Positive values indicate permit imports, negative values indicate permit exports.

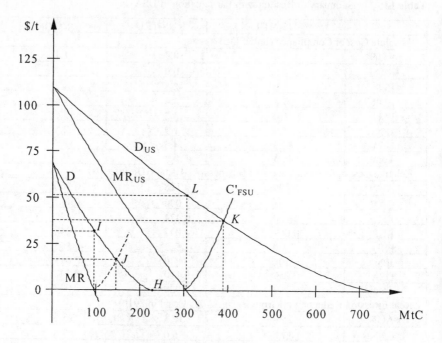

Figure 8:   Graphical Exposition of Results.

3.6   Conclusions

In Section 3 we have investigated the environmental and economic implications of
U.S. withdrawal from the Kyoto Protocol, accounting for hot air and monopoly
supply of emission permits by the Former Soviet Union. Whereas market power
has no environmental impact for U.S. compliance, it prevents the Kyoto Protocol
from boiling down to business-as-usual for the case of U.S. withdrawal. Excess
costs of market power in absolute terms decline from 2.6 bn USD for U.S. compliance to 0.9 bn USD for U.S. withdrawal. In relative terms, however, excess cost
increase from 40% for U.S. compliance to 100% for U.S. withdrawal. As we
pointed out, side-payments could be a relatively cheap policy mechanism for non-
U.S. OECD countries to double the environmental effectiveness of Kyoto (without
U.S.) and bypass the problems of hot air and market power.

There are several caveats to our paper. First, our analysis does not cover a further
commitment period after 2012, which might influence the behaviour of parties in
the first commitment period, e.g. through strategic banking of emission permits.
Second, we have not considered the possibility of lowering market power by
opening up emission trading to non-Annex B countries via the Clean Development
Mechanism (CDM). Third, we have not incorporated the benefits of emission

reduction into the efficiency analysis of market power. All these issues are potentially important but – for the time being – bear large uncertainties with respect to an appropriate parameterisation for applied analysis.

3.7   Appendix A: Algebraic Model Description

This Section provides an algebraic summary of the partial equilibrium model for permit trade underlying the simulations. We begin with the model formulation for a competitive system of permit trade without the occurrence of hot air. Second, we show how hot air can be accounted for. Finally, we lay out the set-up for the case of monopolistic permit supply.

A.1 Competitive Permit Trading

Under competitive permit trading, all countries i are price takers. Each country minimises its compliance costs to some exogenous target level k_i. Compliance costs equal the sum of abatement costs and the costs of buying carbon permits; in the case of permit sales, the second term becomes negative, which means that the country minimises the cost of abatement minus the income from selling permits. Costs are minimised subject to the constraint that a country meets its exogenous reduction target, in other words: A country's initial endowment of permits plus the amount of permits bought or sold on the market (q_i) may not exceed the emission target level k_i:

$$\min_{q_i} \; C_i\left(\overline{e_i} - e_i\right) + P \cdot q_i \tag{2}$$

$$s.t. \; e_i = k_i + q_i,$$

where

C_i denotes the abatement cost function for reducing carbon emissions,

$\overline{e_i}$ stands for the business-as-usual emissions,

e_i are the actual emissions, and

P is the permit price taken as exogenous.

The first order condition for the cost minimisation problem is given by:

$$C_i'\left(\overline{e_i} - e_i\right) = P. \tag{3}$$

In the optimum, the price taking countries abate emissions up to a level where their marginal abatement costs (C') equal the permit price. Total costs of reducing emissions to the overall target level $K = \sum_i k_i$ are minimised, since all opportunities for exploiting cost differences in abatement across countries are taken.

A.2 Accounting for Hot Air

A country with hot air (h_i) minimises costs of abatement minus income from selling permits ($q_i - h_i$, $q_i < 0$):

$$\min_{q_i} \; C_i \left(h_i + \overline{e_i} - e_i \right) + P \cdot q_i \tag{4}$$

$$s.t. \;\; e_i = k_i + q_i - h_i \,.$$

The amount of hot air equals the difference between the emission target and the business-as- usual emissions:

$$h_i = k_i - \overline{e_i} \,. \tag{5}$$

The first order condition yields:

$$C_i' \left(h_i + \overline{e_i} - e_i \right) = P \,. \tag{6}$$

The existence of hot air does not change the cost-efficiency property of unrestricted competitive permit trading since marginal abatement costs are still equalised. However, hot air sold on the permit market does not imply any effective (real) emission reduction in the hot air countries. The occurrence of traded hot air, therefore, results in an increase of overall emission compared to a situation without international permit trade.

A.3 Monopolistic Permit Supply

Monopolistic permit supply is characterised as a situation where one country (denoted 'm') – in our case the hot air country FSU – has supply power in the permit market while all other countries, denoted as fringe 'f', behave as price takers. The fringe countries, thus, minimise their compliance costs given the permit price set by the monopolist. They emit carbon until the marginal costs of abatement equal the permit price:

$$C_f' \left(h_f + \overline{e_f} - e_f \right) = P \,. \tag{6'}$$

The aggregate permit demand of the fringe, which is in total a net importer of permits, is:

$$Q_F (P) = \sum_f q_f (P) \,. \tag{7}$$

The monopolist sets its permit supply ($q_m < 0$) to minimise abatement costs minus income from permit sales:

$$\min_{q_m} C_m\left(h_m + \overline{e_m} - e_m\right) + P \cdot q_m \tag{8}$$

$$s.t. \quad e_m = k_m + q_m - h_m$$
$$P = P(Q_F)$$

where P is the inverse demand function of the fringe countries. As illustrated in Figure 8, the first order condition of the cost minimisation problem indicates that the monopolist sets marginal abatement costs equal to marginal revenue:

$$C'_m\left(h_m + \overline{e_m} - e_m\right) = P - P'(Q_F) \cdot q_m. \tag{9}$$

Marginal abatement costs are accordingly not equalised between the fringe countries (Equation 6') and the monopolist (Equation 9), resulting in overall efficiency losses due to market power.

3.8   Appendix B: GHG Emission Reduction Targets

Table 14:   GHG Emission Reduction Targets.

	Label[a]	Original Kyoto Targets (OLD)[b] (% of 1990 GHG Emissions)	Revised Targets (NEW)[c] (% of 1990 GHG Emissions)
Australia	AUN	108	110.7
Austria	EUR	87	92.9
Belgium	EUR	92.5	93.8
Bulgaria	EIT	92	95.2
Canada	CAN	94	107.9
Croatia	EIT	95	95
Czech Republic	EIT	92	94.1
Denmark	EUR	79	81.1
Estonia	FSU	92	94.7
Finland	EUR	100	107.8
France	EUR	100	103.9
Germany	EUR	79	80.7
Greece	EUR	125	133.1
Hungary	EIT	94	97.8
Iceland	EUR	110	118
Ireland	EUR	113	116.2
Italy	EUR	93.5	95.3
Japan	JPN	94	99.2
Latvia	FSU	92	98
Liechtenstein	EUR	92	107.9
Lithuania	EUR	92	96.5
Luxembourg	EUR	72	79.6
Monaco	EUR	92	93
Netherlands	EUR	94	95.2
New Zealand	AUN	100	107
Norway	EUR	101	105.3
Poland	EIT	94	96.5
Portugal	EUR	127	130.7
Romania	EIT	92	96.2
Russian Federation	FSU	100	105.7
Slovakia	EIT	92	96.3
Slovenia	EIT	92	100.4
Spain	EUR	115	118.9
Sweden	EUR	104	109.5
Switzerland	EUR	92	96.6
Ukraine	FSU	100	102.4
United Kingdom	EUR	87.5	88.8
United States	USA	93	96.8

[a] Label of aggregate model region which includes the respective Annex B country. [b] UNFCCC (1997).
[c] Estimates by the European Commission accounting for sink credits based on UNFCCC (2001).

4   Investment Risk

4.1   Introduction

Cooperation between the industrialised and the developing world through joint implementation of GHG emission abatement promises substantial economic gains to both parties. As long as the costs for GHG mitigation that industrialised countries have committed to are lower in developing countries, it makes economic sense that developing countries undertake abatement projects in return for funds from industrialised countries which receive emission credits counting to their domestic emission targets. This basic idea of cost-effectiveness led to the clean development mechanism (CDM) under the Kyoto Protocol accommodating project-based emission reductions in developing countries to exploit the potential for low-cost abatement. Emission crediting provides market-based incentives to invest in climate-friendly (i.e. emission mitigation) projects since emission reductions can be sold on international permit markets, thus recovering higher initial investment costs. Many policy makers consider project-based emission reductions as an important instrument to promote sustainable development with respect to improved environmental quality as well as better economic performance of developing countries since it helps to attract larger amounts of foreign direct investment. Yet, there are concerns that the potential benefits of project-based abatement measures may be substantially reduced by risk concerns of investors associated with abatement projects in developing countries. In addition, the uneven distribution of investment risks and abatement possibilities could produce a (politically undesired) shift in comparative advantage of emission abatement stacked against least-developed countries that typically bear high investment risks and have rather limited abatement possibilities due to low emission levels (Wirl et al., 1998).

To what extent do risk considerations reduce the potential for cost savings to industrialised countries? What are the implications of risk for the magnitude and distribution of benefits from project-based emission trading among developing countries? This Chapter provides quantitative insights into the relative importance of risk preferences for project-based emission crediting with developing countries. It is structured as follows. Section 4.2 describes in more detail the nature of investment risks in emission crediting. Section 4.3 illustrates the potential implications of risk accounting and describes the empirical estimation of investment risks. Section 4.4 discusses policy scenarios and results. Section 4.5 concludes.

4.2   Investment Risks in Project-Based Emission Crediting

CDM projects involve cross-border investments by industrialised countries in order to generate emission credits for subsequent sale on international credit markets or for transfer emission credits (Grubb et al., 1999). The investor provides debt and equity financing of the mitigation project in exchange for the claims on the project and the net cash flow it produces (financial return). The sale of permits from climate-friendly projects makes it possible to recover higher-investment costs of mitigation projects vis-a-vis 'conventional' projects.

Potential investors interested in participating in emissions reduction projects taking place in developing countries may hesitate because of investment risks. Three main categories of risk can affect the performance of project-based emissions crediting: (i) *technological risks* that are tied to the process of production and refer to uncertain output quantities; (ii) *economic risks* that refer to uncertain input and output prices; and (iii) *political risks* that arise from uncertainty about property rights on the assets of the revenue streams and involve tax changes or, as the most drastic example, expropriation. Risk diversification by investors may be achieved via investments in different countries, technologies and project types. For our analysis, we assume that the risks in emission crediting are predominantly country-specific, i.e. the variations in the profits of single projects are mainly due to the economic or political conditions in the project's host countries. Investors invest in 'conventional' projects that yield a return greater than the minimum acceptable hurdle rate, i.e. the return on a risk-free investment plus a risk premium. Obviously, investors will demand a higher rate of return, i.e. a risk premium, for risky projects, compared to risk-free options. Investors will undertake investments induced by domestic emission limitations as long as their perceived return is positive, i.e. the price received for the emission credit sold on international permit markets is higher than the associated (risk adjusted) marginal abatement cost in the project's host country.

To estimate risk premia at both the country and project level, different techniques may be applied. Dailami and Leipziger (1999) provide e.g. an econometric analysis of past projects. Saini and Bates (1984) give an overview over various methods for the analysis of country-specific investment risk, which is the predominant risk category in mitigation projects. For our analysis, we use interest rate spreads between long-term government bonds of the developing country where the emission abatement project is located (risky country) and the US (as a risk-free reference country) to determine the developing country's risk premium. This approach is motivated by several studies showing that interest spreads carry substantial information for determining country risk (e.g. Edwards, 1986). Our calculations are based on data from the International Monetary Fund's International Financial Statistics (IFS) (IMF, 2000). The descriptive statistics of the country-specific risk premiums for different regions are given in Table 15. The bond yield spreads quantify the fraction of the generated credits that drop out due to project failure.

Table 15:   Descriptive Statistics of Bond Yield Spreads τ.

Regions	IFS Countries	Obs.	Mean	Median	Std. Dev.	Skew	Kurtosis	Max	Min
AFR	Malawi, South Africa, Namibia, Zimbabwe	264	0.051	0.061	0.041	-0.507	2.092	0.135	-0.043
ASI	Thailand, Korea, Malaysia, Singapore, Sri Lanka	264	0.028	0.026	0.017	0.297	2.134	0.069	-0.005
CHN	China	144	0.042	0.034	0.028	0.207	1.937	0.110	-0.004
IND	India	86	0.061	0.061	0.014	-0.095	2.195	0.088	0.031
MPC	Mexico, Morocco	34	0.016	0.012	0.013	0.484	2.075	0.039	-0.005
MSA	Venezuela, Jamaica, Antilles, Honduras, Chile	264	0.062	0.048	0.067	1.536	6.946	0.407	-0.025

Source: Böhringer and Löschel (2002b).

4.3   Analytical Framework and Parameterisation

Figure 9 illustrates the central effects of investment risks on the emission credit market in a simple three-country partial equilibrium framework. The effects are similar to those of transaction costs (Stavins, 1995). There is some industrialised country that faces total abatement requirement of T. It can fulfil its obligations by either domestic abatement or by investments in abatement projects abroad. The demand curve D for emission credits from abroad is determined by the marginal abatement cost curve of the industrialised country. On the other hand, there are two (unrestricted) project host countries with marginal abatement cost functions c_i' ($i = 1,2$) that yield the total supply S of emissions generated through projects.

In the absence of investment risks, the industrialised country demands emission credits generated through projects as long as the price for the credits is below its marginal abatement costs. In the market equilibrium, marginal abatement costs are equalised at price p across domestic abatement activities undertaken in the industrialised country and projects abroad that are hosted in the developing countries. The total amount of emission credits generated by projects abroad is $q = q_1 + q_2$, with q_1 representing projects undertaken in country 1 and q_2 projects undertaken in country 2, respectively. In the cost-effective solution, the industrialised country purchases credits q and abates domestically $T - q$.

Investment risks lead to a different equilibrium than in the absence of investment risks, where marginal abatement costs are equalised across all regions in equilibrium. If investment risks associated with abatement projects are taken into account, the investment decision is governed by the risk-adjusted marginal abatement costs, $\tilde{c}_i'$, which is the effective permit supply curve facing permit demanders. We assume that only investments in country 2 are risky and induce a shift of its effective supply curve in the investor's perspective from c_2' to $\tilde{c}_2'$. Rather than equilibrating marginal abatement costs as is done in the absence of investment risk, the sum of marginal abatement costs and marginal investment risks is equalised. Investment risks raise the costs for the participants in permit trade and thereby unambiguously decrease the volume of permit trading. The new market equilibrium with investment risks is characterised by a higher credit price $\tilde{p}$, which decreases the purchase of emission credits (i.e. the industrialised country's abatement investments) from abroad to $\tilde{q}$ and increases domestic abatement of the industrialised country to $T - \tilde{q}$. Hence, investment risks abroad shift the comparative advantage to domestic actions. In addition, the number of investment projects in the more risky country 2 decreases $(q_2 - \tilde{q}_2)$ while more projects are undertaken in the less risky country 1 $(\tilde{q}_1 - q_1)$ reflecting a shift in comparative advantage towards the less risky host country.

Overall, the potential efficiency gains from permit trade are reduced under risk accounting vis-à-vis a situation where risk is neglected. The true costs of control are higher with investment risks. This stems partly from the resource costs from investment risks and partly from the suppression of permit trade that has been mutually beneficial in the absence of investment risks. The burden from investment risk considerations is unevenly shared between permit demanders and high- and low-risk permit suppliers. The benefits from emission crediting for the industrialised countries and higher risk host countries decrease, whereas low-risk host countries may gain compared to the 'no-risk' situation. Industrialised countries are unambiguously worse off compared to a situation characterised by the absence of investment risks. The industrialised countries have to do more abatement domestically and pay higher prices on the permit market.

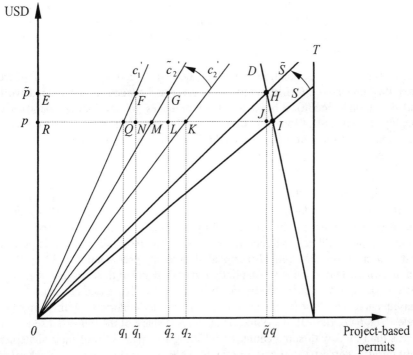

Figure 9:   Effects of Investment Risks.

To quantify the economy-wide implications of risk consideration in multilateral emission crediting, we extend the partial equilibrium model for permit trade outlined in Chapter 4. The analysis is based on marginal abatement cost curves for 13 regions. For the regional marginal abatement cost curves, we use data from the world energy system model POLES (Criqui et al., 1996), which embodies a detailed bottom-up description of regional energy markets and world-energy trade.

4.4   Scenarios and Results

In our expository simulations, we assume a uniform 20% cutback requirement of carbon emissions across industrialised countries vis-à-vis the business-as-usual emission level in 2010 while developing countries remain uncommitted. We compare two scenarios:

GLOBAL   There are no restrictions to where-flexibility. Beyond trading emission rights among each other, industrialised countries can buy emission credits from developing countries through abatement projects. Investment risks are neglected.

RISK   Investors are aware of investment risks. They are risk-neutral and discount emission credits purchased through CDM projects with the mean risk value of the developing country where projects are undertaken.[28]

Table 16 reports the simulation results for the two scenarios. Unrestricted where-flexibility under *GLOBAL* through CDM projects between the developed world and developing countries leads to direct revenues to developing countries of roughly 8.4 bn USD. However, these are only the incremental abatement costs from abatement measures. Including additional FDI that would not have occurred otherwise, total investment flows to developing countries may be considerably larger (Zhang and Maruyama, 2001).

It becomes clear that the CDM mechanism could provide substantial financial transfers to the developing world. In total revenue terms, CDM flows under *GLOBAL*, which are purely determined by marginal abatement costs and size of mitigation possibilities, will benefit CHN by far the most, since it has large low-cost abatement options. Global marginal abatement costs amount to 32 USD per ton of carbon. This value is substantially lower than any of the marginal abatement costs associated with purely domestic abatement of industrialised countries.[29] As a consequence, all industrialised countries turn into net importers of emission rights under *GLOBAL*. In total, the domestic abatement share of the industrialised world is less than 50% with some countries fulfilling less than 30% of their abatement duty through domestic mitigation projects: EUR, e.g., achieves only 29.7% of its total abatement requirement of 208 MtC (i.e. 20% of its business-as-usual emissions of 1040 MtC in 2010) domestically. We now turn to the implications of risk in mitigation projects in developing countries. In general, the accounting of risk should result in a reduction of total cost savings from CDM projects, since risk premia increase the costs for emission credits from the investor's perspective. Consequently, domestic abatement action of industrialised countries should rise vis-à-vis the *GLOBAL* scenario. Country-specific risk premia imply non-uniform deductions from the (increased) uniform emission market price across CDM countries (see Section A in Table 16). As has been pointed out in Section 4.3, low-risk countries may benefit from risk considerations at the expense of high-risk countries through both higher effective prices for carbon credits and more CDM projects compared to the case *GLOBAL*. The qualitative reasoning is confirmed by the quantitative results. However, our quantitative results suggest that the risk-induced changes are relatively small. If investors are risk-neutral, i.e. for the sce-

---

[28]   We assume that the risks of emission trading between industrialised countries can be neglected.

[29]   The marginal abatement costs in USD/tC to achieve a 20% reduction of emissions from business-as-usual emission levels in 2010 for the case of purely domestic action are as follows: AUN 74.1, CAN 194.6, EIT 56.2, EUR 169.9, FSU 54.5, JPN 195.3, USA 89.5.

nario *RISK*, the changes are close to negligible (e.g. with respect to country-specific compliance costs, changes as compared to *GLOBAL* are only as high as 3% with total compliance costs increased by 2.4%).

Table 16:   Implications of Investment Risks.

	GLOBAL	*RISK*
A. Marginal Abatement Costs (in USD/tC)		
AUN	32.2	33.0
CAN	32.2	33.0
EIT	32.2	33.0
EUR	32.2	33.0
FSU	32.2	33.0
JPN	32.2	33.0
USA	32.2	33.0
AFR	32.2	31.3
ASI	32.2	32.1
CHN	32.2	31.6
IND	32.2	31.0
MPC	32.2	32.4
MSA	32.2	31.0
B. Cost of Compliance (in m USD)		
AUN	560	569
CAN	895	915
EIT	822	833
EUR	5.549	5.665
FSU	2.221	2.248
JPN	1.809	1.848
USA	8.304	8.451
AFR	-675	-676
ASI	-804	-821
CHN	-5.372	-5.427

Table 16 continued.

	GLOBAL	RISK
IND	-613	-608
MPC	-447	-462
MSA	-475	-474
Total	11.775	12.061
C. Domestic Abatement Share (in % of Total Abatement Requirement)[a]		
AUN	56.1	57.1
CAN	27.1	27.6
EIT	66.9	68.1
EUR	29.7	30.2
FSU	70.1	71.3
JPN	26.0	26.5
USA	48.8	49.7
Total [b]	45.6	46.4

[a] Values below 100% indicate permit imports, values above 100% indicate permit exports.
[b] With respect to total industrialised emissions in 2010.

4.5　Conclusions

We have investigated how risk considerations affect the economic implications of emission crediting. Based on simulations with a simple partial equilibrium model of emission trade, we found that project-based emission crediting in developing countries provides considerable income to developing countries with larger low-cost abatement options. Our quantitative results show that the incorporation of country-specific investment risks induces rather small changes to the magnitude and distribution of benefits from project-based emission trading vis-à-vis a situation where investment risks are neglected. This holds for the case of risk-neutral investors that discount emission credits purchased through CDM projects with the mean risk value of the developing country where projects are undertaken.

Böhringer and Löschel (2002b) provide a much more comprehensive assessment of the potential implications of investment risks where they incorporate alternative risk attitudes of investors. Their analysis shows that, if investors go for high safety of returns, there is a noticeable decline in the overall volume of emission crediting and the associated total economic benefits. Differences in risk across developing countries then become more pronounced with converse implications for high-risk and low-risk developing countries. While low-risk developing countries attract higher project volumes and benefit from higher effective prices per emission credit compared to a reference scenario without risk, the opposite applies to high-risk countries. The – politically undesired – shift in comparative advantage of emission abatement penalising high-risk, typically least-developed, countries may become dramatic if risk-averse investors perceive large differences in project-based risks across countries. In this case, only very cheap mitigation projects in high-risk countries will be realised, driving down the respective country's benefits from emission crediting to the advantage of low-risk developing countries.

References

Aït-Sahalia, Y. and M.W. Brandt (2001), Variable Selection for Portfolio Choice, *The Journal of Finance* 56 (4), 1297-1351.

Alexander, G.J. and A.M. Baptista (2002), Economic Implications of Using a Mean-VaR Model for Portfolio Selection: A Comparison with Mean-Variance Analysis, *Journal of Economic Dynamics and Control* 26, 1159-1193.

Arrow, K.J. (1965), *Aspects of the Theory of Risk-Bearing*, Helsinki.

Bach, S., C. Bork, M. Kohlhaas, C. Lutz, B. Meyer, B. Praetorius, and H. Welsch (2001), *Die ökologische Steuerreform in Deutschland: Eine modellgestützte Analyse ihrer Wirkungen auf Wirtschaft und Umwelt*, Heidelberg.

Baumol, W.J. (1963), An Expected Gain-Confidence Limit Criterion for Portfolio Selection, *Management Science* 10 (1), 174-182.

Berndt, E.R. and M.A. Fuss (1986), Productivity Measurement with Adjustments for Variation in Capacity Utilization and Other Forms of Temporary Equilibrium, *Journal of Econometrics* 33, 7-29.

Böhringer, C. (2000), Cooling Down Hot Air – A Global CGE Analysis of Post-Kyoto Carbon Abatement Strategies, *Energy Policy* 28, 779-789.

Böhringer, C. (2001), Industry-Level Emission Trading Between Power Producers in the EU, *Applied Economics* 34 (4), 523-533.

Böhringer, C. (2002), Climate Politics From Kyoto to Bonn: From Little to Nothing?, *The Energy Journal* 23 (2), 51-71.

Böhringer, C. and A. Löschel (2002a), Assessing the Costs of Compliance: The Kyoto Protocol, *European Environment* 12, 1-16.

Böhringer, C. and A. Löschel (2002b), *Climate Policy Induced Investments in Developing Countries – The Implications of Investment Risks*, ZEW Discussion Paper 02-68, Mannheim.

Böhringer, C. and A. Löschel (2003), Market Power and Hot Air in International Emission Trading: The Impacts of U.S. Withdrawal from the Kyoto Protocol, *Applied Economics* 35 (6), 651-664.

Böhringer, C. and T.F. Rutherford (2002a), Carbon Abatement and International Spillovers, *Environmental and Resource Economics* 22 (3), 391-417.

Böhringer, C. and T.F. Rutherford (2002b), *In Search of a Rationale for Differentiated Environmental Taxes*, ZEW Discussion Paper 02-30, Mannheim.

Böhringer, C. and T.F. Rutherford (2004), Who Should Pay How Much? Compensation for International Spillovers from Carbon Abatement Policies to Developing Countries – A Global CGE Assessment, forthcoming in: *Computational Economics* 23 (2).

Böhringer, C., J. Jensen, and T.F. Rutherford (2000), Energy Market Projections and Differentiated Carbon Abatement in the European Union, in: Carraro, C. (Ed.), *Efficiency and Equity of Climate Change Policy*, Dordrecht, 199-220.

Böhringer, C., T.F. Rutherford, A. Pahlke, U. Fahl, and A. Voß (1997), Volkswirtschaftliche Effekte einer Umstrukturierung des deutschen Steuersystems unter besonderer Berücksichtigung von Umweltsteuern, *IER-Forschungsbericht* 37, Stuttgart.

Bose, R.K. and M. Shukla (1999), Elasticities of Electricity Demand in India, *Energy Policy* 27, 137-146.

Bovenberg, A.L. (1997), Environmental Policy, Distortionary Labour Taxation, and Employment: Pollution Taxes and the Double Dividend, in: Carraro, C. and D. Sinisalco (Eds.), *New Directions in the Economic Theory of the Environment*, Cambridge, UK.

Buchner, B., C. Carraro, and I. Cersosimo (2001), *On the Consequences of the U.S. Withdrawal from the Kyoto/Bonn Protocol*, FEEM Nota di Lavoro 102.2001.

Burniaux, J.-M. (1998), How Important Is Market Power in Achieving Kyoto?: An Assessment Based on the GREEN Model, in: OECD (Ed.), *Economic Modelling of Climate Change*, OECD workshop report.

Burniaux, J.-M., G. Nicoletti, and J. Oliveira-Martins (1992), *GREEN, A Multi-Sector, Multi-Region General Equilibrium Model for Quantifying the Costs of Curbing CO₂ Emissions: A Technical Manual*, Working Papers 116, OECD Economics Department, Paris.

Buttermann H.G. and B. Hillebrand (1996), *Sektorale und regionale Wirkungen von Energiesteuern*, Untersuchungen des RWI 19, Essen.

Cansier, D. and R. Krumm (1996), Joint Implementation: Regimespezifisches Optimalverhalten im Kontext umweltpolitischer Grundprinzipien, *Journal of Environmental Law and Policy* 19, 161-181.

Conrad, K. and J. Wang (1993), Quantitative Umweltpolitik: Gesamtwirtschaftliche Auswirkungen einer CO_2-Besteuerung in Deutschland (West), *Jahrbücher für Nationalökonomie und Statistik* 213, 308-324.

Criqui, P. et al. (1996), *POLES 2.2., JOULE II Programme*, European Commission DG XVII – Science Research Development, Brussels.

Criqui, P., F. Cattier, P. Menanteau, and M.-C. Quidoz (1996), *POLES 2.2. Reference Guide*, Institute of Energy Policy and Economics, Grenoble.

Criqui, P., S. Mima, and L. Viguier (1999), Marginal Abatement Costs of CO_2 Emission Reductions, Geographical Flexibility and Concrete Ceilings: An Assessment Using the POLES Model, *Energy Policy* 27 (10), 585-602.

Dailami, M. and D.M. Leipziger (1999), *Infrastructure Project Finance and Capital Flows: A New Perspective*, Economic Development Institute Working Paper, Washington, D.C.

Damodaran, A. (1999), *Estimating Country Premiums*, NYU Working Paper, New York.

DIW (1994), *Ökosteuer – Sackgasse oder Königsweg? Wirtschaftliche Auswirkungen einer ökologischen Steuerreform*, Expertise Commissioned by Greenpeace, Berlin.

DOE (Department of Energy) (2001), *International Energy Outlook*, Washington, D.C.

EC (1999), *Preparing for Implementation of the Kyoto Protocol*, COM(1999)230, http://europa.eu.int/comm/environment/docum/99230_en.pdf.

Edwards, S. (1986), The Pricing of Bonds and Bank Loans in International Markets, *European Economic Review* 30, 565-589.

Ellerman, A.D. and A. Decaux (1998), *Analysis of Post-Kyoto CO_2 Emissions Trading Using Marginal Abatement Curves*, MIT Joint Program on the Science and Policy of Global Change Report 40.

Ellerman, A.D. and I.S. Wing (2000), Supplementarity: An Invitation for Monopsony, *The Energy Journal* 21 (4), 29-59.

Ellerman, A.D., H.D. Jacoby, and A. Decaux (1998), *The Effects on Developing Countries of the Kyoto Protocol and CO_2 Emissions Trading*, MIT Joint Program on the Science and Policy of Global Change 41.

Godby, R. (2000), Market Power and Emissions Trading: Theory and Laboratory Results, *Pacific Economics Review* 5 (3), 349-363.

Goulder, L.H. (1995), Environmental Taxation and the Double Dividend: A Reader's Guide, *International Tax and Public Finance* 2, 155-82.

Grubb, M., C. Vrolijk, and D. Brack (1999), *The Kyoto Protocol: A Guide and Assessment*, Royal Institute of International Affairs, London.

Hahn, R.W. (1984), Market Power in Transferable Property Rights, *Quarterly Journal of Economics* 99, 753-765.

Harrison J., M. Horridge, and K.R. Pearson (2000), Decomposing Simulation Results with Respect to Exogenous Shocks, *Computational Economics* 15 (3), 227-249.

Hutton, J. and A. Ruocco (1999), Tax Reform and Employment in Europe, *International Tax and Public Finance* 6, 263-288.

IEA (1996), *Energy Prices and Taxes, Energy Balances of OECD and Non-OECD Countries*, Paris.

IMF (International Monetary Fund) (2000), *International Financial Statistics*, Washington, D.C. (CD-Rom).

IPCC (International Panel on Climate Change) (1996), *Climate Change 1995: Economic and Social Dimensions of Climate Change, Contribution of Working Group III to the Second Assessment Report of the Intergovernmental Panel on Climate Change*, Cambridge, MA.

Jackson, T. (1995), Joint Implementation and Cost-Effectiveness Under the Framework Convention on Climate Change, *Energy Policy* 23, 117-138.

Janssen, J. (2000), Implementing the Kyoto Mechanisms: Potential Contributions by Banks and Insurance Companies, *Geneva Papers on Risk and Insurance Issues and Practice* 25 (4), 1-17.

Janssen, J. (2002), Risk Management of Joint Implementation and Clean Development Mechanism Projects through Carbon Investment Funds, in: Albrecht, J. (Ed.), *Instruments for Climate Policy: Limited Versus Unlimited Flexibility*, Cheltenham, 148-169.

Jepma, C.J. (1995), *The Feasibility of Joint Implementation*, Dordrecht.

Jorgenson, D.W. and M. Nishimizu (1978), US and Japanese Economic Growth, 1952-1974: An International Comparison, *Economic Journal* 88, 707-726.

Jorion, P. (2001), *Value at Risk: The New Benchmark for Managing Financial Risk*, New York.

Krutilla, K. (1999), Environmental Policy and Transactions Costs, in: van den Bergh, J.C.J.M. (Ed.), *Handbook of Environmental and Resource Economics*, Cheltenham, 249-264.

Kuik, O., P. Peters, and N. Schrijer (1994), *Joint Implementation to Curb Climate Change: Legal and Economic Aspects*, Dordrecht.

Löschel, A. and Z.X. Zhang (2002), The Economic and Environmental Implications of the US Repudiation of the Kyoto Protocol and the Subsequent Deals in Bonn and Marrakech, *Weltwirtschaftliches Archiv – Review of World Economics* 138 (4), 711-746.

Malueg, D.A. (1990), Welfare Consequences of Emission Credit Trading Programs, *Journal of Environmental Economics and Management* 18, 66-77.

Manne, A.S. and R.G. Richels (1992), *Buying Greenhouse Insurance: The Economic Costs of CO_2 Emission Limits*, Cambridge, MA.

Markowitz, H. (1952), Portfolio Selection, *The Journal of Finance* 7, 77-91.

McDougall, R.A., A. Elbehri, and T.P. Truong (1998), *Global Trade, Assistance and Protection: The GTAP 4 Data Base*, Center for Global Trade Analysis, West Lafayette.

Misiolek, W.S. and H.W. Elder (1989), Exclusionary Manipulation of Markets for Pollution Rights, *Journal of Environmental Economics and Management* 16 (2), 156-166.

Montero, J.P. (1997), Marketable Pollution Permits with Uncertainty and Transaction Costs, *Resource and Energy Economics* 20, 27-50.

OECD (Organisation for Economic Cooperation and Development) (2002), *Foreign Direct Investment for Development – Maximising Benefits, Minimising Costs*, Paris.

Paltsev, S.V. (2000), *The Kyoto Protocol: Hot Air for Russia?*, Working Paper 00-9, University of Colorado, Boulder.

Pratt, J.W. (1964), Risk Aversion in the Small and in the Large, *Econometrica* 32, 122-136.

Rutherford, T.F. and S.V. Paltsev (2000), *GTAP-Energy in GAMS: The Dataset and Static Model*, Working Paper, University of Colorado, Boulder.

Saini, K.G. and P.B. Bates (1984), A Survey of the Quantitative Approaches to Country Risk Analysis, *Journal of Banking and Finance* 8, 340-356.

Santos, J.A.C. (2001), Bank Capital Regulation in Contemporary Banking Theory: A Review of the Literature, *Financial Markets, Institutions and Instruments* 10 (2), 41-84.

Sartzetakis, E.S. (1997), Tradeable Emission Permits Regulations in the Presence of Imperfectly Competitive Product Markets: Welfare Implications, *Environmental and Resource Economics* 9 (1), 65-81.

Sinn, H.-W. (1989), *Economic Decisions under Uncertainty*, Heidelberg.

Sorrell, S. and J. Skea (1999), Introduction, in: Sorrell, S. and J. Skea (Eds.), *Pollution for Sale: Emissions Trading and Joint Implementation*, Cheltenham, 1-24.

Springer, U. (2002), *International Diversification of Investments in Climate Change Mitigation*, Diskussionsbeitrag Nr. 100, University St. Gallen.

Stavins, R.N. (1995), Transaction Costs and Tradable Permits, *Journal of Environmental Economics and Management* 29 (2), 133-148.

Steward, R., D. Anderson, M.A. Aslam, C. Eyre, G. Jones, P. Sands, M. Stuart, and F. Yamin (2000), *The Clean Development Mechanism: Building International Public-Private Partnership Under the Kyoto Protocol. Technical, Financial and Institutional Issues*, New York and Geneva: United Nations.

Telser, L.G. (1955), Safety First and Hedging, *The Review of Economic Studies* 23, 1-16.

Tietenberg, T., M. Grubb, A. Michaelowa, B. Swift, and Z.X. Zhang (1999), *International Rules for Greenhouse Gas Emissions Trading: Defining the Principles, Modalities, Rules and Guidelines for Verification, Reporting and Accountability*, New York and Geneva: United Nations.

Torvanger, A. et al. (1994), *Joint Implementation Under the Climate Convention: Phases, Options and Incentives*, Cicero Report 1994:6, Oslo.

UN (1997), *Kyoto Protocol to the United Nations Framework Convention on Climate Change*, FCCC/CP/L.7/Add.1, Kyoto.

UNFCCC (United Nations Framework Convention on Climate Change) (1992), *United Nations Framework Convention on Climate Change*, New York, 9 May 1992, in force 21, March 1994.

UNFCCC (1997), *Kyoto Protocol to the United Nations Framework Convention on Climate Change*, FCCC/CP/L.7/Add.1, Kyoto.

UNFCCC (2001), *United Nations Framework Convention on Climate, Review of the Implementation of Commitments and of Other Provisions of the Convention*, FCCC/CP/2001/L.7, VI, 5.

UNFCCC (2001), *Activities Implemented Jointly under the Pilot Phase*, Fifth Synthesis Report on Activities Implemented Jointly under the Pilot Phase, Note by the Secretariat, FCCC/SBSTA/2001/7, Marrakesh.

Victor, D.G., N. Nakicenovic, and N. Victor (2001), The Kyoto Protocol Emission Allocations: Windfall Surpluses for Russia and Ukraine, *Climatic Change* 49, 263-277.

Welfens, J.P.P., B. Meyer, W. Pfaffenberger, P. Jasinski, and A. Jungmittag (2001), *Energy Policies in the European Union: Germany's Ecological Tax Reform*, Berlin, Heidelberg, New York.

Welsch, H. (1996), Recycling of Carbon/Energy Taxes and the Labour Market: A General Equilibrium Analysis for the European Community, *Environmental and Resource Economics* 8, 141-151.

Westkog, H. (1996), Market Power in a System of Tradeable CO_2-Quotas, *Energy Journal* 17, 85-103.

Westkog, H. (2001), *Why Quota Trade Should Be Restricted: The Arguments Behind the EU Position on Emissions Trading*, CICERO Working Paper 2001:07.

Weyant, J. (Ed.) (1999), The Costs of the Kyoto Protocol: A Multi-Model Evaluation, *The Energy Journal* Special Issue.

Wirl, F., C. Huber, and I.O. Walker (1998), Joint Implementation: Strategic Reactions and Possible Remedies, *Environmental and Resource Economics* 12 (2), 203-224.

Woerdman, E. (2000), Competitive Distortions in an International Emissions Trading Market, *Mitigation and Adaptation Strategies for Global Change* 5 (4), 337-360.

World Bank (2001), *Global Economic Prospects and the Developing Countries*, Washington, D.C.

Zhang, Z.X. and A. Maruyama (2001), Towards a Private-Public Synergy in Financing Climate Change Mitigation Projects, *Energy Policy* 29, 1363-1378.

Trade Liberalisation and Climate Policies

Nikos Kouvaritakis, Nikos Stroblos, Leonidas Paroussos, and Spyridon Tsallas

National Technical University of Athens, 9 Iroon Politechniou str., 15773 Zografou Campus, Athens, Greece
kapros@central.ntua.gr

1 Introduction

1.1 Foreword

The issue of the reduction of the levels of tariff and non-tariff barriers below the ones corresponding to the GATT agreement of 1994 has been raised in the circles of international organisations such as the WTO, the World Bank, etc. Programmes of trade liberalisation based on the reduction of trade barriers within Regional Trade Agreements are leading towards the same direction. The expansion of world trade that is expected to take place due to these reductions is considered by the same groups as an important factor contributing to an increase in world production and poverty reduction especially in developing countries.

When the GATT agreement was under examination, a great number of general equilibrium models was developed aiming at quantifying the consequences of the possible reductions in trade barriers at regional and global levels. Focusing on the provision of answers to specific questions brought forward each time in international forums, these models are forced to examine a narrow segment of reductions of tariff and non-tariff barriers regarding either some specific groups of products (agricultural, textiles) or some specific groups of countries (ASEAN, for instance).

At the theoretical level, the existence of tariffs results in a distorted distribution of resources among products and countries. Therefore, if the hypothetical reduction of tariffs leads to a more effective utilisation of production resources, an expansion of world trade, and an increase of world output, then their abolition is expected to magnify these results.

On the other hand, it is natural for all countries – and even more for the developing ones – to express their increased concerns for the distribution of the predicted benefits. These concerns are nowadays so strong that, as it has been shown by the failure of the 3rd World Trade Organisation Ministerial meeting in Seattle, full liberalisation of external trade remains a hypothetical exercise. Nevertheless, such an experiment is of vital importance in order to test the validity of the arguments of each side. These issues will be considered in the analysis of the first part of this chapter.

It is evident that growth without any changes in the production process leads to more pollution. In recent years key among environmental concerns has been the issue of climate change. The elimination of tariff and non-tariff barriers and the imposition of the emissions restriction policy interact in two ways: On the one hand they act competitively. Trade liberalisation leads to a higher level of economic activity by wiping out distortions of the efficient distribution of resources resulting from the imposition of tariffs. The imposition of emission constraints reduces economic activity by introducing what amounts from the purely economic point of view to a distortion in the markets. Given the uneven impact of these two distortionary factors on countries and sectors of production, the first question brought up is which of the factors prevails at the regional and global levels. From another point of view, these factors can be complementary to each other. In view of the imposition of restrictions on emissions, the evolving question is whether the abolition of tariffs facilitates the abatement effort of the countries or not. We deal with these questions in the second part of this chapter.

1.2   Brief Description of the GEM-E3 Model

In order to study the effects of full liberalisation of international trade and the restriction of emissions in the post-Kyoto period, the latest version of GEM-E3-World general equilibrium model was utilised (Capros et al., 1997) Before presenting the modifications that were made to the model in order to sufficiently respond to the needs of this study, the most important characteristics of the core model are briefly described.

GEM-E3 is a multi-country applied general equilibrium model covering the world divided in 17 regions (Table 1) that are linked through endogenous trade of goods and services. The model considers 4 economic agents (households, firms, government and foreign) and 18 production sectors (and goods) (Table 2). It is based on an entire representation of a Social Accounting Matrix for each region (including Input-Output table and National Accounts), an Investment Matrix per region, a Consumption Matrix per region, and a Trade Matrix at the world level.

Table 1:   GEM-E3 Regional Aggregation.

	Countries and Regions
AUZ	Australia, New Zealand
JAP	Japan
EAS	Korea, Indonesia, Malaysia, Philipinnes, Singapore, Thailand, Vietnam, Hong Kong, Taiwan
CHI	China
IND	India, Shri Lanka, Rest of Asia
NAM	USA, Mexico, Canada
LAM	Argentina, Brazil, Chile, Uruguay, Central America, Caribbean, Rest of South America/Andean Pact
NEU	Denmark, Sweden, Finland
GEU	Germany
BEU	UK
REU	Rest of European Union
OEU	Iceland, Norway, Switzerland, Turkey
CEA	Central European Associates
FSU	Former Soviet Union
NAF	Morocco, Rest of North Africa, Rest of Middle East
AFR	South Africa, Rest of Southern Africa, Rest of Sub Saharan Africa
ROW	Rest of the World

Table 2:   GEM-E3 Sectoral Aggregation and COICOP Classification.

	Products and Sectors		Consumption Categories
1	Agriculture	1	Food, beverages and tobacco
2	Coal	2	Clothing and footwear
3	Oil	3	Housing and water charges
4	Gas	4	Fuels and power
5	Electricity	5	Household equipment and operation excluding heating and cooking appliances
6	Ferrous and non ferrous metals*	6	Heating and cooking appliances
7	Chemical Products*	7	Medical care and health
8	Other energy intensive*	8	Transport equipment
9	Electronic Equipment*	9	Operation of transport
10	Transport equipment*	10	Purchased transport
11	Other Equipment Goods*	11	Communication
12	Other Manufacturing products	12	Recreational services
13	Construction	13	Miscellaneous goods and services
14	Food Industry		
15	Trade and Transport*		
16	Textile Industry		
17	Other Market Services*		
18	Non Market Services		

* Sectors with imperfect competition in the modified model.

Each productive sector in the core model, which coincides with the column of an Input-Output table, is assumed to consist of a virtually infinite number of firms that produce a homogeneous good under perfect competition. The technology of production of all sectors is characterised by constant returns to scale and production functions have nested constant elasticity of substitution specifications. Taking into account the restrictions imposed by technology, each producer tries to maximise his profit and generates a demand for factors of production, which in GEM-E3 are capital, labour, energy, and materials (KLEM-type production function). The quantity of each factor of production is determined endogenously in the model from the interaction of supply and demand in the corresponding markets. In capital markets, the supply of capital for a specific period of time is constant and equal to the stock of capital that is available in the same period. Nevertheless, producers can increase the stock of capital through time by investment expenditures. The ability to invest and, therefore, to determine the available physical stock of capital for the next period is one of the dynamic characteristics of the model.

The investment decisions of producers depend on two factors: The first factor is the quantity of capital possessed by each producer in the current period; the second factor is the desired quantity of capital, which is determined during the profit maximisation process, taking into account a long-run rate of return on capital. The model has two options for the determination of this long-run rate of return: It is either determined exogenously, based on the data available in the base year, or it is set equal to the dual price of the restriction of stability in the current account for each country. The desired quantity of capital is also dependent on exogenous expectations about the evolution of the economy. The producer therefore decides on his future investments comparing the desired with the available quantity of physical capital. The model is capable of dealing with neutral technological progress, as well as labour-, capital-, energy-, and material-augmenting technological progress.

Consumption expenditure, in combination with the supply of labour, is determined in the model during the process of the intertemporal utility maximisation of the representative household under the intertemporal restriction of its income. This is done through a two-stage maximisation: At the beginning, total consumption expenditure and leisure of the households are determined using the steady-state formulation of the above maximisation problem. Indirectly at this stage, the aggregate savings and the supply of labour are determined. At the second stage, under the restriction of total consumption expenditures, a static utility function is maximised in order to determine the demand for the 13 consumption categories. With the utilisation of the Consumption Matrix, these categories are translated into demands for the 18 products that correspond to the level of disaggregation used in this version of the model.

Regarding aggregate demand, the GEM-E3 model uses a nested-Armington (Armington, 1969) specification. At the upper level of this aggregate demand function it is supposed that domestic buyers (producers and consumers) use a composite good that combines domestic and imported goods that are considered as imperfect substitutes. At a second stage, imported goods are distinguished depending on their country of origin.

Given the prices of domestically produced goods and imports, the domestic buyer tries to minimise the cost of the composite good based on the above structure, determining in this way the demand for domestically produced goods and imported goods. The demand for exports is also determined endogenously since it is defined as the sum of the demand for imports of all other countries for the products of one country.

Government behaviour is determined by external factors. Public expenditures are also determined completely exogenously, by supposing that they increase at a specific rate each year. Prices that clear all markets for goods and factors of production are simultaneously determined with the interaction of the supply and demand functions in the framework defined above.

Except from the transactions related to the production sphere, GEM-E3 also covers the distributive transactions that take place in an economy as they are registered in the lower right part of a Social Accounting Matrix. Institutional sectors (households, firms, government, foreign), apart from income they receive from their endowment in factors of production (wages, rents), are involved in transactions that redistribute income, such as taxes, donations, etc. Taking into account all these transactions (productive and redistributive), the savings of each institutional sector that finance its investments are determined. The surplus of each sector is defined as the difference of its savings and investments; in aggregate though, the sum of the surpluses of all sectors in an economy is equal to zero, satisfying the Law of Walras.

Except from the core model, GEM-E3 embodies an environmental module, which connects economic activity to the emissions caused by the use of coal, crude oil, and gas during their production and consumption processes. In the framework of this model, the effects of environmental policies such as taxation, tradable pollution permits, and global constraints on emissions can be analysed.

The modifications made in GEM-E3 for the purposes of the CCGT project have to do with the core model, mainly in the production process and the external sector, while leaving unchanged the environmental module.

The first modification refers to the status and technological conditions under which some productive sectors operate. Specifically, it is assumed that the market structure is imperfectly competitive in the sectors that have a large potential for economies of scale (Capros et al., 1998). These sectors – mainly intermediate and equipment goods industries – are assumed to have a finite number of symmetric firms operating in the market under an oligopolistic market regime. The rest of the sectors have infinite firms under perfect competition.

The introduction of economies of scale in the model was made possible through the adoption of the hypothesis that the total cost function is composed of two parts (Pratten, 1988), one part representing the variable cost and one part representing the fixed cost. Production functions remain the same as in the core model and maintain the property of constant returns to scale. Thus the variable cost part is represented by the marginal cost function. Economies of scale are introduced in the analysis with the inclusion of fixed costs in the model. This part of the cost is independent of the level of production; both the average fixed cost and the average total cost are reduced as the level of production increases, with economies of scale emerging in this sector.

The second modification refers to the homogeneity of the goods produced by firms in the sectors that are characterised by imperfect competition. Specifically, it is assumed that firms in these sectors do not produce a homogeneous good but horizontally differentiated varieties of a product. These varieties are assumed to be imperfect substitutes. The existence of many varieties of a good enables a different specialisation of demand named in modern economic literature as 'love of variety' property (Dixit and Stiglitz, 1977). According to this theory firms and households love variety and prefer the consumption of two units of different varieties of a product rather than the consumption of two units of the same variety. The adoption of the product varieties approach is commonly used in current literature because among other things it makes use of a sort of endogenous growth possible; this is obvious if we consider that, according to the 'love of variety' approach, the same level of utility can be achieved with a smaller amount of differentiated products.

Another modification made to the core of the GEM-E3 model refers to the pricing policy of the firms in imperfectly competitive sectors. As mentioned above, the number of firms in these sectors is finite. The entry of a firm in such a sector depends on the level of demand for its product, which has to cover the total cost of production of this good (fixed and variable). In cases where the demand for the product of this sector is low, the average fixed cost is so big that the newcomer firm ends up with losses. Based on the argumentation above, firms in imperfectly competitive sectors control, to a certain degree, the demand of the sector and have the ability to sell at prices higher than marginal cost. Thus in the model it is supposed that firms in imperfectly competitive sectors price their products setting a mark-up on their marginal cost. This mark-up depends on the perception of the elasticity of demand. Actually the model calculates endogenously three elasticities of demand and, therefore, three mark-up rates. This occurs because the model assumes that the firm sells its products in three markets: home, European, and rest of the world. In this we are incorporating notions of price discrimination. This issue will be brought up in the discussion of the modification of the external sector. The assessment of these three perceived elasticities is made using the Nash-Cournot hypothesis with zero and invariant conjectures. The number of firms existing in each imperfectly competitive sector is also endogenously determined. This is made possible by making the hypothesis that the entry of new firms in a sector is continued until total profits inside the sector turn to zero (Zero-Profit Condition).

The fourth modification refers to the specialisation of demand in the model. This change was necessary in order to broaden and diversify the substitution abilities among products of the same sector coming from different origins. In order to be able to distinguish among different origins of imports, a four-level nested-Armington type function is used (Figure 1). At the first level, the domestic consumer of the product has the ability to choose between the domestically produced good and the imported good regardless of origin. At the second level, since the quantity of the domestically produced good is determined, the decision is made for the distribution of demand for the different varieties of the good produced by home firms according to the 'love of variety' principle. Also at this level, imports are distinguished between imports from Europe and imports from the rest of the world. At the third level, the distribution of imports from Europe to imports from each country inside the region is made, the same occurs for the imports from the rest of the world. At the fourth level, imports from each country are distributed among the different varieties produced by the firms in this country[1].

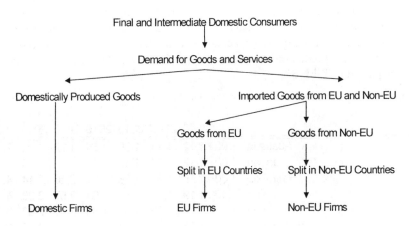

Figure 1:   Market Segmentation in GEM-E3.

1.3   Baseline Assumptions

According to the usual practice in general equilibrium models, the first step in the course of a study is the construction of a business-as-usual scenario, the results of which will be the basis of comparison for all alternative scenarios.

In the majority of cases the analysis is made with static models that are applied in only one period. In these cases, the construction of a business-as-usual scenario is

---

[1]   The complexity of this structure is due to the need for differentiation of the elasticities of substitution coming from the various origins. Since the Armington aggregator is actually a function with constant elasticity of substitution, using only one nesting level would carry the assumption that goods have the same elasticity of substitution regardless of the country of origin.

limited to the calibration of the parameters of the model using the statistical data of the base year. In this way the model embodies the existing structure of the economy and usually requires no further adjustment. However, the 'free trade' and 'soft landing' simulations examined in this study require a different sort of treatment. The base year in the GEM-E3 model is 1995 while the simulations examined refer to the post-Kyoto period (2010-2030). Since, GEM-E3 is a general equilibrium model with several recursive dynamic characteristics, a solution to the above problem would be to solve the model for the 1995-2030 period and consider that the results are composites of a business-as-usual scenario. However, such a practice would be a simple transfer of the structural characteristics of the world economy in 1995 to the world economy in 2030. In order to avoid this solution, exogenous predictions for the evolution of some crucial variables such as GDP and CO_2 emissions have been used by modifying in an appropriate way the structure of the economies of the regions of the model. The above modification was made possible by making reasonable assumptions for the exogenous technological progress and the exogenous expectations about the evolution of the economy. Specifically, the predictions for the evolution of GDP during the 1995-2030 period are displayed in Table 3:

Table 3:   Reference GDP Growth Compared to 1995.

	1995	2000	2005	2010	2015	2020	2025	2030
Australia	1.00	1.12	1.24	1.39	1.54	1.72	1.92	2.14
Japan	1.00	1.12	1.27	1.42	1.59	1.79	2.00	2.24
East Asia	1.00	1.16	1.35	1.58	1.91	2.46	3.14	4.01
China	1.00	1.19	1.36	1.63	2.04	2.57	3.23	4.14
India	1.00	1.14	1.29	1.52	1.83	2.26	2.83	3.71
North America	1.00	1.15	1.30	1.48	1.69	1.91	2.16	2.45
Latin America	1.00	1.13	1.25	1.40	1.56	1.84	2.19	2.66
Nordic Europe	1.00	1.11	1.22	1.36	1.49	1.66	1.83	2.04
Germany	1.00	1.09	1.21	1.33	1.46	1.63	1.79	1.95
UK	1.00	1.10	1.21	1.35	1.50	1.67	1.83	2.02
Rest of Europe	1.00	1.11	1.25	1.38	1.51	1.66	1.84	2.06
Other Europe	1.00	1.14	1.30	1.49	1.74	2.14	2.64	3.25
Central European Associates	1.00	0.93	1.13	1.39	1.70	2.11	2.60	3.18
Former Soviet Union	1.00	0.92	1.15	1.42	1.69	2.10	2.59	3.17
North Africa	1.00	1.12	1.28	1.50	1.82	2.29	2.90	3.73
Africa	1.00	1.19	1.42	1.70	1.98	2.39	2.88	3.54
ROW	1.00	1.13	1.26	1.44	1.65	2.06	2.57	3.15

The evolution of CO_2 emissions was provided by the POLES model (Table 4).

As regards tariff and non-tariff barriers, the application of the rules according to the decisions of international agreements valid as of today is assumed in the business-as-usual scenario.

The basic hypothesis at the world level is that there exists full implementation of the commitments that have been agreed at the Uruguay Round. The most important pieces of information that can be quantified in the framework of the Uruguay Round are tariff and non-tariff barriers imposed on international trade at the world level.

Only the most important regional trade agreements from the viewpoint of international trade have been retained in the business-as-usual scenario. Furthermore, it is assumed that China joins the WTO by 2005.

Table 4:   Reference Growth of CO_2 Emissions Compared to 1995.

	1995	2000	2005	2010	2015	2020	2025	2030
Australia & New Zealand	1.00	1.16	1.19	1.26	1.39	1.48	1.65	1.90
Japan	1.00	0.97	0.94	0.95	0.98	1.00	1.03	1.05
East Asia	1.00	1.19	1.37	1.66	2.04	2.45	2.99	3.53
China	1.00	1.24	1.70	1.99	2.27	2.54	2.85	3.22
India	1.00	1.32	1.88	2.41	3.03	3.70	4.40	5.12
North America	1.00	1.11	1.13	1.20	1.26	1.32	1.36	1.42
Latin America	1.00	1.21	1.28	1.53	1.79	2.07	2.36	2.67
Nordic Europe	1.00	1.13	1.13	1.19	1.31	1.31	1.38	1.38
Germany	1.00	0.99	0.92	0.93	0.97	0.99	1.01	1.00
UK	1.00	1.04	1.02	1.04	1.09	1.15	1.18	1.24
Rest of Europe	1.00	1.08	1.10	1.14	1.20	1.24	1.26	1.27
Other Europe	1.00	1.17	1.29	1.46	1.67	1.88	2.13	2.42
Central European Associates	1.00	0.94	0.94	1.00	1.07	1.13	1.18	1.26
Former Soviet Union	1.00	0.87	0.83	0.93	1.09	1.23	1.35	1.44
North Africa	1.00	1.20	1.29	1.46	1.67	1.91	2.16	2.46
Africa	1.00	0.95	1.29	1.74	2.29	2.86	3.62	4.36
Rest of the World	1.00	0.93	1.20	1.53	1.93	2.47	2.93	3.27
Annex B	1.00	0.97	0.96	1.01	1.10	1.17	1.24	1.29
TOTAL	1.00	1.10	1.21	1.35	1.52	1.68	1.86	2.04

In both the business-as-usual and the policy scenarios special care has been given to the current account of each country, which is significantly affected due to the nature of the exercises of this study. A reduction of tariffs would very probably cause a continuously increasing deficit in the balance of payments mainly for the developing countries. This point is also – directly or indirectly – a permanent source of debate in the negotiations for further liberalisation in international trade in the WTO framework. In order to avert such an evolution in the simulations of the model, it was assumed that the ratio of the current account to GDP remains constant for developing countries for the entire time period under examination. For each country this ratio is equal to the corresponding ratio in 1995, which has been calculated using actual data. The introduction of this restriction to the model results in the endogenisation of the long-run rate of return on capital, as it has been explained in section 1.2. The long-run rate of return on capital affects directly the demand for investment and the demand for durable consumption goods, and indirectly the demand for imports. Thus when the ratio of the current account to GDP tends to diverge from the predefined level, the model increases or decreases imports in order to neutralise such a phenomenon.

2   'Full Liberalisation' Scenario

2.1   'Full Liberalisation' Scenario Assumptions

An experiment assuming totally free trade was designed in order to study the distortion introduced by trade barriers to the world level of production and the resulting welfare losses, as well as to focus on the differences in environmental damages from the evolution of the world trade institutional regime.

The elimination of tariff and non-tariff barriers will normally lead to a reduction in government revenues. In some developing countries, government revenues from tariffs are as high as 10% to 20% of total government revenues. In some studies similar to the present, the need for the imposition of other supplementary measures in order to compensate for the loss of government revenues due to the tariff abolition is discussed (Weisbrot and Baker, 2002). The lack of counterbalance measures in the presence of a hypothetical elimination of tariffs will result in the overestimation of the benefits from free trade because, in essence, this is equal to the provision of consumers with an additional exogenous income. For this reason in most of the models it is assumed that, in parallel to the elimination of tariffs, a lump-sum tax providing the same amount of revenues to the government is imposed. The imposition of another kind of tax on products (sales tax) is not considered appropriate because these taxes distort the distribution of resources. Theoretically, therefore, it would be meaningless to replace the distortionary role of tariffs with an equally distortionary role of taxes on products. The adoption of a lump-sum tax, although it can be introduced in a model relatively easily, is a simplification that is not very realistic. The way that this issue is treated in this study is the following: Three types of buyers of imported goods that benefit from tariff abolition are examined in the model, households that purchase imported consumption goods, producers that import intermediate inputs, and the government that imports public consumption goods. In order to treat the benefit from the elimination of tariffs in a neutral way, we compensate the benefits of all three types of buyers for a reduction on their level of income. This is achieved by increasing the income tax rate for households and firms and reducing public expenditures in a way that the budget deficit of each country remains the same as in the business-as-usual scenario.

2.2   Policy Shocks and Transmission Mechanisms in the GEM-E3-Model

In order to provide insights on the way that the GEM-E3 model responds to the abolition of tariff and non-tariff barriers, the adjustment process of the model following the initial shock is described in Figure 2. The variables, the values of which will initially diverge from the ones of the baseline, are the following:

1. Prices of imports, which will be reduced by the amount of the corresponding tariff rates according to the hypotheses of the scenario, and

2. Capital inputs, which are increased compared to the baseline because the elimination of tariffs in 2010 results in the increase of investments for the period 2010-2030.

In order to decompose the results caused by each of the above factors, it is assumed that no increase of capital inputs takes place initially.

2.3   A Reduction of the Prices of Imports Due to the Elimination of Tariffs

According to the hypotheses of the model, imported quantities of each product are combined with the corresponding domestically produced quantities of the same product through a function of Armington type so as to form a composite good, which is then allocated to consumption, intermediate inputs, and investments.

In Figure 2 the total imports of product i (with price $PIMP^0$) are distinguished, for the sake of the clarity of the presentation, into imports from the North (with price $PIMPN^0$) and imports from the South (with price $PIMPS^0$). During the initial perturbation the price of the domestically produced good i (PXD^*) remains constant, therefore the price of the composite good i (PY) decreases due to the reduction of the prices of the imported goods.

The decrease in the price of the composite good i depends on the following factors:

- The amount of the reduction in the price of imports.

- The elasticities of substitution among goods i with different origin in the Armington function.

- The value shares of goods i with different origin.

Given the differentiation of the above factors by region and good, general conclusions for the exact amount of the reduction of the price of the composite good cannot be drawn.

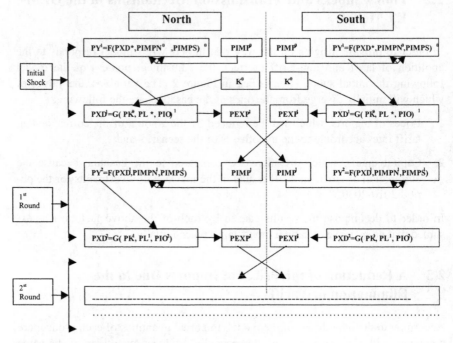

Figure 2:   The Adjustment Process in GEM-E3.

However, it can be concluded with certainty that the reduction of the price of the composite good will be smaller in size than the corresponding reduction in the price of imported products, assuming that there exists a fraction of the composite good that is produced domestically.

More specifically, the higher the value share of the domestically produced good in the total value of the composite good, the smaller is the decrease in the price of the composite good compared to the reduction of the price of the imported goods. In a similar way, the reduction of the price of the composite good i is affected more from the reduction of the price of imports from the country with the bigger value share in the total value of the composite good.

Knowing the reduction of the price of the composite good i at the initial shock and without possessing additional information, the direction of the change in the quantity demanded for the composite good i cannot be foreseen *a priori*. The reductions of the prices of all goods are not uniform due to the different tariff rates, resulting in a substitution effect that decreases the quantities demanded for the goods the prices of which have been reduced less than others. Nevertheless, it can be generally said that the reduction of the prices of imports will cause a substitution of the domestically produced good, increasing (decreasing) the demand for imports more (less) than the demand of the domestically produced good.

As far as production is concerned, products are considered by the model to be produced using technology described by a constant elasticity of substitution (CES) production function that combines capital, labour, and intermediate consumption.

After the initial disturbance, the model goes through a second cycle of adjustments with the production functions as the main axis. Given the payments to capital $(PK^0)^2$, labour (PL*), and the domestic production (PXD*), the reduction – from the previous stage – of the prices of the intermediate inputs (PIO^1) results in the reduction of the marginal cost of production of all goods. An additional effect is the reduction of the fixed cost in the sectors that are structured in a monopolistically competitive way. This reduction of cost generates excess profits in all sectors and, therefore, leads to the entry of new firms in the markets. These adjustments result in the reduction of the price of domestic production PXD*. Using the same arguments, the reduction of the price of domestic production will be smaller than the reduction of the price of intermediate inputs. Furthermore, the bigger the value shares of intermediate inputs in the total value of production, the bigger this reduction will be. The increase or decrease in production of specific products cannot be foreseen without knowing the conditions of substitution of goods in the various uses. Regarding quantities of the factors of production demanded, labour and capital will be partially substituted and so the demand for these inputs will increase less (decrease more) compared to the demand for intermediate inputs.

The reduction in the price of production of a good leads, according to the hypotheses of the model, directly to the decrease in the price of exports (for the exporting country) and the price of imports (for all other countries). At that point a new round of adjustments – with the same qualitative characteristics as the previous round but with smaller reductions in prices – is initiated. This procedure is continued until a new equilibrium is found in the model.

2.4   An Increase in the Initial Capital Inflow

In this case we suppose that the prices of imported goods remain stable, therefore the initial disturbance is created in the domestic production of goods where, given the quantities of labour and intermediate inputs to the production of a good, the increased supply of capital leads to a reduction in its price as well as the price of production of all goods. The reduction in the price of production is smaller than the reduction in the return on capital and is higher when the value share of capital in the total value of production is high.

Referring to external trade, the reduced price of production of a good results, according to the hypotheses of the model, in a reduction of the price of exports in the country that produces the good and, therefore, in a reduction of the price of imports in the country that imports the good. If we take import prices as given, the

---

[2]   It is supposed, as previously, that the initial stock of capital remains the same.

reduction in the price of domestic production leads to a smaller reduction (in percentage terms) of the price of the composite good that can be used for domestic demand.

An a priori prediction of the quantity of a product produced cannot be made without the prior knowledge of the quantitative changes that take place. In the market of factors of production there is a partial substitution of labour and intermediate inputs that increase (reduce by a smaller percentage) the demand for capital compared to the demand for the other factors of production.

2.5   Aggregate Macroeconomic Results at the World Level

The simulated results concerning the main macroeconomic magnitudes at the world level due to the elimination of tariffs are presented in Figure 3. The main finding of the 'full liberalisation' scenario is that the total elimination of tariffs leads to an increase of world GDP and welfare level; this is even stronger in the developing countries. More specifically, world GDP increases by 1.1% compared to the baseline. The GDP in countries of the so-called South grows at about double that rate (1.9%) of the so-called North (0.8%). The main factor contributing to this is the redistribution of world trade in favour of the countries of the South.

The exports of the South increase at a higher rate than its imports contributing to the increase of GDP. On the other hand, the imports of the North increase at a higher rate than its exports, thus moderating the GDP increase in the countries of the North. Moreover, the improvement of the trade balance of the South compared to the North creates the relatively higher increase in the domestic production and investments in the South.

A more detailed analysis of the redistributions in international trade as simulated by the 'full liberalisation' scenario is conducted. Most of the increase in exports (and imports) of the South is due to the increase of the trade among the countries of the South that increases faster than all other bilateral transactions. The increase of the total exports of the North is mainly due to the increased exports to the South and less due to the increase in the trade among the countries of the North. It is also obvious that the improvement in the trade balance of the South is due to the relatively higher increase of the exports of the South compared to the increase of the imports from the North.

The direction of these results can be explained using the arguments stated above. The average percentage of tariffs imposed by developing countries on their imports are almost three times as much as the corresponding percentages in the countries of the North. In general, developing countries impose higher tariffs on their imports compared to the countries of the North in all categories of products both to collect money and to protect the domestic industries from competition. Tariffs on traditional (agricultural, textile, and food) products are also significantly higher than the tariffs imposed on industrial products; it is therefore logical for the transactions among countries of the North to have a small tariff rate because they are composed mainly of industrial products. The average tariff rate for the imports of the North from the South is higher because these transactions are mainly composed of traditional products. Following the same reasoning, the highest average tariff rate is imposed on the transactions among the countries of the South that are composed of agricultural products, foods and textiles.

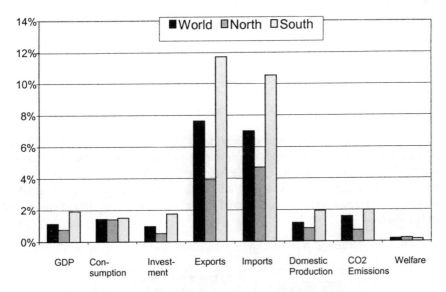

Figure 3:   Full Liberalisation Scenario (% Changes from Baseline in 2030).

Table 5:   Initial Changes in Import Prices and Capital Volume (2030).

	North-North	North-South	South-North	South-South
% Import price change due to tariff abolition	-2.8	-3.3	-9.2	-12.1
Value shares of imports to total domestic demand (%)	4.5	3.9	9.3	5.2
Value shares of domestically produced goods to total domestic demand (%)	91.6			85.5
% Change in Capital volume	0.5			1.5
Value share of capital to total value of domestic production (%)	15.9			21.4
Value share of Labour to total value of domestic production (%)	44.8			33.5
Value share of intermediate consumption to total value of domestic production (%)	39.3			45

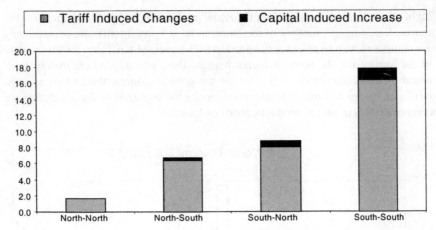

Figure 4:   Full Liberalisation Scenario: Exports (% Changes from Baseline in 2030).

The initial reduction in the price of imports, which creates the strongest effects, will be proportionate to the reduction of tariffs in each market. Therefore, based on the data of Table 5, the prices of the imported goods from the South decrease more than the prices of the imports of the North in all markets. The most significant initial reduction (12.1%) is observed in the trade prices among the countries of the South.

Table 6:   % Changes from Baseline in the Volumes and Prices of Imports (2030).

| | % changes from baseline | | | | | |
| | Tariff Abolition effect | | Capital increase effect | | Total effect | |
	North Imports	South Imports	North Imports	South Imports	North Imports	South Imports
Volumes	(1)	(2)	(3)	(4)	(5)	(6)
North exports	1.6	6.4	-0.1	0.4	1.5	6.8
South exports	7.9	16.2	0.7	1.4	8.6	17.5
Prices						
North exports	-3.6	-10.1	0.3	0.2	-3.2	-9.9
South exports	-6.0	-14.9	0.0	0.0	-6.0	-14.9

In Table 6 (columns 5 and 6) the final reductions in import prices resulting from the simulation under the hypothesis of full tariff abolition are presented. The prices of imported goods decrease in all regions more than the initial reductions due to secondary effects. A comparison of the changes of import prices in Table 5 and Table 6 leads to the conclusion that the secondary effects enhanced the relative reduction of the prices in favour of Southern exports. Consequently, the substitution effects in all markets result in a higher increase of the exports of the South. In Table 6 it is shown that exports of the South to the North increase by 6.8% while the trade among the countries of the South increases three times more.

Table 7:   % Changes from Baseline in the Prices and Volumes of Domestic Demand and Production (2030).

	% changes from baseline					
	Tariff Abolition effect		Capital increase effect		Total effect	
	North	South	North	South	North	South
Volumes	(1)	(2)	(3)	(4)	(5)	(6)
Domesticaly Produced goods	0.5	-0.9	0.1	0.7	0.5	-0.3
Domestic Demand	0.8	1.0	0.1	0.6	0.9	1.6
Prices						
Domesticaly Produced goods	-0.9	-2.5	0.3	0.0	-0.6	-2.5
Domestic Demand	-1.2	-4.1	0.3	0.1	-0.9	-4.1

Similarly, the price of domestic supply decreases more in the markets of the South for two reasons: the first refers to the relatively bigger decrease in the prices of imported goods; the second is that the domestically produced goods have a smaller value share in the South than in the North. The reduced price of the domestic supply, which results after the initial perturbation, causes the reduction of the price of domestic production and exports in the following way: If we ignore initially the increased capital inflow, the reduction of the price of the domestic supply of goods will lead to a substitution of labour and capital for the less expensive intermediate uses in the production process.

The reduction of the price of domestic production and exports is bigger for the South, at this stage of adjustments, for two reasons: The first is that the price of intermediate uses is reduced, according to the arguments stated above, more in the South; the second is that the value share of the intermediate uses is higher in the production of the South. This is logical if we take into account that the production process of the South is less efficient and therefore more expensive in terms of material inputs. The amounts of these changes are presented in Table 8 (columns 1 and 2). The volume of production in the South is increased by 1.9% in order to satisfy the increased demand for exports that has covered the small reduction of domestic demand. The increase of production is powered by the increased utilisation of intermediate inputs by 1.2% and the increased inputs of labour by 0.7%. The substantial reduction of 4.3% in the prices of intermediate inputs resulted in the substitution of capital and labour inputs. It can also be inferred that the substitution effect in the production of the South is stronger than the positive income effect, resulting in lower returns on capital and labour by 0.1% and 1.4% respectively.

The production of the North increases by 0.7% mainly due to the increased contribution of intermediate inputs by 0.6%. In contrast to the South, the positive income effect is greater than the substitution effect, resulting in increased returns to capital and labour by 0.3% and 0.2% respectively.

Table 8:   % Changes from Baseline in Production Function Variables (2030).

	% changes from baseline					
	Tariff Abolition effect		Capital increase effect		Total effect	
	North	South	North	South	North	South
Volumes	(1)	(2)	(3)	(4)	(5)	(6)
Capital	0.0	0.0	0.4	1.7	0.4	1.7
Labour	0.0	0.7	0.1	0.5	0.0	1.2
Intermediate Consumption	0.6	1.2	0.1	0.8	0.7	2.0
Domestic Production	0.7	1.2	0.1	0.7	0.8	1.9
Prices						
Capital	0.3	-0.1	-0.4	-2.9	-0.1	-3.0
Labour	0.2	-1.4	0.4	1.4	0.7	0.1
Intermediate Consumption	-1.2	-4.3	0.3	-0.1	-1.0	-4.4
Domestic Production	-0.8	-2.8	0.3	0.0	-0.5	-2.9

Similar results have been obtained for the adjustments made in the categories of demand other than exports. The reduction in the price of goods creates a positive income effect[3] on the level of consumption, which contributes to increased consumption in both the Northern and the Southern markets. This result is further enhanced from the increase in income caused by the expansion in production. In the same way, the increase in demand leads to the entry of new firms and, therefore, to the increase in the demand for investments. It follows from the above arguments that the South will have a bigger increase in demand for investments.

According to the assumptions of the scenario, the elimination of tariff rates takes place in 2010, thus the increased investments in the subsequent years generate an increased quantity of capital. The qualitative characteristics of the adjustments created by the elimination of tariff rates are the same for all this period. It is reasonable therefore for the investments in the South to increase faster. The total increase of capital is 1.7% for the South and 0.4% for the North compared to the baseline (Table 8). The capital increase in the South results in a significant reduction in the return on capital, which, in addition to the lower returns due to tariff abolition, leads to a final decrease of 3% in its price. On the other hand, the higher volume of capital increases the demand for labour, which leads to higher wages; however, due to the lower price of labour that resulted from the elimination of tariffs, the final increase in wages is only marginal. The capital increase in the North has the same impact on the returns on capital and wages as in the South, though less pronounced. However, because of the higher demand for labour and capital that results from the tariff abolition which increases the prices of both factors of production, the final impact is a marginal decrease in the return on capital and a noticeably higher increase in wages than that in the South. Thus the negative impact from the increased demand for capital on the return on capital is enough to compensate for the positive income from free trade in the North, en-

---

3   When we refer to the positive income effect, we imply the one resulting from secondary adjustments. The income effect from the initial shock has been compensated from the increased income tax rate.

hances the negative impact from trade liberalisation in the South, and favours wages in both regions.

2.6   Sectoral Results at the World Level

At the sectoral level, the results of the simulation for the world are presented in Table 9. The elimination of the substantial tariff burden faced by the traditional sectors (agricultural, textiles and food products) results in the substantial increase of international trade for these products. Therefore, it is important to highlight that imports of agricultural products increase by 24.4% while imports of food products and textiles by 10.7% and 9.4% respectively. It has to be noted that the average tariff rates for these product categories at the world level are as high as 17.5% for agricultural products, 14.5% for food products, and 11% for textiles. The cumulative increase of capital during the period 2010-2030 has enhanced these results, increasing world trade by 1.1% in agricultural products and about 1% in food products. The effects of this capital increase in the trade of textiles are substantially smaller (0.3%).

Table 9:   % Changes from Baseline in World Sector Variables (2030).

	% changes from baseline					
	Imports			Domestic Production		
	Tariff Abolition effect	Capital increase effect	Total effect	Tariff Abolition effect	Capital increase effect	Total effect
Product	(1)	(2)	(3)	(4)	(5)	(6)
Agriculture	24.4	1.1	25.5	0.6	0.7	1.3
Oil	2.5	0.2	2.7	0.3	0.6	0.9
Ferrous and non Ferrous metals	6.9	0.6	7.5	0.1	0.5	0.6
Chemical Products	7.1	0.6	7.7	0.8	0.5	1.2
Other energy intensive	5.2	0.9	6.2	0.2	0.5	0.7
Electronic equipment	5.8	0.3	6.1	0.9	0.2	1.1
Transport Equipment	9.7	0.0	9.7	1.0	-0.1	0.9
Other Equipment Goods	6.3	0.5	6.8	0.3	0.4	0.7
Other Manufacturing Products	10.2	0.6	10.8	0.6	0.5	1.1
Food industry	10.7	0.8	11.5	1.5	0.5	2.1
Textile industry	9.4	0.3	9.7	2.7	0.4	3.1

The highest increase in trade for industrial products is observed in 'Other Manufacturing Goods' (10.2%) and in the 'Transport equipment' category (9.7%).

The textiles sector, according to Table 9, increases production at the world level by 3.1%, percentage that is the highest among all other sectors. The food sector follows with a 2.1% and the agricultural sector with a 1.3% increase. As far as the non-traditional sectors are concerned, the highest increases in production are in the 'Chemical products', 'Electronic equipment' and 'Other manufacturing goods' categories with 1.2% and 1.1% respectively.

An analysis of the structure of tariff rates both at the sectoral and the regional level is needed prior to providing an explanation for these results and analysing the reallocation of external trade and production. Figure 5 assists in this analysis.

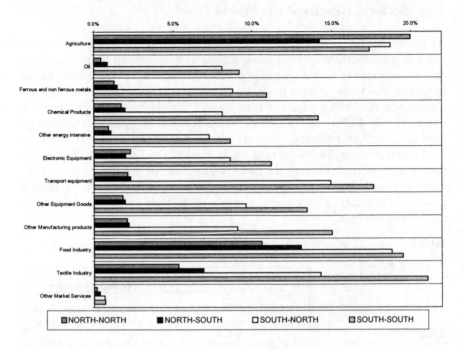

Figure 5:   Full Liberalisation: Average Tariff Rates (2030).

An observation of Figure 5 reveals an enormous differentiation of the tariff rates not only among products but also among regions. Referring to products, tariff peaks[4] are a characteristic of traditional products (agricultural, food, textiles) in all regions. As far as the regions are concerned, it is obvious that the developing countries of the South impose significantly higher tariffs compared to the developed countries of the North. In reality, the majority of the products imported from the countries of the South face tariff peaks, with the textiles as the most marked case; these peaks in the trade among countries of the South exceed 20%. Another characteristic case is agricultural products that face the highest tariff rates in the trade among countries of the North. Moreover, the agricultural products are the only case that the North imposes higher tariff rates than the South. An example is the high protection of US products from European exports. Tariffs imposed on industrial products, except from food products, by the countries of the North are below 5%. With the exception of the 'Electronic equipment' category, imports of

---

4   Tariff peaks are conventionally defined to be tariffs exceeding 15%.

the North from the South have higher tariff rates than the imports among the countries of the North. On the other hand, with the exception of agricultural products, tariff rates imposed on trade among countries of the South are higher than the tariff rates imposed on imports of the South from the North.

The changes in imports from baseline due to the tariff abolition are shown in Figure 6. In general, this tariff structure determines the pattern of the substitutions taking place in the world market in the simulations.

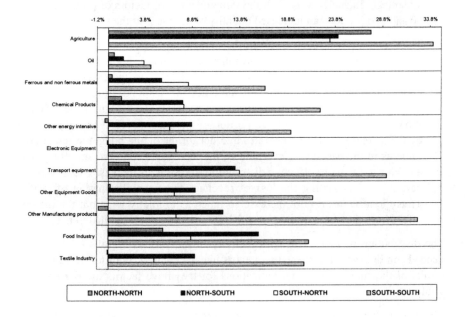

Figure 6:   Full Liberalisation (% Changes of the Volume of Imports from Baseline in 2030).

Two general observations can be made with the assistance of this diagram: the first relates to the developing countries. For almost all goods, trade among countries of the South displays the highest increases. Apart from the increase in the agricultural products sector (33.5%), a significant increase is observed in the trade of 'Other manufacturing goods' (32.6%), 'Transport equipment' (29.3%), and 'Chemical products' (22.6%) categories; these results are in accordance with the tariff structure described above. It has to be noted that trade among countries of the South increases more than 15% for all goods but oil. The second observation concerns only developed countries: Excluding agricultural products, the highest rates of increase for all product categories are observed in imports of the North from the South. Apart from the food products that show the highest increase of 15.8%, substantial increases are achieved in the imports of 'Transport equipment' (13.5%) and 'Other manufacturing goods' (12.6%).

2.7   Aggregate Macroeconomic Results at the Regional Level

According to the economic theory, full liberalisation of world trade results in the increase in world economic activity. This increase is mainly due to:

- The distortion of the distribution of resources both at sectoral and regional levels due to the existence of tariffs, the elimination of which forces each country to specialise in the production of goods in which it has a comparative advantage. In such a way with the same quantity of factors of production it is possible to produce an increased quantity of all goods at the world level.

- The income effect resulting from the reduction of prices of imported goods: with a given level of income consumers can purchase more goods after the elimination of tariffs. The increased demand leads to increased production under the assumption that there are underutilised factors of production that are mobilised towards covering the increased needs. In the design of the scenario it has been assumed that a large portion of this income effect is compensated by the increase in income tax rates in order for the public budget to remain the same as in the baseline. Nevertheless, the increased economic activity generated due to the more effective distribution of resources increases tax revenues, partially compensating the loss of revenues from the elimination of tariffs. Thus the tax rates do not increase so much as to totally wipe out the income effect from the elimination of tariffs but enough to cover the difference.

The distribution of increased world activity in the various regions of the world depends on the weight of these two factors in each country. In order to explain the results of the simulation, some indications for the above factors are presented in Table 10.

The average tariff rates on imports in each region of the world are presented in column 1 of Table 10. Developing regions such as India, the Rest of the World, and China apply a higher tariff protection on their imports, which is expressed through average tariff rates almost 20 times higher than those of the European countries. Among developed countries, Japan has the highest average tariff rate; it is worth mentioning that Japan is one of the few countries of the world that do not participate in any regional agreement.

The scaling of the average tariff rate among countries provides clear indications both for the extent of the distortion in the distribution of resources and for the extent of the income effect created in each country from the tariff abolition. Income from tariff rates for developing countries are a significant part of their GDP, which in the case of the three regions mentioned above exceeds 5%. Tariff abolition therefore increases substantially the purchasing power of the consumers of these countries resulting in an increased level of total demand. One could note that the extensive tariff protection of these countries allows home industries to produce with relatively high cost in sectors where they do not have a comparative advantage. Therefore the high average tariff rates imply a high distortion in the distribution of resources. As it has been explained in Section 2, the heavier is the tariff burden on imports of a country, the bigger are the reductions on the prices of domestically produced goods after the elimination of tariffs. This results in improvement in competitiveness for the products of this country in the international markets, and increased demand for exports.

Table 10:   Aggregate Macroeconomic Results at the Regional Level (2030).

	Average Duty Rate (%)	Change in capital volume (%)	% changes from baseline			
			GDP	Exports	Imports	Domestic Production
	(1)	(2)	(3)	(4)	(5)	(6)
Australia	5.9	0.9	0.9	4.3	7.3	0.9
Japan	8.2	0.6	1.4	7.2	9.3	1.4
East Asia	7.9	1.0	1.8	9.8	8.8	2.0
China	18.4	2.0	2.9	20.4	23.4	3.0
India	28.2	8.1	5.1	40.8	31.0	4.7
North America	3.0	0.3	0.5	4.5	5.0	0.5
Latin America	8.3	0.5	0.9	10.9	9.0	0.9
Nordic Europe	1.2	0.5	0.6	1.6	2.6	0.7
Germany	1.4	0.4	0.6	2.3	3.2	0.7
UK	2.1	0.6	0.8	1.9	3.7	0.8
Rest of Europe	2.1	0.4	0.4	2.9	3.9	0.8
Other Europe	4.6	0.4	1.5	4.4	3.8	1.4
Central European Associates	6.5	1.2	1.5	8.1	5.7	1.5
Former Soviet Union	1.2	0.6	0.6	1.5	2.5	0.5
North Africa	6.4	0.6	1.4	6.6	5.9	1.3
Africa	5.7	2.4	2.1	6.3	6.5	1.9
Rest of the World	24.8	1.1	2.9	40.9	21.3	2.2

The increase in total demand generates increased needs for factors of production and mainly for investments on fixed capital, with the lower prices of the imported capital goods being an additional factor in favour of increased investments. Column 2 of Table 10 shows the increase in capital inputs compared to the baseline that results from the increased investments as simulated by the model for the period 2010-2030. For the reasons mentioned above, it can be observed that the highest increases in capital inputs take place in the countries that have the highest tariff rates. Such increased capital inputs enable a positive response of domestic production to the increased demand generated by the tariff abolition. This ability to expand capital inputs together with the more effective allocation of recourses resulting from the removal of distortions eventually leads to increased overall levels of activity. Figure 7 depicts the positive correlation between the relative percentage of tariffs to GDP and the rate of increase of GDP resulting from the model simulation under discussion.

It is a usual observation in applied research on international trade that international trade increases at a higher rate than GDP. The data of Table 10 strongly support this observation. This attribute has been explained in economic theory in many ways. One of these explanations that is related to the analysis developed in this section refers to the significant reduction of tariffs that has taken place over the last fifty years. The most important interpretations explaining that the reduction of tariffs favours international trade more than domestic production activity are the following:

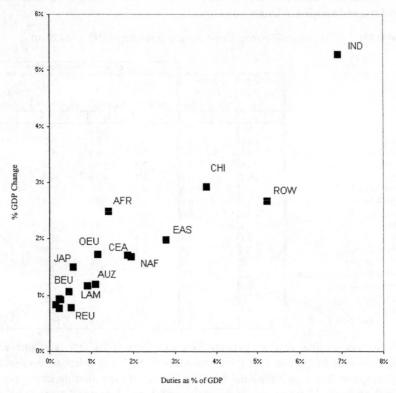

Figure 7:   Relation Between the Reduction of Duties and the Increase of GDP in 2030.

The demand for imports has a higher elasticity than the demand for domestic goods; thus for the same reduction in prices, relatively more quantities of imported goods are demanded. According also to the reasoning developed above, in general equilibrium conditions the prices of domestically produced goods are reduced less than the prices of imports, which is a fact that favours demand for imports even more than domestic production. A second reason is the impact of the "love of variety" characteristic that is taken into account by the model, which acts towards increased demand for imports. According to the 'love of variety' property, the increase in the level of income of the consumer will be directed towards the variety that has the lowest percentage in the composite good. Due to the existence of tariffs, imported varieties comprise a smaller percentage of the composite good than the domestic varieties, thus consumers spend the additional income generated by the elimination of tariffs to buy more of the imported varieties.

3   Climate Policy

3.1   The Kyoto Period

3.1.1   Introduction

In this part of the book, the issues of trade in goods and permits and their implications on welfare under the imposition of restrictions on emissions are studied using the CCGT general equilibrium model. The scenarios examined are differentiated depending on which of the Annex B countries are assumed to comply with the Protocol, the existence of excess emission rights ('hot air') and its utilisation by the Former Soviet Union.

In the scenario simulations it is assumed that the abating countries meet their individually assigned targets according to the Kyoto Protocol inside one club or 'bubble'. These targets are assumed to represent endowments in emission rights that can be traded inside the club.

The examination of these topics is made at two stages. At the first stage the permits traded inside the bubbles are assumed to be supplied under perfect competition. Following an 'echeloning' sequence regarding the number of participating countries, we have examined the implications of the construction of different abatement clubs. At the second stage, it is assumed that the Former Soviet Union supplies its emission rights monopolistically. The summary and main conclusions of the findings for the Kyoto period are provided in the final Section.

3.1.2   Perfectly Competitive Permit Markets

The scenarios that were simulated for the Kyoto period under perfectly competitive permit markets are the following:

- Scenario I (All Annex B countries – AB): All Annex B countries are provided with permit endowments according to the Kyoto Protocol (Table 11) and are assumed to form one abating club. When all Annex B countries participate in the bubble, the overall restriction is equal to the one implied in the Kyoto Protocol.

- Scenario II (All Annex B countries plus the Rest of the World – AB+ROW): As in Scenario I and, in addition, developing countries join the club with a permit allowance that represents their emissions in the baseline. Developing countries were not considered as participants in the Kyoto Protocol; the United States have brought up the implications of the absence of these countries (Rest of the World in this model) as one of the major reasons for their withdrawal. The inclusion of developing countries in the abating club in this scenario is made in order to provide an insight on the usefulness of the clean development mechanisms when there are no transaction costs involved.

- Scenario III (All Annex B countries without the United States – AB-USA): As in Scenario I but excluding the United States. Under the current evolution of the negotiations, the implications of the withdrawal of the United States from the Kyoto Protocol are of vital importance for all countries since the United States are one of the major polluters and their absence could imply a degeneration of the process. This scenario is examined in order to study the effects of the United States withdrawal on the effectiveness of the process and on the cost that the rest of Annex B countries have to bear.

- Scenario IV (All Annex B countries without the United States and the Former Soviet Union – AB-USA-FSU): As in Scenario III but excluding the Former Soviet Union. A usual topic of discussion regarding the Kyoto Protocol is the significance of the 'hot air' endowment of the Former Soviet Union: how these emission rights affect the abatement effort of other participants and the additional costs/benefits this might involve. A first observation that can be made is that it reduces the environmental effectiveness of the process, providing to Annex B countries the option to avoid domestic action without equivalent emissions reduction elsewhere and, therefore, should not be granted to the Former Soviet Union. In this scenario it is assumed that the United States do not sign the Protocol and, for illustrative purposes, that the Former Soviet Union is also excluded.

- Scenario V (Europe and the Central European Associates – EC): The abating club consists of Europe and the Central European Associates with the allocation of permits as in Scenario I. This scenario provides insights on the implications on trade and welfare of the joint abatement effort of an enlarged Europe.

- Scenario VI (Europe Alone – EA): Europe abates alone. In this scenario it is assumed that the Kyoto agreement collapses and that Europe decides to reduce its emissions alone according to its Kyoto target.

All the scenarios above imply an effective emission constraint. This constraint generates a non-negative shadow cost of reducing the last ton of carbon inside the bubble, which is equal to the marginal cost of abatement. When the permit market is perfectly competitive, as it is assumed in this section, the marginal cost of abatement represents the market-clearing price of emission permits.

The carbon value, together with the emission allowances and the level of the emissions attained, determine the value of the transfers due to permit trade among countries and agents in the model. The demand for permits depends on the difference between scenario emissions and emission rights allocated according to the Kyoto Protocol. Abatement flexibility increases with permit market enlargement because it affords wider opportunities for cost-effective abatement options. As it is shown in Table 11, primarily the Former Soviet Union and secondarily the Central European Associates are provided with emission rights that represent more emissions than in the baseline. On the other hand, the smallest permit allowance compared to baseline emissions among Annex B countries is provided to the United States. Among non-'hot air' owners, Australia has the highest permit endowment.

Table 11:   Ratio of Permit Endowment to Baseline Emissions (2010).

United States	0.726
Europe	0.825
Japan	0.797
Canada	0.805
Australia	0.855
Central European Associates	1.028
Former Soviet Union	1.319

The net position of each country in the permit market depends on the initial endowment in emission rights and the relative cost of abatement, which is reflected on the final reduction in emissions in the scenario compared to the baseline. This level of reduction is dependent on the restriction inside the club and not on the difference between the regional allowance in emission rights and baseline emissions. Each country reduces emissions until the marginal cost of reducing one ton of carbon is equal to the permit price. If at this point the amount of the emissions reduced inside the region exceeds the difference between baseline emissions and the Kyoto target, then this country is a net exporter of permits.

The highest restriction on emissions for a club is imposed when Europe alone meets its Kyoto target (17.5% fewer emissions compared to the baseline in 2010). In this case the carbon value is €99 115.11, which is the highest among all scenarios. This price reflects the high cost of reducing emissions inside Europe when no flexibility mechanisms (emissions trading, joint implementation, clean development mechanisms) are offered outside this region.

The carbon value drops to €99 67.31 when the Central European Associates trade permits with Europe, not only due to the 'hot air' provided to Eastern Europe, resulting in an overall constraint representing 86.1% of baseline levels, but also due to the higher abatement potential in this region compared to Europe. The difference between the level of emissions implied by the permit endowment and emissions in the scenario determine if a country is a net seller or purchaser of permits. As is shown in Table 12, the percentage reduction for Central European Associates is twice as big as the reduction in Europe, thus, given their favourable endowment in emission rights, they end up selling permits to Europe.

Table 12:   % Reduction of Emissions Compared to Baseline in all Scenarios (2010).

	AB+ROW	AB	AB-USA	AB-USA-FSU	EC	EA
World	-7.18	-5.88	-0.85	-2.49	-1.51	-1.49
Europe	-2.49	-9.04	-2.67	-13.36	-11.61	-17.52
Central European Associates	-7.21	-20.62	-6.53	-28.15	-24.87	
Japan	-2.21	-8.70	-2.62	-12.36		
Canada	-3.71	-12.30	-3.92	-18.08		
Australia	-4.42	-15.54	-4.86	-20.96		
Former Soviet Union	-5.10	-15.37	-4.50			
United States	-5.05	-15.22				
Rest of the World	-10.61					

In the AB-USA-FSU scenario, where the Central European Associates is the only region providing 'hot air' for trade in the bubble, the restriction of emissions inside the club is 15.7% fewer emissions compared to baseline in 2010. The simulated carbon value for this scenario is €99 82.83. For this price of permits the Central European Associates make the most significant abatement effort among the countries in the club which, combined with their favourable allowance, makes them net sellers of permits. The only non-'hot air' owner that sells permits in this scenario is Australia, which abates substantially more than its 14.5% target. Canada, Europe, and Japan make smaller reductions than those implied by their individual regional targets, thus they end up net purchasers of permits.

The inclusion of the Former Soviet Union in the club (AB-USA scenario) creates a scenario with the lowest restriction in the club (3.6%) compared to baseline emissions in 2010. The simulated carbon value of €99 13.72 is the lowest among all scenarios examined in this part of the book. The 'hot air' owners are the only regions that sell permits in this scenario; the Central European Associates register the biggest emission reductions compared to the baseline and, in combination to their endowment in excess emission rights, they are net sellers of permits. The Former Soviet Union reduces its emissions less than Australia; however, the differences in their assigned targets as percentages of their baseline emissions in 2010 result in their opposite positions in the permit market: The Former Soviet Union is a net seller of permits and Australia is a net purchaser of permits. Canada, Europe, and Japan are net purchasers of permits because they reduce their emissions less than implied by their individual assigned targets.

The overall restriction in the club in the AB scenario represents 86.6% of baseline levels, with a simulated carbon value of €99 57.95. At this level of carbon value, apart from the 'hot air' owners, Australia is also a net seller of permits because it makes an emission reduction bigger than that implied by its target.

The enlargement of the permit market with the inclusion of the developing countries in the bubble (AB+ROW scenario) results in an overall constraint representing 92.8% of baseline levels. At the simulated price of permits of €99 18.07, developing countries, which have a target equal to their baseline emissions, register the
biggest emission reduction, thus they sell permits. The 'hot air' owners reduce
their emissions more than the other Annex B countries; given their favourable
permit endowments, they are net sellers of permits in this scenario. The rest of the
Annex B countries reduce their emissions less than it is implied by their targets,
thus they purchase permits.

In order to appreciate the importance of these net flows for the individual regions,
Table 13 below gives the percentage of the value of permit sales (+) / purchases
(-) in total private consumption.

Table 13:   Permit Sales/Purchases as % of Private Consumption in All
Scenarios (2010).

	AB+ROW	AB	AB-USA	AB-USA-FSU	EC
Europe	-0.04	-0.07	-0.03	-0.05	-0.06
Central European Associates	0.20	1.46	0.14	2.74	2.00
Japan	-0.04	-0.07	-0.03	-0.07	
Canada	-0.09	-0.13	-0.07	-0.04	
Australia	-0.04	0.02	-0.03	0.13	
Former Soviet Union	0.96	3.89	0.72		
United States	-0.10	-0.17			
Rest of the World	0.10				

The 'hot air' owners (the Former Soviet Union and the Central European Associates) have a positive income inflow whenever they are participating in the abatement effort. This transfer of income is maximised for the Former Soviet Union
when all Annex B countries participate in the process (AB scenario) because the
carbon value is the highest among the scenarios that they are inside the club. The
maximum for the Central European Associates is reached in the AB-USA-FSU
scenario, because this scenario has the highest permit price among the ones they
participate.

The United States make significant emission reduction when they participate;
however, their permit endowment represents a smaller percentage of the baseline
emissions compared to all other countries, this is why they have the highest relative transfers.

Canada, which does not make substantial emission reduction when it participates,
has also an allocation of emission rights that represents significantly fewer emissions than in the baseline, thus the resulting transfer of income is significant.

In the least-cost allocation of the reduction of emissions in the model, Japan
makes the smallest abatement effort implying that this region is characterised by
costlier abatement options. Moreover, its permit endowment covers considerably

fewer emissions than in the baseline. Nevertheless, this transfer of income does not represent more than 0.07% of their total private consumption; this is due to the fact that the emissions produced in Japan per unit of consumption in the baseline are substantially fewer than in the other regions.

Australia has relatively high abatement potentials, which, in combination to the favourable permit endowment (see Table 11) results in small losses (or even gains) in income from permit trade.

Europe has a relatively favourable allocation in emission rights but also relatively low abatement potentials. This region is in all cases a net purchaser of permits but the expenditures for permits do not exceed 0.07% of total private consumption expenditure.

Countries are not affected in a uniform way by the restriction imposed on emissions and the resulting transfers of income due to permit trade. The distortion of the relative prices of goods has a different impact on each region due to the differences in consumption and production patterns. The higher prices of fuels paid by both final consumers and firms initiate a substitution process towards less carbon-intensive fuels and products. Coal, which has the highest emission factor among fuels, is substituted by oil and gas; furthermore, energy-intensive inputs are substituted by less energy-intensive inputs, labour, and capital.

The economic agents in the model adjust to the cost that is introduced by the restriction of emissions by responding to the altered prices of goods, services, and factors of production by changing their consumption patterns of intermediate and final goods for firms and households respectively. In equilibrium, the changes in the consumption mix, given the new prices, correspond to the maximum level of profits and welfare for firms and households respectively.

The sum of all adjustments occurring in the demand for sectoral output in the presence of the carbon value is mirrored in the activity levels (Table 14). Sectoral activity takes into account the impacts of the carbon value on the prices of fuels, the relative prices of production of each sector, and the income effects generated by the different levels of dependence of the production and consumption patterns on fuels.

Table 14:   % Changes in Production Compared to Baseline in the AB Scenario (2010).

	Annex B	Non-Annex B
Energy-Intensive Industries	-0.9	1.6
Coal	-18.0	-7.0
Refined Petroleum and Coal Products	-7.0	1.6
Crude Oil	-3.8	-3.0
Natural Gas	-9.2	-2.7
Electricity	-5.3	1.3
Rest of Industry	-0.1	0.0

The most important role in the adjustment towards the new equilibrium is played by energy sectors. The demand for coal is significantly influenced by the imposition of a carbon value. The demand for oil and gas is also substantially affected, but less than coal due to the lower emission factor of these fuels compared to coal. The fuel mix used for electricity generation in each region determines the increase in the price of electricity and the resulting reduction in the demand for this sector.

The reduction in the production of energy-intensive industries, which are affected by the higher prices of energy, reaches almost 1% due to the fact that the amount of fuels used in their production process comprises a big portion of their total intermediate inputs.

Concerning the demand for the rest of industries sector, the low consumption of fuels and energy-intensive products as a share of their total intermediate inputs results in changes that are not significant.

The welfare of the representative agent in the model is based on the level of consumption, which is positively dependent on wages, rents on capital and resource endowments, and taxes, while it is negatively dependent on expenditures on investment and government consumption.

The combination of baseline emissions, emission allowances, the relative ease of abatement, and the carbon value determine the net transfers of income to the sellers of permits, which is the initial 'shock' to the different agents and economies in the model. Thus permit sales are a positive income inflow to the selling country that can be used to increase consumption of domestically produced goods and imported goods, as well as to increase productive capacity through investment.

The abatement costs and the different relative prices refine the changes in income from permit sales/purchases, adjusting the economies to a new equilibrium where choices are optimised in view of the new economic conditions.

The carbon value imposed on fuels inside the abating club increases the prices faced by the consumer (households as final consumption and firms as intermediate inputs) of all goods depending on their consumption (and its composition) of energy and energy-intensive inputs. These higher prices stimulate a partial substitution of these goods for others whose increases in prices are lower. Therefore consumption shifts towards less energy-intensive patterns inside the club.

The higher prices of domestic consumption lead to a lower level of demand, thus the prices paid to producers are lower than in the baseline. In such a case these lower prices create a comparative advantage for the countries inside the club because it results in relatively lower export prices for these countries.

On the other hand, households in non-abating countries increase their consumption of energy because it becomes less expensive than in the baseline. For the same reason, firms outside the club substitute non-energy inputs for energy inputs in the production process. The lower prices of energy in non-abating countries reduce the cost of production in all sectors, each depending on the amount of fuels used in the production process as a percentage of total intermediate inputs. The new price level also implies that the price of goods as faced by the final consumer, offered both in the domestic and international markets, is lower than in the baseline.

Final consumers and firms in abating countries substitute domestically produced goods for imports because they become relatively less expensive. This means that the reduction in the demand for domestically produced goods due to the higher prices caused by the imposition of the carbon value is enhanced even further.

The lower prices of fossil fuels outside the club lead to a higher level of total domestic demand in these countries, pushing the level of total production upwards.

The cost of production in energy-intensive sectors in non-abating countries is reduced due to the lower internationally traded prices of fuels. This is why all abating countries have higher imports from and lower exports to non-abating countries (Table 15). The imports of energy-intensive products in the Former Soviet Union and the Central European Associates from countries in the club are increased compared to baseline for two reasons: On the one hand these regions loose their comparative advantage in the production and exports of energy-intensive products they have in the baseline (which is due to their low energy cost), and on the other hand they have a higher income due to the sales of permits.

The higher level of production in the countries outside the club also involves higher emissions than in the baseline: This is the 'carbon leakage' effect, which is an important factor in determining the overall environmental impact and, furthermore, assists in comparing the efficiency of each policy. The impact of carbon leakage on the reduction of emissions in the abating club is shown in Figure 8. The total length of each bar shows the hypothetical reduction of emissions if carbon leakage was not present.

Among the scenarios simulated in this part of the book, the EA scenario has the highest carbon leakage measured in terms of emission increases of non-abating regions as a percentage of the reduction in the abating club (34.2%). The joint abatement effort of Europe and the Central European Associates, due to the amount of 'hot air' available in this region, involves a lower target for the abating club, thus a smaller reduction of emissions, but the smaller amount of carbon leakage leads to a final reduction that is slightly better than when Europe abates alone.

Table 15: % Change from Baseline in the Volume of Imports of Energy-Intensive Products (2010).

Exporter	Importer: Europe	Japan	Canada	Australia	Central European Associates	Former Soviet Union	United States	Rest of the World
Europe	-0.06	-0.37	-0.88	-0.03	0.86	3.72	-0.45	-0.67
Japan	-0.19		-1.02	-0.17	0.69	3.56	-0.59	-0.80
Canada	-0.34	-0.63		-0.31	0.52	3.37	-0.80	-0.96
Australia	-1.25	-1.53	-2.03	-1.27	-0.43	2.47	-1.62	-1.86
Central European Associates	-4.73	-5.16	-5.56	-4.77	-4.06	-1.35	-5.15	-5.33
Former Soviet Union	-8.35	-8.87	-9.22	-8.48	-7.75	-5.11	-8.78	-8.80
United States	1.03	0.70	0.18	1.04	1.92	4.82		0.39
Rest of the World	1.25	0.92	0.41	1.26	2.15	5.05	0.84	0.61

The carbon leakage measured in terms of emission increases of non-abating regions as a percentage of the reduction in the abating club is also high when neither the United States nor the Former Soviet Union participate in the club (33.3%). In AB-USA and AB scenarios carbon leakage is significantly lower compared to the AB-USA-FSU scenario, reaching 26.2% and 18.1% respectively. The enlargement of the permit market in the AB+ROW scenario, where no carbon leakage exists by definition, leads to the biggest reduction in global emissions (7.2%).

The welfare implications of each scenario are presented in Table 16. The changes in welfare have the same direction as the net transfers of income in the permit market. Exceptions to this rule are Canada, Australia, and developing countries for the scenarios where they are inside the abating club, and the Former Soviet Union for the scenarios where it is outside the abating club.

Canada, Australia, and developing countries are heavily dependent on the production and exports of energy and energy-intensive products; the imposition of the restriction in the club reduces significantly both the domestic demand and the demand for exports of the sectors that comprise a large portion of their total production. This reduction in their production reduces the demand for their resource endowments, thus their rents, lowering the welfare of the representative agent.

The Former Soviet Union, which is a major exporter of energy and energy-intensive products, faces a reduction in the demand for exports of these products compared to the baseline. The returns to its resources are thus reduced due to the lower level of demand for the energy sectors, resulting in a lower level of welfare.

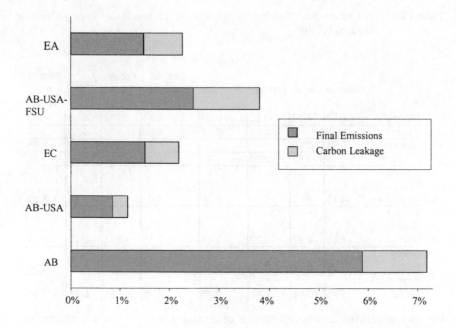

Figure 8:   Final Reduction of Emissions and Carbon Leakage in all Scenarios (2010).

The highest cost for Europe is observed when it meets its Kyoto target alone (0.48%). The rents for resource endowments are reduced in all countries, with the most pronounced reduction occurring in the abating region. The higher level of production in all regions but Europe leads to the increase in the demand for labour and capital, which increases wages and returns on capital. In Japan, the United States, and the Central European Associates this income is enough to compensate for the lower rents of fossil fuels, thus these regions are better off than in the baseline. This is not the case for the rest of the countries that end up with a lower level of welfare.

Table 16:   % Changes in Welfare from Baseline in All Scenarios (2010).

	AB+ROW	AB	AB-USA	AB-USA-FSU	EC	EA
Europe	-0.02	-0.18	-0.06	-0.36	-0.32	-0.48
Central European Associates	0.28	1.17	0.11	1.58	1.07	0.02
Japan	0.01	-0.13	-0.05	-0.27	0.04	0.05
Canada	-0.29	-0.72	-0.14	-0.54	-0.02	-0.02
Australia	-0.27	-0.40	-0.13	-0.41	-0.04	-0.04
Former Soviet Union	0.87	3.69	0.74	-0.48	-0.37	-0.33
United States	-0.09	-0.23	0.00	0.00	0.01	0.01
Rest of the World	-0.08	-0.09	-0.02	-0.06	-0.03	-0.05

The cost for Europe is lower when it forms a bubble together with the Central European Associates. The same arguments as in the EA scenario are valid for the rest of the regions, with the Central European Associates realising a significant increase in their welfare due to the revenues from permit sales.In the AB scenario the 'hot air' owners are the only regions with a higher level of welfare compared to the baseline; this is due to the revenues from the sales of permits that are enough to compensate for the significantly lower rents of their resource endowments and their returns on labour and capital due to the lower level of demand and production.

The exclusion of the United States from the club produces results of the same direction as in the AB scenario, though of a smaller magnitude due to the lower carbon value: The Former Soviet Union and the Central European Associates have smaller gains and the rest of the regions smaller losses.

In the AB-USA-FSU scenario the results on welfare of the AB-USA scenario are enhanced, though not reaching their levels in the AB scenario, with the exception of the Former Soviet Union. Its exclusion from the abating club leads to a higher level of production in this region compared to the AB scenario and lower compared to the baseline due to the lower demand for exports. The increase in the production of non-energy sectors compared to the baseline increases the demand for labour and capital and their returns; this additional income though is not enough to compensate for the lower rents to their energy endowments, thus it has a substantial loss in welfare.

In the AB+ROW scenario it is not only the 'hot air' owners but also Japan that have a higher level of welfare. This is due to the income from permit sales that the representative agent in Japan receives for the permits sold in the internal market that compensate for the lower wages and returns on capital because of the lower level of demand and production. The rest of the Annex B regions have a lower welfare for the same reasons as in the AB scenario. In developing countries the revenues from permit sales partially compensate for the losses in the returns of factors of production and resources, thus the Rest of the World ends up with marginally smaller losses compared to the AB scenario.

Compared to the AB scenario, all countries without excess emission rights have smaller welfare losses or even gains in the AB+ROW scenario and the 'hot air' owners have smaller gains because of the lower carbon value.

In the case that the United States do not participate in the abatement effort, the level of welfare in this country does not change from baseline. The cost of compliance for all non-'hot air' owners and the gains of the Former Soviet Union and the Central European Associates are reduced. If we further exclude the major 'hot air' supplier, the welfare implications on the participating regions and developing countries increase while the United States do not experience a change in welfare from baseline.

3.1.3   Monopolistic Permit Supply

In this section it is assumed that the Former Soviet Union supplies its 'hot air' monopolistically. The monopolist can control the supply of permits, meaning that it can increase or decrease the supply of permits in order to maximise its benefits from permit trade. Since the lower the supply of permits, the higher their internationally traded price, it would be profitable for the Former Soviet Union to restrict its supply in order to increase the revenues from permit sales, as long as its sales do not fall faster than the price increases. Such a practice increases the carbon value and thus the cost of implementation of the Kyoto Protocol.

In situations of limited permit supply, there are two markets for permits: the domestic market (of the Former Soviet Union) and the international market (of the club). In general, the carbon value in the domestic market is lower (or even zero) than in the international market. As the monopolist increases the supply of permits in the international market, the permit price is reduced in the international market and increased in the domestic market. In a partial-equilibrium model, the solution to this market of emission rights would be the point where the Former Soviet Union maximises revenues from sales of permits. However, in a general equilibrium model, where all markets are interconnected and the effects from a change in one market are reflected in all the other markets, the optimum solution is given by the point where the Former Soviet Union maximises its level of welfare; this point is usually not the same as the revenue-maximisation level.

The methodology used for these simulations is the following: To start with, the Former Soviet Union is allowed to sell only a small portion of its 'hot air' endowment in the international permit market. This portion is gradually increased in small steps until perfect competition supply is reached. The optimum position for the monopolist is obtained at the supply 'step' where its welfare is maximised. Clearly when the supply of the monopolist is lower the net exporters of permits will have higher benefits from permit sales and permit importers can be expected to have higher welfare losses.

The scenarios that were simulated for the Kyoto period under imperfectly competitive permit markets are the following:

- Scenario VII (All Annex B countries – AB_IC): As in Scenario I but with the Former Soviet Union supplying its 'hot air' monopolistically. This scenario was simulated in order to examine the impacts of possible restrictive practices of the Former Soviet Union in permit markets in the abatement effort of Annex B countries.

- Scenario VIII (All Annex B countries without the United States – AB-USA_IC): As in Scenario III but with the same assumption for the Former Soviet Union as above regarding the utilisation of its 'hot air'. In the absence of the United States for the abatement process the percentage of the 'hot air' inside the club is bigger, thus its utilisation has a higher impact on the determination of the permit price.

- Scenario IX (Europe, the Central European Associates, and the Former Soviet Union – ECF_IC): As in Scenario V with the addition of the Former Soviet Union and monopolistically structured permit market.

3.1.3.1   AB_IC Scenario

When the Former Soviet Union does not supply any emission permits for trade (point A in Figure 9), then the situation is identical to a scenario where all Annex B countries apart from the Former Soviet Union meet their Kyoto targets inside one club. In this scenario the carbon value is €99 110.85, making the abatement effort very costly. The cost in terms of welfare for Japan, the United States, and Europe is significant (0.25%, 0.29%, and 0.35% respectively), higher for Australia & New Zealand (0.47%), and very high for Canada (1.06%).

The Central European Associates decrease their emissions from baseline by more than a third, leading to significant gains in welfare by 2.79% because of the high revenues from permit sales.

The Former Soviet Union has not only no revenues from permit sales but also significantly decreased demand for exports of fossil fuels, meaning lower total demand and production. This has a negative impact on the level of welfare of 0.73%. The Rest of the World is marginally worse off by 0.13% for the same reasons.

As the supply of emission rights increases, all regions in the club – apart from the monopolist – face a continuously decreasing carbon value. When welfare is maximised for the monopolist (point B in Figure 9), all countries in the club apart from the Former Soviet Union reduce their emissions slightly more than in the perfect competition scenario (point C in Figure 9) due to the higher carbon value. However, the abatement effort made by the Former Soviet Union is much lower (reduction of 9.7% instead of 15.4% for the perfectly competitive market). These results are due to the fact that the price for emission rights in the club is also higher than in the perfect competition scenario, at €99 66.02, but differs from the price in the internal permit market of the Former Soviet Union, which is only €99 38.94. The aggregate reduction in the global emissions is 5.87%, which is slightly smaller than in the perfect competition scenario not only due to the marginally increased emissions of the Rest of the World (higher carbon leakage) but also because of the increased emissions of the monopolist compared to the perfect competition case: These two effects combined exceed the additional emission reduction made by the rest of the regions in Annex B.

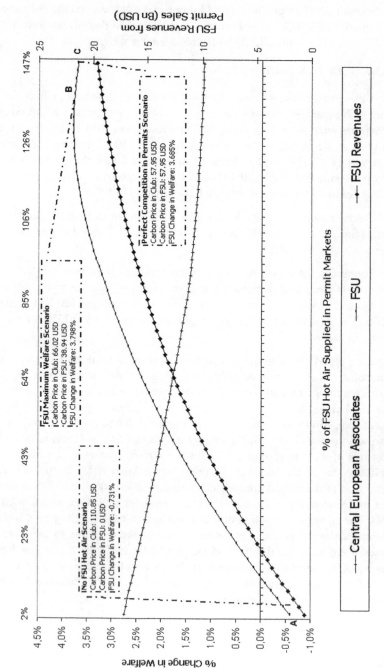

Figure 9: Annex B – Abatement with Imperfect Competition in Permit Markets.

The welfare implications are similar to the perfect competition case though amplified due to the higher carbon value (Table 17). The Rest of the World has also lower welfare level because of the lower demand for energy exports that leads to lower demand for – and therefore the rents paid to – their energy endowments.

Table 17:   % Change in Welfare from Baseline in the AB and AB_IC Scenarios (2010).

	AB	AB_IC
World	-0.11	-0.12
Europe	-0.18	-0.21
Central European Associates	1.17	1.22
Japan	-0.13	-0.15
Canada	-0.72	-0.76
Australia	-0.40	-0.41
Former Soviet Union	3.69	3.80
United States	-0.23	-0.24
Rest of the World	-0.09	-0.09

The Central European Associates act as a 'free rider' in this permit market structure, since they realise increased revenues from emission right sales compared to the case where the Former Soviet Union supplies its rights perfectly competitively, without reducing the amount of permits it sells in the international market.

The Former Soviet Union acts monopolistically, discriminating perfectly the price it charges for carbon permits sold inside and outside the region, therefore it benefits both from the higher price it receives for the emission rights it sells in the international permit market and the lower price – meaning lower cost of abatement – inside the region. The welfare increase achieved in this region is higher, but not substantially so, compared to the perfect competition scenario.

Overall, the cost of implementing the Kyoto Protocol in all Annex B countries when the Former Soviet Union uses monopolistic practices in the permit market is 0.12% lower welfare for the world.

The demand for fossil fuels decreases in Annex B countries due to their higher consumption prices. The demand for the products of the rest of the sectors decreases in all regions, except from the demand for the rest of the industry sector in the Former Soviet Union that increases because it becomes relatively less expensive than the other sectors of the economy due to its low consumption of fuels. The only non-abating region, the Rest of the World, has increased demand for the products of all sectors due to the lower cost of energy.

3.1.3.2   AB-USA_IC Scenario

The benchmark case in the study of the monopolistic permit supply is the compliance of all Annex B countries with the Kyoto Protocol, meaning that they are supplied with emission rights as many as they are provided by the agreement, with the exception of the United States, which is what seems to be the most likely arrangement.

When the Former Soviet Union supplies no 'hot air' in the international permit market (point A in Figure 10), then the only excess emission rights available in the market for trade are those of the Central European Associates. The welfare in this region increases by 1.58% due to the €99 82.83 paid for each permit sold in the market. The welfare level of the rest of the regions is reduced due to the high cost of abatement.

The effort needed to comply is reduced as the Former Soviet Union allows for a fraction of its 'hot air' to be traded internationally, lowering in this way the world price of emission permits. When supplying about 66% of its 'hot air' (point B in Figure 10), revenues from sales are maximised for the monopolistic supplier at a substantially lower carbon value of €99 37.47, giving 1.11% higher welfare for the Former Soviet Union.

The rest of the countries in the club face a lower cost of abatement, due to the lower price per emission right they have to pay; their cost in terms of welfare is about half of what it is when the Former Soviet Union is not supplying any permits. The Central European Associates gain only 0.35% in welfare due to the lower amount of revenues from sales of permits.

By increasing the supply of 'hot air' to 72% of its endowment (point C in Figure 10), the Former Soviet Union maximises its level of welfare at 1.12% despite the fact that the revenues from permit sales are lower. This is due to the fact that the demand for imports from the Former Soviet Union is higher compared to point B due to the lower carbon value inside the club. This increased demand for exports of the Former Soviet Union increases the production of fossil fuels inside this region, leading to higher payments to resources and higher income from taxation in private consumption, output, imports, exports, and intermediate consumption. Due to the lower carbon value the revenues from permit sales are lower for the Central European Associates, thus their increase in welfare (0.28%) is smaller than in point B. The other regions in the club, facing a lower permit price, have a smaller reduction in welfare. The slightly decreased level of welfare compared to the baseline of the Rest of the World is due to the lower demand for fossil fuels globally and, therefore, to the lower rents paid to resource endowments.

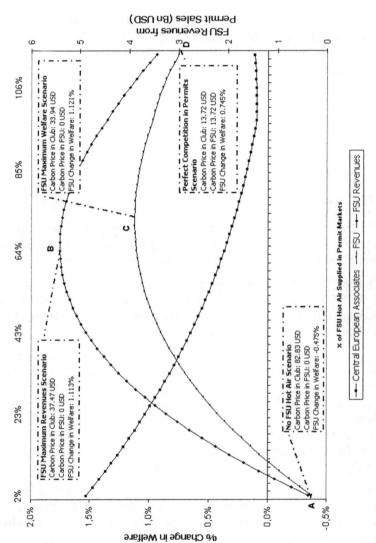

Figure 10: Annex B – USA with Imperfect Competition in Permit Markets.

The reduction of global emissions of 1.22% is small but it is higher than when we do not allow for monopolistic practices on behalf of the Former Soviet Union. The countries of the club reduce their emission levels significantly, except from the major 'hot air' supplier that increases emissions by 1.4% compared to the baseline, which is a substantial deviation from the 4.5% reduction in emissions of the perfect competition scenario. This is due to the higher demand for (and consumption of) fossil fuels inside the Former Soviet Union. Emissions also increase by the non-participants, the United States and the Rest of the World, leading to a high carbon leakage effect.

The point meaning that the supply of permits is perfectly competitive (point D in Figure 10) is reached when the Former Soviet Union reduces its baseline emissions by 4.5%, selling about 114% of the excess emission rights they were endowed with. The lower demand for fossil fuels inside the Former Soviet Union compared to point C results in the lower rents to fuel endowments, thus lower level of welfare.

3.1.3.3   ECF_IC Scenario

The abatement effort of Europe and the Central European Associates has different effects on welfare depending on the availability of excess emission rights from the Former Soviet Union and the way this 'hot air' is manipulated.

The 'hot air' available in this club exceeds the amount of emissions that have to be reduced in Europe according to the Kyoto Protocol (the restriction in the club is non-binding). If the Former Soviet Union does not restrict the supply of permits, the carbon value is driven to zero because supply exceeds demand.

When no carbon permits are sold from the monopolistic supplier (point A in Figure 11), then the abatement effort is expensive for Europe and very profitable for the Central European Associates, gaining more than 1% in terms of welfare. The carbon value inside the club increases the price of fuels, thus the demand for domestic and imported energy is reduced; The resource endowment of the Former Soviet Union receives lower rents due to the decrease in the demand for fossil fuels in the abating regions; welfare, therefore, is negatively affected by 0.37% although no abatement is made inside the region.

As the supply of carbon permits increases due to the fact that more 'hot air' becomes available from the Former Soviet Union, the value of carbon permits decreases, making the abatement effort less costly for Europe. On the other hand, the welfare of the Central European Associates decreases as the supply of the monopolist increases due to the lower revenues from permit sales, thus they are worse-off compared to point A. The Former Soviet Union gains not only from the increase in carbon revenues but also from the smaller decrease in the rents paid to their resources; this is due to the smaller decrease in the demand for exports of fossil fuels inside the club as the carbon value drops.

Revenues from emission rights sales are maximised for the Former Soviet Union (point B in Figure 11) when supplying 39.3% of their 'hot air' endowment at €99 30.86 with a resulting change in welfare of 0.48%. At that point the Central European Associates gain only 0.22% and Europe is better off than when no 'hot air' was available because they pay less than half the permit price.

The optimum choice for the Former Soviet Union, however, is not that level of supply of emission rights, as it would be in a partial-equilibrium model; by supplying 6.2% more of their 'hot air' endowment (point C in Figure 11), they find their revenues decreasing due to the lower price of €99 26.03 but the increase in the rents paid for their resources is enough to compensate for the lower permit sales. Again, the Central European Associates loose revenues due to the lower price, ending up with just a 0.15% overall gain in welfare, while Europe complies to the Kyoto Protocol with a cost of only 0.14%.

The carbon value is €99 26.03 for Europe and the Central European Associates, and zero for the Former Soviet Union due to the abundant emission rights available inside the country that have not been offered in the international permit market because they would lower their price thus reducing the revenues from permit sales. In other words, the increased offer of permits would result in a lower welfare level for the Former Soviet Union.

The overall effect in global emissions is weakened due to the carbon leakage effect, which is noticeably high in this case.

Any increase from point C on in the supply of permits leads to lower welfare level for both suppliers due to the sharp decline in the price of emission rights. The total amount of 'hot air' from both regions exceeds the demand for permits by Europe, therefore when the Former Soviet Union supplies more than 85% of its 'hot air' endowment, the price of permits drops to zero and the scenario is identical to the baseline.

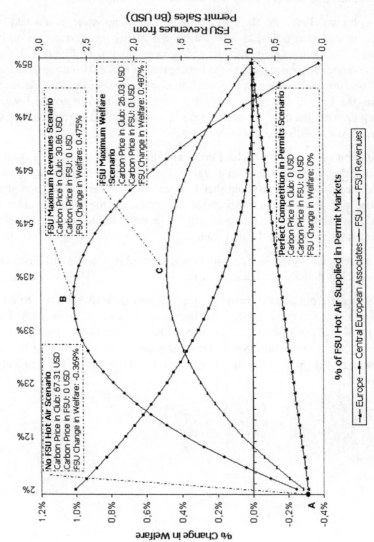

Figure 11: EU, Central European Associates, and Former Soviet Union with Imperfect Competition in Permit Markets Scenario.

3.1.4   Welfare Implications and Environmental Effectiveness

It can be generally expected that emission abatement policy carries a cost in terms of welfare losses and that such losses increase more than linearly with the size of the reduction implied by the policy. It is also generally accepted that within a competitive emission permit market the wider the effort is spread the smaller these losses are likely to be since the scope of cost effective emission reduction options is enlarged. The analysis using computable general equilibrium models however can go beyond these generally accepted principles and look at secondary welfare effects that arise from the fact that economies are interconnected through international trade in a manner that the adjustment to a constraint in one country/region may have repercussions on the economies and ultimately the welfare of other countries/regions even when the latter do not participate in the abatement effort. Such secondary effects have been exposed in the previous sections and materialise mainly through movements in prices of the goods directly affected by the abatement effort (fossil fuels), energy-intensive products as well as other goods that, from a first look, are relatively immune to the changes implied by the abatement effort.

The issues addressed in this section are:

- Taking total welfare and environmental impacts (direct and indirect) what can be said in terms of the environmental efficiency implied in the different scenarios examined?

- To what extent restrictive practices in the market of internationally traded permits affect this environmental efficiency?

The environmental impact and the cost of abatement per ton of carbon in terms of welfare are presented in Table 18. The first column shows the percent reduction in world emissions implied by the scenario and includes carbon leakage effects. The second and third columns show the average cost in terms of welfare (consumption) loss per ton of carbon reduced in 2010 for the World and EU 15. The European Union is shown separately because it is the subject of special focus of the CCGT project and has been retained on all the abatement clubs considered. The scenario with the highest environmental effectiveness and the lowest cost in welfare is the AB+ROW case, which is equal to the implementation of the Kyoto Protocol together with clean development mechanisms free of transaction cost. This result is due to the fact that the abating countries take advantage of the least expensive way to abate all around the world, thus lowering the cost of compliance significantly. Furthermore, the higher prices of fuels do not generate any substitution effects towards the increase of energy imports because all countries are abating, thus the lack of carbon leakage prevents the overall environmental impact from shrinking.

Table 18:   % Change in Emissions from Baseline and Cost in Private Consumption per Ton of Carbon in Each Scenario (2010).

	Total Emission Reduction	Cost Per ton of Carbon	
	% changes from baseline	World	Europe
AB	-5.88	60.53	27.15
AB+ROW	-7.18	20.19	2.19
AB-USA	-0.85	74.67	65.90
AB-USA-FSU	-2.49	206.73	123.71
EC	-1.51	186.44	183.42
EA	-1.49	298.03	275.37
AB_IC	-5.87	67.51	31.13
AB-USA_IC	-1.22	158.23	121.09
ECF_IC	-0.69	145.01	177.37

Not surprisingly the scenario with the highest environmental effectiveness and the lowest cost in welfare is the AB+ROW case. Such a scenario apart from offering a wider option of cost effective emission reduction options also minimises the perturbation to the world economic and trade system and avoids carbon leakage. Less obvious however is the extent to which such an arrangement could be environmentally efficient (one third of the average cost compared to the all Annex B case) and the even greater efficiency in terms of EU effort. Unfortunately this scenario is purely hypothetical.

The withdrawal of the United States from the Kyoto process dramatically reduces the environmental impact mainly because of the increased significance of 'hot air' in the remainder of the club. However, the efficiency of abatement in terms of worldwide welfare loss is not substantially increased. The cost per ton to the EU however more than doubles.

Excluding additionally the Former Soviet Union improves the environmental impact (mainly through the removal of hot air) but increases very substantially the cost both for the World and the EU.

Were the EU to attempt to meet its target alone (with the rest of the world undertaking no abatement effort) both the environmental impact would be small (-1.5% decrease in world emissions) and the cost per carbon abated very high and naturally borne overwhelmingly by the EU. On the other hand including the Accession countries would leave the environmental impact intact (despite the inclusion of hot air available in these countries) while average costs are reduced by more than one third.

The exercise of monopolistic practices by the FSU in the context of Annex B wide Club would leave the environmental impact unaffected the restriction of supply being almost exactly compensated by additional carbon leakage in developing countries. On the other hand the increase in average abatement costs would be almost insignificant. The effects of restrictive practices are very different in the context of a reduced market (excluding the USA): Reducing the hot air available enhances the environmental impact but average abatement costs approximately double. Monopolistic practices are necessary in the case when all non-European signatories of the Protocol drop out of the process if any environmental impact is to be preserved. The cost to the EU in this case however remains high.

3.2   The Post-Kyoto Period: 'Soft-Landing' Scenario

3.2.1   'Soft-Landing' Scenario Assumptions

The 'soft-landing' scenario used in this study is based on the definition of Criqui and Kouvaritakis (1997). It is a realistic scenario, taking into account the differences among countries in the emissions per capita (reflecting the responsibility for the reduction of pollution) and GDP per capita (reflecting the ability to afford the cost of abatement). The abatement effort is gradual and the horizon of emission stabilisation and eventual reduction depends on both rates mentioned above. Annex B countries, for instance, which have high emissions per capita rate and also high GDP per capita, have tight targets from the beginning of the post-Kyoto period. On the other hand, developing countries have a smoother path of reduction of emissions, as implied by the amount of permits they are supplied compared to their baseline. Consequently, emission allowances are calculated based on the initial situation of each country that determines its ability and responsibility to abate.

The reduction schedule is based on the soft-landing CO_2 only-'only' scenario of the Greenhouse Gas Emission Control Strategies project[5] (Criqui, 2002). The emission rights allocated in the framework of the 'soft-landing' scenario are presented in Table 19. Annex B regions are assumed to form an abating club for the Kyoto period and all countries are assumed to join this club in 2015 and thereafter.

A market for pollution permits is created when a limited amount of 'property rights' on emissions are distributed to the economic agents. These represent a right to pollute equal to the amount of emission rights owned by the polluter. These rights can be traded among economic agents (and among all countries).

The emission permits are distributed according to a grandfathering principle to the firms and to the households of each country. Economic agents have then to compare the cost of reducing emissions below their endowment, to the benefit from selling their permits to the market.

---

[5]   Research Project N° EVK2-CT-1999-00010, Thematic Programme: Environment and Sustainable Development of the DG Research (Fifth Framework Programme), EU.

Table 19:   Emission Rights in the 'Soft-Landing' Scenario.

	1995	2010	2030
Australia & New Zealand	1.00	0.99	0.89
Japan	1.00	0.90	0.64
East Asia	1.00	0.00	2.83
China	1.00	0.00	2.82
India	1.00	0.00	5.09
North America	1.00	0.00	0.97
Latin America	1.00	0.00	2.86
Nordic Europe	1.00	0.91	0.76
Germany	1.00	0.88	0.61
UK	1.00	0.93	0.79
Rest of Europe	1.00	0.98	0.78
Other Europe	1.00	0.00	1.98
Central European Associates	1.00	0.93	0.86
Former Soviet Union	1.00	0.85	0.72
North Africa	1.00	0.00	2.40
Africa	1.00	0.00	4.20
Rest of the World	1.00	0.00	3.83

The underlying assumption of perfectly competitive permit markets that has been made in this version of the GEM-E3 model implies that the carbon value is the shadow price of the globally imposed restriction. The extent of the reduction of emissions in each country depends on the relative ease of abatement: The reduction of the emissions of a country with relatively low cost of abatement is bigger than that of a country with relatively high cost of abatement regardless of their endowments in permit rights. More specifically, the reduction of emissions is made up to the point that the cost of reducing an additional ton of CO_2 is equal to the world permit price. The difference between the regional allocation in emission rights, which depends on the scenario assumptions for the regional endowments, and the volume of emissions of a country, determines the amount of permits that are sold or purchased by this country.

3.2.2   The Adjustment Process

In order to explain the impacts of the policy of restriction on emissions on the various macroeconomic variables, the resulting changes have to be separated into initial systemic disturbances and secondary effects. These initial disturbances can be assessed by making some preliminary analysis of the abatement potential in the different regions in conjunction with other factors that affect the market for permits.

3.2.2.1   *Initial Systemic Disturbances*

The magnitude of the changes generated by the initial systemic disturbances is bigger than the ones initiated by the secondary effects. This is also a necessary condition in order for a general equilibrium model to converge to a new equilibrium point. The introduction of a restriction in the market for emission permits, which is part of the environmental module embodied in the core model, causes initial disturbances both in the supply and in the demand of goods and services.

On the supply-side, the initial disturbance refers to the prices of the energy inputs due to the burden of the carbon value imposed on these inputs. The imposition of the same carbon value to all countries leads to different increases in the prices of fossil fuels for two reasons. The first is that the three primary fuels (coal, oil, gas) examined in the model have different CO_2 emission factors: Coal has the highest factor, followed by oil and gas. The bigger is the amount of coal as a percentage of the bundle constituting the energy input, the higher is the increase in the price of this bundle. The second reason is that fossil fuels have a different price in each region. The prices of energy inputs in countries that have significant reserves of energy resources are often lower. The same occurs in countries that have low tariffs and taxes on fossil fuels. Thus the imposition of the same burden results in a higher increase in the prices of fossil fuels in the countries with the lower price levels of these goods. The magnitude of the impacts of the initial disturbance on the supply-side of each country is displayed in column (1) of Table 20.

The highest increases in the unit cost of energy are observed in the Former Soviet Union, the Central European Associates, and China due to both the high percentage of coal in the energy bundle of these regions and to the low prices of energy inputs inside these regions. It is evident that the different increases in the unit cost of energy depend on the various impacts that the above factors have on each country. The relatively lower prices of coal and oil in the Former Soviet Union and the Central European Associates compared to China increase the unit energy cost more than in China despite the fact that coal is a significantly smaller part of their energy bundles. On the other hand, the smallest increase in the unit cost of energy is observed in Latin America, where oil is a big part of the energy bundle but comes with a high price. The same comments *mutatis mutandis* can be made for the major oil producers such as North Africa-Middle East, Africa, and East Asia. Among developed countries, the highest increase in the unit cost of energy is observed in North America mainly due to the relatively lower taxes imposed on these inputs in this region.

The initial disturbance on the demand-side is caused by the sales and purchases of emission rights. These transactions affect the demand factors in two ways: On the one hand they increase (decrease) the disposable income of households, increasing (decreasing) the part that goes to consumption. On the other hand these transactions are transfers to (from) the external sector, affecting the current account of each country. For the simulations of this study, the restriction of stability of the ratio of the current account to GDP for developing countries was imposed. This was achieved by allowing the model to endogenously change the level of the real interest rate that results as the dual price of this restriction. When a developing country sells permits – with its GDP, imports, and exports remaining stable – its current account tends to improve, violating the restriction. The compensating mechanism acts towards reducing the real interest rate of this country and thus increasing its imports until the restriction is met. Imports increase indirectly through the increase of consumption and investment. Consumption increases because with a lower real interest rate current consumption is preferable than future consumption. Therefore savings are reduced in favour of consumption. Investment increases because the reduction in the real interest rate lowers the cost of financing investment projects. This initial increase in demand, given the domestic supply and the prices of imported goods, generates an increase in the prices of domestically produced goods and an increase in imports. The opposite adjustments occur in the case that a developing country purchases permits. The distribution of emission rights and the relative ability of each country to reduce its emissions as well as the level of the carbon value determine the amount and direction of sales and purchases of permits. In countries with relatively low cost of abatement and relatively favourable initial allocation of permits such as India and China, the sales of permits are substantially high. Conversely, in countries with relatively small quantities of emission rights compared to their baseline emissions such as the Former Soviet Union, the amount spent on the purchases of permits is highly significant, having the anticipated consequences on the disposable income and the current account.

3.2.2.2   Secondary Effects

On the supply-side, the higher cost of energy inputs results in an increase in the cost of production of goods and services. However, the increase in the cost of production will be lower than the increase in the price of the energy inputs because the prices of the other cost elements increase less than the prices of fossil fuels. A higher increase in the cost of production is faced by sectors that are more energy-intensive, such as electricity, ferrous and non-ferrous metals, chemicals, etc. The higher cost of energy inputs initiates substitution mechanisms in the production process. These substitutions will occur not only between fossil fuels, depending on the emission factor of each fuel, but also between energy inputs and other non-energy-intensive inputs. The result of these substitutions is the significant reduction in the demand for all three primary fuels and mainly for coal, which has the highest emission factor. Substitutions – to a smaller extent – and a noticeable reduction in demand will occur also in the case of energy-intensive products.

Table 20: Changes in the Unit Energy Cost and the Share of the Value of Net Exports of Permits in Disposable Income (2030).

	Unit Energy Cost % change from baseline (1)	Value of Net Exports of Permits % share of disposable income (2)
Australia	49.9	-0.8
Japan	22.1	-0.1
East Asia	30.0	-0.3
China	112.0	2.6
India	73.2	4.0
North America	74.7	-0.1
Latin America	18.5	0.3
Nordic Europe	37.1	-0.2
Germany	48.2	-0.1
UK	45.6	-0.2
Rest of Europe	40.4	-0.2
Other Europe	24.7	-0.1
Central European Associates	113.1	-0.5
Former Soviet Union	114.1	-2.4
North Africa	36.8	0.3
Africa	20.3	0.7
Rest of the World	36.9	0.6

On the demand-side, the increase in the prices of fossil fuels results in their substitution in consumption for other non-energy products. This reduction will be even bigger for the countries the disposable income of which is decreased due to purchases of permits. The opposite takes place in the case of the net sellers of permits, where this reduction is partially compensated. A comparison of the increase in the unit energy cost in all countries and the change in disposable income (see Table 20) leads to the conclusion that the substitution effect is substantially more important than the income effect, resulting in reduction in the demand for all fossil fuels in all countries.

The increase in the price of energy has an impact on the prices of durable goods, affecting the decisions of the consumer. Specifically, in the model it is supposed that the producer combines the use of durable goods with energy in order to produce a composite service such as heating, cooking, and transport, thus the price of energy is a part of the user cost of durables. This means that an increase in the price of energy reduces the demand for durable consumption goods.

The imposition of the same carbon value in all countries, as it has been mentioned above, results in higher increases of prices of fossil fuels in the regions with relatively less expensive energy goods. This occurs mainly in the countries that are major producers of fossil fuels. The effect of the abatement scenario on these countries is to create a comparative disadvantage vis-à-vis the rest of the countries. This comparative disadvantage is very pronounced with respect to energy-intensive sectors, with a noticeable reduction in exports of these goods too. An important channel of diffusion of this comparative disadvantage is electricity and domestic transport, which make a marginal contribution to international trade but constitute a significant input for the rest of the sectors.

On the other hand, countries with relatively high energy prices before the imposition of the restriction on emissions gain a comparative advantage in energy-intensive sectors.

The reduction of production in the energy-intensive sectors initiates a reduction of employment and of the level of capital employed. The resulting surplus in the labour force puts a pressure on the labour market, forcing wages to lower levels. The same occurs in the capital markets. The reductions in wages and employment are bigger in more labour-intensive countries. A part of the surplus labour force is absorbed in other sectors that are not affected substantially from the burden on energy inputs. These sectors according to economic theory are labour-intensive sectors such as agriculture, food industry, textiles, and market and non-market services. The countries that are more labour-intensive gain a comparative advantage in these sectors. Similar adjustments occur for capital in the capital-intensive sectors.

3.2.2.3   Abatement Potentials

The abatement process can also be viewed from the prism of Marginal Abatement Cost Curves (MACCs), which is one of the most widely used tools for evaluating different emissions trading schemes. It has been shown in many studies and is a conclusion of the present scenario evaluation that MACCs are to a great extent independent of the participation or not of a country in a market scheme for sales and purchases of emission permits as well as to the distribution of permits to the various countries that participate in this market (Ellerman and Decaux, 1998). They are mainly dependent on the economic structure of a country; a change in their position in the two-dimensional space reflects a change in the effectiveness of this structure. Such a change occurs, for instance, with the tariff abolition as simulated in the model. In computable general equilibrium models, when a restriction on emissions of a country is imposed, the carbon value results as a dual value of this restriction. In this study, the MACCs are derived by repeated simulations of the GEM-E3-World model under alternative assumptions for the global emission restriction. A pair of carbon value and abated emissions for each country is generated in each simulation. The MACC for each country is then the locus of these pairs in the two-dimensional space.

A representative picture of the differences in the emissions abatement potential of each region as they are depicted by the MACCs can be found in Figure 12.

In Figure 12 the absolute reduction of emissions is shown on the horizontal axis and the carbon value on the vertical axis. This presentation assists mainly in the evaluation of the distribution of emissions abatement by region. The absolute quantity of emissions abatement depends to a great extent on the magnitude of the production activity of a region. Based on this criterion, the significant emissions abatement potentials existing in regions such as North America can be explained. However, the magnitude of the production activity is not sufficient to provide a satisfactory explanation for the relative position of the MACC of each region in Figure 12. North America, for instance, with GDP seven times as much as the one of China, has lower emissions abatement potential for all carbon values. The same observation can be made for Japan, which, having one of the highest GDPs in the world, has low emissions abatement potentials in absolute terms. An alternative presentation would be to show the percentage reduction in emissions compared to the baseline on the horizontal axis (Figure 13). This depiction provides even further insights on the relative abatement potential of various regions. The potential according to which a country is capable of reducing emissions at a certain point in time mainly depends on the intensity and the composition of energy products used in production and consumption. A country that uses energy inputs relatively more intensively in its production process has a higher abatement potential compared to other countries. Under the assumption that there exist two countries with the same composition of energy inputs (coal, oil, gas), which differ in terms of production and consumption intensity of these energy inputs, the marginal product of energy inputs and, therefore, their price in the more energy-intensive country is lower than in the less energy-intensive country. Something similar occurs in consumption due to declining marginal utility. When two countries face the same carbon value then the price of fossil fuels in the energy-intensive country will increase relatively more, resulting in more extensive substitution of energy inputs and, thus, a bigger reduction in emissions.

The average ratios of energy inputs to output by region in the business-as-usual scenario are presented in Table 21. According to Table 21, China uses coal with significantly higher intensity than the rest of the countries, with a coal to output ratio three times as much as India, and twenty three times higher than North America. Oil is also used with great intensity.

India and the Former Soviet Union are among the regions with high energy intensity but with a composition of energy products different to that of China. The relatively high emissions reduction potential of these regions is due to the high intensities primarily in oil and secondarily in natural gas.

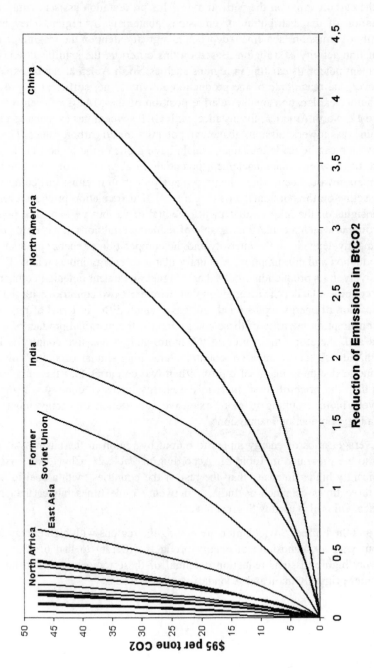

Figure 12:   Reduction of Emissions in Absolute Terms by Region (2030).

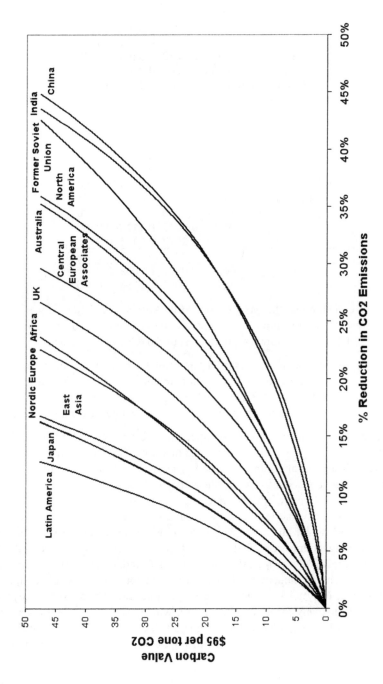

Figure 13:   Reduction of Emissions in Percentage Terms by Region (2030).

Table 21:   Energy to Output Ratio in Baseline Projections (2030).

	Coal	Oil	Gas
Australia	0.0020	0.0172	0.0063
Japan	0.0003	0.0064	0.0039
East Asia	0.0017	0.0340	0.0073
China	0.0212	0.0296	0.0016
India	0.0087	0.0501	0.0130
North America	0.0009	0.0106	0.0055
Latin America	0.0009	0.0382	0.0097
Nordic Europe	0.0008	0.0099	0.0018
Germany	0.0017	0.0024	0.0018
UK	0.0010	0.0106	0.0047
Rest of Europe	0.0005	0.0070	0.0020
Other Europe	0.0012	0.0118	0.0065
Central European Associates	0.0032	0.0194	0.0068
Former Soviet Union	0.0031	0.0321	0.0271
North Africa	0.0003	0.0605	0.0060
Africa	0.0019	0.1115	0.0106
Rest of the World	0.0072	0.0191	0.0137
WORLD	0.0022	0.0182	0.0055
North	0.0008	0.0082	0.0040
South	0.0051	0.0390	0.0085

The relative position of the MACC for North America in Figure 13 can be explained by both the magnitude of economic activity and the substantial energy intensities in this region compared to the rest of the developed countries.

Among developed countries, Australia has a relatively high abatement potential because it has the highest coal to output ratio among countries of the North as well as high intensities for the other two fuels, while Japan and the European countries have relative low abatement potentials due to their low intensity in energy inputs.

A significant observation that can be noticed from Figure 12 and Figure 13 is that in some cases the MACCs of two countries intersect. This means that up to a certain level of carbon value, one country has higher emissions reduction potential compared to another country while the opposite is true thereafter. This, for instance, occurs in terms of the relative abatement potentials between China and India; for a carbon value less than €99 20, India has higher emissions abatement potential than China while for a price of permits higher than €99 20, China is the one with the higher emissions abatement potential. This inversion is due to the fact that China is relatively more carbon intensive than India and is able to substitute coal for other energy inputs with lower emission factors. On the other hand, India, due to the relatively lower carbon intensity, will be forced to substitute beyond a certain level relatively more quantities of oil, which offers lower emissions abatement potential because it has a lower emission factor than coal. Nevertheless, in terms of absolute levels as it is shown in Figure 12, China has higher emissions abatement potential than India for all levels of carbon value because of the bigger size of the production activity in this country. This characteristic is likely to affect the results of different emissions trading schemes.

3.2.3   World Emissions Profile

Under the assumptions made the global restriction for the Kyoto period (up to 2010) results in a carbon value of €99 14.25 at the end of the implementation period. The reduction in global emissions is 2% compared to the business-as-usual scenario.

In 2015 most of the non-Annex B regions are provided with emission rights that represent more emissions than they have in the baseline. The emission rights of Annex B countries stand at substantially lower levels than their baseline emissions. Given the availability of cheaper abatement options in non-Annex B countries, this enlargement of the permit market results in a reduction of the carbon value in 2015 compared to 2010 to €99 4.82.

Table 22:   % Change of Emissions Compared to Baseline in the 'Soft-Landing' Scenario.

	2015	2020	2025	2030
Australia & New Zealand	-21.0	-31.9	-42.3	-53.3
Japan	-18.4	-25.3	-32.4	-38.8
East Asia	-2.0	-6.3	-14.0	-19.9
China	2.4	2.6	-2.7	-12.6
India	2.6	3.8	2.7	-0.3
North America	-10.5	-18.0	-24.6	-31.4
Latin America	13.2	19.0	16.8	7.3
Nordic Europe	-24.0	-32.7	-39.4	-43.7
Germany	-21.7	-29.3	-35.4	-39.2
UK	-15.7	-23.4	-30.4	-36.4
Rest of Europe	-20.1	-27.7	-33.9	-38.7
Other Europe	-0.2	-3.3	-9.6	-19.1
Central European Associates	-19.4	-23.4	-27.1	-31.6
Former Soviet Union	-28.0	-37.9	-45.1	-50.1
North Africa	6.4	9.3	6.5	-3.0
Africa	3.6	6.7	2.2	-2.6
Rest of the World	6.0	8.8	9.9	13.0

In 2020 the permit allocations to the Annex B countries become increasingly tight and the amount of excess emission rights ('hot air') provided to the non-Annex B countries is increased only marginally. The higher demand for permits cannot be compensated by the slightly increased supply of permits, thus the resulting carbon value increases. Given that the restriction of emissions becomes tighter towards the end of the implementation period, the permit price for 2030 reaches €99 19.44.

The overall restriction in emissions in the 'soft-landing' scenario results in a reduction of 19.7% compared to the baseline in 2030.

Among developed countries, which are net importers of permits in 2030, Australia registers the most significant loss of income. According to the construction of the 'soft-landing' scenario, given that Australia has high ratios of GDP per capita and emissions per capita, the permit allocation for this country is lowest compared to the baseline among all regions. The rest of the developed countries, due to the amount of the emission rights they are supplied, spend no more than 0.15% of their GDP on purchases of internationally traded permits.

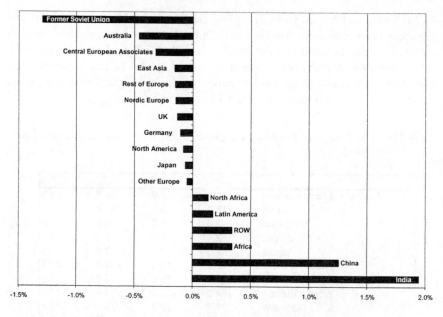

Figure 14:   'Soft-Landing' Scenario: Net Exports of Permits as % of GDP (2030).

The scenario assumes that, although the Former Soviet Union is provided with permits covering its baseline emissions for the Kyoto period, the emission rights it is given for the post-Kyoto period represent substantially fewer emissions than in the baseline; this explains why their spending on permit imports reaches 1.3% of their GDP in 2030.

Among the rest of the developing countries, the Central European Associates and East Asia are the only regions that are net importers of permits. The rest of the developing countries are net sellers of permits; in the case of India and China the income flow represents 1.9% and 1.2% respectively. This is due to the fact that, as it is shown in Table 22, the permits provided to these countries do not correspond to substantially fewer emissions than in the baseline. In addition, following the discussion above, the relative cost of abatement for these countries displayed in

Figure 12 and Figure 13 is the lowest among all regions. Thus the profits for these countries from the sales of permits, as it is explained in Figure 14, are relatively high.

3.2.4   Macroeconomic Results

The macroeconomic results generated by the simulation of the 'soft-landing' scenario at the world level are displayed in Figure 15. As is explained previously, referring to the supply-side, the imposition of the same carbon value in all regions generates different increases in the energy cost in each country, with the low energy cost users facing the highest consequences. The income inflow from the sales of emission rights increases the demand for goods and services of the net exporters for permits while the opposite occurs for the net importers of permits.

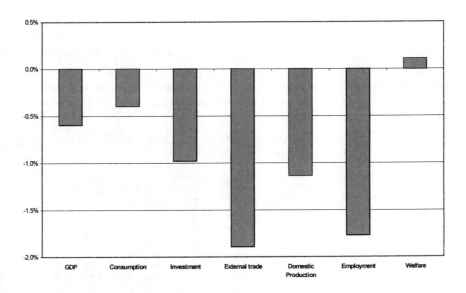

Figure 15:   The Macroeconomic Results of the 'Soft-Landing' Scenario (% Changes from Baseline in 2030).

At the world level the impact of the first factor is reflected in the reductions of GDP, international trade, and employment. The burden on the price of fossil fuels increases the general price level, reducing disposable income of households and resulting in the reduction of production activity and employment. In parallel, it generates a reduction in the level of total productivity by distorting the distribution of resources both geographically and sectorally. The second factor acts towards the redistribution of world income from the developed to the developing countries. Given the higher propensity of the lower income households to consume, this redistribution of income increases the demand for consumption goods in developing regions. It also lowers the savings of most developed countries in a way that, at the world scale, a shift from investment towards consumption goods is observed. A considerable part of global activity takes place in sectors that are severely affected by the increased cost of energy inputs but, on the other hand, are not significantly involved in international trade. Such sectors are the production of electricity, domestic transport, market services, and construction. The expenditures made for the products of these sectors are largely inelastic, thus the reduction in the income spent on purchases of goods with higher elasticity is relatively bigger. This results in the more significant reduction in the demand for products with higher elasticities that are also involved in international trade. At the world level this trend is expressed through the bigger reduction of international trade than GDP.

At the regional level, the macroeconomic results of the 'soft-landing' scenario are displayed in Table 23. The reduction of production activity observed at the world level is also present at the regional level but with substantial deviations in the distribution of the magnitude of the reduction in each country. Based on the argumentation developed previously, the bigger reductions occur in countries that are specialised in the production and exports of energy and energy-intensive products due to the inexpensive energy inputs in the business-as-usual scenario, a situation that is radically altered by the imposition of the carbon value.

Table 23: The Macroeconomic Results of the 'Soft-Landing' Scenario at the Regional Level (% changes from baseline in 2030).

	GDP	Exports	Imports	Domestic Production	Employment	Wage	Return on Capital	Welfare
Australia	-0.6	1.5	-2.6	-1.18	-0.02	-1.00	-2.76	-0.42
Japan	0.1	0.6	-1.1	-0.06	-0.06	1.67	1.75	0.00
East Asia	-0.4	0.0	-1.6	-0.89	-0.25	-0.71	-0.87	-0.19
China	-3.5	-10.1	-0.6	-5.37	-2.56	-8.60	-12.48	0.70
India	-3.5	-24.8	1.5	-6.23	-2.96	-5.23	-2.12	1.35
North America	-0.5	-1.6	-2.2	-0.96	-0.17	0.78	-0.41	-0.06
Latin America	-0.3	-3.5	-0.1	-0.64	-0.41	1.88	0.49	0.07
Nordic Europe	0.0	0.2	-1.0	-0.24	-0.07	1.11	0.95	-0.11
Germany	0.1	0.4	-1.1	-0.12	-0.08	1.06	0.87	-0.04
UK	-0.2	0.1	-1.2	-0.52	-0.12	0.80	0.20	-0.08
Rest of Europe	0.1	0.4	-1.4	-0.23	-0.09	0.88	0.69	-0.07
Other Europe	-0.1	0.0	-0.2	-0.32	-0.23	1.85	0.88	0.01
Central European Associates	-1.5	-2.3	-2.6	-2.05	-0.51	-1.08	-3.38	-0.21
Former Soviet Union	-6.1	-4.3	-11.9	-7.74	-2.20	-8.22	-15.20	0.19
North Africa	-0.9	-2.2	0.0	-1.33	-0.88	0.95	-1.84	0.10
Africa	-2.1	-5.4	-2.2	-3.54	-1.56	-3.20	-5.09	0.22
ROW	-0.1	-4.7	0.8	-0.48	-0.99	0.00	1.19	0.32

On the supply-side, the significant reduction of production inevitably lowers the demand for labour and capital, and leads to a reduction of wages and returns on capital, which are translated into lower value added and GDP. Since the reduction of emissions is achieved by substituting energy and energy-intensive inputs for less energy-intensive inputs, labour, and capital, intermediate consumption is reduced more than value added. Given that domestic production is the sum of intermediate consumption and value added, the reduction in GDP is smaller than the reduction in domestic production.

On the demand-side, the results are diversified depending on the net position of each country in the market for permits. In the case of regions such as China, India, the Rest of the World, North Africa-Middle East, Africa, and Latin America, which are net exporters of permits, the relatively higher increase of the cost of production in these countries is expressed through the lower demand for domestically produced goods both in domestic and foreign markets, resulting in the reduction of imports at a rate smaller than that of the reduction of exports. The income inflow from the sales of permits widens the deficit in the balance of trade even further because it initiates the increase of consumption that is covered with imports due to the substantial reduction in domestic production. In some cases, such as that of India and the Rest of the World, the income effect from the sales of permits in consumption is so big that imports actually increase. On the other hand, in regions such as the Former Soviet Union, the Central European Associates, and East Asia, which are net importers of permits, the adjustment on the demand-side follows a different path. The trade in the permit markets worsens the current account of these countries. In order to meet the restriction of the current account, imports must be reduced at a rate bigger than that of the reduction of exports. This is achieved with adjustments both on the demand- and on the supply-side. The adjustment on the demand-side is induced in the following way: The disposable income of households is reduced not only due to the reduction of the quantities of primary factors of production (labour and capital) employed and their returns but also due to the expenditures for the purchase of emission rights. This generates a reduction in the demand both for domestically produced goods and for imported goods. The lower demand for domestically produced goods reduces their prices; this reduction in some product categories is such that it compensates for the comparative disadvantage stemming from the relatively higher cost of energy. On the supply-side, the adjustment will take place in the specialisation in labour-intensive goods, which are favoured due to the surplus of labour created by the lower production of fossil fuels. Sectors the production process of which gains a comparative advantage in this way experience increased exports. The final result is that the rate of increase of exports in these countries is higher than the rate of increase of imports. In the case of East Asia, which is traditionally specialised in the production of labour-intensive goods, exports are marginally increased.

The significant reductions in the returns on capital cause a redistribution of demand from investment goods to consumption goods. This impact, in combination to the increase of the disposable income of households from the sales of permits and the higher propensity to consume of the lower income households, results in an increase of consumption in developing countries.

The production activity of developed countries is reduced with rates considerably lower than those of the developing regions. This occurs because of the following reasons:

- The increase in the unit cost of energy in these countries is smaller, as it follows from the discussion above.

- Their more modern technologies allow for an easier substitution of energy inputs for other 'cleaner' inputs.

- Their production structure is more diversified and less dependent on energy and energy-intensive activities, as it is the case in developing countries.

The relatively smaller increase in the cost of production in these countries leads to a gain of comparative advantage in the domestic as well as in the foreign markets. This leads to an increase of exports and the reduction of imports for all developed countries but North America. The improvement in the balance of trade in North America is brought about by a reduction of imports bigger than the reduction of exports. The increased revenues from international trade compensate to a great extent for the payments for the purchase of permits.

The reduction in domestic production of fossil fuels releases labour and capital that are directed towards energy-intensive sectors, in which developed countries have increased their comparative advantage. Since these sectors are more labour- and capital-intensive than the energy sectors, the marginal products of labour and capital increase, resulting in the increase of their returns. This outcome is observed in all developed countries except for Australia, the coal sector of which has a substantial reduction in production and is more capital-intensive than the energy-intensive sectors. The relatively big quantities of labour and capital released from this sector in Australia exert high pressure on the corresponding markets, leading to the reduction of wages and returns on capital. In developing countries, the increased rent on capital favours relatively investment expenditures, which decline less than consumption.

From the analysis above, two flows of income between developed and developing countries can be distinguished. These flows have the opposite direction and generate different results. The first flow of income starts from developing countries and is expressed by the deficit of their balance of trade that contributes to the reduction of their GDP. The recipients of this income are the developed countries, which direct this income towards investments due to the increased rents on capital; thus the reduction in their GDP is smaller than that of the developing countries. The second flow of income starts from the developed countries in the form of purchases of permits from the developing countries. Due to the decreased return on capital in developing countries, this income is directed towards consumption. When imports increase, the level of welfare of the households increases but GDP decreases. Thus welfare is a more appropriate measure for the impacts of the abatement effort to the consumer than the activity level, which to a large extent reflects the increased effort undertaken by a net purchaser of permits towards increased exports in order to finance this spending.

Examining the impact of the abatement effort on welfare, there is a clear pattern between the net position of a country in the market for permits and the welfare impacts on this country: the higher the sales (expenditures) the higher the gains (losses) in welfare. The only region that deviates from this pattern is the Former Soviet Union. This is due to the fact that the Former Soviet Union, as well as the Central European Associates and East Asia, do not follow the pattern of flows of income of investment and consumption as described above. These countries have an improved balance of trade and purchase permits, thus have the same pattern of flows of income with the developed countries. However, due to the reduction in the return on capital, final expenditure in these countries is directed towards consumption, as in the developing countries. In the case of the Former Soviet Union, the considerable improvement in the balance of trade and the significant decrease in the rent of capital lead to an increase in consumption and welfare. On the other hand, the limited impact of the above factors in the Central European Associates and East Asia lead to the reduction of consumption at a rate smaller than that of investment, resulting in the reduction of the level of welfare.

3.2.5 Sectoral and Country Results

This section deals with the simulated redistribution of world activity among countries and sectors. The initial disturbance refers to the sectors of primary fuels, thus the quantitative effects on these are the most pronounced. Given that the expectations for the direction of the changes in these sectors are met, the results of the GEM-E3 model do not differ in substance from the outcomes of other partial or general equilibrium models. Given that primary fuels are a significant input in the production process, the initial disturbance is diffused to the rest of the sectors of production generating a partial re-structuring in production and external trade. The magnitude of the secondary effects, apart from the magnitude of the initial disturbance, also depends on the intensity of utilisation of various inputs in the production of goods, as well as the relative position of each country in the production at the world level. These two factors are affected to a great extent by the hypotheses that have been embodied in the baseline scenario.

Energy products[6]

Energy products carry the main weight of the emissions restriction policy and, as expected, the demand for and production of these products are reduced.

The most significant reduction is observed in the production of coal, which has the highest emission factor among all primary fuels. Significant, although of a smaller

---

6 It has to be noted that, according to the aggregation adopted in the model, there is no distinction made between crude and distilled oil, thus each unit of the "oil" product in the model includes a mix of both of these products in the same ratio as in the base year (1995). The same note can be made for gas.

magnitude, are the reductions in the level of production of the other two primary fuels.

The most significant reductions in the production of coal and gas take place in countries that are the major producers of these products, as is the case for China, North America, and India for coal, and North America and Former Soviet Union for gas. Coal and gas in these countries is mainly consumed domestically, thus the reduction of production is primarily driven by the reduction in domestic demand. On the other hand, the production of oil in North Africa-Middle East, which is one of the major producers of these products, is reduced with relatively low percentages. This is due to the fact that they produce oil with a lower cost than their main competitors, and gain a share in world market for oil, resulting in a small reduction of domestic production (Figure 16).

A relatively big reduction in the world production is observed in the electricity sector due to the intensive use of primary fuels. The burden on the price of electricity, together with the following reduction in the demand, is heavier in countries such as China, North America, and India, where the production is based mainly on the use of coal.

Energy-intensive sectors

The prices of energy-intensive products, due to their dependence on fossil fuels inputs, increase more than the prices of all other non-energy sectors of the economy. The increases in the price levels are differentiated by good and country depending on its composition and the prices of energy inputs of each product. In all countries but the Former Soviet Union, ferrous and non-ferrous metals exhibit the highest increases in prices compared to the rest of energy-intensive products due to the relatively higher consumption of coal inputs in their production process. Gas is used more intensively than coal in the production of ferrous and non-ferrous metals in the Former Soviet Union. Given that chemical products in the Former Soviet Union are more gas-intensive than ferrous and non-ferrous metals, the price of the former increases more than that of the latter. The most significant increases in the prices of energy-intensive products are observed in countries with low cost of production such as China, India, Latin America, and North Africa-Middle East. These countries increase their share in world production over time in the baseline scenario due to their low prices of primary fuels. The relatively higher burden on these countries due to the imposition of a common carbon value results in the partial substitution of these products both in the domestic and the international markets.

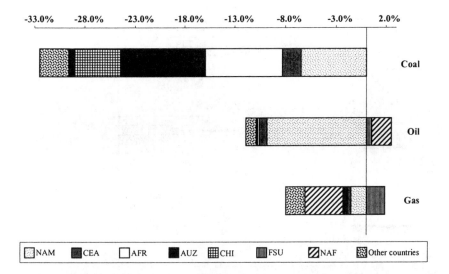

Figure 16:   Decomposition of the Changes in the World Level of Exports of Energy Products (2030).

The exception to this tendency is the Former Soviet Union, which registers an increase in the production and exports of ferrous and non-ferrous metals. This is due, on the one hand to the intensive use of cheap gas (as opposed to heavily penalised coal), and on the other to the significant reduction of non-energy costs of production (substantial reductions of wages and returns on capital).

An additional reason for the lower demand for energy-intensive products in developing countries is the lower demand for investment goods. Ferrous and non-ferrous metals and chemical products are significant inputs for equipment goods (electronic, transport, other), and cement (included in the other energy intensive goods sector) is a significant input for the construction sector. For the opposite reasons developed countries such as Japan, Germany, and North America, which are the major producers of energy-intensive products, increase their production and gain a share in the world export markets of these products.

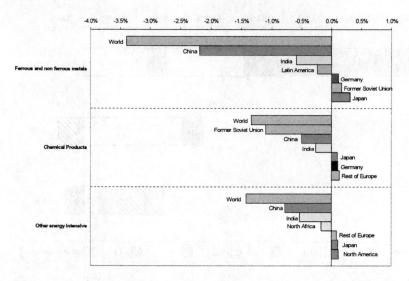

Figure 17:   Decomposition[7] of the Changes in the World Production of Energy-Intensive Products (2030).

Investment goods – durables

Noticeable reduction in the world production and international trade is observed in the sectors producing investment goods. In the case of transport equipment and other equipment goods, the reductions in production both at the regional and at the world levels are bigger than the reductions in the production of some energy-intensive products such as chemicals. This is due to the fact that the assumptions of the 'soft-landing' scenario have both direct and indirect impacts on the factors affecting demand and supply of these products.

On the supply-side, the impacts are indirect: these products, being more energy-intensive than the economy as a whole, face more intensively the considerably higher cost of the energy and energy-intensive inputs. Low-cost energy producers have the most severe consequences in this case.

On the demand-side, impacts are both direct and indirect: The direct impact refers to the increase in the price of consumption of durable goods (electronic equipment, transport equipment, other equipment goods), which, according to the hypotheses of the model, depends on the prices of fuels. Indirectly, the demand for investment goods is affected by the redistribution between consumption and savings caused by the transfers of income from permit sales and purchases. For durable goods, the combination of higher cost of production and consumption results in the reduction of production in all countries. This reduction is bigger for the low-

[7]   Each bar represents the contribution of each region in the change in world production.

cost energy producers due to their increasing comparative disadvantage both in the domestic and the international markets.

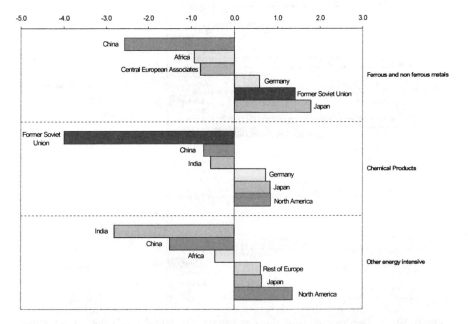

Figure 18:   Decomposition of the Changes in the World Exports of Energy-intensive Products (2030).

The Former Soviet Union, the exports of durable goods of which increase substantially, is the exception of this rule for two reasons: The first is the significant reduction in wages and returns on capital that compensate for the increased cost of energy and energy-intensive inputs. The second reason is the significant reduction of domestic demand (mainly intermediate consumption and investments), thus more output becomes available for exports.

In developed countries the reductions in production and exports of these goods are only marginal. In some cases such as North America and Australia, exports increase as a result of the combination of increasing comparative advantage and the confinement of domestic consumption expenditures. The production in the construction sector is reduced in all countries due to the lower investment expenditures in all countries. This reduction is bigger in developing countries due to the redistribution of expenditures towards higher consumption. The sector of other manufacturing products is affected only indirectly in this simulation. The comparative advantage of developing countries, in combination to the bigger reduction of their investment expenditures, results in the reduction of production and exports. Developed countries increase their production in order to meet the higher domestic demand for investments as well as the increased demand for imports from developing countries.

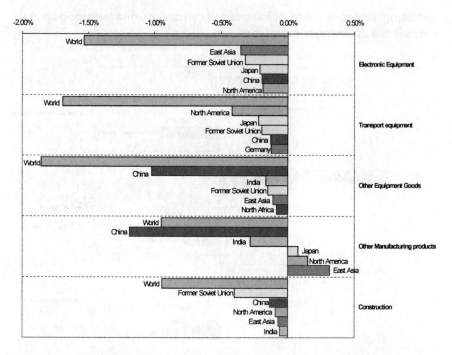

Figure 19:   Decomposition of the Changes in the World Production of Investment
Products (2030).

Traditional consumption goods

On the supply-side, consumption goods face the lightest burden from the higher
prices of energy inputs compared to the rest of the sectors in the economy because
of the low intensity with which these inputs are used. On the other hand, given
that traditional goods are primarily labour-intensive and secondarily capital-
intensive products, their costs of production are significantly affected by the
changes in wages and returns on capital. The most noticeable reductions of wages,
combined with the relatively higher labour-intensity of consumption goods in
developing countries, results in the bigger reduction of the cost of production in
these countries. Excluding the food and textile industries in India, the reduction of
wages compensates for the higher prices of energy inputs, leading to a lower cost
of production of traditional consumption goods.

On the demand-side, these products are favoured by the redistribution of expenditures towards higher consumption levels, while the opposite occurs in developed
countries. The result of these adjustments is the increase of production of traditional goods in developing countries and a corresponding decrease in the developed countries. At the world level this is translated into the increase in the production of agricultural and food products, and a marginal reduction in the produc-

tion of textiles mainly due to the substantial reduction in the production of these goods in India. The highest increases in production take place in China and the Former Soviet Union, where the biggest reductions in wages occur. These two countries have the highest increase in exports of traditional consumption products. On the other hand, in the majority of developed countries the exports of these goods decrease.

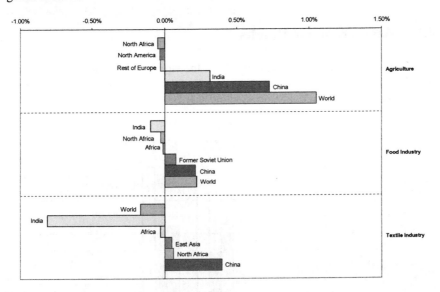

Figure 20:   Decomposition of the Changes in the World Production of Traditional Consumption Products (2030).

4   The Effects of Free Trade in Emissions Abatement: 'Full Liberalisation & Soft-Landing' Scenario

In this part of the book we will examine the impact on the results of the model of a combination of shocks: the elimination of tariff and non-tariff barriers and the imposition of the emissions restriction policy. The main question that is addressed is whether the abolition of tariffs facilitates the abatement effort or not. A similar question is brought up in the literature regarding the discussions over the 'Double Dividend' hypothesis. These discussions examine if the level of welfare of a country increases in the case that the revenues from the imposition of a carbon tax are used for the reduction of other taxes. In this study, such a direct correlation between the reduction of tariffs and revenues from the sales of permits is not possible due to the design of the scenarios. The financing of the reduction of tariffs is an issue of the public sector while the transactions regarding permits take place among private sector agents (firms and households). Furthermore, the 'full liberalisation' scenario requires that tariff and non-tariff barriers are totally eliminated and not reduced up to the point that the loss in tariff revenues is equal to the gain from the revenues from permit sales. Nevertheless, the results of the simulated scenario from the GEM-E3 model provide useful insights for the impact of tariff abolition on the abatement effort of each country.

4.1   Macroeconomic Results

The macroeconomic results stemming from the simulation of the 'full liberalisation & soft-landing' scenario (FL&SL) are, as expected, a synthesis of the results of the 'full liberalisation' and 'soft-landing' scenarios.

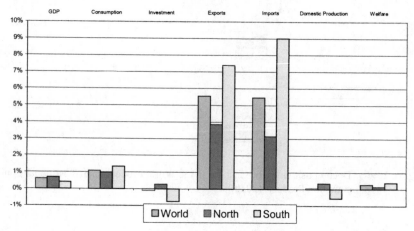

Figure 21:   Results of the 'FL&SL' Scenario at the Macroeconomic Level (2030).

The elimination of tariffs results in the increase of world production of all goods, and specially of the traditional consumption goods (agriculture, food industry, textiles) due to the tariff peaks existing in these sectors. The significant differences existing in the tariff burden between countries of the North and the countries of the South result in the higher increase in the production of these goods in developing countries. The imposition of the restriction on emissions reduces significantly the economic activity at the world level, with the burden placed mainly on energy and energy-intensive sectors. At the country level, the imposition of the same carbon value in all countries has the most significant impact on the low energy-cost producers, the majority of which belong to the developing countries. The higher burden on the prices of developing countries is translated in a reduction of their relative advantage and their shares in world exports in the international markets. The transfers of income in the form of purchases and sales of emission permits, in combination to the restriction on the current account of developing countries, redistribute expenditures of countries towards consumption goods in developing countries and towards investment goods in developed countries, with the corresponding adjustments in welfare. The favourable impact of the tariff abolition on the level of prices and the increase in consumption expenditures create an increased demand for the goods of traditional consumption sectors in developing countries. However, given that the sectors that are negatively affected from the increased cost of energy constitute the largest portion of economic activity of these countries, total domestic production is reduced and their trade balance becomes negative. This results in the increase of GDP in developed countries with rates higher than those of developing countries.

4.2   Sectoral Results

The elimination of the relatively low tariffs imposed on primary fuels is not enough to compensate for the significant burden on their prices from the imposition of the carbon value, thus the demand for and production of primary fuels is reduced significantly both at the regional and global levels. The reduction in the production of coal is bigger in the South mainly due to the size of Chinese production. In international markets, given that Australia is the major exporter of coal, the reduction in the exports of coal in the North is bigger than that of the South. The significant shares of North Africa-Middle East and the Former Soviet Union in the world exports of oil explain, following the argumentation of the 'soft-landing' scenario, the increase in the exports of oil in the South. The significant dependence of the electricity sector on coal mainly in developing countries (China, India, and the Former Soviet Union) overrides the increase in the demand for electricity coming from the increased economic activity due to tariff abolition, resulting in the reduction in the production of electricity at the world level.

The production of energy-intensive products at the world level is reduced or increased only marginally. The contribution of developing countries to this evolution is significant; in these countries demand decreases for two reasons: The first is that the higher burden on energy inputs in the countries of the South creates a comparative disadvantage in the production of energy-intensive products, resulting in the reduction in the demand for exports of energy-intensive products. The second reason is the reduction of investments, which are the main source of domestic demand for energy-intensive products.

The adjustments in the case of investment goods are more complex: The demand for investments increases in developed countries while it is reduced in the countries of the South. Moreover, the prices of durable goods (transport and other equipment goods) intended for consumption purposes increase due to the higher prices of primary fuels, reducing the demand for these products in all countries. Therefore domestic demand for durable goods intended either for consumption or investment purposes decreases in the countries of the South. The elimination of the relatively high tariffs imposed on the transactions among countries of the South increases the demand for exports but not enough to compensate for the reduction in domestic demand. The result of these adjustments is the reduction of domestic production of durable goods in developing countries. In developed countries the increase in the demand for durable goods for investment purposes as well as the increase in the demand for exports are enough to offset the reduction of demand for consumption purposes, resulting in a higher level of domestic production for these goods.

Table 24:   % Changes from Baseline in Domestic Production (2030).

	Full Liberalisation			Soft Landing			Soft Landing & Full Liberalisation		
	World	North	South	World	North	South	World	North	South
Agriculture	1.9	1.8	2.0	1.0	-0.2	1.9	3.1	1.4	4.2
Coal	1.5	-0.4	2.2	-36.3	-32.4	-37.6	-36.3	-33.2	-37.3
Oil	1.5	1.2	1.7	-9.6	-16.6	-5.2	-8.5	-15.8	-4.0
Gas	1.0	0.7	1.3	-11.4	-11.8	-10.9	-10.7	-11.3	-10.0
Electricity	1.2	0.8	1.7	-6.0	-3.0	-10.3	-5.1	-2.2	-9.1
Ferrous and non ferrous metals	1.3	0.9	1.8	-3.4	1.0	-8.3	-2.2	2.1	-7.0
Chemical Products	1.6	1.0	2.7	-1.3	0.7	-4.8	0.2	1.8	-2.5
Other energy intensive	1.2	0.5	2.4	-1.4	0.7	-5.2	-0.3	1.3	-3.2
Electronic Equipment	1.4	0.1	3.8	-1.5	-0.7	-3.0	-0.3	-0.8	0.5
Transport equipment	0.9	1.7	-1.3	-1.7	-1.3	-2.9	-0.9	0.3	-4.2
Other Equipment Goods	1.2	0.7	2.0	-1.9	-0.2	-4.8	-0.7	0.6	-3.0
Other Manufacturing products	1.5	-0.3	4.3	-0.9	0.6	-3.4	0.5	0.4	0.5
Construction	0.8	0.5	1.6	-0.9	-0.3	-2.3	-0.2	0.2	-0.9
Food Industry	2.3	2.1	2.6	0.2	0.0	0.6	2.6	2.3	3.2
Trade and Transport	1.2	0.8	2.0	-0.8	-0.5	-1.6	0.4	0.4	0.3
Textile Industry	3.3	0.6	5.5	-0.2	0.1	-0.4	3.2	0.8	5.2
Other Market Services	0.8	0.8	0.9	-0.1	-0.2	0.2	0.8	0.7	1.1
Non Market Services	0.1	0.4	-0.6	0.1	0.0	0.4	0.7	0.4	1.4

Table 25:   % Changes from Baseline in Exports (2030).

	Full Liberalisation			Soft Landing			Soft Landing & Full Liberalisation		
	World	North	South	World	North	South	World	North	South
Agriculture	26.1	25.1	27.2	0.0	-1.0	1.1	27.0	23.0	31.5
Coal	1.8	-2.1	6.4	-32.5	-30.5	-34.9	-32.2	-32.8	-31.5
Oil	2.9	2.7	3.0	-9.4	-22.0	2.2	-7.0	-19.9	4.8
Gas	1.5	-1.6	2.3	-6.1	-14.8	-3.7	-4.5	-16.2	-1.3
Ferrous and non ferrous metals	7.7	4.2	10.6	-1.2	6.8	-7.9	6.3	12.2	1.3
Chemical Products	8.2	4.0	13.3	-2.5	3.7	-10.2	5.3	8.1	1.9
Other energy intensive	7.4	2.0	12.6	-2.2	6.1	-10.2	4.7	8.7	0.7
Electronic Equipment	6.6	2.1	9.7	-1.8	-1.3	-2.1	4.6	0.5	7.4
Transport equipment	9.9	6.7	21.4	-1.8	-1.6	-2.5	7.7	4.8	18.6
Other Equipment Goods	7.6	3.8	13.2	-2.0	0.3	-5.3	5.3	4.0	7.1
Other Manufacturing products	11.5	2.0	16.2	-2.7	3.3	-5.8	7.9	5.6	9.1
Food Industry	11.9	6.9	17.7	-0.3	1.2	-2.0	11.7	8.1	15.7
Textile Industry	9.9	2.1	12.6	-0.4	0.9	-0.8	9.6	2.9	11.9

At the world level the production of durable goods is reduced due to the significant decrease of production in the countries of the South. An increase in the production and exports of electronic equipment in developing countries and a reduction in the production and exports of these goods in developed countries is observed; this is due to the fact that countries such as China and East Asia have gained a comparative advantage in the production of these goods at the expense of Japan and North America. The significant reduction of wages caused by the reduction of production activity in China and East Asia reduce significantly the cost of production of electronic equipment, which is labour-intensive in these countries. The production in the construction sector, the product of which is almost exclusively used for investment purposes, drops in the countries of the South and increases in developed countries, following the course of investments in these regions.

4.3   The Effects of Trade Liberalisation on the Abatement Effort

The increase in production activity caused by the tariff abolition results in a greater use of coal, crude oil, and gas as intermediate inputs for the production of goods and as final goods for household consumption, therefore more emissions are produced both at regional and world levels. More specifically, world emissions are increased by 1.6%. As is shown in Table 26, about 60% of the increase in emissions comes from China and India while only 10% from European regions. This is due to the relatively higher increase in activity in China and India as a consequence of trade liberalisation.

The increase in emissions notwithstanding facilitates the abatement effort through a more efficient allocation of resources. As shown in Table 27, tariffs on primary fuels are substantially lower than on non-fuels, thus the prices of non-fuels face a bigger reduction. This means that the substitution towards non-fuel goods is more pronounced. The increased production activity also favours the increase of investments for the entire 2010-2030 period, thus capital inputs are higher in the 'FL&SL' scenario, increasing the substitution ability of primary fuel inputs.

The changes induced by trade liberalisation are in a way equivalent to a change in the shape of the implicit Marginal Abatement Cost Curve. For illustration purposes, a comparison of the abatement effort between the 'soft-landing' and the 'FL&SL' scenarios is shown in Figure 22. Point B shows the quantity of emissions in the baseline, which, according to the projections used for the simulations, reaches 44.4 billion tons of CO_2. Point T shows the target quantity of emissions in the 'soft-landing' scenario, which is 35.6 billion tons of CO_2. In the 'soft-landing' scenario the carbon value is gradually increased up to the point P ($€_{99}$ 19.4) in order to reduce emissions so that the target is met. Diagrammatically, this gradual adjustment takes place along the curve BM. The tariff abolition results in the increase of emissions compared to baseline represented by the distance BA. The quantity of emissions in the 'full liberalisation' scenario (point A) is 45 billion tons of CO_2.

Table 26:   Changes in Regional Emissions in the 'Full Liberalisation' Scenario Compared to Baseline (2030).

	Changes from Baseline (%)	Contribution to Total Increase from Baseline (%)
Australia	1.1	0.9
Japan	1.4	2.3
East Asia	1.5	8.3
China	2.1	27.9
India	4.5	28.8
North America	0.5	5.7
Latin America	1.0	2.9
Nordic Europe	0.9	0.3
Germany	0.7	0.9
UK	1.0	0.9
Rest of Europe	1.2	3.4
Other Europe	1.4	1.1
Central European Associates	1.6	2.4
Former Soviet Union	0.7	3.8
North Africa	1.1	4.1
Africa	1.9	4.9
Rest of the World	2.0	1.4

In the 'FL&SL' scenario the target quantity of emissions is assumed to remain the same as in the 'soft-landing' scenario, thus the reduction achieved in the 'FL&SL' scenario is bigger. Nevertheless, this reduction is obtained with almost the same carbon value ($€_{99}$ 19.5) as in the 'soft-landing' scenario. The fact that in the 'FL&SL' scenario a bigger emission reduction is achieved at almost the same marginal cost is a measure of the positive impact of tariff abolition on the global emission abatement effort.

At the regional level, the measurement of the increase in the effectiveness in emission reduction can be illustrated with the use of country-specific MACCs. An increase in the effectiveness in emission reduction means that the same quantity of abated emissions is achieved with a lower carbon value or that the MACC of each country moves to the right (Figure 23). In order to measure the improvement of the ability to abate, the MACCs are re-estimated for the case that the emissions restriction policy is combined with the full liberalisation of international trade (see Appendix).

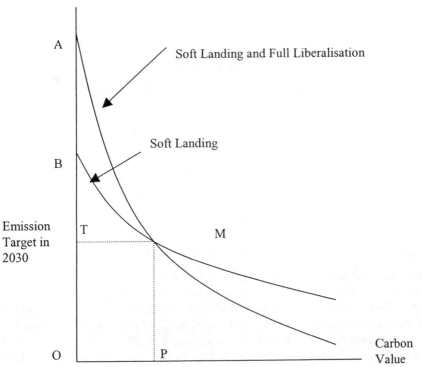

Figure 22:   A Comparison of the Abatement Effort Between the 'Soft-Landing' and 'FL&SL' Scenarios.

The comparison of the two sets of MACCs shows that the curves have moved to the right for each country. The measurement of this shift for each country is based on the percentage reduction on the carbon value resulting from the replacement of the abated quantities of emissions in 2030 with the ones of the 'soft-landing' scenario[8].

---

[8]   The distance AC is equal to the common carbon value for all countries resulting from the 'soft landing' scenario in 2030 and the distance 0C is equal to the abated emissions of the corresponding country. Thus the percentage reduction we refer to is equal to the rate $100 \cdot \left(\frac{AB}{AC} - 1 \right)$.

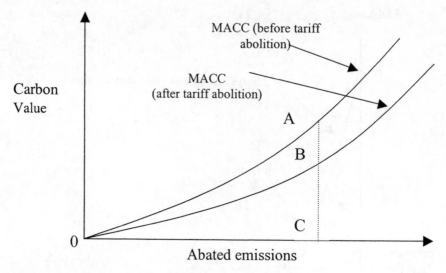

Figure 23:   The Impact of Trade Liberalisation on MACCs.

The results of this exercise are displayed in the third column of Table 27. According to the data of Table 27 and the argumentation above, the highest gains in terms of effectiveness in the reduction of emissions is found in countries with the highest tariff rates in the baseline. The size of tariffs is a measure of the distortion in the allocation of resources and also of the extent of adjustments that take place due to the trade liberalisation. In India and the Rest of the World, which have high tariff rates in the baseline, the same emission reduction is achieved with lower carbon values due to tariff abolition. On the other hand, the adjustments in European countries are almost negligible due to the low tariffs they impose on their imports.

5   Conclusions

The main result obtained from the analysis of the scenario involving the full liberalisation of international trade is that the total elimination of tariffs leads to an increase in world GDP and welfare level. This corresponds with expectations derived from trade theory. However the pace of trade liberalisation in recent decades (which has been extended into the Baseline Scenario) has raised questions as to further potential for gains and our analysis points to the conclusion that they still exist. Furthermore most of the potential benefits from full liberalisation of international trade seem to be concentrated on developing countries where most of the doubts concerning its desirability have been expressed.

According to this scenario's results most of the increase in trade (both imports and exports) in developing countries is due to an increase in exchanges among these countries that increase faster than other bilateral transactions. The increase in total exports of developed countries is mainly due to increased exports to developing countries and less to the increase in the trade among developed countries.

Table 27:   The Impact of Trade Liberalisation on the Abatement Effort (2030).

	Primary Fuels Average Tariff (%)	Non-Fuels Average Tariff (%)	% Change in Carbon Value due to Tariff Abolition
Australia	0.1	6.1	-2.0
Japan	0.6	8.6	-2.8
East Asia	4.9	8.1	-4.1
China	3.5	18.8	-5.9
India	16.9	30.1	-20.6
North America	1.4	3.0	-2.2
Latin America	10.2	8.1	-5.8
Nordic Europe	0.1	1.2	-2.6
Germany	0.1	1.5	-1.6
UK	0.1	2.1	-1.9
Rest of Europe	0.2	2.1	-3.3
Other Europe	4.2	4.6	-4.0
Central European Associates	2.2	6.6	-6.4
Former Soviet Union	0.0	1.2	-2.3
North Africa	5.3	6.4	-3.6
Africa	1.3	6.0	-4.8
Rest of the World	20.4	25.1	-11.8

The biggest increases in investments take place in the countries that have the highest tariff rates, enabling a positive response of domestic production to the increased demand generated by the elimination of tariffs. This ability to expand capital inputs together with the more effective allocation of recourses resulting from the removal of distortions eventually leads to a positive correlation between the relative percentage of tariffs to GDP and the rate of increase of GDP.

The observation that international trade increases at a higher rate than GDP is strongly supported by the results of GEM-E3. It can be mainly attributed to the 'love of variety' property incorporated in the model. Due to the existence of tariffs, imported varieties comprise a smaller percentage of the domestic demand than the domestic varieties, thus consumers spend the additional income generated by the elimination of tariffs to buy more of the imported varieties.

At the sectoral level, the elimination of the substantial tariff burden imposed on imports of goods from traditional sectors (agricultural, textiles and food products) results in a substantial increase of international trade in these products.

Concerning Climate Change policies for the Kyoto horizon a number of cases have been examined. They involve alternative configurations for participation in Clubs of abating regions with a common target corresponding to Kyoto commitments for the respective regions. Abatement is paradigmatically assumed to take place under a regime of a full tradable permit market involving all abating agents within the Club, benefits from permit sales accruing to the consumers in the respective regions. Since the model used is a computable general equilibrium model, the costs and benefits include abatement costs, costs and benefits from purchases/sales of permits as well as secondary impacts, notably those arising from changes in the terms of trade and re-allocation of economic activity in different sectors and countries.

In all cases examined where developing countries do not participate in an abating Club and therefore incur no direct costs they end up with diminished welfare due to secondary effects in the form of reduced prices and volumes of their energy and energy intensive exports.

A withdrawal of the United States from the Kyoto process apart from reducing the environmental impact of the process and endangering the whole process (55% clause) signifies a considerable increase (2.5 to 4 times) of the average cost to the EU per ton of CO_2 avoided worldwide. This result is to a large extent due to carbon leakage effects (lower fossil fuel prices and higher polluting activity in non-participating regions).

Inclusion of the Former Soviet Union naturally blunts the environmental impact because of the so called 'hot air' effects but at the same time enhances the efficiency of the abatement effort in the EU (the average cost to the EU per ton of CO_2 avoided worldwide falling to between a half and two thirds of their levels when the Former Soviet Union did not participate). Such reductions are less important if the Former Soviet Union does not bring into the market the totality of its excess permits.

The Former Soviet Union stands to gain overall from inclusion in the Club of abating countries. Such gains are very substantial in cases when the USA is also participating but remain non-negligible for other configurations especially when the Former Soviet Union does not trade all its excess permits.

When not participating in a Club the Former Soviet Union experiences losses in economic terms compared to the zero worldwide abatement reference case. These losses result from the fact that the Former Soviet Union is a major energy and energy-intensive product exporter and suffers from lower export prices and higher import prices (worsening of terms of trade) without the benefit of net permit sales. In this sense non-inclusion for the Former Soviet Union is a worse case even than the complete collapse of the Kyoto process and considerably worse than inclusion in an abating Club.

Were the EU to attempt meeting its Kyoto commitments alone with its Central European Associates the prospect of inclusion of the Former Soviet Union would render the exercise meaningless since it is very likely that the sum of the targets will be above reference (no abatement) levels. Former Soviet Union participation in such a Club can only be envisaged in the context of limitations to Former Soviet Union excess permits used. Such a scenario would bring considerable economic benefits (compared to the EU/CEA alone case) to both the EU and the Former Soviet Union. It would however be accompanied by a corresponding reduction in environmental effectiveness.

A number of cases were examined where the Former Soviet Union was assumed to participate in a Club acting as a monopolist in restricting the supply of excess permits in order to maximise its benefits. It was found that the restriction that maximised the value of permit sales did not correspond to the point of maximum welfare. In most cases the latter represented a less restrictive stance where some loss in net sales was compensated by gains in welfare arising from trade effects. In general such imperfect competition in the permits market was found to increase the cost of abatement at the world level although such increases were small when the abating Club was large (involving the whole of Annex B).

For the post-Kyoto period an abatement scenario of the 'soft-landing' type has been considered. Such scenarios take into account current emission patterns and increasingly tighten individual country emission budgets depending on income and emissions per capita. The aim has been to extend the climate change policy analysis beyond the Kyoto commitment period when it can be reasonably assumed that developing countries participate in the abatement effort. Again free trade in permits without transaction costs was assumed generating a unique carbon value for the world. Two major factors contribute to differentiation of impacts across regions: a) though unique this carbon value generates differential impacts on energy costs in the different regions, depending on carbon intensity but also on differential energy prices incorporated in the Baseline scenario, and b) the income inflow from the sales of emission rights increases the demand for goods and services of the net exporters of permits while the opposite occurs for the net importers of permits.

At the world level the impact of the first factor is reflected in the reductions of GDP, international trade, and employment. The burden on the price of fossil fuels increases the general price level, reducing disposable income of households and resulting in the reduction of the production activity and employment. In parallel, it generates a reduction in the level of total productivity by distorting the distribution of resources both geographically and sectorally. The second factor acts towards the redistribution of world income from the developed to the developing countries. Given the higher propensity to consume of the lower income households, this redistribution of income increases the demand for consumption goods in developing countries, lowers the savings of most developed countries in a way that, at the world scale, a shift from investment towards consumption goods is observed.

Two flows of income having the opposite direction and generating different results between developed and developing countries can be distinguished. The first flow of income starts from developing countries and is expressed by the deficit of their balance of trade that contributes to the reduction of their GDP. The recipients of this income are the developed countries, which direct it towards investments due to the increased rents on capital; thus the reduction in their GDP is smaller than that of the developing countries. The second flow of income starts from the developed countries in the form of purchases of permits from the developing countries. Due to the decreased return on capital in developing countries, it is directed towards consumption. When imports increase, the level of welfare of the households increases but GDP decreases.

The energy products carry the main weight of the emissions restriction policy and, as expected, the demand for and production of these products are reduced both at the regional and global levels. Similar impacts are obtained for energy intensive sectors.

On the supply-side it is consumption goods that face the lightest burden from the higher prices of energy inputs. On the other hand, given that traditional goods though not energy-intensive are labour-intensive and to a lesser extent capital-intensive products, their costs of production are significantly affected by the changes in wages and returns on capital. The most noticeable reductions of wages, combined with the relatively higher labour-intensity of consumption goods in developing countries, result in the bigger reduction of the cost of production in these countries. On the demand-side, these products are favoured by the redistribution of expenditures towards higher consumption levels, while the opposite occurs in developed countries. The result of these adjustments is the increase of production of traditional goods in developing countries and a corresponding decrease in the developed countries.

In order to examine possible impacts of trade liberalisation in view of climate change policy a scenario was constructed combining tariff abolition with the post-Kyoto global constraint scenario discussed above.

As was mentioned earlier, tariff abolition leads to increased productive activity worldwide which would result in a greater use of coal, crude oil, and gas as intermediate inputs for the production of goods and as final goods for household consumption. This means that emissions in the liberalisation scenario stood at a level 1.5% higher than the Baseline. About 60% of the increase occurs in China and India while only 10% in European regions corresponding to the relatively higher increase in the production activity in China and India. Imposing the emission constraint therefore implies that reductions at the world level must be deeper. However, the carbon value obtained is substantially the same as in the abatement case without trade liberalisation. This is mainly due to important side effects of liberalisation that permits an increase in investment in developing countries and a more efficient allocation of resources worldwide. Such changes are equivalent to a rightward shift of the implicit marginal abatement cost curves. The highest profits in terms of effectiveness in the reduction of emissions are found in countries with the highest tariff rates.

Appendix: Marginal Abatement Cost Curves

In a simulation of a market for emission permits of a computable general equilibrium model, there are two factors playing a crucial role for the resulting outcome: the determination of the total abated quantity of emissions and the distribution of emission rights to the participating countries. With the assistance of the MACCs the ways through which these factors affect the outcome are explained.

Let there be a permit market with two participating countries (A and B) as it is shown in Figure 24. The total quantity abated is represented by the distance 0_A0_B on the horizontal axis of the diagram. The starting point of the axes for country A is 0_A and the abated emissions increase to the right. In the same way, the starting point of the axes for country B is 0_B and the abated emissions increase to the left. $MACC_A$ and $MACC_B$ stand for the MACCs for countries A and B respectively. For the sake of the presentation, emission rights are expressed as the difference of the amount of emissions according to the allocation of permits in the scenario and baseline emissions. From Figure 24 it can be inferred that country A has the right to produce 0_AA less emissions than in the baseline (the same stands for the distance 0_BA for country B).

The least-cost combination of the reductions of emissions in the two countries as it is defined in a computable general equilibrium model is achieved at the point of intersection of the two MACCs. At this point the marginal abatement costs of the two countries are equal by definition, meaning that country A will reduce its emissions by 0_AR and country B by 0_BR. The common carbon value for the two countries resulting from the model is equal to PP. Under the technological conditions existing in each country and expressed by the MACCs, the main factor affecting the carbon value and the distribution of emissions in a permit market is the total quantity of emissions from the overall restriction. An increase in the overall restriction on emissions is equal in this example to a shift of the starting point of the axis for country B from the point 0_B to the point 0^*_B and a parallel shift of $MACC_B$ to $MACC^*_B$. As it is expected this tighter constraint will generate an increase in the carbon value. It is also expected that in the least-cost combination of the reduction of emissions, the most significant emission abatement will be made by the country with the MACC that has the higher elasticity; in terms of Figure 24 this is the country with the steepest MACC. This can be proved diagrammatically in the following way: Supposing that the two countries have the same MACCs, both countries would reach the same reduction in emissions which would be equal to half of the total quantity of emissions according to the overall restriction[9]. If we assume that the slope of $MACC_B$ is reduced, meaning that it rotates counterclockwise around the point 0_B then at the new equilibrium country A reaches a bigger reduction of emissions compared to country B.

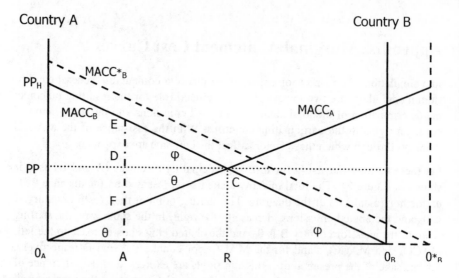

Figure 24:   MACCs and the Mechanism of Emissions Abatement.

Given the least-cost allocation of the reduction of emissions the initial distribution of emission rights to the participating countries, shown by point A, determines the sales and purchases of emission permits among countries. In Figure 24 it can be observed that country A, for the given distribution of emission rights, is a net exporter of permits. The quantity of permits sold by country A to country B is equal to the distance AR. For this sale country A receives the amount represented by the area ADCR, while the total cost of abatement for the same quantity is provided by the area AFCR. Therefore the profit for country A from the sales of permits is represented by the area of the triangle DFC. In a similar way, country B pays for the purchase of AR emission rights the amount represented by the area ADCR while the cost of abatement for this country if it had been abating alone would be the area of the trapezoid AECR. The profit for country B is represented by the area of the triangle CDE. It can be proved that the country that has the

---

[9]   The triangle 0AC0B is isosceles and therefore its height is also its median.

flattest MACC (indicating higher abatement potentials) has the highest profit[10] from this transaction. In the case that country A is provided with emission rights enough to cover its emissions in the baseline, then the line EA in Figure 24 shifts to the position O_APP_H.

In order to construct a MACC in the framework of the current study, several simulations under alternative hypotheses as for the restriction on emissions of each country were examined using the GEM-E3 model. With the resulting carbon values and abated emissions, the existing relationship between these two variables in each country was estimated econometrically. The functions have been approximated by 2nd and 3rd degree polynomials of the form:

$$PP = \alpha_3 \cdot \Delta E^3 + \alpha_2 \cdot \Delta E^2 + \alpha_1 \cdot \Delta E$$

where PP : Carbon value

ΔE : Abated CO_2 emissions (in billion tons)

Table 28:   Estimates for MACCs by Region in the 'Soft-Landing' Scenario (2030).

	α_3	α_2	α_1	R^2
Australia	2674.4000	73.3550	95.6120	0.9999
Japan	0.0000	670.6600	125.1100	0.9998
East Asia	0.0000	66.6230	24.8580	0.9998
China	0.4756	-0.2090	3.4105	0.9999
India	4.8397	-0.8302	5.7284	0.9998
North America	0.9644	-0.1694	6.0689	0.9999
Latin America	0.0000	419.5700	73.8660	0.9999
Nordic Europe	0.0000	11494.0000	375.3600	0.9995
Germany	0.0000	866.3600	118.2700	0.9996
UK	0.0000	930.5600	89.0670	0.9999
Rest of Europe	0.0000	168.2600	50.5620	0.9998
Other Europe	0.0000	2057.1100	176.1100	0.9997
Central European Associates	0.0000	373.0300	17.6120	0.9982
Former Soviet Union	3.5469	4.3654	13.9270	0.9999
North Africa	0.0000	116.1900	55.8480	0.9999
Africa	-54.4840	149.7100	55.3330	0.9998
Rest of the World	0.0000	3270.6000	129.6700	0.9991

---

[10]   In terms of Figure 24 this means that triangle DFC has a bigger area than the triangle DCE if the angle ϑ is bigger than the angle φ. It is true that $DF = CD \cdot \tan(\vartheta) > DE = CD \cdot \tan(\varphi)$, thus

$$\frac{1}{2} \cdot DF \cdot CD = \frac{1}{2} \cdot CD^2 \cdot \tan(\vartheta) > \frac{1}{2} \cdot DE \cdot CD = \frac{1}{2} \cdot CD^2 \cdot \tan(\varphi)$$
.

Table 29:   Estimates for MACCs by Region in the 'FL&SL' Scenario (2030).

	a_3	a_2	a_1	R^2
Australia	2561.8000	77.3120	93.9740	0.9999
Japan	0.0000	649.7300	121.9100	0.9998
East Asia	0.0000	63.6610	23.9490	0.9998
China	0.4508	-0.2218	3.2537	0.9999
India	4.0970	-1.4132	5.0986	0.9998
North America	0.9400	-0.1760	5.9641	0.9999
Latin America	0.0000	398.9300	70.2510	0.9999
Nordic Europe	0.0000	11270.0000	363.9100	0.9995
Germany	0.0000	851.5900	116.5700	0.9996
UK	0.0000	908.5100	87.9210	0.9990
Rest of Europe	0.0000	163.1900	48.7690	0.9998
Other Europe	0.0000	1967.4000	169.5600	0.9997
Central European Associates	0.0000	352.0300	16.0810	0.9981
Former Soviet Union	3.2631	4.7041	13.3730	0.9998
North Africa	0.0000	112.4100	53.7900	0.9999
Africa	-57.9800	149.9200	51.2810	0.9998
Rest of the World	0.0000	2958.5000	110.6400	0.9990

References

Armington, P.S. (1969), A Theory of Demand for Products Distinguished by Place of Production, *IMF Staff Papers*, No. 16, 159-178.

Capros P., T. Georgakopoulos, D. Van Regemorter, S. Proost, T. Schmidt, and K. Conrad (1997), The GEM-E3 Model for the European Union, *Journal of Economic & Financial Modeling* 4 (2&3), special double issue, 51-160.

Capros, P., T. Georgakopoulos, D. Van Regemorter, and D. Willenbockel (1998), Aggregate Results of the Single Market Programme, in: *General Equilibrium Macro-Economic Ex-Post Evaluation of the EU Single Market Programme*, Office for Official Publication of the European Communities.

Criqui, P. (2002), *Greenhouse Gas Emission Control Strategies: Full Scientific Report*, submitted to DG Research.

Criqui, P. and N. Kouvaritakis (1997), *Les coûts pour le secteur énergétique de la réduction des émissions de CO₂: une évaluation internationale avec le modèle POLES*, Grenoble: IEPE.

Dixit, A.K. and J.E Stiglitz (1977), Monopolistic Competition and Optimum Product Diversity, *American Economic Review*, 67, 297-308.

Ellerman, A.D. and A. Decaux (1998), *Analysis of Post-Kyoto CO₂ Emissions Trading Using Marginal Abatement Curves*, MIT Joint Program on the Science and Policy of Global Change, Report No. 40, Cambridge, MA.

Pratten, C. (1998), A Survey of the Economies of Scale, in: European Commission (Ed.), *Studies on the Economics of Integration: Research on the Costs of Non-Europe*, Vol. 2, Luxembourg.

Weisbrot, M. and D. Baker (2002), *The Relative Impact of Trade Liberalization in Developing Countries*, CEPR Discussion Paper.

Druck: betz-druck GmbH, D-64291 Darmstadt
Verarbeitung: Buchbinderei Schäffer, D-67269 Grünstadt